Context and Text

Method in Liturgical Theology

Kevin W. Irwin

Context and Text

Method in Liturgical Theology

A PUEBLO BOOK

The Liturgical Press   Collegeville, Minnesota

A Pueblo Book published by The Liturgical Press

Design by Frank Kacmarcik, Obl.S.B.

Library of Congress Cataloging-in-Publication Data

Irwin, Kevin W.
    Context and text : method in liturgical theology / Kevin W. Irwin.
    p.   cm.
    ''A Pueblo book.''
    Includes bibliographical references.
    ISBN 0-8146-6125-4
    1. Catholic Church—Liturgy. 2. Catholic Church—Doctrines.
    3. Theology—Methodology. I. Title. II. Title: Liturgical
    theology.
    BX1970.I7583 1994
    264'.02'001—dc20   93-28747
                                                                         CIP

To Gerard J. Békés, O.S.B.

Contents

Preface

Twenty-five years after the promulgation of *Sacrosanctum Concilium*, the Constitution on the Sacred Liturgy of Vatican II, Mark Searle wrote a brief assessment of our failures and achievements in implementing it. He pointed to the need for a new "liturgical movement" to deepen the renewal underway, especially spiritually and theologically. Toward the end of that essay he writes:

"[A]ny revival of the liturgical movement must seek to reopen the dialogue with systematic theology. There is hardly any serious theological issue which does not surface, in one way or another, in the liturgy: theological epistemology, God-language, theological anthropology, ecclesiology, salvation history, even the issues of critical theology, shaped as they are by particular cultural contexts. A new liturgical movement cannot avoid such issues as they arise in liturgical practice."[1]

In the same year that the Liturgy Constitution was promulgated, the famous Orthodox (liturgical) theologian Alexander Schmemann stated that "the problem of the relationship between worship and theology is on the theological agenda of our time."[2] At the same time he said "although the existence of the problem is certain, it is still difficult to define it."[3]

That the relationship of liturgy and theology was certainly part of the agenda about the reform of Roman Catholic liturgy enunciated in the Liturgy Constitution is clear. These include its assertions of the priority of the study of liturgy in theological schools (n. 16) and the principle that the reform of the liturgy should be undertaken in light of theological, historical, and pastoral investigations (n. 23).[4]

Despite the spate of writing concerning liturgical theology[5] in the past twenty-five years,[6] Mark Searle's assessment remains valid—there is still a great need for dialogue between liturgists and theologians.[7] Among other things this dialogue can concern how to articulate the theology of what occurs in the act of liturgy, how to appropriate liturgy as a source for systematic theology, how to use the liturgy as a basis for articulating moral and spiritual theology (understanding that these are closely united) or how to develop a new and more adequate approach to sacramental theology. In this latter case liturgists see in the revised liturgical rites a whole new horizon within which to develop a theology of the sacraments that transcends the conventional post Tridentine Roman Catholic divorce between liturgy and sacramental theology.[8] In addition, some contemporary theologians will argue for a "doxological" theology that relies on the liturgy (among other things) for stimulus and corrective to an overly intellectual doctrinal theology.[9]

This book is situated within the present debate over liturgical theology in at least three ways. First, it concerns *method* for the study of liturgy in general, specifically its theological component. Second, it explores the meanings which the term *liturgical theology* can have. These include (1) "theology *of* the liturgy" in the sense of a theological description of what occurs in the act of worship, (2) "theology *drawn from* the liturgy," thus making liturgy a theological source along with other "sources" for theology such as scripture, teachings of theologians past and present and statements of the magisterium,[10] and (3) (as an extension of "theology drawn from the liturgy") the moral and spiritual *implications* derived from engaging in liturgy. Third, our study is situated at the present stage of liturgical renewal when the revised ritual forms are being evaluated and critiqued and newer forms of liturgical rites are both called for and proposed,[11] including the agenda for ongoing liturgical reform, revision and inculturation from the perspective of engaging in what is often termed "critical liturgical theology."[12]

The chief concern of this book is methodological. In our view contemporary liturgical method is itself still in a stage of maturing.[13] Our contribution is intended to underscore the theological depth inherent in and proper to the liturgy and to indicate some conclusions that can be drawn from it, especially because some of the (very helpful) contemporary historical investigations of the liturgy have tended not to emphasize these themes.[14] At the same time we will argue that an appreciation of the historical evolution of the Church's liturgy can lead to a rich theology derived from varied yet complementary liturgical usages.[15]

In addition, our principal concern will be to articulate how the study of liturgy is essentially *pastoral theology* in the sense that it concerns reflection on *enacted* liturgical rites which shape the faith and life of believing participants.[16] The historical, theological, and pastoral investigation of the liturgy required by the Constitution on the Sacred Liturgy forms the background and part of the rationale for this work. This book intends to offer some principles about how to interpret the various aspects of liturgy in relation to each other (e.g., texts, symbols, ritual gestures) in a theological way and to articulate some theological and spiritual implications derived from liturgy. Its chief contribution will be to propose and exemplify such an investigation from the perspective of a liturgical-theological reflection on the Church's liturgical praxis.[17]

One particular reason why I think this book is necessary at present concerns the nature of the present postconciliar reformed liturgy[18] where variety and flexibility are built into its structure and is evident in celebration. Since many comparatively recent approaches to liturgical theology in this century from liturgists (e.g., Lambert Beauduin, Odo Casel, Cipriano Vagaggini) and statements of the magisterium (e.g., *Mediator Dei*) presumed a fixed liturgy inherited from Trent, the present task involves moving beyond these methodological approaches in order to propose a method for engaging in liturgical theology given the present liturgical reform.[19] Especially significant methodological approaches by authors such as Salvatore Marsili, Aidan Kavanagh, and Geoffrey Wainwright as well as those by Albert Houssiau and Gerard Lukken (from rather different perspectives) have been especially influential on my thought and on the method described and used in this book.[20]

The book is divided into three parts. Part 1, entitled "Relating Liturgy and Theology," deals with historical perspectives on this relationship (chapter 1) and observations on method for developing contemporary liturgical theology (chapter 2). Part 2, entitled "Context is Text: Theology of Liturgy," proposes a method for articulating a theology of the act of liturgy dealing with Word, symbol, euchology and the liturgical arts (discussed specifically in chapters 3 through 6). Part 3, entitled "Text Shapes Context:

Liturgical Theology," discusses the contribution which theology derived from liturgy can make to contemporary discussions about the nature of theology, to the method used in ecumenical sacramental conversations (chapter 7) and to spirituality derived from liturgy (chapter 8).

In describing their recent works on "liturgical theology" both Geoffrey Wainwright (in *Doxology*) and Edward Kilmartin (in *Christian Liturgy*) indicate the built in limitations of even these substantial contributions to liturgical-theological method. I need to do the same. This book concerns sketching the history of the liturgy/theology relationship, proposing a method for part of what is meant by "liturgical theology," applying a methodological proposal to interpreting the component elements of liturgical rites and indicating some implications of liturgical theology for the craft of theology in general, for ecumenism and for spirituality. However, in writing (as in preaching) it is important to decide what *not* to say! Among the things not sufficiently addressed here are the formulation of a precise method derived from the social sciences for interpreting and evaluating liturgical performance,[21] the role of imagination and affectivity in both liturgical performance and liturgical theology and how to assess the liturgical assembly's engagement in both liturgy and in developing theology derived from it.

By intention the present work is decidedly Roman Catholic. It regularly draws on and refers to the present post Vatican II liturgical rites as the primary locus for liturgical theology. At the same time, however, the present work reflects deep ecumenical concerns, particularly those explicitated in chapter 7 regarding dialogue about sacraments. I hope this book will be an invitation to others to join in the task of developing a method for doing liturgical theology. What I present here are directions toward this end.

I am grateful to a number of people for their helpful discussions of method for liturgical theology over the past five years. These include colleagues from the "Liturgical Theology" study group of the North American Academy of Liturgy and from the "Sacramental/Liturgical Theology" continuing seminar of the Catholic Theological Society of America as well as colleagues and students at The Catholic University of America. Because of their particularly important contributions in individual discussions, in reading detailed outlines, and portions or all of this finished manuscript I should like to thank Gerard Békés, Andrew Ciferni, Katherine

Dooley, Rita Claire Dorner, Regis Duffy, Peter Fink, Edward Foley, Gordon Lathrop, Gerald O'Collins, Gabriel O'Donnell and David Power.

For financial contributions to my sabbatical fund I wish to thank in particular the Bauman, McCann and Robmar Foundations as well as the Faculty Research Fund of The Catholic University of America. Finally I wish to thank many friends in Washington, D.C., and elsewhere who offered invaluable personal support for *and diversion from* the writing of this book. During my sabbatical year (1991-92) they were very understanding of the new way I found to "tell time"—not month by month but chapter by chapter. I am sure they will all agree that the worst "time" was the *ides* of each chapter!

Finally a word about the man to whom I dedicate this book. I first met Fr. Gerard J. Békés, O.S.B., when I was a doctoral student at Sant' Anselmo (Rome). During the spring term, 1975, I enrolled in a seminar he led on ecumenical dialogue on sacraments and found him an insightful and wise guide through the then newly-developing and maturing plethora of documents of bilateral and multilateral consultation. One outgrowth of the seminar was the topic for my doctoral thesis. Another was working with Fr. Békés as my doctoral mentor. From that time at Sant' Anselmo, continuing through rather regular contact in the intervening years, and most recently in the drafting stages of this book I have always held him in highest esteem as an inspiring teacher, a judicious mentor, a wise man, a gracious gentleman and a holy monk. From the beginning I knew that this man spoke of what he knew from the inside, namely that he believed what he taught and that his belief and thought were shaped by deep penetration into the mystery of God. I gratefully dedicate this work to him with deep admiration and abiding affection.

Solemnity of All Saints, 1992
Washington, D.C.

Notes

1. Mark Searle, "Renewing the Liturgy—Again," *Commonweal* 115 (November 18, 1988) 622.

2. Alexander Schmemann, "Theology and Liturgical Tradition," in *Worship In Scripture and Tradition*, ed. Massey H. Shepherd (New York: Oxford University Press, 1963) 165.

3. Ibid. 166. See, Walter J. Burghart, "A Theologian's Challenge to Liturgy," *Theological Studies* 35 (1974) 240 where he addresses "the liturgist as theologian." "[A] dangerous chasm still yawns between liturgy and theology. In our context here, I am not so much concerned over the damage done to theology by its neglect of the Church's liturgical experience, by its failure to take seriously the age-old adage *Lex orandi—lex credendi*. I agonize much more over the converse tragedy, over the hurt to liturgy when too few liturgists are profound theologians."

4. For a helpful review of other conciliar and post conciliar documents in the same vein see, Giorgio Bonaccorso, *Introduzione allo studio della Liturgia* (Padova: Edizioni Messagero Padova, 1990) 29–43.

5. The first use of this term is commonly cited as from M. Cappuyns in both "Liturgie et théologie," *Questions Liturgiques* 19 (1934) 249–272 and "Liturgie et théologie," in *La vrai visage de la liturgie. Cours et conferences des semaines liturgiques* (Louvain: Mont Cesar, 1938) 175–209, esp. 199 where he cites the influence which Lambert Beauduin had on him regarding the relationship between liturgy and theology.

6. For a summary and assessment of the writing of I. H. Dalmais, C. Vagaggini, L. Bouyer, S. Marsili, G. Lukken, A. Houssiau, A. Schmemann, G. Wainwright, A. Kavanagh, P. Fink, E. Kilmartin, D. N. Power, and M. Collins on liturgical theology see, Kevin W. Irwin, *Liturgical Theology. A Primer* (Collegeville: The Liturgical Press, 1990) 18–63.

7. Among others, see the helpful introduction and collected essays in *Liturgie—Ein vergessenes Thema der Theologie?*, ed. Klemens Richter (Freiburg: Basel, 1987).

8. For helpful insights on this relationship see, among others, Cor Traets, "Orientations par une théologie des sacrements," *Questions Liturgiques* 53 (1972) 97–118, idem. "Rite et liturgie sacramentelle," *Questions Liturgiques* 55 (1974) 11–31, Albert Houssiau, "La liturgie, lieu privilegie de la théologie sacramentaire," *Questions Liturgiques* 54 (1973) 7–12, idem. "La redécouverte de la liturgie par la théologie sacramentaire (1950-1980)," *La Maison Dieu* no. 149 (1982) 27–55, and Aidan Kavanagh, *On Liturgical Theology* (New York: Pueblo Publishing Co., 1984) 41, 46 and 76 and passim. For a particularly thorough example of both method and application see, Salvatore Marsili, "Teologia della celebrazione dell'eucaristia," in *Eucaristia. Teologia e storia della celebrazione. Anamnesis 3/2* (Casale Monferrato: Marietti, 1983) 11–186 and idem. *Mistero di Cristo e Liturgia dello Spirito*, ed., Maria Anselma Abignente (Vatican City: Libreria Editrice Vaticana, 1986).

9. See chapter 7, below. This is not to ignore the contemporary debate over "God-language" which has raised the fundamental issue of the adequacy of language to speak about God and to God. A premise throughout this book is that all liturgical language can hope to provide is the least inadequate terminology for and about God and that an appropriate doxological cast to such language in theology is provided by the liturgy.

10. This distinction between a theology of liturgy and theology derived from liturgy is commonly made. See, for example, Pedro Fernandez, "Liturgia y teologia. Historia de un problema metodologico," *Ciencia tomista* 99 (1972) 139, James Empereur, *Models of Liturgical Theology* (Bramcote/Nottingham: Grove Books, 1987) 7, Thomas Fisch, "Schmemann's Theological Contribution to the Liturgical Renewal of the Churches," in *Liturgy and Tradition*. Theological Reflections of Alexander Schmemann, ed. Thomas Fisch (Crestwood: St. Vladimir's Seminary Press, 1990) 6, K. W. Irwin, *Liturgical Theology* 64–68, and idem. "Liturgical Theology," in *New Dictionary of Sacramental Worship*, ed. Peter E. Fink (Collegeville: The Liturgical Press, 1990) 724–725.

11. An example of this process is the revision of the English language funeral rite from the Latin original of 1969, through the first English edition translated by the International Commission on English in the Liturgy (hereafter referred to as "ICEL") of 1975, to the present (second) English edition approved by Rome in 1987 and promulgated in the U.S.A. in 1989.

12. See, the particularly influential essay of Angelus Haussling, "Die kritische Funktion der Liturgiewissenschaft," in Hans B. Meyer, ed., *Liturgie und Gesellschaft* (Innsbruck: Tyrolia Verlag, 1970) 103–130. In addition see, among others, David N. Power, "People at Liturgy," *Twenty Years of Concilium—Prospect and Retrospect. Concilium Vol. 170*, eds. Paul Brand, Edward Schillebeeckx and Anton Weiler (Edinburgh: T. and T. Clark, 1983) 8–14 and Adrien Nocent, "I tre sacramenti dell'iniziazione cristiana," *Anamnesis 3/1 I Sacramenti* 74–94, 117–130, 193–203. While the three meanings of liturgical theology articulated here may be regarded as a summary of the present understanding of liturgical theology in general, some authors offer their own variations. For example, Julian Lopez Martin, "La fe y su celebracion," *Burgense* 23 (1982) will speak of the theological understanding of liturgy itself, the place of liturgy within the framework of theology in general and the mutual relationship of liturgy and catechesis for the pedagogy of the faith (143).

13. Among others see, Franco Brovelli, "Storia del movimento liturgico nel nostro secolo: dati, attese e linee di approfondimento," *Ephemerides Liturgicae* 53 (1985) 217–238, esp. 223 where he states that a solidification of methodological approaches to liturgy is in order, especially as these concern the interrelationship between liturgy on the one hand and culture, theological reflection, pastoral problems, religious customs, civic observances and the local church on the other. He admits that the intuitions about what ought to be factored into liturgical study are more clear at present than is an articulated method for liturgical study.

14. The critique by Francois Vandenbroucke of the first edition of *L'Eglise en prière* is a case in point. After acknowledging where the authors of the various

sections of this volume did address theological aspects of the liturgy, Vandenbroucke argues that their treatment of theological aspects of liturgy was decidedly insufficient. See, F. Vandenbroucke, "Sur la théologie de la liturgie," *Nouvelle Revue Théologique* 92 (1970) 135. Bruno Cardinali offers a trenchant critique of the second edition of this same work in "La nuova edizione de *L'Eglise en priére*," *Rivista Liturgica* 73 (1986) 704–712. After providing an overview of the contents of the four volumes he indicates his deep concern about what the work lacks. He argues that the lack of sufficient theological exploration of the liturgy really requires that the work be subtitled "introduction to the study of the evolution of the liturgy," because he insists that the book lacks sufficient anthropological and theological focus (709–711). He asks why Dalmais' helpful treatment of the relationship between *lex orandi* and *lex credendi* is so brief in a work of 1250 pages and why his insights are not verified throughout, especially in the sections on Eucharist and the other sacraments (710). For helpful presentations of the importance of history for liturgical method and for the way historical liturgical study discloses theological meanings see the essays by Pierre Marie Gy, *La liturgie dans l'histoire* (Paris: Les Editions du Cerf, 1990) noting the "Preface" by Jacques Le Goff (5–10) containing helpful insights about relating history and theology in liturgical studies. Also see, Robert Taft, "The Structural Analysis of Liturgical Units," *Worship* 52 (1978) 314–329, esp. 314–318, idem. "Liturgy as Theology," *Worship* 56 (1982) 113–117 and idem. "Response to the Berakah Award: Anamnesis," *Worship* 59 (1985) 305–325, esp. 311–314. The recent publication of Matias Augé's, *Liturgia. Storia, celebrazione, teologia, spiritualità* (Milano: Edizioni Paoline, 1992) is an example of a helpful synthetic approach to theological and pastoral themes inherent in the (revised) liturgy.

15. See below, chapter 2, 57–62. For a useful *apologia* for the function of history in sacramental theology see, Louis Marie Chauvet, "Place et fonction de l'histoire dans une theologie des sacrements," *Revue de l'Institute Catholique* 24 (1987) 49–65.

16. See, Margaret Mary Kelleher, "Liturgy as a Source for Sacramental Theology," *Questions Liturgiques* 72 (1991) 28–29 where she writes "liturgical texts do not become liturgy until they are performed by concrete local assemblies, and it is in the performance that meaning is actually created, communicated, and sometimes even transformed."

17. This phrase is used by G. Bonaccorso, *Introduzione* 43 to describe his approach to liturgical method in this important monograph which both reflects and in some ways transcends the stated purposes of the method employed at the Liturgical Institute of Santa Giustina in Padua (Italy).

18. From the outset I should like to acknowledge the awkwardness of a phrase used throughout—"the present reformed liturgy." This phrase is chosen over "the liturgy," which term could signify a "fixed" rite. The phrase is also used in order to suggest the ongoing refinement of the contemporary postconciliar reform of the liturgy, including its ongoing indigenization.

19. For a very helpful summary of the debates at Trent about liturgical pluriformity, the Roman uniformity imposed after Trent, the Chinese rites

controversy and the intended pluriformity of the present reform see, Giuseppe Alberigo, "Dalla uniformità liturgica del concilio di Trento al pluralismo del Vaticano II," *Rivista Liturgica* 69 (1982) 604–619.

20. We would agree with the observations of Armando Carideo in "Urgenza e significato di una rinnovata ricerca sui fondamenti biblici della Teologia liturgica," *Rivista Liturgica* 65 (1978) 589–590 who states that before the Council the evolution of liturgical theology underscored the need for reform of liturgical celebration; after the Council the reform of liturgical celebration has given urgency to the need to articulate an adequate appreciation of the theological meaning of liturgy, especially of actual celebrations.

21. Important, although tentative, first steps in this direction are offered by the continuing work of various study groups of the North American Academy of Liturgy on how the social sciences contribute to liturgical method, as well as the published studies of liturgical performance by the Georgetown Center for Liturgy, Spirituality and the Arts (see, Lawrence J. Madden, "Introduction," *The Awakening Church, Liturgical Renewal, 1963–1988* [Collegeville: The Liturgical Press, 1992] 1–10) and by Mark Searle and David Leege, "The Celebration of Liturgy in the Parishes," and "Of Piety and Planning: Liturgy, the Parishioners and the Professionals," *Notre Dame Study of Catholic Parish Life*, Reports 5 and 6 (August 1985 and December 1985).

Part 1

Relating Liturgy and Theology

Chapter 1: **Historical Perspectives**

Historical overview of the relationship between liturgy and theology emphasizing modern and contemporary theologians and magisterial statements.

Chapter 2: **Method**

Introduction of book's thesis, summarized by the phrase *context is text—text shapes context,* and consideration of the parameters of this work within broader consideration of method for liturgical theology in general.

Chapter 1

Historical Perspectives

The phrase ascribed to Prosper of Aquitaine *ut legem credendi lex statuat supplicandi* ("the law of prayer grounds the law of belief")[1] has become something of a theme statement for many contemporary authors concerned with liturgical theology, often preferring this original formulation to the shortened *lex orandi, lex credendi* ("the law of prayer [is] the law of belief"). The purpose of this chapter is to explore the original meaning of this key phrase and to describe the relationship between liturgy and theology through Vatican II. As we will see, this relationship can mean giving priority to liturgy over theology, giving priority to theology over liturgy and to the mutual relation of liturgy and theology.[2]

The method employed here will be historical. The first part of the chapter presents how precursors and contemporaries of Prosper of Aquitaine used the liturgy for theological purposes. Next is a discussion of the original setting and meaning of *ut legem credendi lex statuat supplicandi* from Prosper's own writings. This is followed by an overview of how representative patristic and medieval authors used the liturgy for theological purposes, principally what today we would call moral, spiritual and systematic theology. Particularly notable here will be how the liturgy grounded the understanding of sacraments. The mutual relationship between liturgy and theology will be noted especially in the next section dealing with how some Reformers and the bishops at Trent viewed the task of the reform of the liturgy. That there is much contemporary interest in liturgical theology is evident in the final section of the chapter dealing with a review of representative liturgists and theologians as well as a brief overview of magisterial statements through Vatican II.[3]

Prosper of Aquitaine's maxim that the Church's prayer grounds the Church's belief is the first succinct articulation of what had, in fact, already been an accepted premise of theological argument. Evidence as early as Hippolytus' *Apostolic Tradition* and the positions argued by Tertullian, Origen, Cyprian and Augustine are commonly cited as examples of recourse, prior to Prosper, to the Church's liturgy to ground the articulation of its faith. Such recourse was done in a variety of ways including ritual structures, sacramental practices and prayer texts. For example, Hippolytus' argument in the *Apostolic Tradition* was to establish the outline to be followed for praying the Eucharistic anaphora,[4] Tertullian referred to the Church's penitential practices in order to distinguish pardonable from not pardonable sins[5] and Augustine frequently referred to the Church's actual liturgical practice, specifically initiation rites, or parts of the Eucharist such as prayers of the faithful, the Our Father or texts of final blessings to counter the Pelagian heresy.[6] In addition, the exploration of the meaning of such central theological tenets of Christian belief as the mystery of the Trinity, the divinity of Jesus, original sin and the need for grace were very frequently derived from their articulation in the Church's liturgy.[7] The way the Church enacted the liturgy clearly influenced how the Church articulated and described its belief.

Prosper of Aquitaine

The argument of the *Indiculus* of Prosper of Aquitaine was intended to counteract the errors taught by the semi-Pelagians, some of whom were particularly influential in Gaul.[8] His argument here on the necessity of grace finds a parallel text in another of Prosper's works, *De vocatione onmium gentium.*[9] However, here the practice of the Church is set alongside the text of 1 Tim 2:1-6: "first of all I urge that supplications, prayers, intercessions and thanksgivings be made for all. . . ." The argument in the *Indiculus* about justification deriving from God's grace is based principally on a summary of decrees of the Holy See about this doctrine. Prosper argues that next in rank after such decrees are the liturgical prayers which the priest prays which are in accord with apostolic tradition and which the whole Catholic Church employs. This introduces the statement *ut legem credendi lex statuat supplicandi,* the assertion of which leads to a description of the traditional Good Friday intercessions which contain prayers for a variety of people who need the grace of God for a variety of reasons. He cites specifically heretics who need to receive the true catholic faith, schismatics who need the grace of charity that will lead them to the (true) way, sinners who need the grace of penitence, and finally catechumens who need to be brought to the sacrament of regeneration (baptism).[10] Prosper understands that the value of liturgical prayer derives from its conformity with apostolic tradition; its theology is also reliable because of this same apostolic origin.[11] Bernard Capelle will put this statement in line with evidence from the *Didache*, Hippolytus' *Apostolic Tradition*, the Syrian *Didascalia* and the *Apostolic Constitutions* as examples of how the liturgy carried great theological weight. However, especially in this period, liturgy is not marked by textual or ritual fixity; rather, he argues, it as capable of change, evolution and development. While the main structure of the liturgy remained the same, there is a decided interplay and variability of liturgical forms, texts and explanations depending on contemporary controversies and local circumstances.[12] The theological weight of these texts rests upon their conformity with the apostolic faith.

In the *Indiculus*, Prosper argues that the authority of the liturgy did not rest on a specified body of texts derived from the apostolic witness.[13] Here he simply indicates three things: (1) who should be prayed for, (2) what grace is needed for them, and (3) that theological weight is given to these prayers because the whole Church prays for these needs. Hence many commentators distinguish between the theology reflected in the prayers from prayer texts themselves in establishing the value of Prosper's adage. This is a valuable distinction since the prayers are merely alluded to; they are not cited in full. In making this distinction what is commonly asserted is that the evidence proving the error of the semi-Pelagians about the necessity of grace derives not from liturgical prayer *texts* per se but from the *fact* that the Church's liturgical rites include prayer asking that God's grace (in differing ways) would come upon heretics, schismatics, sinners and catechumens.[14] Karl Federer maintains that the theological importance of the Good Friday intercessions referred to by Prosper derives from the fact that they are the Church's chief evidence that prayer for God's grace reflects the Church's belief that the needed grace comes from God.[15] Thus Prosper's argument is in the Augustinian tradition about the need for God's grace to initiate, sustain and complete justification.[16] Prosper's point in referring to the Good Friday intercessions is that in asking that God's grace come to various groups of people the Church asserts its belief (against the Pelagians) that it is grace and not works that leads to salvation.[17] The basis for this argument is the theology reflected in these prayers, not necessarily the specific prayer texts used.[18]

Hence Prosper's dictum *ut legem credendi lex statuat supplicandi* in its original setting means that the liturgy manifests the Church's faith.[19] The statement's reference to the apostolicity of liturgy means that liturgy is a theological source to the degree that it is founded on Scripture and is the expression of a praying Church. Prosper's reference to liturgical texts also implies an appreciation that such texts are poetic, symbolic and more fully existential than rational in composition and style.[20] Thus a proper interpretation of Prosper's valuable adage about the Church at prayer is based on what occurs in the *liturgical event* of Good Friday and it respects the particular genre of liturgical prayer. (As will be noted below, it is far from the kind of textual fundamentalism that plagued some nineteenth century authors' use of liturgical prayers as "proof texts" for doctrine.[21]) A valid interpretation rests on the presumption that the *fact* of the Church's engagement in *rites,* not just texts only, grounds the articulation of the Church's belief. Prosper's argument is also in line with much other patristic evidence that reflects flexibility in liturgical rites and that respects flexibility in interpreting these rites theologically.[22]

Patristic Use of Liturgy for Theology

Patristic literature reflects a liturgical-theological relationship in a number of ways,[23] three of which are of particular import here. The first, and for our purposes the most important, concerns the tradition of mystagogia enshrined in the mystagogic catecheses, that is patristic explanations of the sacraments tied directly to what was spoken and what occurred in the liturgy. The second concerns homilies on liturgical feasts, which explanations help to form the theological understanding and meaning of feasts and seasons.[24] The third concerns theological writings rooted in liturgical practices, for example (as already noted above) Augustine's use of liturgical rites in *De baptismo* and *De peccatorum meritis et remissione et de baptismo.*

As has been argued regarding Prosper of Aquitaine, the authority of the liturgy in the patristic era was not that of a simple deposit transmitted intact. In addition, the *lex orandi* both reflected a living theology and supported a response to liturgy in Christian living. Hence, to use the liturgy to explain the meaning of sacraments resulted in a rich and pluriform sacramental theology (including what may be termed "sacramental ethics"). In order to give proper weight to the authority of the liturgy as a *locus theologicus* in the patristic age Bernard Capelle argues for the following principles of interpretation: (1) study the evidence of the liturgical rite itself, including texts, (2) ascertain its provenance, and (3) investigate how it has been interpreted (then and since).[25] One could draw out the meaning of this last principle by emphasizing the importance of comparing a given liturgical rite with others in both East and West. In addition, without these second and third steps a proper understanding of the authority of the liturgy is severely limited (not to say distorted) because of the potential for textual fundamentalism foreign to the patristic era during which variety in liturgical ritual and in theological meaning flourished. It is commonly held (especially today in light of the present revision of the Rite for the Christian Initiation of Adults) that the patristic era offers a model of how mystagogia should function in the sense of developing the theology and catechesis of sacraments through commentaries on the liturgical rites.[26] At the same time the very variety found in such catecheses invites creativity today in the way that mystagogia can and should function since these catecheses did not (and could not) result in a uniform liturgical/sacramental theology.

For example (generally speaking) the liturgical structure of the Eucharist included (some form of) entrance rite, proclamation of Scripture readings, homily, intercessions, presentation of gifts, proclamation of the anaphora and distribution of Communion. The mystagogic catecheses based on the liturgy of the Eucharist concerned commentaries on the rites, including Scripture texts (particularly those associated with the Eucharist), the anaphora and the eucharistic species. Instances of liturgical pluriformity in this period included the shape of both the introductory and dismissal rites, the choice of Scripture readings, as well as the structure, length, style and theological themes of the anaphora.[27] This liturgical pluriformity was usually more easily seen in the anaphora structure and the comparatively more elaborate anaphora content in the East where themes only briefly noted in the West were more fully enshrined in Eastern texts.[28] Structurally this meant greater emphasis on the epiclesis, for example, and much more elaborate and lyrically rich language throughout the anaphora itself. Theologically the themes receiving greater stress in the East included, for example, praise for creation, more elaborate exploration of the mystery of the Trinity as well as greater emphasis on soteriology and the paschal mystery. Also the prevalent influence of neo-Platonism formed an important philosophical background for the developing Eucharistic catechesis and teaching, particularly in mystagogia.[29] However, liturgical variety was not limited to the East; the varied parts of the Roman Canon attests to the same phenomenon in the West.[30] In fact the differences in the text of the Canon on which Ambrose based part of his catechesis in the *De Mysteriis* and *De Sacramentis* exemplify Western liturgical variety.

Another example concerns the liturgical theology of initiation found in the mystagogic catecheses. By common consensus the mystagogic catecheses of Cyril of Jerusalem offer one example of how the enacted liturgy of the Easter Vigil established the theological explanation of the sacraments of initiation.[31] In accord with Capelle's process of interpretation (noted above) it is important to note that Cyril's explanations rest on the whole complexus that is the liturgy. Among these are the cosmic symbolism of (the directions) East and West, symbolic actions of water bathing and chrism anointing, texts of the renunciation of satan and profession of faith, texts of prayers, Scripture readings (e.g., Rom 6:3-14) and descriptions of ceremonies as a whole. Hence the sources for liturgical theology are many, varied and firmly liturgical in the sense of being components of the ritual action of initiation comprising water immersion, chrismation, and Eucharist. The liturgical theology which derives from such a complexus of liturgical elements can be characterized as (1) *biblical-theological* in the sense of interpreting the Scripture texts with which each of the five catecheses begins, as (2) *systematic* in terms of the theology of initiation which results from commenting on the rites, for example illumination and ecclesial belonging, and (3) *ethical* in terms of the kind of new life which results from sacramental initiation and which ought to be reflected in life.

Capelle's concern to establish the provenance of a liturgical document is important when considering Cyril's catecheses because obviously the architecture of the Church of the Holy Sepulchre influenced both the rites themselves in terms of what was able to be carried out at the Easter Vigil and the liturgical theology derived from the rites. Another aspect of determining its provenance concerns a comparison of the Jerusalem initiatory rites with other contemporary Eastern and Western rites.[32] Such a comparison again demonstrates liturgical pluriformity within stability of liturgical structures. A particularly intriguing example concerns the liturgical theology of postbaptismal anointings, which itself also raises the question of the shift from chrismation to "confirmation," as well as the differences in liturgical practice and theology between the East and West (to use general categories).[33]

In addition, the fact that the prevailing neo-Platonism served as a philosophical background for Cyril's liturgical theology needs to be factored into a consideration of provenance.[34] Here a comment on the kind of language used in the liturgical catecheses is in order, to demonstrate both the influence of neo-Platonic thought and how there was a fluidity in such usage. Yarnold notes that Cyril continually uses the term "sign" in relation to the reality of Christ. In Cyril, "sign" does not mean the absence of the thing signified. Rather "it is the sacramental sign which makes present an aspect of Christ's incarnate life so that we share in it. Baptism symbolizes his sufferings and makes them present; The Eucharist does the same for his body and blood."[35] What adds to the pluriformity motif, however, is that not all patristic authors use the same terms to describe the sign/reality relationship. Terms such as *typos* (type), *eikon* (symbolic imitation), *antitypon* (antitype/sign) and *symbolon* (foreshadowing) can be used almost interchangeably in relation to *aletheia* (reality), *ontos* (reality) and *alethos* (truly).[36] The prevailing theological idea here is soteriological, understood in two senses. First it concerns the work of salvation Christ accomplished. The second, intrinsically related to this, and from our perspective a key theological aspect of liturgy, is the Church's participation in the very act of redemption. This is to suggest that through the liturgy the present Church takes part in the same saving event of (accomplished) redemption through the means native to liturgy—particularly words, gestures and symbols—to the extent that a new event of redemption is experienced. For example, in a neo-Platonic framework the Eucharist is regarded as a "copy," the means through which contemporary communities share in the "original" exalted Lord. Here "copy" conveys a reality not equal with the (now) exalted Lord, but by no means any less "real" a participation in the life of the exalted Lord. In the liturgical theology of the patristic era "symbolic reality" is a helpful way of describing the value of liturgical participation which is the present Church's chief means of participating in the paschal and Trinitarian mysteries.[37]

What is important to note from the methodological point of view in the patristic era is that Prosper's adage captured the sense that the liturgy grounded much of the theology, particularly the sacramental theology, through this period. Two tentative applications for our project can be derived from studying this period, one methodological, the other theological. From this period we learn that it is liturgy as *enacted rites* that serves as the primary source for theology. The hermeneutical principle that we shall argue throughout (specifically in chapter 2) concerns maintaining the cohesiveness and cogency derived from interpreting liturgy as *enacted rites*, not merely independent words and/or symbols. The theological insight derived from this era concerns a theology of sacraments that is rich and multifaceted. That initiation means (among other things) illumination, adoption, purification, enlightenment, filiation, cleansing, renewal, rebirth, incorporation into the paschal mystery and incorporation into the life of the Trinity is based on and derived from the liturgy. This example suggests the application that the more that contemporary theologies of initiation both use the liturgy as its primary source and appropriate insights from previous eras which interpreted such rites (principally the patristic era) the richer it will be in developing initiation theology. What was codified in Prosper of Aquitaine's adage is clearly a reflection of the important liturgical theology of the whole patristic era.

Medieval Relationship Between Liturgy and Theology

Because of his obvious preeminence in this period, two aspects of the teaching of Thomas Aquinas, the representative author for this period, will be discussed here: the relationship between liturgy and theology in general (particularly sacramental theology) and how the liturgy was used specifically as a source for sacramental theology. The specific term *liturgia* was foreign to Aquinas' usage, largely because this Greek-inspired term had dropped out of common usage and was only reappropriated in the second half of the sixteenth century.[38] Rather, Aquinas's teaching on the relationship of liturgy to theology is found in his treatment of the allied terms *ceremonia, cultus, devotio, minister, ministerium, munus, mysterium, obsequium, officium, offerre, religio, ritus,* and *sacramentum.*[39] To the specific question of how Aquinas understood liturgy as a source for theology[40] (admitting that the word "liturgy" is anachronistic) it is clear that Aquinas regarded liturgy as one of the Church's *auctoritates* and not as a *locus theologicus* (this would mean a diminishment). Aquinas distinguished among three authorities: (1) the doctrine and the practice of the Church, (2) the apostolic tradition, i.e., the teaching of the Fathers transmitted in the Church's life, and (3) sacred Scripture. He understands the liturgy to be a major part of the first of these *auctoritates* along with councils and papal teachings.[41] He argues that this is an appropriate understanding of the liturgy since in the liturgy the faith and life of the Church is manifested.[42]

The clearest expression of Aquinas' liturgical interest is found in his discussion of the relationship between Christian cult and the Trinity, the action of the Spirit, the mystery of Christ and the ecclesial reality of sacraments.[43] Despite the experienced diminishment of popular participation in sacramental liturgy (especially when compared with the patristic era) Aquinas repeatedly asserts the ecclesial reality of sacraments from objective and subjective perspectives emphasizing the *fides ecclesiae,* the *actus ecclesiae,* the *intentio Ecclesiae,* and the *ritus ecclesiae* in sacramental activity.[44] Here Aquinas' assertion that the prayer of the Church takes priority over the private prayer of individual believers would not be surprising considering his own mendicant observance emphasizing communal celebration of the Eucharist and the hours.

Regarding the theological explanation of sacraments, the scriptural Word proclaimed at sacramental liturgy and the Scriptures as containing some foundations for sacraments, continue to have an important role in Thomas's sacramental teaching as they did in the patristic era. Thus the close association of Word and rite seen in patristic liturgy and catecheses was sustained, at least to some extent. Thomas stands in line with Augustinian sacramental teaching emphasizing that it is the Incarnate Word who gives power to sacramental words.[45] However, Aquinas gives particular attention to the "sacramental words" spoken by the priest at the core of the rite, most usually in connection with sacramental symbols such as water, bread and wine, etc. He sees these words as a spiritual factor that gives precision to the significance of the symbolic action or material element in use. It is in this way that he adopts the terminology of "matter" and "form" to describe the Augustinian contention that the element and the Word together comprise a sacrament.[46]

A matter of some debate among those who comment on Aquinas' sacramental teaching concerns his notion of symbol as related to his more customary use of *signum*. Even at its most minimal understanding Aquinas' insistence on the necessity and importance of "matter" in sacramental liturgy refers to the grounding of sacraments in symbolic engagement. Authors debate the significance of the difference between "sign" and "symbol" in Aquinas. Pedro Fernandez will assert that Aquinas' use of *signa* over *symbola* is the result of a linguistic adjustment and that *signa* should not be understood as having a theological meaning different from that of *symbola*.[47] The reality effected in sacraments is fundamentally a faith expression done through Word and sacramental gesture in order to continue the redemptive work of Christ, particularly our sharing in the passion and the paschal mystery. For Aquinas the reality both *signified and caused* by the sacrament is concretized in the grace of justification.[48] A chief legacy of Thomas to subsequent sacramental theology is his assertion *sacramenta significando causant*. Contemporary and subsequent theories of sacramental causality need to be measured in relation to this Thomistic adage.[49]

While medieval authors would sustain the important patristic insight that sacraments were a source of healing, they gave it a new dimension by focusing more directly on individuals and their eternal salvation.[50] The exact causes for this are hard to ascertain precisely, but the lessening of liturgical participation and (later) the black death were contributing factors. Aquinas is particularly faithful to liturgical expression when he discusses the triple temporal dimension of grace: past, present and future. This links with his understanding of sacraments. He states: "hence as a sign a sacrament has a threefold function. It is at once commemorative of that which has gone before, namely the Passion of Christ, and demonstrative of that which is brought about in us through the Passion

12

of Christ, namely grace, and prognostic, i.e., a foretelling of future glory."[51]

Even the rather elusive notion of sacramental character receives something of a liturgical dimension in Aquinas.[52] He asserts that character is oriented to participation in the (exterior) cult of the Church—*relatio ad ecclesiam*. This is also reiterated when he speaks of sacraments of the New Law containing a double objective: remedy for sins and a spiritual perfection that pertains to the worship of God.[53] The specific relationship of cult and character in Aquinas concerns believers' participation in the priesthood of Christ. He distinguishes active from passive participation; active participation comes through orders, passive participation derives from baptism and confirmation.[54] Here one sees the influence of the way the liturgy was celebrated with increasing emphasis on the work of the ordained for the baptized. This is clearly exemplified both in baptism and Eucharist with the priest acting *in persona Christi*.[55]

With the demise of the adult catechumenate, the rise of *quam primum* infant baptism and the concomitant ritual adjustments (or lack of adjustment) to suit this new pastoral need, it is not surprising that scholastic initiation theology emphasized what the rite accomplished for the child. The removal of original sin received due emphasis in Aquinas. However other aspects of initiation theology from the patristic era continued to exert their influence through important notions such as illumination, filiation, life in the Trinity, experiencing the paschal mystery etc. The effects of water baptism were explored in a rather balanced way. Initiation meant far more than the removal of sin, and of the obstacles that impede humanity's appropriation of salvation. Initiation was the chief means of transforming and perfecting human beings so that they could take part in Christian worship.[56] Baptism initiated one into the priestly people who offer to God the glory of Christ himself.[57]

Scholastic Eucharistic theology as exemplified in Aquinas' teaching[58] combines a theology of Eucharist with a theology of priesthood because it is through the priest's words and actions that the Eucharistic species comes about, both for Communion (at least of the priest, less so for the community) and for Eucharistic adoration. The patristic emphasis on symbol and symbolic language that could uphold the reality of Eucharistic presence through a word like *figura* now diminishes (especially after the Berengarian controversy). Categories from Aristotelian thought were used to explain the difference between presence "in truth" and presence "in figure." The previous contention that the "truth" was seen in the "figure" was replaced by increased emphasis on the phrase "either in figure or in truth." Hence, Aquinas will distinguish between "figures" and "sacraments."[59] Despite this shift in terminology (understood to be necessary at the time)[60] one must credit Aquinas with sustaining a Eucharistic teaching that avoided both a "crassly realistic" approach or a "merely spiritual" approach. He also sustained some emphasis on sacramental sign in the Eucharist, although this was decidedly diminished from that of the patristic era.

To the specific question of how the liturgy served as a source for sacramental theology it may be asserted that some measure of influence continued, but in a manner different from the patristic era. For example, initiation theology reflected the contemporary emphasis on *who* was initiated, *when* and *how*. The comparatively complete and elaborate descriptions from patristic sources of the catechumenate, initiation liturgy and liturgical theology now waned because adult initiation ceded to the more common practice of infant initiation. Hence the Lenten rites of the catechumenate and their catechetical instructions were telescoped into a baptismal rite for children held at one time.[61] In the West the separation of water baptism from chrismation influenced the development of a theology of confirmation which was at least distinguished, if not separated, from baptism. (This was not the case in the East where the sacraments of initiation were kept together, whether for adults or children, both ritually and theologically.[62]) Similarly, Aquinas's theory about confirmation was clearly influenced by the thirteenth-century practice of administering confirmation in late childhood[63] and his approach to anointing of the sick reflected the contemporary practice of delaying this anointing until one was near death.[64]

While it is clear that medieval theologians were preoccupied with a systematization of sacraments less influenced by the rites themselves when compared to the patristic era, nevertheless one can also say that the sacramental practices of the day continued to play an important role in medieval understandings of sacraments. The *lex orandi* was not absent; it was understood in a different way. It is important to be fair to Aquinas' teaching in that it reflected the needed systematization of theology at the time and yet sustained some measure of reference to liturgical practice, if not the full liturgical reality assumed in the patristic age. Just as the liturgy was not the sole source for theology in the patristic era (recalling the use of Scripture, the teaching of other Fathers and neo-Platonism) so for Thomas liturgy was regarded as one of the *auctoritates* for theology alongside Scripture and Aristotelian philosophy. Undoubtedly commentators on Aquinas and later Thomists did something of an injustice to the careful, balanced and measured scholastic theology he produced. Somewhat later descriptions of the mechanistic understanding of the priest's role in sacraments and the devotional practice of Eucharistic adoration as opposed to sharing in Eucharistic Communion, would affect medieval Eucharistic theology and piety. Eucharistic practices such as the private Mass and the stipend system were hardly prime examples of what Eucharistic Liturgy should be. Yet it was these practices above all that would influence both the sacramental theology and piety of this era.[65] Liturgy continued to influence theology but more as rites performed *for* the people, than *by* and *with* the community.

Reformation and Trent: Relating Liturgy and Theology

The risk of generalization about what are very complex matters is invariably the danger inherent in dealing with the period of the Reformers and Trent. Particularly because theological reasons and concerns influence the way the liturgy was changed by both the Reformers and in the Catholic Church after Trent, skillful guides are needed to assess the important persons and evidence concerning our specific interest about relating liturgy and theology. One such guide is Geoffrey Wainwright.

With regard to the Reformation specifically, Wainwright asserts that "the Protestant Reformers sought a root-and-branch cleansing of medieval western doctrine and its liturgical expression."[66] He argues that the basis for this cleansing was largely theological (based on the Scriptures) and that such an approach was not new. His helpful sketch of "doctrinal control over liturgy in the early Church" (in chapter 8) is based on his working assumption that the couplet *lex orandi, lex credendi* can be and has been interpreted to mean that liturgy can influence theology and that theology can influence liturgy.[67] Here he demonstrates the important example of doctrinal concerns in the great prayer of Eucharistic thanksgiving.[68] In another example he adopts Jungmann's thesis about the anti-Arian motif as having "the profoundest effects on the Church's liturgy."[69] He then cites examples from the Augsburg Confession, the preface to the *Book of Common Prayer* and the *Forme des prières* of John Calvin to show how this movement sought to establish correct, biblical, teaching in the liturgy.[70] Wainwright argues persuasively that the Protestant tradition gave appropriate priority to *lex credendi* when it came to forms of existing worship that needed correction. He argues that this should be regarded favorably especially because, from the time of the early Church, doctrinal control had to be exercised over the liturgy. This became especially necessary at the Reformation when the Reformers purged the existing liturgical rites of non-scriptural assumptions, usages, and references.[71]

Wainwright will admit, however, that "there is undoubtedly a strong streak of didacticism in the reformed rites."[72] But such a charge should not be made of Wainwright's own appreciation of liturgy since he repeatedly maintains that liturgy is first of all a living ritual action directed toward the experience of God. Despite his reliance on liturgical texts (especially hymns reflecting his own worship tradition[73]) Wainwright appropriately argues against a liturgy that is overly didactic.

For our purposes, Wainwright's argument about historical precedent for doctrinal influence on shaping forms of worship and the example of the Reformers in this regard is most helpful. The relationship of the *lex orandi* to the *lex credendi* is more continuous and dialectical than is sometimes assumed. It is clear that the liturgy at the time of the Reformation was in great need of reform, needing specific adjustments that were theologically accurate and authentic. In the *Apostolic Constitution* promulgating the Roman Missal after Vatican II Pope Paul VI cited Pius V's constitution *Quo primum* promulgating the Roman Missal after Trent where the pope alluded to the necessity of reforming the liturgy by noting that "the study 'of ancient manuscripts in the Vatican library and elsewhere' . . . helped greatly in the correction of the Roman Missal."[74]

In addition to the voices and initiatives of the Reformers, Roman Catholics were also keen on initiating such a reform,[75] sometimes looking toward liturgical reform as a prime means for unifying the Church. Yet the debates at Trent should not be understood to require either ecclesiological or liturgical uniformity. The decrees of Trent themselves also sanctioned specific, local rites. This meant that the liturgy used by any religious community or non-Roman Western rite that was in existence for over two hundred years could remain a local usage.[76] When Trent dealt with liturgical reform at first it was an empirical approach that concerned specific abuses.[77] Later they called for the (Roman) revision of two key books. the Missal and the Breviary.

The Fathers at Trent evidenced oscillation in the reform of the liturgy, however. In addition to sanctioning local usages they required that liturgical reforms were to be approved by the pope, not by individual bishops, which approval was to be in accord with the decrees and direction of the Council itself.[78] Later on (for a variety of reasons) this came to mean a tenacious uniformity defended as essentially good for the faith. What occurred with the publication of the Roman Breviary (1568) and the Roman Missal (1570) was a liturgical reform not from the council but from Rome, which reform led to a Romanization of the Western Church.[79] This has rightly been judged a liturgical uniformity hitherto unknown[80] in the sense that while formerly liturgical rites were evaluated for orthodoxy, now the Holy See was to take significant initiative in adjusting and regulating rites. The publication of a *Roman* Breviary and Missal would insure their being taken seriously.

It was especially after the Council of Trent that a clear separation developed between the liturgy and sacramental theology. In the wake of the Tridentine concern for rubrical precision in the doing of the liturgy, demonstrated by the printing of rubrics in the Roman Missal and Ritual, liturgy became equated with the external performance of the Church's rites. Sacramental theology was incorporated into manuals of dogmatic theology which paid little attention to the rites themselves as a theological source. The sacramental discussions in such manuals focused on the Reformation debates about causality, the number of sacraments and their institution.[81] The divorce between the *lex orandi* and *lex credendi* was exemplified in the division of what had been a single area of study into two: liturgy and sacramental theology. Thus what resulted was a rather legalistic understanding of liturgy with sacramental theology assigned to dogmatic tracts. Most theological manuals after Trent were highly apologetic in tone and many were merely compilations of Tridentine decrees with some commentary. This resulted in imbalanced tracts whose content was severely limited since Trent dealt with *ad hoc* issues regarding sacraments. In fact, its decrees were never intended to be a complete sacramental theology or to disclose a complete theology of a particular sacrament.[82] However, given the need to reassert Roman Catholic teaching, it was understandable that subsequent theological manuals would reiterate and sometimes explain, but rarely go beyond, the parameters set by Trent's decrees. Given the pervasiveness of this attitude after Trent, it is not surprising that some authors in the early evolution of the liturgical movement can now be criticized for an almost exclusively apologetic approach to liturgical sources whereby liturgical texts were used as "proofs" and doctrinal authoritative statements.[83] In fact, what they were doing was imitating a post-Tridentine approach to Catholic theology derived from the manuals.

From our methodological interest it is clear that a relationship existed between liturgy and theology at and after Trent, with the greater weight being given to how correct theology influenced the reform of the Western liturgy. Y. Brilioth will assert that "liturgy and doctrine always influence one another in a variety of ways, and the formulae of worship come to embody the conclusions of theological speculation."[84] This was certainly true during the Reformation and at Trent.

Modern Theologians

What broke through the post Tridentine rubrical understanding of liturgy and sacraments was undoubtedly historical study of the evolution of rites and their theological interpretation.[85] Since the historical study of liturgy was concomitant with the revival of interest in the Fathers of the Church, it is not surprising that historical research explored how a study of the patristic era most especially could disclose a theology of liturgy not then commonly appreciated. By this time the categories of "matter and form" in sacramental theology from Aquinas on (given the Aristotelian framework for his theology) came to be understood in very minimalistic and legalistic ways. With the advent of historical interest in liturgy clear advances were made into exploring the theological meaning of liturgical rites.

The name of the abbot of Solesmes, Prosper Guéranger (1805–1875) is synonymous with nineteenth-century historical and pastoral writing on liturgy. His principal works concerned both historical and theological foundations for appreciating the liturgy in *Institutions liturgiques*[86] and his multi-volume commentary on the liturgical calendar, *L'Année liturgique.*[87] After a comparatively brief section on definitions and the importance of liturgical study in the *Institutions*, Guéranger sets forth a rather detailed review of the historical evolution of the Western liturgy.[88] That Guéranger's interest was also pastoral is seen in his repeated references to the beauty, dignity and mystical character of the liturgy.[89] However, Guéranger's writing also showed him to be a fierce champion of a rather clericalized liturgy and Roman centralization of the liturgy, to the point of calling neo-Gallican initiatives in liturgy "anti-liturgy."[90] Whatever the critical assessment of Guéranger, his work will remain a landmark in the evolving historical study of liturgy, which study also contained important theological insight.[91]

The early decades of the twentieth century mark important years for the growing liturgical movement. Its chief concerns were both historical study and the pastoral appreciation of liturgy (especially through active participation) of the Church's (official) prayer. Louis Bouyer will credit Lambert Beauduin (1873–1960) with beginning the liturgical movement in this century with his celebrated lecture at the Malines (Belgium) conference in 1903.[92] Beauduin's interest was primarily the ecclesiological aspects of the liturgy, specifically the renewal of the Church through an appreciation of what liturgy is and does in the Church. This is coupled with his keen pastoral zeal in renewing liturgical celebration as a source of spirituality for the people.[93] With regard to the relationship between liturgy and theology, Beauduin will not hesitate to state that liturgy expresses the "theology of the people" and "dogma spoken by our mother [the Church]."[94] He begins his *Essai de manuel fondamental de liturgie* by stating that if theology is the science about God and of divine things, it is clear that liturgy rightly pertains to this science.[95]

Beauduin will assert directly that dogma is to liturgy what thought is to the orator, what the ideal is to the artist, and what the soul is to the body. The first condition of the cult is that it be *true.*[96] He notes that liturgy does not propose dogmas as theses, but that the liturgy assimilates dogma into its formulas, rites, chants and symbols. On the other hand, liturgy renders to dogma the service of giving terminology to dogmas; liturgical books are a theological source of the first value.[97] Beauduin underscores his characteristically ecclesial understanding of the liturgy when he states (1) that the theological value of liturgy derives from its being the testimony of all the Churches and has been used for generations in the worship of God[98] (2) that liturgy is the catechism of the people, and when he argues (3) that liturgy is important in order to prevent spirituality from becoming too individualistic.[99] This ecclesiological concern is deepened in Beauduin's assertion that the ultimate end and goal of all liturgical cult is the Church's life in the Trinity, described as an economic Trinitarian theology expressed and experienced in the liturgy.[100]

Beauduin's lasting legacy regarding the developing thought on liturgical theology is his emphasis on the interrelationship between liturgy and theology and his emphasis on ecclesiology as the essential foundation for the theology of liturgy. Not surprisingly, when Beauduin cites the liturgy specifically it is most usually the texts of prayers or chants. Positively this shows his deep knowledge and reverence for such texts. Negatively it can be interpreted to be a kind of liturgical textual fundamentalism. Beauduin is not alone in this kind of usage.[101] To be fair, however, a kind of "proof text" method is reflected in much dogmatic theology contemporary with Beauduin.

Beauduin's ecclesiological vision of the liturgy was shared and expressed creatively in a number of the writings of Romano Guardini (1885–1968).[102] Equally pastoral in his concern that the celebration of the liturgy have its effect on the moral and spiritual lives of its participants,[103] Guardini's work has rightly been characterized as a liturgical theology with a particularly systematic slant.[104] For Guardini the liturgy is the *lex orandi* for every kind of prayer; it is the supreme (but not the unique) form of prayer. The liturgical participant is part of the unity of the believing community, that is the Church.[105] The liturgy, with its appropriate "style" and its special symbolism, is at once joyful and serious, and always the profound expression of the Church offering believers a way to live daily life based on this privileged communal experience of God.[106] For Guardini the celebration of the liturgy was important, but it was also indispensably linked to a "liturgical *life*," understood as the necessary consequence of liturgical celebration.[107]

To this ecclesial self-expression Guardini will emphasize that the liturgy should be understood and experienced as the memorial event of the paschal mystery of Jesus.[108] He argues the liturgy is a special "epiphany" of the saving realities of creation, the incarnation and the Church.[109] To this notion of epiphany Guardini adds the pivotal term "memorial," understood as the saving act of Christ already fully accomplished in history yet perennially manifest through the liturgy. Thus the liturgy is the moment when Christ's act of redemption is experienced anew, which experience is not a repetition but a renewal of redemption for the sake of the Church.[110] Thus Guardini refrains from psychological descriptions of the redemption experienced through liturgy; he prefers the term "actualize."[111]

Guardini argues that historical research is only one component of his method for exploring his vision of pastoral liturgy.[112] He firmly insisted throughout his writings on what he calls liturgical education and liturgical formation.[113] For Guardini this concerns a deep appreciation for the *epiphany* of liturgy, emphasizing especially its Christological and ecclesial aspects. In terms of liturgical theology this would mean that the experience of the Church's *lex orandi* should assimilate the Church into this privileged expression of redemption.[114] One might term this a profound *appreciation* of liturgy as the epiphany in the Church of the memorial of Christ's redemption. At the same time, Guardini is not to be charged with archaism or a rigidly fixed notion of liturgical forms. Hence, during the Second Vatican Council he argued for a liturgical reform that was faithful to tradition but which also addressed what had been lacking in the present (Tridentine) liturgy. One such example concerns the experience of the Word at worship and an appropriate theology of the Word of God as expressed in liturgy.[115]

The clear Christological emphasis in Guardini's work is also at the center of Odo Casel's (1886–1948) influential theology of liturgy as *Mysteriengegenwart* and his study *Das christliche Kultmysterium*. Casel was concerned to break through then operative neo-Scholastic theories of grace which tended to compartmentalize growth in the spiritual life according to categories of uncreated and created grace. His study of patristic authors and of pagan mystery cults enabled him to find a way to express Christian liturgy as the mystery of Christ himself present and effective for the good of the Church.[116] For Casel the Christian mystery is threefold. First it is God "considered in himself, as the infinitely distant, holy, unapproachable. . . ."[117] Second it is Christ himself, the mystery in person "because he shows the invisible godhead in the flesh."[118] Third, "since Christ is no longer visible among us, in St. Leo the Great's words: 'what was visible in the Lord has passed over into the mysteries'."[119] Thus he asserts that the subject of this book is "the meaning of the divine mystery and the meaning of Christian worship in the Christian scheme." For him the apex of Christian revelation is Christ as a *mysterium,*

"as St. Paul means the word, a revelation made by God to man through acts of god-manhood, full of life and power; it is mankind's way to God made possible by this revelation and the grace of it communicating the solemn entry of the redeemed Church into the presence of the everlasting Father through sacrifice, through perfect devotion; it is the glory that blossoms out of it. At the mid-point of the Christian religion, therefore, stands the *Pasch,* the passage which the Son of God who appeared in the flesh of sin, makes to the Father."[120]

This Christological emphasis in liturgy leads to an ecclesiological emphasis as well. "The Church, not yet brought to her completion, is drawn into this sacrifice of his; as he sacrificed for her, she now takes an active part in his sacrifice, makes it her own, and is raised thereby with him from the world to God, and glorified."[121] Casel's argument in *The Mystery of Christian Worship* expands on these central insights. The book is replete with references to patristic authors (such as Cyril of Jerusalem and Gregory Nazianzen)[122] reflective of Casel's appreciation for the way the patristic era appreciated the theology of liturgy.

Casel's theories were groundbreaking at the time (but are rather commonplace in liturgical understanding today) and his work influenced many others (for example Salvatore Marsili will not hesitate to note that he was a disciple of Casel's).[123] He has also been criticized. Louis Bouyer will criticize Casel's work on the basis of his definition of *mysterium.* Bouyer argues that there is a world of difference between pagan Hellenism and Christianity in the way each uses this term. *The* mystery in Christianity is Christ, the revealer of God's wisdom, as revealed in Christ the Word and Christ the crucified. Nothing of the esoteric ritual of pagan Hellenism ought to be used when trying to comprehend Christ as mystery.[124]

Three other criticisms are germane. One concerns Casel's understanding of the Church. Given the advances in prior writing in the Liturgical Movement (e.g., Beauduin) about the active participation of the community in liturgy (as endorsed by popes such as Pius X) it is surprising that Casel's notion of Church as participant in the mystery of Christ would be comparatively objective and institutional in the sense that it stresses more the Church as the locus for experiencing the mystery of Christ rather than as active participants in Christ who are thus changed and become more Christ-like.[125] A certain cultic and ecclesiological self-consciousness may thus be said to mark Casel's theology of liturgy. Second, as has been noted by others,[126] is the regrettable absence of a pneumatological emphasis to this important theological synthesis. Given the fact that Casel used so many patristic sources, it is surprising that their pneumatological and Trinitarian emphases would not find their way into his theory. These two criticisms are connected in that the one influences the other; more emphasis on the Church could easily lead to emphasis on the Trinity and vice versa. The third criticism is the lack of precision in Casel's citations from patristic authors.[127] However, in sum, from the point of view of liturgical theology it is clear that Casel's important contribution was to present a theology of the liturgy based on an actualization of the mystery of Christ through the liturgy.

Anton Baumstark's (1873–1960) work *Comparative Liturgy* (still) stands as a classic description of the evolution of liturgical method from the 1930's. Baumstark asserts that the subject matter of liturgy belongs to theology; its method is empirical and grounded in history.[128] By "comparative method" Baumstark means the empirical investigation of the "origins and variations of the changing forms of this enduring substance of eternal value [the liturgy]."[129]

Baumstark asserts and then substantiates two antitheses: uniformity versus variety in the liturgical life and in each of its forms; and second, austerity versus richness.[130] He argues that as one goes back in history variety in liturgical forms increases. Here he cites various examples of Eucharistic prayers in the East and differences among sacramentaries in the West. In addition he argues that as the liturgy evolved its original brevity and simplicity led to greater richness and prolixity.[131] He argues for the importance of a comparative method that includes both a study of liturgical rites and of liturgical texts. With regard to textual study he argues for rigorous philological investigation. He observes that the later a text is the more "liturgical prose becomes charged with doctrinal elements."[132]

It is not surprising that Baumstark's principles of liturgical study and "laws of liturgical evolution" would find a congenial home with other liturgists who have seen the historical study of liturgy as a key to understanding. Baumstark's focus on texts was made easier for students of liturgy considering the publication in this century of important sacramentaries, pontificals, *ordines*, lectionary lists and the like. While Baumstark addresses the need to deal with "liturgical action," his work emphasizes more fully the textual aspects of liturgy (which he calls "liturgical prose" and "liturgical poetry"). What we would now regard as something of a flaw is succinctly capsulized in Botte's rather straightforward caution about "being duped by words."[133] However, this is not meant to denigrate in any way the important synthesis of liturgical method offered and exemplified in *Comparative Liturgy*. Baumstark's knowledge of the sources and his power of synthesis are laudable. That his method remains discussed and to some degree is still used as a foundation of liturgical study evidences why this work can be called a classic.

The work of three systematic theologians is worth recalling here to note that not just liturgists were concerned to preserve an appreciation of the relationship between liturgy and theology. In his ranking of theological sources in *La foi et la théologie* Yves Congar will place liturgy after Scripture and the magisterium and before Church Fathers, Church discipline and theologians.[134] He asserts that the liturgy is not an arsenal of arguments, but that it is the *didascalia* of the Church. Liturgy is first and foremost the means through which one penetrates into, and thus experiences, the paschal mystery.[135] Most interesting methodologically and from the point of view of appreciating what liturgy is, Congar suggests that beyond texts the sources of liturgy include epigraphy, archeology, iconography, and the practice of the Church.[136] In *Tradition and Traditions* Congar elaborates on liturgy more fully and asserts that it is "the expression of a Church actively living, praising God and bringing about a holy communion with him."[137] Fundamentally, liturgy is a sacred action containing the intimacy of a living experience. In it the Church expresses its faith "hymning it, practicing it, in a living celebration wherein too, it makes a complete self-giving."[138] Congar goes on to underscore the uniqueness of liturgy by stating that the liturgy "does not insert Christ's work merely by proclamation and teaching but through the unique and *sui generis* reality of the sacramental order; it is able to assume the form of a present reality, at once hidden and revealed, and active . . . ."[139] He understands liturgy to disclose means germane to a ritual action—symbols and rites—more than the mind can grasp about the reality of God.[140] The advantage of Congar's brief references to liturgy is that they occupy an important place in his method and theology. He understands liturgy as a pluriform action, the complexity of whose nature one must respect when trying to interpret it for theological purposes.[141]

A second systematician to be credited with articulating the place of liturgy in delineating the sources of revelation is Edward Schillebeeckx. In *Revelation and Theology* he asserts that "in addition to the universal councils of the Church, liturgical prayer, as the official prayer of the Church, is one of the most characteristic expressions in which the unanimity of the Church's faith . . . can be made external in a truly authentic manner."[142] At base Schillebeeckx underscores the uniqueness of liturgy by stating that "sacramental liturgy is nonetheless in principle an act of the Church's teaching authority. . . ."[143] Schillebeeckx is careful to assert (along with Pius XII) that the liturgy does not necessarily *give rise to dogma;*[144] rather the liturgy *manifests* dogma.[145] He argues that while "dogma and liturgy are constantly acting and reacting on each other . . . a deeper knowledge of faith does not of itself bring about a development in liturgical rites."[146]

As far as ranking the importance of liturgy as it relates to theology Schillebeeckx will (understandably) respond with a Thomistic spin. He argues that the liturgy's manifestation of dogma

"coincides with what Aquinas called the *consuetudo ecclesiae* ('practice of the church'), which was, in his opinion, more important in resolving theological questions than the doctrine of theologians or even of the church fathers, because liturgical practice is the most characteristic manifestation within the church of the church's faith, together with the church's explicit and solemn declarations of dogma."[147]

Most likely because his discussion is even briefer than Congar's, Schillebeeckx's argument is helpful yet limited. One would have wanted a fuller explanation of what he means by saying that liturgy is an *act* of the Church's teaching authority. One would also have wished for a more complete description of what he means by liturgy and what comprises the liturgy (especially its non textual aspects).

In the *Mysterium Salutis* encyclopedia, A. Stenzel offers a carefully crafted consideration of how liturgy functions as one of the means whereby revelation is transmitted. In this setting it is significant that he places liturgy ahead of kerygma (and Christian art) as modes of transmitting revelation. For him liturgy is a *locus* of theology primarily because it is a particular expression of Christ's high priesthood which sanctifies its participants.[148] His argument is historical in the way he reviews how liturgy has been essentially linked to dogma and how the Church's faith has been expressed through the liturgy's use of doxologies and symbols.[149] In light of Pius XII's statement in *Mediator Dei* he argues that liturgy is best understood as witness and commentator on the faith. Thus he inserts into this discussion how the liturgy is a profession of faith, which faith profession the liturgy is meant to foster.[150] Stenzel is quite careful to underscore that the relationship between liturgy and theology is really indirect since the direct object of the liturgy is not so much teaching, or the transmission of truths—it is concerned with experiencing the reality of salvation in Christ.[151] Here he cites a number of patristic authors to indicate the ways in which the liturgy has traditionally functioned as this experience of faith. He then uses the example of anamnesis to underscore the way liturgy expresses and transmits the faith.[152]

What is helpful in Stenzel's argument is his careful historical review of the adage from Prosper of Aquitaine, his setting this study within the contemporary framework of how liturgy and theology are interrelated and how he carefully ascribes to liturgy a unique role in the expression of faith as it functions primarily as an experience of salvation. Thus he articulates how faith must necessarily function as a foundation for linking liturgy and theology. It is notable that this discussion of liturgy and theology is followed by an elaborate discussion of how kerygma is linked to dogma, again with a proper emphasis on faith and the transmission of faith through revelation expressed in and through the Church.

Church Pronouncements

That the notion of *lex orandi* was not absent from magisterial teaching since Trent is evident in the references which Herman Schmidt traces to the "law of prayer."[153] That it forms at least part of source for dogmatic theology is also clear in the cataloging provided by Ph. Oppenheim.[154] With regard to papal teachings, Schmidt notes, for example, the statements regarding *lex orandi* of Sixtus V (1587), *Immensa aeterni* establishing the Congregation of Rites, and Pius IX (1854) and *Ineffabilis Deus* on the dogma of the Immaculate Conception.[155] The latter is particularly significant given its temporal coincidence with Guéranger and the fact that Protestant writers will cite this as among the more problematic instances of *lex orandi* grounding *lex credendi*.[156]

In his review of papal references from Trent to Pius XII, Herman Schmidt notes that Sixtus V (in 1587) and Pius IX (in 1854) each referred once to the *lex orandi* basing the *lex credendi*. He then ascribes two references to Pius XI (1925, 1928) and three to Pius XII (1943, 1947, 1950).[157] Clearly Pius XI's first usage is among the more significant pronouncements (in *Quas primas* establishing the feast of Christ the King)[158] where he stated that "the liturgy . . . is the most important organ of the ordinary magisterium of the Church. . . . (*legem credendi lex statuit supplicandi*). The liturgy is not the *didascalia* of this or that individual, but the *didascalia* of the Church."[159]

However, it is Pius XII's use of a variation on this adage in *Mediator Dei* which proves fertile ground for liturgists and theologians since it is found in an encyclical on the nature of the sacred liturgy itself. The adage is found in two places: par. 45 *lex orandi lex credendi* and par. 47 *lex credendi legem statuat supplicandi*.[160] Clearly the first citation conforms with the precedents discussed in this chapter. The second presents a new twist, especially for Roman Catholics, in the sense that here Pius XII acknowledges an interrelation between *orandi* and *credendi* and refrains from giving absolute priority to *lex orandi*.[161] Commentators will argue that the pope's adjustment of the classic adage was intended to counteract the use of the phrase by Modernists such as George Tyrell.[162]

What is most helpful about this encyclical is its articulation of a theology of liturgy in an unprecedented document in the then burgeoning Liturgical Movement.[163] One of the chief characteristics of the theology of liturgy articulated here is its christological focus, with special emphasis on soteriology and sanctification derived from Christ's humanity.[164] The addition of a notable ecclesiological dimension to Pius XII's understanding of liturgy is found in the instruction on music in liturgy, *De Musica sacra et de sacra Liturgia* (1958). Here the liturgy is described as constituting the public cult of the mystical body of Christ, head and members, a sentiment derived from Pius XII's *Mystici Corporis*.[165] However, on other matters, the instruction is rather juridical in tone, somewhat akin to some of the language in *Mediator Dei*.

Clearly, the Constitution on the Sacred Liturgy of Vatican II introduced a new phase in understanding what liturgy is and how the liturgy ought to be celebrated with "full, conscious and active participation" of the faithful as "the aim to be considered above all else" (n. 14).[166] As we noted[167] this constitution places important emphasis on the theological dimensions of liturgy. Besides giving priority to the study of liturgy in theological schools it articulates the overriding principle that the reform of the liturgy should be undertaken in light of theological, historical, and pastoral investigations.[168]

Cipriano Vagaggini will remark that the Constitution has no desire to offer a rigorously technical definition of the liturgy.[169] Therefore one needs to look at its descriptions of what is accomplished in the liturgy to understand liturgy's theological foundations. Commentators generally agree that par. 7 is foundational here for its emphasis on liturgy as an exercise of the high priesthood of Christ, that by means of signs, humanity is sanctified and that the liturgy is enacted by the whole body of Christ, head and members. With regard to the theological dimensions of the liturgy more specifically par. 10 is particularly instructive. The often quoted phrase that the liturgy is "the summit toward which the activity of the Church is directed; at the same time it is the fountain from which all her power flows" is not cultic self-consciousness, because almost immediately the balance of the text underscores the apostolic nature of the Church as it is fed at the liturgy and that the liturgy joins the Church together in unity and love. As Church documents have asserted since Pius X, the liturgy concerns both the glorification of God and the sanctification of humanity. Clear ecclesiological emphases of the liturgy are underscored in the Liturgy Constitution par. 2 and 26 (among others) which understandings reflect an ecclesiology of communion unlike the kind of juridical ecclesiology that marked *Mediator Dei*.[170] While many of the subsequent statements on the Constitution may be read as comparatively legalistic in tone, their purpose overall is to reform the liturgy to foster the "full, conscious, and active participation in liturgical celebrations called for by the very nature of the liturgy" (par. 14).

In light of our methodological interest here, three main points can be made about the Liturgy Constitution. First, there is clear affirmation of the *theological* value of liturgical celebration, which emphasis happily transcends the comparatively juridical and rubrical assertions of that preceded it (even in this century). Second, the consideration of liturgy as a central moment in the Church's life helps to contextualize liturgical celebration within and as an essential focus in the Christian life while maintaining its status as "summit and source" of the Church's life. Third, the ecclesiological emphasis of liturgy leads to raising the question about the way the liturgy is celebrated so that active participation is effected and the Church grows into full stature in Christ.[171]

The theological emphasis on liturgy of the Liturgy Constitution is found in other Vatican II documents, among which are the Dogmatic Constitution on the Church and the Decree on Ecumenism. The Constitution on the Church emphasizes the interrelationship between sacraments and the building up of the body of Christ generally speaking (par. 7) and of the interrelationship between Eucharist and the building up of the local Church in particular (par. 26). Significantly, such assertions require an appreciation of the dynamic and active presence of Christ in liturgy. The Decree on Ecumenism reiterates the theme of unity derived from the liturgy by emphasizing how the Eucharist is the particular locus for building up the body of Christ, the Church (par. 2).

While this overview is merely indicative (and by no means exhausts the teaching of Vatican II on the theology of the liturgy)[172] at least three points can be made about how ground-breaking the teaching of Vatican II is regarding the theology of liturgy. First, in light of these decrees it is clear that the Church wishes to over-come any dichotomy between the cult of liturgy and the self-sacrifice involved in living the cult of the Christian life (recall Rom 12:1 about offering one's body as a living sacrifice). Second, the kind of ecclesiology of liturgy articulated here transcends any vestiges of a clericalized or sacralized understanding of liturgy. These statements assert how the liturgy is incarnated within the culture of various peoples (which insight leads necessarily to the inculturation agenda). Third, the Christian life is understood to be a unified whole, one life with ordinary and special moments, among which are times to engage in liturgy (see Liturgy Constitution, par. 9) which is understood as a particular means of building up the body of Christ, until its members are called from this world to the Father's house (see Liturgy Constitution, par. 8).[173]

Because of his unique role in implementing the prescriptions of Vatican II on reforming the liturgy a review of Paul VI's reflections on *lex orandi lex credendi* is in order.[174] In three addresses between 1966–1970 to the Consilium charged with implementing the liturgical reform Paul VI referred to this topic directly placing emphasis on how theology should be a constant guide in reforming liturgical texts. In the 1966 address he stated that "intense effort must be brought to bear on the agreement of the *lex orandi* with the *lex credendi*, so that in its meaning [liturgical] prayer preserves the riches of dogma and religious language is suited . . . to the dogmatic realities it bears. . . ."[175] In the 1968 address he stated that "since the *lex orandi* must be in harmony with the *lex credendi* and serve to manifest and corroborate the faith of the Christian people, the new prayer formulas you are preparing cannot be worthy of God unless they are the faithful reflections of Catholic teaching."[176] In the 1970 address he noted the work of the group in having "striven to see to it . . . that theology more strongly influences liturgical texts for a closer correspondence between the *lex orandi* and the *lex credendi*."[177]

On three other occasions the pope returned to this theme more generally. In an instruction to a general audience in 1969 on the new order of Mass (which instruction was clearly aimed to allay fears about its implementation) he stated that in the new Mass "the equation between the *lex orandi* and the *lex credendi* has [not] been jeopardized."[178] In another general audience address in 1975 he stated more positively that "we must all hold fast and joyously to the conviction that the *lex orandi* (rule of prayer) possesses in the *lex credendi* (rule of faith) its guiding light and measure."[179] In an address to a consistory in 1977 the pope spoke of the beneficial effects of the liturgical reform. In a rather strong exhortation about conformity to the established norms of the liturgical reform he stated "otherwise the essence of dogma and obviously of ecclesiastical discipline will be weakened, in line with the famous axiom, *lex orandi, lex credendi.* We therefore call for absolute loyalty so that the rule of faith may remain safe."[180] The pope's statements both sustain the value of the *lex orandi* and emphasize how correct theology should be preserved in liturgical prayer. If "orthodoxy" can and should mean both "right praise" of God and "right belief" in God,[181] then the pope's statements may be said to sustain both meanings. (Toward the end of his pontificate the French "Traditionalist" movement under Archbishop Marcel Lefevbre was likely a strong catalyst leading Paul to insist on the doctrinal correctness of the reformed liturgy and also to insist on strict conformity in implementing the new liturgy. The importance of ecclesiology was very much at the heart of Montini's theology. That he would seize upon the ecclesiological dimensions of liturgy is not surprising; the Lefevbre schism only heightened this concern.)[182]

This admittedly selective overview of the origins and evolution of the notion of the law of prayer grounding the law of belief evidences a broad evolution in interpreting Prosper of Aquitaine's adage "let the law of prayer establish the law of belief." It also establishes many nuances attached to the very notion of liturgical theology. Our distinction (noted in the Preface) between liturgy as a theology of liturgy (i.e., a theological exploration of what occurs in liturgy) and as a source for theology has been helpful in the review of literature offered here since authors variously use "liturgical theology" to refer to either or both (or even other) meanings. Yet, the weakness inherent in the distinction is that it can separate what are really two parts of one reality. The review of traditional sources cited in this chapter attests to how important it is to appreciate these two dimensions of engaging in liturgical theology. In the chapters that follow both realities, a theology of what occurs in liturgy and liturgy as source for theology will be borne in mind and are essential to our argument.

In trying to underscore the priority of the *lex orandi* in doing theology many of the authors reviewed here have tended to emphasize liturgical *texts*. The positive value of this emphasis is that it gives due weight to texts which have been crafted over centuries of Church life and prayer and which are essential to the ritual enactment of liturgy.[183] The negative side, however, is the danger of using liturgical texts as "proof texts" and of textual fundamentalism. Liturgy is far more than texts. Liturgy is an enacted communal symbolic event with a number of constitutive elements and means of communication, including, but not restricted to, texts. Hence in succeeding chapters (specifically three through six) we will articulate a hermeneutic of liturgical texts that gives them due weight but which does not isolate them from their native setting in which they function as central means of communicating divine praise and divine truth through the symbolic, communal act of liturgy. The danger of textual fundamentalism has been noted as important.[184] Here it is sufficient to underscore the fact that liturgy is an evolving reality whose main contours have been shaped by liturgical tradition, but whose component elements have been and continue to be adapted and adjusted. The inculturation agenda focuses this even more strongly today. The task here is to strive for a balance that includes evolving forms within an accepted ritual structure with texts, gestures, symbols and environment open to adjustment. Hence part of what will be argued in what follows concerns such evolution within the continuity of liturgical tradition.

The succeeding chapters are intended to shed light on an elusive task—how to develop liturgical theology based on the multifaceted *event* called liturgy.

Notes

1. This phrase (sometimes rendered *ut legem credendi statuat lex supplicandi*) found in the so-called *Capitula Coelestini* (statements added to a letter of Pope Celestine I, dated in the early fifth century, also called the *Capitula* or *Auctoritates de gratia*) is now generally ascribed to Prosper of Aquitaine's *Indiculus* as written between 435–442. See, Philippus Oppenheim, *Principia theologiae liturgicae* (Turin: Marietti, 1947) 77, M. Pinto, *O valor teologico da liturgia*. Coleccao "Criterio" 27. (Braga: Livraria Cruz, 1952) 98–100, E. Portalié, "Célestin I.

Lettre contre les Sémipelagiens et les Capitula annexés," *Dictionnaire de théo-logie catholique* 2, 2052-2053, Paulus Renaudin, "De auctoritate sacrae liturgiae in rebus fidei," *Divus Thomas* 13 (1935) 41-54, Wilhelm DeVries, "Lex sup-plicandi, lex credendi," *Ephemerides Liturgicae* 47 (1933) 48-58, esp. 48-54, Paul De Clerck, " 'Lex orandi, lex credendi,' Sens originel et avatars historiques d'un adage équivoque," *Questions Liturgiques* 59 (1978) 194-196, as well as the same author's extended study *La "prière universelle" dans les liturgiques latines anciennes. Témoinages patristiques et textes liturgiques.* Liturgiewissenschaftliche Quellen und Forschungen, no. 62 (Münster: Aschendorff, 1977) 88-89. On the original text and a standard interpretation of its usefulness for liturgical the-ology see Mario Righetti, *Manuale di storia liturgica*, 4 vols., 2nd ed. (Milano: Ancora, 1950) 1:23-27.

2. One example of how authors will argue whether priority ought to be given to liturgy or theology derives from their interpretation of *statuat* in this for-mula. On the notion of the "mutual relation" between liturgy and theology see, Pedro Fernández, "Liturgia y teologia. Una cuestion metodologica," *Ecclesia Orans* 6 (1989) 261-283.

3. See my own summary and assessment of representative contemporary authors in *Liturgical Theology: A Primer*. For other helpful reviews see, Franco Brovelli, "Per uno studio della liturgia," *Scuola Cattolica* 104 (1976) 567-635, esp. 591-635 and Pedro Fernandez, "Liturgia y teologia. Historia de un problema metodologico," *Ciencia tomista* 99 (1972) 135-179.

4. See, Jose Manuel Bernal, "Liturgia y Orthodoxia," *Phase* 17 (1977) 56-58 and Bernard Capelle, "Autorité de la liturgie chez les Pères," *Recherches de théologie ancienne et médiévale* 21 (1954) 10-11.

5. See, J. M. Bernal "Liturgia y orthodoxia," 58-60, B. Capelle, "Autorité," 12-13, J. Lopez Martin, "La fe," 164 and Eloi Dekkers, "Creativité et ortho-doxie dans la *Lex Orandi*," *La Maison Dieu* n. 111 (1972) 23-24.

6. B. Capelle, "Autorité," 8-9, I. H. Dalmais, "La liturgie," 286, E. Dekkers, "Creativité," 25-26 and J. Lopez Martin, "La fe," 164. For a thorough explo-ration of Augustine's use of the liturgy see, Jean-Albert Vinel, "L'argument liturgique opposé par Saint Augustin aux Pélagiens," *Questions Liturgiques* 68 (1987) 209-241.

7. See the helpful summary by M. Cappuyns, "Liturgie et théologie," (*Ques-tions Liturgiques*). For a brief discussion of how Origen used the liturgy see, Dekkers, "Creativité," 24-26. For Cyprian see, I. H. Dalmais, "La liturgie et le dépot de la foi," in *L'Eglise en prière. I, Principes de la liturgie* (Paris: Desclée, 1983, Ed. nouvelle) 286, P. De Clerck, "Lex orandi, lex credendi," 204-205, P. Fernandez, "Liturgia y teologia," 154, and J. Lopez Martin, "La fe," 164.

8. See, E. Portalié, "Celestin I. Lettre," *DTC* 2, 2059. For a helpful compari-son of Prosper's text with texts from the Gallican liturgy see, P. Oppenheim, *Principia theologiae liturgicae* 78-80. Also see, M. Cappuyns, "L'origine des Capitula pseudo-célestiniens contre le semi-pélagianisme," *Revue Bénédectine* 41 (1929) 156-170.

9. *De vocatione omnium gentium*, 1, 12. For explanation and commentary see, Karl Federer, *Liturgie und Glaube, Eine theologiegeschichtliche Untersuchung.* Paradosis IV. Legem credendi lex statuat supplicandi (Fribourg: Paulusverlag, 1950) 15–16.

10. See, P. L. 50, 531–535 conveniently reproduced in Portalié, "Célestin," *DTC* 2057.

11. See, B. Capelle, "Auctorité," 7.

12. Ibid., 18.

13. B. Capelle, "Auctorité," 10–11.

14. See, DeClerck, "Lex orandi" 195–96, Karl Federer, *Liturgie und Glaube,* 19–41 and Miguel M. Garijo Guembe, "Réflexions pour une dialogue entre l'orthodoxie et le catholicisme á propos de l'adage 'lex orandi—lex credendi' " in A. Pistoia and A. Triacca, eds., *La liturgie, son sens, son esprit, sa methode. Liturgie et théologie.* Conferences St. Serge 28. (Rome: Edizione Liturgiche, 1982) 73.

15. Federer, *Liturgie und Glaube* 15–16.

16. M. M. Garijo Guembe, "Réflexions," 74.

17. For a consideration of how this theology that countered semi-Pelagianism accorded with Augustinian orthodoxy, see, "Célestin I," *DTC* 2, 2060 where E. Portalié specifies that Prosper's theology accords with Augustine's *Letter 217* and *Ad Vitalem,* n. 2, 26 (P. L. 33, 978).

18. DeClerck, "Lex orandi" 202; Federer, *Liturgie und Glaube* 13.

19. P. Fernandez, "Liturgia y theologia," 153.

20. DeClerck, "Lex orandi," 206.

21. See below, this chapter 19–20.

22. For a review of the debate between Pelagius and Augustine that involves flexibility in liturgical forms and prayers as these influence liturgical theology see, J. A. Vinel, "L'argument liturgique" 209–241, esp. 236. Also see, B. Capelle, "Autorité" 18–21.

23. For a useful, general explanation of the patristic use of the liturgy see, Vittorino Grossi, "I Padri della Chisea e la teologia liturgica," *Rassegna di Teologia* 24 (1983) 126–137.

24. Some of these are preserved in the revised Office of Readings in the present Liturgy of the Hours, a classic example of which is the present assignment of the first of St. Leo the Great's sermons on the Nativity (*Sermo 1 in Nativitate Domini,* 1–3, P.L. 5, 190–193) to Christmas. For a useful collection of many such homilies as they help to explain the theology of the liturgical year see, *Liturgical Practice in the Fathers,* eds. Thomas K. Carroll and Thomas Halton (Wilmington: Glazier 1988).

25. Capelle, "Autorité" 21.

26. See, among others, Enrico Mazza, *Mystagogy,* A Liturgical Theology in the

Patristic Age, trans., Matthew O'Connell (New York: Pueblo, 1989).

27. For a useful overview of these ritual and theological differences see, Hans Bernhard Meyer, *Eucharistie*. Geschichte, Theologie, Pastoral. Handbuch der Liturgiewissenschaft 4 (Regensburg: Friedrich Pustet, 1989) Chapter 3 ''Vom Herrenmahl zur Eucharistiefeier,'' and chapter 4 ''Die Ritusfamilien des Ostens und des Westens,'' 87-164. A helpful comparison summary of the Antiochean and Alexandrian anaphoral structure is on p. 133. For a collection of such texts and appropriate comparisons within and among liturgical families see, Anton Hanggi and Irmgard Pahl, *Prex Eucharistica*. Textus e Variis Liturgiis Antiquioribus Selecti (Fribourg: Editions Universitaires, 1968) as well as R. C. D. Jasper and G. J. Cuming *Prayers of the Eucharist:* Early and Reformed, third ed. (New York: Pueblo, 1987).

28. For a helpful comparison table of the Antiochean and Alexandrian anaphoral structure see, H. B. Meyer, *Eucharistie*, p. 133. For a brief but helpful description of the anaphora of St. Basil and (what its author calls) its liturgical theology as one example of Byzantine usage see, Giuseppe Ferrari, ''La dimensione teologica nella liturgia de S. Basilio,'' *Nicolaus* 8 (1980) 138-140.

29. See, Alexander Gerken, *Teologia dell'eucaristia* (Alba: Edizioni Pauline, 1977) 65-104 (translated from the second edition of *Theologie der Eucharistie* [München: Kösel-Verlag GmbH, 1976].)

30. See, for example, Allan Bouley, *From Freedom to Formula*. The Evolution of the Eucharistic Prayer from Oral Improvisation to Written Texts. Studies in Christian Antiquity, no. 21 (Washington: Catholic University of America Press, 1981).

31. These are sometimes simply called the ''Jerusalem Catcheses'' because Cyril's authorship is not always agreed to. A convenient edition of the Greek text and a translation are found in F. L. Cross, ed., *St. Cyril of Jerusalem. Lectures on the Christian Sacraments* (London: SPCK, 1951). It is significant that three readings from these catecheses are used at the Office of Readings in the present Liturgy of the Hours from Thursday through Saturday of the Easter octave.

32. See the helpful summary of both Eastern and Western rites of the period in Bruno Kleinheyer, *Sakramentliche Feiern I*. Die Feiern der Eingliederung in die Kirche. Gottesdienst der Kirche. Handbuch der Liturgiewissenschaft, 7, 1 (Regensburg: Verlag Friedrich Pustet, 1989) 57-95. Note especially pp. 80-81 for a very helpful table comparing the initiation liturgies of the East after Nicea: the Byzantine, Armenian, West Syrian, Maronite, East Syrian/Chaldean and Coptic.

33. Useful tools for this kind of study are Hugh M. Riley, *Christian Initiation*. Studies in Christian Antiquity, Vol. 17 (Washington: Catholic University of America Press, 1974) and E. Mazza, *Mystagogy*.

34. See the brief but helpful comment by Edward Yarnold, *The Awe-Inspiring Rites of Initiation*. Baptismal Homilies of the Fourth Century (Slough: St. Paul, 1971) 94.

35. See, Yarnold, *Awe-Inspiring Rites*, 93.

36. Ibid.

37. See, A. Gerken *Eucaristia* 70–80.

38. Pedro Fernandez, "Liturgia y theologia en la 'Summa' de Santo Tomas," *Angelicum* 51 (1974) 383.

39. Ibid. Also see, Joseph Lécuyer, "Réflexions sur la théologie du culte selon saint Thomas," *Revue Thomiste* 55 (1955) 339–362 and Liam G. Walsh, "Liturgy in the Theology of St. Thomas," *The Thomist* 38 (1974) 557–583.

40. See, among others, P. M. Pinto, *O Valor teologico* 270–290, and H. Hering, "De loco theologico liturgiae apud Sanctum Thomam," *Pastor Bonus* 5 (1941) 456–464.

41. P. Fernandez, "Liturgia y teologia," 411.

42. Ibid., 417.

43. Ibid., 384.

44. Ibid. Also see, J. Espeja, "La Iglesia, comunidad liturgica segun Sto. Tomas," *Teologia Espiritual* 27 (1965) 487–499.

45. *S.T.* IIIa, q. 66, 5 at 3. See, P. Fernandez, "Liturgia y teologia," 394.

46. See, ibid., 393–95 and Liam G. Walsh, *Sacraments of Initiation*. Theology Library Series 7 (London: Geoffrey Chapman, 1988) 33.

47. See, ibid., 396 and idem. "Teologia de la liturgia en la 'Summa' de Santo Tomas," *Ciencia tomista* 101 (1974) 272.

48. P. Fernandez, "Liturgia y teologia," 398.

49. See, *De Veritate* q. 26, a 4, ad 13 and ST IIIa, 62 a 1, ad 1.

50. Hence the importance of Peter Lombard's introduction to his sacramental theology (noting that an individual received healing) from *Quatuor Libri Sententiarum*, Book Four, Distinction 1: "The Samaritan who tended the wounded man, applied for his relief the dressings of the sacraments, just as God instituted the remedies of the sacraments against the wounds of original and actual sin" from Elizabeth Rogers, trans. and ed., *Peter Lombard and the Sacramental System* (Merrick: Richwood, 1976, reprinted from 1917 original) 79. Lombard's teaching here is not new. However, what followed was new in that almost immediately he engages in a rather elaborate systematic treatment of sacraments and their effects (especially compared to the patristic era). Lombard was the first to introduce the notion of "cause" into western sacramental theology, a term which would figure into most scholastic treatments of sacraments with various theories flourishing about causality (including, among others, "moral" and "instrumental," from representatives of the "Franciscan" and "Dominican" schools).

51. *S.T.* IIIa, 60, 3. Translation from *Summa Theologiae*, Vol. 56. The Sacraments. Blackfriars edition of Latin text and English translation. (New York: McGraw-Hill, 1975) 11–13.

52. See, Christopher Kiesling, "The Sacramental Character and the Liturgy," *The Thomist* 27 (1963) 385–412.

53. Ibid., 407. *S.T.* IIIa, 63, 5 obj. 3 and 63, 1.

54. Ibid., 410, S.T. IIIa, 63, 2.

55. See, among others, J. Lecuyer, "Réflexions" 349 and 359.

56. This is, in fact, a hallmark of scholastic theology of sacramental character, as argued, among others, by Piet Fransen.

57. See, "Introduction," *The Sacraments. Summa Theologiae*, xxiii. Aquinas' treatment of baptism is in *S.T.* IIIa, qq. 66–71, and of Confirmation is q. 72.

58. *S.T.* IIIa, 73–83.

59. *S.T.* IIIa, 70, 2.

60. See, A. Gerken, *Teologia dell'eucaristia*, 105–110, on the change to "thing-thinking" requiring the shift in Eucharistic terminology.

61. For a helpful description of the changes in initiation rites from the fourth century through the ritual of Paul V see, among others, Adrien Nocent, "I tre sacramenti dell'iniziazione cristiana," in *Anamnesis 3/1*, 41–68.

62. See, among others, J. D. C. Fischer, *Christian Initiation: Baptism in the Medieval West* (London: SPCK, 1965).

63. See, Thomas Aquinas, *S.T.* IIIa, 72. For a most useful study of how liturgy influenced Thomas' teaching on initiation and see, Nathan Mitchell, "Dissolution of the Rite of Christian Initiation," in *Made, Not Born* (Notre Dame: University of Notre Dame Press, 1976) 50–82.

64. Thomas Aquinas, Supplement to *Tertia Pars* Q. 32.

65. See, David N. Power, "Order," in Francis Schüssler Fiorenza and John P. Galvin, eds., *Systematic Theology. Roman Catholic Perspectives*, Vol. II (Minneapolis: Fortress Press, 1991) 277–279.

66. *Doxology. The Praise of God in Worship, Doctrine and Life. A Systematic Theology* (New York: Oxford University Press, 1980) 263.

67. The points of difference between Wainwright and Aidan Kavanagh on this issue are indicated in K. W. Irwin, *Liturgical Theology* 46–47.

68. *Doxology* 253–255.

69. Ibid., 257. It should be noted that today not all would agree with Jungmann's thesis (for example, Emil Lengeling) or at least its entirety or the extent of the anti-Arian motif in editing liturgical texts.

70. *Doxology* 264–270.

71. Ibid., 251. See Wainwright's review of Aidan Kavanagh's *On Liturgical Theology* in *Worship* 61 (March 1987) 183.

72. *Doxology* 267.

73. About which more will be said below, chapter 6, 237–246.

74. Paul VI Apostolic Constitution on the new Roman Missal, *Missale Romanum*, translation from *Documents on the Liturgy 1963-1979. Conciliar, Papal, and Curial Texts* (Collegeville: The Liturgical Press, 1982) hereafter cited "DOL" n. 1358:

"No one should think, however, that this revision of the Roman Missal has come out of nowhere. The progress in liturgical studies during the last four centuries has certainly prepared the way. Just after the Council of Trent, the study 'of ancient manuscripts in the Vatican library and elsewhere,' as St. Pius V attests in the Apostolic Constitution *Quo primum*, helped greatly in the correction of the Roman Missal. Since then, however, other ancient sources have been discovered and published and liturgical formularies of the Eastern Church have been studied."

75. See the very helpful historical and ecclesiological analysis of the situation around the time of Trent in Giuseppe Alberigo, "Dalla uniformità liturgica," 604-606.

76. Ibid., 608-609.

77. Ibid., 606.

78. Ibid., 610.

79. Ibid., 613.

80. Jo Hermans, "L'etude de la liturgie comme discipline théologique. Problèms et méthods," *Revue théologique de Louvain* 18 (1987) 344.

81. Among other examples, see Pierre Dens, *Tractatus de sacramentis in genere* (Mecheln, 1850) containing a brief tract on sacraments obviously intended for seminarians.

82. Among other valuable studies, see those of Andre Duval collected in *Des sacrements au Concile de Trente* (Paris: Cerf, 1985).

83. See, Franco Brovelli, "Fede e Liturgia," *Nuovo Dizionario di Liturgia* 544.

84. Yngve Brilioth, *Eucharistic Faith and Practice, Evangelical and Catholic*, trans., A. G. Hebert (London: SPCK, 1930, reprinted 1965) 16. See, William Nicholls, *Jacob's Ladder: The Meaning of Worship*, Ecumenical Studies in Worship, No. 4 (Richmond: John Knox Press, 1958) 10: "Thus the theological endeavors and surest foundations of those who take part in them feed their minds constantly at the liturgy. . . . Conversely, however, the form and expression of the litrugy itself, at any given time must be subject to the criticism of theology."

85. See Alexander Schmemann, *Introduction to Liturgical Theology*, trans. Asheleigh Moorhouse (London: The Faith Press, 1966) 10 about the theological meanings of rites; also see the classic work of Anton Baumstark *Comparative Liturgy*, 3rd ed. rev. by Bernard Botte, English ed. by F. L. Cross (Westminster: Newman Press, 1958).

86. *Institutions liturgiques, I, II, III* (Le Mans-Paris, 1940-51). The fact that Guéranger published a number of short articles defending his positions indicates the controversial nature (at least at the time) of his project. See, among

others, "Valeur dogmatique de la liturgie," *Auxiliaire Catholique* 5 (1846) 96–119.

87. These highly influential, multi volume works were begun in 1941 (*L'Avent liturgie*) and were translated into German, Italian, and English.

88. In the helpful abridged version, *Institutions liturgiques. Extraits* (Montreal: Editions de Chire, 1977) the preliminary section is 17–23 and the historical section is 23–290.

89. Among others, see J. Hermans, "La liturgie," 347.

90. Ibid., 348 and fn. 25 citing *Institutions liturgiques*, t. 1 and t. 3.

91. See, Cuthbert Johnson, *Prosper Guéranger (1805–1875): A Liturgical Theologian* An Introduction to his liturgical writings and work. Analecta Liturgica 9 (Rome: Studia Anselmiana, 1984).

92. Louis Bouyer, *Liturgical Piety* (Notre Dame: University of Notre Dame Press, 1955) 56–64.

93. Among Beauduin's more important works are *La piété de l'Eglise* (Louvain: Mont-César, 1914) and his articles under the title "Essai de manuel fondamental de liturgie," in *Questions liturgiques*. His ecclesiological and pastoral contribution to the liturgical movement are acknowledged by many contemporary authors including Burkhard Neunheuser, Salvatore Marsili, Anscar Chupungco et. al.

94. *La piété* 40, 93.

95. "Essai de manuel fondamental de liturgie" *Questions Liturgiques* 3 (1912–13) 56–66, 143–148, 201–209, 271–280.

96. "Essai de Manuel Fondamental [I]," *Questions Liturgiques* 3 (1913) 143.

97. Ibid., 144–145; see, Roger Aubert, "Liturgie et Magistère ordinaire," *Questions Liturgiques* 33 (1952) 6.

98. Ibid., 145–146.

99. Ibid., 147–148.

100. "Essai [II]" 271–279.

101. See, among others, the emphasis on texts only in M. Cappuyns, "Liturgie et théologie," 249–272.

102. See, H. Mercker, ed. *Bibliographie Romano Guardini (1885–1968). Guardinis Werke. Veroffentlichungen uber Guardini* (Paderborn: F. Schöningh, 1978).

103. See, J. Hermans, "La liturgie," 349–350.

104. See, H. W. Gartner and M. B. Merz, "Prolegomena," 170.

105. From Guardini's *Vom Geist der Liturgie*. Ecclesia Orans 1 (1918), cited in Burkhard Neunheuser, "La liturgie dans la vision de Romano Guardini," in *La liturgie, son esprit* 182.

106. Ibid., 183.

107. See, "Ein Wort zur liturgischen Frage," translated and published as "Lettre de Romano Guardini a S. Exc. l'eveque de Mayence," *La Maison Dieu* n. 3 (1945) 23.

108. See, Neunheuser, "La liturgie" 185.

109. Ibid., 186.

110. These insights are taken from Guardini's programmatic essay on method in liturgical study in the *Jahrbuch für Liturgiewissenschaft* 1 (1921) and summarized in Neunheuser, "La liturgie," 186.

111. Neunheuser, "La liturgie," 187.

112. See, J. Hermans, "La liturgie," 350.

113. See, for example, "Liturgische Bildung," in *Liturgie und liturgische Bildung* (Würzburg, 1966) 19–125.

114. This concern comprises a major part of his letter of 1964, cited in fn. 107.

115. See, Guardini, "Der Kultakt und die gegenwartige Aufgabe der Liturgie," in *Liturgie und liturgische Bildung* (Würzburg, 1966) 9–18; see also, H. W. Gartner and M. B. Merz, "Prolegomena," 170.

116. Casel will be criticized for an over reliance on theories derived from mystery religions (see below, fn. 128). For our purposes his theology of liturgy is important, which theology can be detached (if not totally extracted from) Casel's use of pagan cultic practices.

117. Odo Casel, *The Mystery of Christian Worship*, ed. Burkhard Neunheuser (Westminster: Newman Press, 1962) 5.

118. Ibid., 6.

119. Ibid., 7.

120. Ibid., 13.

121. Ibid.

122. Among many other references and quotations, Casel uses Cyril's third mystagogical catechesis (17) and Gregory's Easter sermon (49).

123. See, Anscar J. Chupungco, "Salvatore Marsili: Teologo della Liturgia," in *Paschale Mysterium*, Studi in memoria dell'Abate Prof. Salvatore Marsili, Studia Anselmiana 91, Analecta Liturgica 10, ed. Giustino Farnedi (Rome: Editrice Anselmiana, 1986) 15.

124. Louis Bouyer, review of French edition of *Le Mystère du culte* in *La Maison Dieu* n. 80 (1964) 242–243.

125. *Pace* Pedro Fernandez, "La liturgia, quehacer theologico. Estudio sobre una definicion," *Salamanticensis* 20 (1973) 223.

126. See, for example, the last part of Dalmais' treatment of Casel in *L'Église en priere* Vol. I, 281.

127. L. M. McMahon, "Towards a Theology of the Liturgy: Dom Odo Casel and the Mysterientheorie," *Studia Liturgica* 3 (1965) 146.

128. *Comparative Liturgy,* third edition, rev. B. Botte, English ed. F. L. Cross (Westminster: Newman Press, 1958).

129. Ibid., 2.

130. Ibid., 15.

131. Ibid., 17 and 20.

132. Ibid., 60.

133. See, B. Botte, "Foreword to the Third Edition," *Comparative Liturgy* viii.

134. Yves Congar, *La foi et la théologie.* Le Mystère chrétien, I. (Paris: Desclée, 1962) 145–146.

135. Ibid., 147.

136. Ibid., 147.

137. *Tradition and Traditions,* trans. Michael Naseby and Thomas Rainborough (New York: Macmillan, 1966) 427.

138. Ibid., 428–429.

139. Ibid., 430.

140. Ibid., 433.

141. A criticism one could lodge concerns Congar's statement that the liturgy has remained virtually intact since Gregory the Great (*Tradition and Traditions* 429). If by this the author means basic ritual structures then one can readily agree. But if he means most of its (even preconciliar) content then the statement needs to be critiqued precisely because of the kind of information gleaned from the historical study of liturgy.

142. *Revelation and Theology* Volume One (New York: Sheed and Ward, 1967) 218.

143. Ibid., 219.

144. Ibid., 220. He asserts that this phrasing was designed to avoid teaching what the Modernists taught. See discussion of *Mediator Dei* below, 27–29.

145. Ibid., 220.

146. Ibid., 221.

147. Ibid., 221.

148. A. Stenzel, "Les Modes de transmission de lá Revelation," *Mysterium Salutis, L'Église et la Transmission de la Revelation,* Vol. 3 (Paris: Cerf, 1969) 161.

149. Ibid., 165.

150. Ibid., 166.

151. Ibid., 174.

152. Ibid., 177.

153. Herman Schmidt, "Lex orandi, lex credendi in recentioribus documentis pontificiis," *Periodica* 40 (1951) 5–28, where he traces references through Pius XII.

154. P. Oppenheim, *Principia*, xiii–xix.

155. H. Schmidt, "Lex orandi," 6–7.

156. Geoffrey Wainwright (among others) is ill at ease with such arguments; see, *Doxology*, 235–240, 259–260. For more serene appreciations see C. Vagaggini, *Theological Dimensions of the Liturgy*, trans., W. Jurgens (Collegeville: The Liturgical Press 1976) 509–510 and Wilhelm De Vries, "Lex supplicandi, lex credendi," *Ephemerides Liturgicae* 47 (1933) 48–49, 56–57.

157. Herman Schmidt, "Lex orandi, lex credendi," 5–28. He summarizes the formulas as follows (7): *Legem credendi lex statuat supplicandi* (Pius XI, Pius XII), *Legem credendi lex statuit supplicandi* (Pius XI), *Lex credendi legem statuat supplicandi* (Pius XII), *Lex orandi lex credendi* (Pius XII), and *Lex precandi lex credendi est* (Pius XII).

158. The irony should not be lost here as liturgists commonly assert the problematic nature of trying to "establish" an "idea" feast.

159. *Acta Apostolicae Sedis* 17 (1925) 598. Also see, Annibale Bugnini, *Documenta pontificia ad instaurationem spectantia* (Rome, 1953) 70–71, Cipriano Vagaggini, *Theological Dimensions of the Liturgy* 512, H. Schmidt, "Lex orandi," 7, and G. Guembe, "Réflexions," 74. Given the title of his article it is not surprising that Roger Aubert would draw particular attention to this statement to set up his argument which deals with using the liturgy as a theological source, in "Liturgie et Magistere ordinaire," *Questions Liturgiques* 33 (1952) 5 (as a subtitle) and 6–7 which gives the citation in context.

160. *AAS* 39 (1947) 540–1.

161. See, among others, P. Fernandez, "Liturgia y teologia," 167.

162. See, among others, E. Schillebeeckx, *Revelation and Theology* 220 and M. M. Garijo Guembe, "A propos," 76. Also see, George Tyrell, *Lex orandi, or Prayer and Creed* (London, 1903) and *Through Scylla and Charybdis on the Old Theology and the New* (London, 1907).

163. G. Guembe, "Réflexions," 75, H. Schmidt, "Lex orandi," 8.

164. Emphasized, among others, by P. Fernandez, "La liturgia," 253.

165. Ibid., 254.

166. *DOL* n. 14.

167. See, Preface, p. ix.

168. Constitution on the Sacred Liturgy n. 16: "the study of the sacred liturgy is to be ranked among the compulsory and major courses . . . in theological faculties . . . [it is to] be taught under its theological, historical, spiritual, pastoral and canonical aspects. Moreover, other professors, while striving to expound the mystery of Christ and the history of salvation from the angle proper to each of their own subjects, must nevertheless do so in a way that will clearly bring out the connection between their subjects and the liturgy. . . ." N. 23 of the Constitution states "that sound tradition may be retained, and yet the way remain open to legitimate progress, a careful

investigation is always to be made into each part of the liturgy to be revised. This investigation should be theological, historical and pastoral."

169. C. Vagaggini, "De principiis generalibus ad Sacram Liturgiam instaurandam atque fovendam" *Ephemerides Liturgicae* 78 (1964) 238.

170. P. Fernandez, "La liturgia," 258. Also see, F. Brovelli, "Per uno studio," 573.

171. See, F. Brovelli, "Per uno studio," 575.

172. For a review of other important references to the theology of liturgy in the documents of Vatican II see, F. Brovelli, "Per uno studio," 569–581 and P. Fernandez, "La liturgia," 261–270.

173. P. Fernandez, "La liturgia," 271.

174. For a brief introduction to Paul VI's appreciation for liturgy prior to being elected pope see, Franco Brovelli, "Movimento liturgico e spiritualità cristiana," *Rivista Liturgica* 73 (1986) 481–484.

175. "Address to the members and *periti* of the Consilium" 13 October, 1966, translation from *DOL* n. 632.

176. Address to the members and *periti* of the Consilium," 14 October 1968, *DOL* n. 670.

177. "Address to the members and *periti* of the Consilium on the occasion of its first plenary meeting," 10 April 1970, *DOL* n. 690.

178. *DOL* n. 1759.

179. *DOL* n. 551. For a succinct and helpful commentary on this text see, Luis Alessio, "La liturgia y la fe," *Notitiae* 15 (1979) 578–583.

180. *DOL* n. 578.

181. About which more will be said below, especially chapter 7, pp. 266–278.

182. For a helpful treatment of the parallels between the post Tridentine and post Vatican II reforms of the liturgy see, René Bornert, "Pour une interprétation comparative de la réforme liturgique," *Questions Liturgiques* 67 (1986) 1–32.

183. For a helpful glimpse into how Pope John Paul II has used liturgical texts in his teachings see, Achile M. Triacca, "L'uso delle citazioni liturgiche nel magistero extraliturgico di Giovanni Paolo II," *Notitiae* 24 (1988) 790–816.

184. A somewhat dated example of an attempt to argue a helpful liturgical theology that is almost exclusively concerned with texts is D. Barsotti, *Liturgia e Telogia* (Milan, 1956).

Chapter 2

Method

The purpose of this chapter is to introduce the thesis and parameters of our effort in the rest of this book and to situate our work within the broader consideration of method for liturgical theology in general. The chapter is divided into three unequal parts. The first section offers some distinctions and definitions about liturgy in general as these bear on our argument. The second section articulates how the term "liturgical theology" can be understood in light of (but not limited to) the historical overview given in chapter one and how it will be understood here. The third section articulates three elements that underlie our approach to liturgical theology as it is argued in succeeding chapters.

I. Liturgy and Theology: Definitions and Distinctions

A basic premise for this chapter is that liturgy is fundamentally *orthodoxia prima,* a theological event. In essence, liturgy is an *act of theology,* an act whereby the believing Church addresses God, enters into a dialogue with God, makes statements about its belief in God and symbolizes this belief through a variety of means including creation, words, manufactured objects, ritual gestures and actions. The many and multifaceted components of liturgy include words (principally Scripture and euchology) symbols and gestures, all expressed within a rite whose intrinsic structure has an inherent logic. To comprehend liturgy requires that one regard highly the value of the theologically rich words and symbols used in liturgy, which words and symbols are inherently metaphorical, polyvalent, often ambiguous and always oriented toward engagement in and appropriation of the mystery of the living God manifest and experienced in the liturgy. Hence liturgy is an *act of theology* in the sense that its statements and actions are addressed *to* God and are made *about* God. Liturgy is *orthodoxia prima* in the sense that it is first order doxological address to and about God. Understood in this way, the act of liturgy is *primary* theology in the sense that the experience of liturgy concerns direct address to God and encounter with God.

Secondary theology is reflection on the act of liturgy as primary theology. Generally speaking for our purposes liturgical theology is secondary theology. The distinction between *theologia prima* and *secunda* is made by a number of contemporary authors and can be regarded as rather firmly established.[1] In particular it is used in the methodological work of Gerard Lukken and David Power on liturgical theology. Lukken holds that the liturgy is both *theologia* and *orthodoxia prima*.

"In the early Church and especially in the East, the liturgy was known as *theologia prima* and dogmatic speculation as *theologia secunda*. The first meaning of 'orthodoxy' was also right praise (*ortho-doxia*) in the liturgy and it is only in the secondary, derived sense that it came to mean right teaching. It is therefore quite legitimate to speak of an *orthodoxia prima* and an *orthodoxia secunda*."[2]

Lukken maintains that the liturgy is quite properly the first source and norm of faith from which correct teaching is derived. Since the liturgy is the Church's self-expression through a complex, ritual act of words and symbols, the liturgical expression of faith is more immediate and direct than an intellectual expression or justification of faith in theological argument or dogmatic pronouncement. He balances this view by acknowledging that *theologia secunda* can and should stand as an important corrective to the liturgy "without which the Spirit is always in danger of being extinguished in the liturgy. A relationship of constant dialogue between *theologia* and *orthodoxia prima* and *secunda* is essential if we are to ensure that the liturgy does not once again become isolated from the faith of the Church."[3]

David Power places the distinction between *theologia prima* and *secunda* within the larger context of what he considers to be three interrelated and important realities: (1) the spiritual experience of Christian revelation, (2) the symbolic and devotional expression of this experience which mediates the spiritual experience in a living way, and (3) the scientific interpretation of the spiritual experience and of symbolic expression, explaining its presuppositions and categories. For Power *theologia prima* is located in the second of these elements and *theologia secunda* is in the third. He believes that the "symbolic and the theoretical are complementary and need one another."[4]

For our purposes the distinction between the act of liturgy as *theologia prima* and systematic reflection on the liturgy as *theologia secunda* will be maintained. In addition to distinguishing *theologia prima* from *secunda* we will continually refer to an additional component, *theologia tertia*, which underscores the essential relatedness of liturgy to living the Christian life. In our understanding tertiary theology derives from both the primary theological act of liturgy and its derivative reflection in secondary theology. It concerns the spirituality and moral life dimension of liturgy in terms of living the spiritual life in congruence with the mystery of God and the gospel values experienced and celebrated in liturgy. In our view *theologia tertia* draws out what is intrinsic to *lex orandi, lex credendi* in that the rule of prayer reflects both the rule of belief and the rule of right living.[5]

II. Understandings of Liturgical Theology[6]

In light of the distinctions made above, in our view "liturgical theology" can mean both a theology of liturgy and theology drawn from liturgy, with the latter including moral and spiritual theology.

(1) Theology of Liturgy. This term describes what Christian liturgy is and what it does in terms of actualizing the reality of Christ's paschal mystery for the Church, gathered and enlivened by power of the Holy Spirit. Through the liturgy contemporary believers are drawn into the paschal mystery and experience redemption through it. This is to view the liturgy as a ritual enactment in the believing Church of the transtemporal event of Christ's dying and rising (which happened once in history but which, by its nature is not bound by time and space categories) through the particular means proper to the liturgy. As fundamentally a *memorial action* the liturgy is the manifestation of this unique paschal mystery for the sake of contemporary congregations gathered in faith as this saving event is renewed through the words and gesture, myth and symbol, narrative and ritual (among other things). This is to

46

suggest that liturgy is essentially a privileged means, not of reenacting the past redemptive deeds of Jesus, but of being drawn into them in such a way that a new act of salvation occurs here and now for contemporary believers precisely because they engage in the act of memory that is liturgy.[7] Therefore a high theological value is placed on the Church's *orandi* because of the way liturgical prayer describes how contemporary faith communities experience anew and continually reappropriate Christ's redemption.

The following theological principles underpin this understanding of liturgy. First, liturgy is essentially *anamnetic* (the opposite of "amnesia") of the paschal mystery in ritual actions through which Christ's high priesthood and intercession for humanity's salvation are continually made manifest. Here we understand anamnesis to be linked directly to Christ's high priesthood (Liturgy Constitution no. 7). Liturgy is anamnetic in the sense that it combines the past redemptive deeds of Jesus (obedient life, humiliation, suffering, death, resurrection, ascension) and draws the contemporary Church into a unique and ever new experience of these redemptive deeds through the words and symbols of liturgy even as the Church yearns for redemption's eschatological fulfillment in the kingdom. All liturgy bridges the past, present and future of the Church in Christ. Recalling the helpful distinctions of Aquinas (noted in chapter 1)[8] we can say that liturgy is commemorative of Christ's redemption accomplished once for all in the past, it is demonstrative of Christ's redemption in the present and prognostic of the final consummation of redemption in the kingdom at the end of time. Liturgical anamnesis makes Christ's act of redemption present in order to enable the contemporary Church to experience here and now an event of grace predicated on Christ's once-for-all act of redemption.

With regard to the Church's *orandi* this is to assert that the traditional phrases from the euchology (term originally meaning "prayer book" or "sacramentary" but which we will use more generally to refer to the Church's prayer texts, *orandi*) on Christmas and Easter are of central theological importance. The use of the repeated designation *hodie* in the antiphon to the canticle of Mary at evening prayer on Christmas day ("Christ the Lord is born *today*; *today* the Savior has appeared. Earth echoes songs of angel choirs, archangels' joyful praise. *Today* on earth his friends exult: Glory to God in the highest, alleluia")[9] and the phrase "Christ is born for us: come let us adore him"[10] as the invitatory to the Liturgy of the Hours on Christmas asserts that each year the Church rejoices once more in the birth of the Messiah in such a way that on this very day a new event of grace occurs. Similarly, to respond to the first reading at the Eucharist and to the Scripture readings at morning and evening prayer on Easter (and through the Easter octave) by using the temporal designation *haec dies* and the text from Psalm 118:24: "This is the day the Lord has made; let us rejoice and be glad, alleluia"[11] also underscores how Christ's act of salvation, accomplished once and for all time, occurs still, here and now in the liturgy, which liturgical experience is a new event of redemption.

Second, liturgy is essentially *epicletic* in that it derives from and is dependent upon the action and power of the Holy Spirit. In every act of liturgy it is the Holy Spirit who transforms faith communities through their liturgical experience of the paschal mystery. In our view the classic theology of liturgical epiclesis in terms of invoking the Spirit to transform symbolic elements used in liturgy (bread, wine, oil, chrism etc.) and to transform the worshipping community into a more complete corporate manifestation of the body of Christ in unity is an example of this essential foundation for the theology of liturgy. The fact that epicletic prayers classically use the subjunctive is illustrative. To pray "let your Spirit . . . ." speaks of the Church's need to *invoke* the Spirit. It also speaks of the Church's faith in the Father's providence to send the Holy Spirit upon the Church gathered in worship to enable its participants to enact the liturgy. It is the Spirit who initiates, sustains and will bring liturgy to its fulfillment in the kingdom. Thus, we understand all notions of "power" in liturgy to be analogous and that those ordained and installed to liturgical ministries act by virtue of the encompassing power of the Holy Spirit, not their own power.[12] Thus what really matters first and foremost in every act of liturgy is what God accomplishes among us through Christ in the power of the Spirit. All ministerial discussions are appropriately contextualized within the parameters of the ways in which the celebrating assembly is incorporated into the mystery of the Trinity through worship and is continually sanctified by the liturgy through the power of the Spirit.

Third, liturgy is essentially *ecclesiological*. It is always an act of the Church's self-understanding and self-expression.[13] All liturgy is accomplished by, with and in the Church assembled at prayer. From among the significant statements of the Liturgy Constitution about the ecclesiology of liturgy, two are particularly notable: n. 14 about fostering "full, conscious and active participation" in the liturgy and n. 26 "liturgical services are not private functions, but are celebrations belonging to the Church, which is the 'sacrament of unity' (citing Cyprian). . . . [L]iturgical services involve the whole Body of Christ; they manifest it and have effects upon it. . . ."[14] To stress the ecclesiology of liturgy is to stress theologically the particularly soteriological aspect of liturgy. The Church at prayer is the Church in need of redemption; through the liturgy it experiences its hoped for redemption. Furthermore, when the Church celebrates the liturgy it partakes in the mystery of the Trinity in the sense that the essential interrelatedness of three persons in God is again made manifest in the liturgy in a way that both invites and draws its participants into greater and deeper communion in the life of the Triune God. The communion among the persons of the Trinity is thus shared through the liturgy with the praying Church.

Especially in light of the essentially anamnetic, epicletic and ecclesiological nature of liturgy we want to assert the importance of understanding liturgy as a unique way for the worshiping assembly to experience Christ's mediation of salvation and the Spirit's power to sanctify and unify the Church. To assert that the liturgy is the Church's central act of corporate prayer is to argue that liturgy is a unique, but not exclusive, locus for the Church's experience of God.[15] The Spirit enables the Church to celebrate liturgy, at which time the Church becomes an event, and the event of liturgy makes the Church more fully itself as the body of Christ on earth. Liturgy occurs at the intersection of the vertical (God to us) and the horizontal (Church communion); both these realities occur because of the presence and activity of the Holy Spirit. Liturgy is the event that constitutes the Church, which event becomes a *kairos* of salvation.

From the anamnetic-Christological, epicletic-pneumatological and ecclesial-soteriological aspects thus asserted, we will argue that there is a significant difference theologically between experiencing the paschal mystery in liturgy and personal meditation on Christ's passion, death and resurrection. The former enacts these saving events; the latter derives from them and, in comparison, only reflects on them. The former experience always gives birth again and again to the Church. The latter is open to the defect of leading to a privatized appreciation of these sacred events which the liturgy by its nature cannot endorse. The essentially communal experience of God through liturgy implicitly critiques any prayer forms or spirituality which focus only on individuals.[16] The craft of doing liturgical theology necessarily focuses on how the Church's central saving mysteries are uniquely experienced in and through the liturgy. For our purposes in this book these three factors—anamnesis (of Christ), epiclesis (in the Spirit) and ecclesiology (in the community of the redeemed)—together bear upon our understanding of what is implied by a "theology of liturgy."

(2) Theology drawn from the liturgy. This meaning of liturgical theology concerns how the means of communication and interaction in liturgy, especially words and symbols, can be utilized as a generative source for developing systematic theology. This would mean that concepts in systematic theology can be fruitfully explored from data found in liturgical rites. Examples of this include how the reformed rites (including General Instructions) image the very being of God (literally "theology," speech about God) how they describe the being and redemptive work of Christ (Christology, soteriology), how they describe the being and work of the Holy Spirit (pneumatology), how they image the Church (ecclesiology) and how they describe and reflect on our need for grace (Christian anthropology) especially as grace is experienced and mediated through liturgy.[17] One of the desired results of the kind of liturgical study called for in the Liturgy Constitution (no. 16) would be met if the liturgy is thus mined for the way it deals with these central aspects of Christian faith and theology.

For example, if one were to reflect on the way Christ is imaged in the liturgy one would come up with a variety and pluriformity of titles and usages. Such a study would mine the meaning of terms such as "redemption," "sanctification," "forgiveness," and "reconciliation" since such frequently used terms in the liturgy describe our need for Christ and image how his salvation is enacted through liturgy. Here the disciplines of Christian anthropology and Christology would appropriately converge as both derive from reflection on what happens in liturgy and how the

50

liturgy itself describes it. Methodologically, the point here would be to utilize liturgy as a source for systematic theology in such a way that systematic theology is intrinsically connected to the act of worship.

With regard to sacramental theology specifically, if one were to probe the eucharistic liturgy to discover the theological meaning of Eucharist (understanding that "Eucharist" can be both a verb and a noun in terms of what the Church *does* and what it *receives*) one would explore how the eucharistic memorial actualizes Christ's paschal mystery and how this actualization deepens our progressive assimilation into the mystery of God through Christ. These notions are thoroughly traditional in Eucharistic theology but were often eclipsed in the Reformation and post-Tridentine debates over Eucharistic presence and sacrifice. This is not to suggest a mere functional theology of the Eucharist. It is rather to reassert the value of articulating a number of complementary ways of understanding what occurs in the Eucharist. The unique experience of the Eucharist appropriately emphasizes the assembly's transformation into the body of Christ by the sacrament of Christ's body and blood. This intrinsic ecclesiological aspect of the Eucharist can stand alongside objective descriptions of Christ's presence in the Eucharistic sacrifice (which descriptions do not necessarily refer to the Church's participation in this sacrificial meal).

In addition, theologizing from the liturgy requires a reexamination of the sources of concepts in Christian theology and of the ways these concepts are developed. This issue touches on the important distinction frequently made today between "symbolic" and "technical" language. If the words, symbols, gestures, and rites of the liturgy are essentially metaphorical, then one needs to admit that such modes of expression are essentially "symbolic"[18] and will often be less precise than the more technical language of dogmatic assertions.[19] This itself however may be an important contribution to the ways in which contemporary liturgical and systematic theologians approach their work. The language of the liturgy is oriented to encounter and to the appropriation of the mysteries celebrated. To assert the value of theologizing about the Eucharist from the liturgy would be to reassert how the language about the Eucharist and the Eucharistic reality are oriented to the Church's experience of the Eucharist, part of which is described in what follows.

(3) *Doxological Theology.* This understanding of liturgical theology has been more hinted at than delineated in full in recent theological writing.[20] In such an understanding systematic theology would have a doxological cast to it (in the sense of thanks, praise, and acknowledgment) and reflect the belief of the theologian, particularly as subject of the liturgical action.[21] This is to suggest that the very nature of theology ought to be oriented to praise and the acknowledgment of God in both prayer and reflection as opposed to theology which tries to describe (much less define) sacred realities.[22] What is operative in this approach to theology is the important notion of how the *mystery* that is God and that is of God is experienced through both liturgy and theology.

The distinction made above by Gerard Lukken is operative here. The first meaning of *orthodoxy* is "right praise." A derived meaning is "correct belief." In our understanding a doxological theology derives from the Church's prayer in praise of God. What is constructed on this basis is an "orthodox" set of beliefs, that is, beliefs that are based on "right praise" and also reflect correct teaching.

One application of this approach to the theological enterprise in general would be to require theology to be both reflective of the act of faith expressed in the liturgy as well as rigorously scientific because the liturgical experience leads to second order reflection in theological discourse. Related to this is the understanding that in doing theology the theologian expresses what he or she experiences and believes and in delineating this as theology the theologian hands on what he or she believes for the good of others, particularly in developing their own faith. Liturgy is an event of salvation; the faith brought to the liturgy is deepened by the liturgy. This implies the involvement of the whole person in the act of liturgy and of doing theology. It relates to self-appropriation in theology of what occurs in the liturgy. This kind of theology would emphasize notions of conversion and growth in the faith as well as growth in understanding. Such an approach to theology in general offers an especially fruitful approach to ecumenical dialogue and ecumenical theologizing on sacraments (some of which is specified below in chapter seven).

III. Method in Liturgical Theology

Among the reasons why a new method is needed for liturgical theology today are the following two. It was asserted in chapter 1 that some approaches to liturgical theology from Trent through this century emphasized liturgical texts almost exclusively. To be fair, however, some authors like Anton Baumstark did emphasize that liturgy was more than texts and that the whole "liturgical action" needed to be explored theologically. However, it is still true that the seminal efforts in this century in liturgical theology emphasized the interpretation of texts. Contemporary emphasis on *liturgy as event* sets the framework for a new method in liturgical theology.[23] Another reason why a new method for engaging in liturgical theology is necessary is the nature of the present reform of the liturgy in Roman Catholicism and in other Christian Churches—a reform characterized by variety and options, especially when compared with the fixed post-Tridentine rites. The primary *locus* for articulating our methodological approach to liturgical theology is the present reformed liturgy. Specific aspects of the reform which need to be borne in mind when delineating a method for liturgical theology include the variety and flexibility of rites and texts within a ritual structure as well as the necessity of inculturating[24] even this reformed liturgy. On one level the variety possible in the reformed liturgy concerns *how* the liturgy is prepared and actually celebrated. The next level (of particular interest here) concerns how the celebration of the reformed liturgy is used as the source for liturgical theology developed from rites that are not uniform. Hence attention moves beyond the texts found in ceremonial books to the shape and component elements of actual liturgical celebration, including texts.[25]

Because of these factors our argument is that liturgical theology must be based on the *data* provided in the revised liturgical books, noting especially options and flexibility in the rites, as well on their *use* in actual celebration. For liturgies in the past this means assessing data from a number of sources in order to fill out the evidence found in liturgical-ceremonial books only. For contemporary liturgical study it is helpful that work is underway utilizing allied disciplines, especially the social sciences, to develop an appropriate method for liturgical theology. Important examples of this kind of methodological discussion at present include the ongoing work of study groups of the North American Academy of Liturgy.[26] On the European side one important example is the liturgical method developed and exemplified in the Pastoral Liturgy Institute of Santa Giustina in Padua (Italy).[27]

Two main concerns comprise the agenda for this book on method in liturgical theology. The first concerns the theology of liturgy discussed in Part 2 of this book. The second concerns theological and spiritual implications of engaging in the liturgy, discussed in Part 3. Methodologically, our concern with the theology of liturgy (Part 2) will be to consider how to provide a theological interpretation of the constitutive elements of the liturgy—Word, symbol, euchology, liturgical arts—as these elements are experienced in relation to each other in liturgical celebration. Of particular interest here is the fact that liturgy is an enacted ritual of the faith community of the Church through which the Church seeks a personal encounter with God through Christ in the Spirit. The fact that this liturgical encounter in faith is expressed through a number of means germane to liturgy as ritual requires that proper tools of interpretation be applied that respect the nature of liturgy containing "kerygmatic-prophetic" and "doxological-symbolic" elements, the former stressing verbal communication, the latter stressing symbolic engagement.[28]

In Part 2 our thesis is that for an adequate liturgical theology one must examine the component parts of liturgical rites—texts, symbols, actions and gestures—both in relation to each other and also in light of the times and places when and where communities were or are engaged in these rites. This is to assert that liturgical rites are only adequately understood and interpreted theologically in relation to their experienced context. Briefly put, the first part of our thesis is that *liturgical context is text*, in the sense that *context* provides the source—*text*—for developing liturgical theology. In our understanding *context* means the following three things.

First, *context* means the historical evolution of a given liturgical rite in order to determine its origin, component parts, and variations in history both liturgically and theologically. The purpose of this study is to uncover the theological meanings which the rite has traditionally conveyed as well as to distinguish aspects of the rite that are essential from those that are peripheral. Second, *context* means an examination of the present reformed rites to determine whether the contemporary celebration of these rites in specific contexts expresses what is actually envisioned in the published rites. This means examining liturgical acts as a whole where words, symbols, and gestures are interpreted and understood in relation to each other.[29] In addition, this meaning of context seeks to determine the extent to which the setting for liturgy (i.e., assembly, environment) and the conducting of liturgy (i.e., preaching, music, gestures, other means of participation) facilitates and enhances the assembly's appropriation and understanding of the scriptural texts, prayers, symbols and gestures of the liturgy. The third notion of *context* argued here shifts attention from what is experienced in liturgy to what is often termed the critical function of liturgical theology.[30] Here the contemporary cultural and theological context of liturgical celebration will be noted in order to explore ways of determining the adequacy of the present liturgical rites and of adapting them to a variety of changing ecclesial and cultural settings.

In general, to state that liturgical *context is text* is to adjust the focus in liturgical theology from a philological-theological study of liturgical texts (e.g., sacramentaries, pontificals, ordos) to discussing these sources in light of their celebration, both past (to the extent possible)'and present. To the extent possible the focus for *lex orandi, lex credendi* concerns *lex agendi* as the most adequate theological locus, where *lex agendi* means enacted rites as theological source. The proposal made here is intended to recontextualize liturgical sources and to use sources together to develop liturgical theology. The particular focus of our argument will argue that when *context* is understood to comprise the three aspects of historical evolution, reformed rites and contemporary critical function, then *context* becomes the *text* in the sense of the primary source for developing liturgical theology.

Methodologically our concern with the second of our agenda items, the theological and spiritual implications of engaging in liturgy (Part 3) concerns some of the ways that the act of liturgy can influence the shape of theology, ecumenical dialogue and living the moral, spiritual life (chapters 7 and 8). One contribution of liturgical theology to systematic theology as discussed in chapter seven is the preservation of theology as disclosive of the mystery of God, and not as defining or determining God's self-disclosure. Liturgical theology is one way of redirecting theology as intrinsically oriented toward confession, thanksgiving and the praise of God. Chapter 8 will concern what we have called *theologia tertia*, the ethical and spiritual dimensions of liturgy, which in our view is an intrinsic part of liturgical theology. This is to suggest that the *lex orandi, lex credendi* axiom requires attention to the *lex vivendi* beyond actual celebration to how what is celebrated and believed is reflected in how the Church lives its faith. Hence in our view the two foci of *lex orandi* and *lex credendi* yield a third part of the equation: *lex vivendi*, or life relation of the liturgy.[31] Such an understanding of liturgical theology can help to reunite the doing of liturgy with living Christianity, lest the craft of liturgy be understood only as engaging in Church ceremonial. Cultic preoccupation appropriately accedes in this understanding of *vivendi* to an emphasis on a proper understanding of liturgy that is concerned with Christian conversion understood as a response to the challenge of the gospel, ratified in cult and reflected in life.

If the first part of our thesis concerning the theology of liturgy is *context is text*, then the second part of our thesis on theology and spirituality derived from liturgy is *text shapes context*. Here *text* signifies the data derived from our investigation of the theology of liturgy (Part 2) as this data is examined and applied to the specific issues of doxological theology, ecumenical sacramental conversations and spirituality. Our argument is that the liturgy provides a unique and essential methodological component for the theological and spiritual issues specified in chapters 7 and 8 (and for others not discussed here). Hence the usefulness of the phrase *text shapes context* in the sense that the theology of liturgy (*text*) necessarily shapes the theology and spirituality of those who participate in the liturgy (*context*). We understand the theological interpretation of the *constitutive elements* of the liturgy (Word, symbol, euchology and the arts) to have *constitutive implications* for Church life, specifically its engaging in theological reflection and leading the spiritual life based on its engagement in the liturgy. Put another way, we understand there to be an *ongoing dialectical relationship* between *text* and *context* where the ecclesial and cultural settings in which the liturgy takes place—*context*—influence the way we experience and interpret the liturgy—*text*. But just as *context* influences how the *text* of liturgy is interpreted, the other side of the equation concerns how that data we call *text* necessarily influences the Church's theology, spirituality and life—*context*.

In succeeding chapters our argument will repeatedly include the value of liturgical tradition in interpreting the present reformed liturgy, the theological dynamics inherent in and theological value of the present liturgy and a critique of the revised rites in light of both liturgical tradition and the exigencies of contemporary need.

Hence, an examination of what we have termed three components of liturgical context now follows: historical evolution, contemporary reform, and critical liturgical theology.

(1) Historical Evolution of Rites. Part of the context that is brought to bear in every liturgical act is provided by the evolution of liturgical forms and, at least implicitly, of the evolution of understandings about liturgy and of liturgical theologies. To study the history of liturgy is to study a history of evolving liturgical forms as well as variety and complementarily in the theological interpretation of the rites celebrated.[32] In the Western liturgy this variety is the result of several historical factors among which are cultural (differences in the mentality of participants), theological (care to insure correct theology) and linguistic (changes in the language used). This kind of investigation also differentiates those aspects of worship that are essential from those that are peripheral.[33]

Our concern here is to establish the importance of understanding the evolution and theological meaning of liturgical forms the combination of which we understand to comprise "liturgical tradition." Clearly, the Church's actual liturgical tradition cannot be determined without historical study and reflection. In this connection the description by Robert Taft of the importance of history for the method used in liturgical studies and liturgical theology is most useful.

"And so history is a science not of past happenings, but of present understanding. . . . [H]istory is not events, but events that have become ideas—and ideas are of the present. The past does not change, but we do, which is why the work of history is always of the present, and never done. Liturgical history, therefore, does not deal with the past, but with tradition, which is a *genetic vision of the present*, a present conditioned by its understanding of its roots. And the purpose of this history is not to recover the past (which is impossible), much less to imitate it (which would be fatuous), but to *understand liturgy* which, because it has a history, can only be understood in motion, just as the only way to understand a top is to spin it."[34]

In addition Taft offers the important comment about method that deals with the knowledge derived from its application.

"Knowledge is not a collection of facts but the perception of their interrelation, and knowledge advances not so much from the discovery of hitherto unknown data as from the perception of new relationships that permit the elaboration of new patterns or systems. . . . So a method is just a way of approaching and organizing the raw information we possess."[35]

For Taft the study of liturgy, like every other branch of theology, requires that students bring to it several skills—including historical, philological and conceptual—in the search to uncover meaning. By using these skills liturgical studies are thus ordered to intelligibility, to understanding the act of worship being investigated.[36]

Taft wisely asserts that the historian's task is to uncover the Church's tradition which "is the Church's self-consciousness now of that which has been handed on to it not as an inert treasure, but as a dynamic principle of life."[37] He argues that in order to gain a proper understanding of liturgical tradition we need "to integrate into our work the methods of the relatively recent *pieta popolare* or *annales* schools of Christian history. . . . What we find embedded in liturgical manuscripts was embedded in a sociocultural ambience outside of which it cannot be understood as liturgy."[38] In order to do this the historian "must be immersed in the total life of the period under study. So we need histories of liturgy written from a new perspective, with time and place rather than ritual as their controlling factor."[39] In this connection the outline and scope of Herman Wegman's *Christian Worship In East and West* is illustrative. Wegman most usually introduces each chapter by describing the liturgical evolution of that period by first describing "historical data" and "cultural data" in light of which he then discusses liturgical evolution, including changes in rites and structures.

In light of our thesis that *context is text* a number of questions need to be raised about the data derived from historical research. A first question asks what texts, symbols, gestures, music, and art were used in the liturgy and who spoke, sang, or participated in them. Implicit here is the question of the extent to which the assembly participated in liturgy through movement, symbolic action, singing and speaking. A second question asks what kinds of sources were used to compose the liturgy. Implicit here is the concern to determine the biblical foundation (as the essential source) of the imagery and metaphors used in ritual language. This investigation seeks to determine to what extent the evolving rites are influenced, or even controlled, less by the scriptures than by contemporary theological controversies or prevailing currents in contemporary spirituality. G. G. Willis's statement is illustrative.

"From the emergence of the collect form in the fifth century it has been the general Roman rule that collects, secrets, and postcommunions are addressed to the Father through the mediation of the Son. The Council of Hippo (393) and the third Council of Carthage (397) ordain that the prayers at mass are to be addressed to the Father. This regulation was made at a time when the content of the prayers was still at the discretion of the celebrant and not authoritatively prescribed by the Church."[40]

Implicit here is the question of correct doxology and orthodox prayer. A third question asks how do the various components of liturgical rites relate to one another (e.g., scriptural proclamation, blessing prayer, acclamations, chants, other music etc.) and how each component is interpreted in relation to the others. This is to acknowledge the various genres of communication that together comprise the act of worship—proclamation of texts, gestural use of symbols, communal participation in song etc. For example, a proper interpretation of the introit and communion antiphons at the Eucharist requires understanding the kind of melodies assigned to these texts (e.g., chant), not just the words of the texts, lest the study of what were experienced as sung texts be confined to a study of words only. Not to investigate melody as well as text would be to change the nature of one of the genres of communication that constitute the liturgy.[41] A fourth question concerns the determination whether and how the descriptions of liturgical ceremonial (e.g., in patristic sources or ordos) reflected what was actually celebrated lest more weight be given to how a rite is described (grand or simple) as opposed to how it was actually experienced.

In addition to studying liturgical history and liturgical tradition in light of the contemporary cultural and socio-political situation, such an investigation needs to study the relationship between liturgy and contemporary theology on the one hand, and between liturgy and contemporary spirituality on the other. For example, one would need to study medieval books of hours as devotional sources used by laypersons at the same time that the liturgy of the hours was adapted and celebrated by the mendicant orders, e.g., Franciscans, Dominicans etc. This shift from an exclusive concern for ritual evolution enhances liturgical study because it is a move in the direction of recontextualizing, and therefore being most faithful to, the liturgical sources themselves. This approach is also necessary in order to make appropriate judgments about liturgical theology since such judgments need grounding in the empirical data of the liturgical event.

Related to this consideration is the notion of the normativity of liturgical tradition. This is to suggest that contemporary liturgical rites have developed in history and have experienced evolutions that need to be brought to bear when interpreting or critiquing present liturgical forms. Liturgical tradition both grounds the contemporary reform and ought to guide further adaptation in order that what is presently experienced is truly part of an organic development. For example Taft's own method in studying the Eucharist[42] attests to how the skilled liturgiologist is equipped to make the most poignant observations about contemporary liturgy and liturgical theology precisely because of the breadth of background derived from the historical and theological study of the liturgy—which in our understanding means liturgical tradition.

The perdurance in liturgical tradition of certain symbolic actions (e.g., bathing in water for baptism) and the ritual and theological importance attached to the proclamation of the blessing prayer (e.g., over water in baptism) means that this evidence can be used to correct those rites which have neglected ample use of either (this kind of) symbolic action or blessing text. Thus liturgical tradition may be said to have provided the means whereby the preconciliar liturgy, which had often minimized sacramental liturgy to categories of matter and form in celebration and theology, was changed at the reform *in the light of liturgical tradition* to maximize symbols and to expand on the use of blessing prayers. For baptism this means giving preference to immersion over infusion for the baptismal washing and in blessing water at every baptism with an extensive blessing prayer as opposed to the use throughout the year of water blessed annually at the Easter Vigil.

A pertinent example of how a study of the evolution of various eucharistic prayers in East and West can help our appreciation of the anaphora prayer form and can inform a contemporary critique of the anaphoras presently in use is that of Louis Bouyer in *Eucharist*.[43] Our method, however, would frame such a discussion differently. While Bouyer presents an impressive summary and interpretation of a wealth of Eucharistic prayer texts, his method limits interpretation to texts only. The author deals with what the texts themselves say, not with the way these texts functioned or function in the liturgy in relation to other things such as scriptures proclaimed, or participation of the faithful in receiving Communion or other rites participated in by the congregation. In addition, Bouyer does not deal with how these texts were proclaimed (whether in Latin or the vernacular, whether aloud or silently, whether sung or spoken) or whether they were understood by the congregation during the act of liturgy. While Bouyer's work is an impressive example of part of the method proposed here in the sense that historical study involves textual study and an awareness of how rites developed, what is also essential is how a community experiences what it is doing liturgically. Therefore, for a proper interpretation of the Eucharistic liturgy as a source of Eucharistic theology one would have to determine, among other things, the primacy and adequacy of the proclamation of the Word, what music accompanied the rite, who participated in the music (e.g., Eucharistic acclamations), what the anaphora texts said, how much of it was comprehended by the assembly, and what were the rites of Communion, including who was invited to share in the Eucharistic bread and wine.

In the light of these questions the kind of method employed by Nathan Mitchell in his work on the Eucharist, *Cult and Controversy*,[44] is a move in the right direction. With regard to liturgy and popular piety, Mitchell's observations about the relationship between liturgy on the one hand and Eucharistic exposition, benediction, and processions on the other are pertinent. He maintains that these devotions enabled people to be drawn into the Eucharistic mystery at a time when the liturgy did not facilitate such access. This example demonstrates that one needs to be careful in determining *a priori* what constituted ''liturgy'' in the sense of what was experienced as ''the work of the people'' as opposed to what liturgical rituals said was the work of the people. Communities present at liturgy were often engaged in personal and devotional prayer, not in the texts of the liturgy; yet they were usually conscious of the actions of the ritual taking place. Could not this visual engagement itself be termed liturgical participation? One needs to be careful about assessing how people did or did not participate in the liturgy in history.[45] Such questions are most significant in evaluating the contemporary liturgy since one of the stated aims of the liturgical reform is the integration of popular piety with the liturgy.[46] Recent research, however, reveals how elusive this task is and the depth behind many practices of popular piety.[47]

For our thesis, therefore, an essential and important component of the present liturgical context is determined by liturgical tradition, understanding liturgical history to be a chief, but not the only component. Methodologically it is important to emphasize that tradition is something not in the past but the present shaped by past experience. This acknowledges the conserving function of ritual in terms of Christian identity. Liturgy and liturgical theology are not created anew in each age; they are products of evolution in history coupled with ongoing theological and pastoral reform and renewal.

(2) Contemporary Liturgical Reform. Chief among the stated aims of the present liturgical reform was the concern to provide rites that facilitate full and active participation, particularly through rites that could be more easily comprehended (Liturgy Constitution, nos. 14, 21).[48] The task of determining whether the present reforms actually do reflect these aims can be aided by the thesis *context is text* precisely because active participation cannot be measured merely by determining whether a correct *rite* has been published. Key issues here concern to what extent the present rites as implemented and practiced function to facilitate popular participation and comprehension, and to what extent contemporary celebrations of liturgy conform to the revised rites themselves.

One way of dealing with the kind of variation in interpretation of the present liturgy is by way of what might be called a hermeneutic of *dynamic dialectic.* This is to suggest that an interpretation of each element of a given liturgical celebration relies on an appreciation of its place within the rest of the celebration and that this location and interrelationship, at least in part, if not in large measure, determines its meaning. The notion of *dialectic* here is called *dynamic* because at various times the same text, symbol or gesture from a given rite can take on a new meaning because the *context* has changed or because a given ritual component (e.g., text, symbol, gesture) is given greater or lesser prominence at a given liturgy. An historical example here concerns the theological precision of the Roman Canon articulating the various aspects of Christ's paschal mystery vis-a-vis a piety that emphasized only Christ's passion. Part of what led to this dissonance was the fact that the words of the Roman Canon with their own theological precision were likely not heard or understood by the assembly. Rather, rubrical directions (the silent Canon, double genuflections at the consecration) and devotional practices mitigated this. Another kind of example concerns the interpretation of the sign of peace at a reconciliation service or at an ordination liturgy, in which settings it takes on meanings not customarily associated with it at a normal Eucharist. Hence texts and gestures within the whole context of a liturgy (Eucharist) or the varying contexts in liturgy for the same gesture (sign of peace) must be factored into an adequate hermeneutic for liturgical theology.

While the word "performance" can contain the negative connotation of leaving liturgical communities passive during a rite, it can be a useful term to indicate the fact that *how a rite is conducted* ("performed") does have an important bearing on how the liturgy engages the assembly's participation. It is certainly an historical anomaly that for centuries the text proposed as the Church's norm for Eucharistic worship and understanding—the Roman Canon—was not audible by the assembly and was not proclaimed in the vernacular. Here performance clearly mitigated the kind of comprehension expected in the liturgy. Thus the distinction between reformed *rite* and *context* is important to sustain since contemporary liturgical contexts may well mitigate comprehension and participation—the very things which the reform sought to achieve.[49] In addition to the kind of ecclesial and cultural factors in the liturgical context which influence performance, and thus participation in and comprehension of the liturgy, other factors affecting comprehension include the physical setting in which the liturgy takes place, the arrangement of assembly in that environment, the use of music, ministries, and symbolic actions.[50]

For example, with regard to the arrangement of the assembly and (what today is commonly termed) the environment, while the

Roman Canon and new Eucharistic prayers use the pronoun "we" to articulate the prayer of the whole assembly, the very arrangement of the assembly can speak more about individuals at prayer than communal worship. Furthermore, with regard to music, if the texts sung at the Communion rite refer to individual reception or to adoration, then the music in which the people participate will reflect messages at variance with those inherent in the Eucharistic rite which at this point emphasizes the communal sharing in the Eucharist, one of whose purposes is to build up the Church as the body of Christ. In addition, with regard to ministries, the performance of a ritual by a single priest celebrant as opposed to liturgy engaging the varied liturgical roles envisioned and demanded by the present rites speaks a message at variance with the notion of the Church at prayer as clearly articulated in the revised liturgical rites (both the texts of the rites of Eucharist and ordination themselves and their accompanying General Instructions). In this regard, it would be an interesting exercise to trace the understanding of the phrases from the Roman Canon *et omnium circumstantium* and *et plebs tua sancta* in light of our thesis. If these texts were originally heard and comprehended by Eucharistic assemblies it was not long afterwards that the assembly became physically distant from the sanctuary with the result that the physical act of hearing such a text was difficult. In addition, hearing this text proclaimed from the sanctuary of a mammoth cathedral provides a far different experience from that of hearing the same text in a parish church, in a small chapel or at a domestic liturgy.[51] Related to this is the posture which the assembly assumed (kneeling or standing) while these phrases were spoken. While an obvious barrier to comprehending the meaning of the gathering of the Church around the altar had been the fact that the language of the Canon was Latin, one could argue that some contemporary liturgical contexts make full comprehension of these same texts impossible precisely because contexts (e.g., physical arrangements) so influence how texts are heard.

The other side of the coin about context as an essential factor in understanding texts is how the present liturgical *rites* (that is General Instruction, Lectionary readings, prayer texts, gestures, and symbols) function as normative and as a critique of inadequate *contexts* for contemporary liturgical celebration. An example of the normative value of the reformed rites concerns the primacy of the assembly in the conduct of and for the theology of the liturgy. The very fact that the assembly is continually referred to in the General Instruction and throughout the present Eucharistic rite signals a shift from the Tridentine missal which directed the actions of sanctuary ministers only (in ways that were rubrically self-conscious). Therefore the emphasis on actualizing the assembly's role in the contemporary liturgy and understanding liturgical ministers as functioning in communion with and on behalf of the assembly signals a shift in how the liturgy is to be experienced and understood. This same evidence also signals a shift in the liturgical theology of the Eucharist from objective presence in the elements only to communal transformation through the Eucharistic enactment of the paschal mystery, which enactment presumes sharing in the transformed gifts of bread and wine.

For example, the fact that every revised ritual states where and how the roles of reader and deacon are to function liturgically is itself a theological statement about how the Church is to be imaged in liturgy—through a variety of roles serving the assembled community. Liturgical theologians rightly capitalize on such directives as indications of a shift in liturgical ministry away from the medieval eclipsing of liturgical roles into that of the priest. When such ministers do not function in the liturgy and roles are again collapsed into one (or even to a few) then the *texts* of the reformed liturgy function as appropriate critiques of those *contexts*. One could argue, therefore, that the reformed liturgy is normative in the sense that inadequate contexts need to be corrected in the light of what the rituals disclose about the ecclesiology of liturgy. One reason why some texts are simply not "heard" is that some liturgical contexts (environment, music, ministries, performance etc.) are simply not congruent with the vision and guidelines of the reformed rites.

The normative value of the reformed rites also indicates that one's interpretation of texts used liturgically is not relative. The meaning is grounded in the revised rites as used liturgically and as bearers of a rich liturgical and theological tradition which tradition is brought to bear as they are used at present. Hence liturgical rites must be interpreted in a way that respects their nature as intended for ritual use and as bearers of theological meanings disclosed principally in liturgical celebration itself.

For example, the present Mass formula for the solemnity of

Corpus Christi reflects traditional themes of the theology of Eucharist. These include Eucharist as memorial (opening prayer), Church unity and peace (prayer over the gifts), present participation in the Eucharist as an eschatological sign (prayer after Communion), as well as images of the effects on the Church of participation in the Eucharist (prefaces for the Holy Eucharist). The Scripture texts from the Lectionary are classic in the sense that they emphasize Old Testament images of feeding (during the Exodus in Deut 8:2-3, 14-16 and Exod 24:3-8) and examples of offering sacrifice (Melchizedek offering bread and wine Gen 14:18-20), of theological expositions about Christ as high priest (Heb 9:11-15), the ecclesiological dimensions of Eucharistic participation (1 Cor 10:16-17 and 1 Cor 11:23-26) and gospel texts about Jesus as the bread of life (John 6:51-58), as host at the Last Supper (Mark 14:12-16, 22-26) and feeding the crowds superabundantly with twelve baskets left over (Luke 9:11-17). Obviously these texts afford abundant material for preaching on this feast. Sermons not derived from these sources, perhaps emphasizing individual piety or the priest's power to consecrate, are implicitly critiqued by the Lectionary itself. When viewed against liturgical tradition as a whole these texts function as normative in the sense that they ground the theology and preaching on Corpus Christi (especially anamnetic and ecclesiological aspects) and they offer a critique of Eucharistic theologies and pieties as well as notions of ordained ministry that are individualistic or merely "power" oriented.

Investigation into what actually occurs at liturgy and (to the extent possible) how what occurs is appropriated by the gathered community is most useful especially since this method can help assess what has actually been implemented and the extent to which the revised rites are truly normative in the sense outlined above. A first question here would be *whether or not* the envisioned liturgical reform has taken place. The kind of approach used in studying the Eucharist in the Order of Mass Study,[52] and in studying liturgy more generally in the Notre Dame Study on Parish Life[53] are significant (if not unflawed) in the sense that they open up avenues for a thorough assessment of reactions to the reforms as they are actually experienced. A second question concerns the possibility of interpreting the elements of liturgy (word, gesture, symbol, song, etc.) in relation to each other for a liturgical hermeneutic that studies *texts in context*.

A particularly poignant example of a facet of the liturgical reform (influenced by liturgical tradition) in the present sacramental rites which needs evaluation in light of actual celebrations is the proclamation of the Word and the act of preaching.[54] Since one of the stated purposes of the Lectionary reform is greater variety in texts heard and preached, one could ask how much variety is experienced in the texts proclaimed at sacramental celebrations, for example infant baptism. To overuse one text, even one suggested in the ritual itself (i.e., Matt 28:18-20) could mitigate one of the intentions of the reform in terms of providing a variety of readings. Further, one needs to ask how well homilies relate the Scripture readings with the sacramental act that accompany them. Are Word and sacrament experienced as and perceived to be correlative? Do baptismal homilies contain any reference to the intrinsic connection between Scriptures proclaimed and bathing in water?

Another example of liturgical reform that needs evaluation would be the use of gestures in celebrating initiation.[55] While the rituals of both adult and infant baptism clearly give preference to immersion over infusion,[56] one could ask to what extent immersion has in fact replaced the pouring of water. Another important aspect of gestural involvement presumed in the revised rite of baptism concerns the assembly's processing from entrance of the Church, to gathering to hear the Word, to font for water baptism and to altar for Eucharist (or for the Lord's Prayer) and conclusion. Some assessment about whether and how communities are actually engaged in such ritual movement would be important to determine whether what is presupposed in the rite actually takes place.

Our thesis about *context is text* and a *dynamic dialectic* for interpretation is advanced here in two ways. First, it requires that liturgical units be interpreted in relation to each other and that the whole liturgical event itself be regarded as an essential component in interpreting liturgical texts, symbols, and gestures. Crucial in this first stage is the actual liturgical celebration.[57] Second, the postconciliar rites set a standard and measure against which to evaluate present liturgical practice. This is to suggest that the rites as revised present a minimum standard of how to celebrate liturgy—a standard that is marked by option, flexibility and direct relationship with the given liturgical assembly.

(3) *Liturgical Adaptation and Critical Liturgical Theology.* It was noted above that the nature of the present liturgical reform is oriented to adaptation and indigenization depending on varying local circumstances. This needs to be kept in mind when considering the normative value of the revised rites. By their nature the present rites contain options and choices within ritual structures that are to be determined in light of the varying settings for celebration. For example, the General Instruction on the Roman Missal states that "the pastoral effectiveness of a celebration depends in great measure on choosing readings, prayers, and songs which correspond to the needs, spiritual preparation and attitude of the participants. This will be achieved by an intelligent use of the options described below" (GIRM no. 313). Anscar Chupungco will argue that the paragraphs 37–39 of the Liturgy Constitution provide the rationale for the kind of flexibility found in each of the rites revised since Vatican II. He (among others) then argues that paragraph 40 opens the door to a far greater liturgical change, namely to a wide ranging adjustment of liturgical structures and rites in light of varying cultural needs. This process has been variously described as "indigenization," "acculturation," and "cultural adaptation."[58]

The present liturgy therefore can be termed both a reform as well as the basis from which to work toward ongoing indigenization of the liturgy. Once the reformed liturgy as envisioned and enunciated in the revised rites is in place then the indigenization imperative (to use Anscar Chupungco's term) is to be undertaken. This process has seen some, although comparatively few, results in practice. Among the many factors that comprise the indigenization task which cause this process to be slow are questions about what is meant by the statements of the Liturgy Constitution that in the reform of the liturgy the "Church does not wish to impose a rigid uniformity" (no. 37) and that in adapting the liturgy "the substantial unity of the Roman rite" is to be preserved (no. 38). Another factor is the fact that efforts toward indigenization continue along with development in the theoretical underpinnings as to why indigenization needs to be undertaken in the first place.[59]

For our thesis about *context* this means that the historical study of the liturgy discloses variety in liturgical forms on which basis the contemporary inculturation agenda functions to provide greater variety in liturgical forms provided that the "substantial unity of the Roman rite" is preserved. Since the contemporary liturgical reform was to be done in light of historical, theological and pastoral investigation (Liturgy Constitution n. 16) the contribution of historical study is most significant here in that it grounds variety in liturgical forms, some of which are based on cultural differences. (Recall here the discussion in chapter one about the patristic era and the varied structures of the eucharistic anaphora and in particular the differences between those of the East and those of the West.) On these bases (among others) one can argue that variety and complementarily of liturgical forms in the present reform is grounded in liturgical tradition, substantiated in the rites of the present reform, is clearly experienced in practice and leads necessarily to greater indigenization of liturgical rites. For our purposes the methodological question that emerges concerns how to develop an adequate method for liturgical theology with these factors in mind. In other words, the contemporary issue concerns how to develop a liturgical theology on the basis of not only pluriform rites, but also on the basis of rites being adapted to changing situations in accord with the indigenization agenda.

One of the factors involved in indigenization but which also has a life of its own concerns what we have already referred to as "critical liturgical theology." Here the question of the *adequacy* of the present reformed rites comes into play. The task of developing liturgical theology in the light of ongoing liturgical reform becomes all the more important since ritual changes almost always both reflect and influence shifts in contemporary theology and spirituality. There is a reciprocity between liturgy and theology that operates in ritual evolution (exemplified in much of liturgical history) and in the ritual changes occurring at present in the sense that changed liturgical rites often reflect developments in theology and it is equally true that changed rites can (and should) influence theology and spirituality. This is to say that the reintroduction in the present of an ancient liturgical practice or text, merely because it is well attested in the tradition, is to introduce the possibility of liturgical anachronism at least stylistically, if not substantially. The present state of liturgical reform invites liturgical theologians to assess the adequacy of the contemporary reform in light of tradition, contemporary theology, Church teaching, and present pastoral needs. Implicit in such an assessment is the acknowledgment of the provisionality as well as the formative nature of liturgical forms; both these factors invite critical assessment of the present rites. Our method takes into consideration the precedent from Prosper of Aquitaine himself who argued not from fixed forms and texts but from a ritual structure that emphasized the value of intercessory prayer. The precedent established by the fact of Good Friday intercessory prayers grounded the theological value of that kind of praying. In our understanding the contemporary reform presents us with a restored vision of what comprises ritual forms. It does not present us with a fixed and unchangeable set of texts and rites. Thus engaging in critical liturgical theology is an imperative toward improving the present reformed liturgy.

Among the theological factors which need to be incorporated into such study and revision are recent advances in anthropology, ecclesiology, Christology, penumatology, Trinity, and eschatology. For example, some of the growing pains with liturgical indigenization are correlative with the contemporary tensions experienced with ecclesiology in general, specifically how local Churches relate to each other, to the Church universal and, in particular, to Rome. Another example is the crucial issue of theological language and names for God, which issue needs to be dealt with squarely in ongoing revision, especially because of the formative nature of liturgical prayer.[60]

A clear example of how knowledge of liturgical tradition, linked with contemporary theology, helps cast a critical eye on the present liturgical reforms concerns the way the Holy Spirit is imaged and operative in the present Roman liturgy. Liturgical and sacramental theologians such as Edward Kilmartin rightly lament the absence of a strong pneumatology in Western sacramental liturgy and theology in general.[61] Clearly one can legitimately criticize the present Roman liturgical rites for their comparatively inadequate pneumatology. Here advances from Scripture and the theology of the person and work of the Holy Spirit would be most helpful in ongoing revisions of a Western euchology that remains primarily Christocentric. The result of theology influencing liturgy would be an improved euchology and, derivatively, an improved theology of liturgy and systematic theology influenced by and/or derived from the liturgy.

As part of the research into how actual liturgical assemblies understand the working of the Spirit in worship, one could inquire about the extent to which people actually "hear" the newly restored Eucharistic epiclesis in the anaphora and appreciate its theological meaning, given the Western preoccupation with the institution narrative.[62] In addition, in accord with our thesis, a major factor in hearing such texts may not be the words of the anaphora themselves but rather liturgical art and architecture which stress images of Christ (specifically crucifixes and stations of the cross) as opposed to art depicting images or the work of the Spirit.

The tradition of allowing for liturgical pluriformity and variety within liturgical tradition could be most useful when providing for the (sometimes vastly) different needs of worshipers in terms of self expression, patterns of bodily involvement and habits of singing because of varied cultural backgrounds. For example, the advantage of the Eucharistic rite developed in Zaire is that it takes into consideration the involvement of whole persons in worship; it is not just concerned with texts.[63]

An example of how liturgical tradition can be brought to bear in critiquing the present liturgy concerns the contemporary Eucharistic prayers in use in the Roman rite. Liturgists have critiqued the use of the same structure for all the new prayers,[64] the inadequacy of the theology of creation in them,[65] the limited use of acclamations during the anaphoras (especially when compared with many Eastern formulas)[66] and the symbolic gestures during the prayer which still tend to highlight the institution narrative in a way that often exalts its position "out of context" with the rest of the prayer.[67] In addition, in the light of our comments above about respecting the various genres of communication in the liturgy, one needs to be aware that traditionally parts (some would argue even all) of the Eucharistic prayers were sung[68] and that Eucharistic acclamations are ranked as chief among the liturgical units to be sung by the assembly. In addition recent research (some of which was undertaken in an ecumenical framework) indicates a wide variety of possibilities for anaphoral structures.[69] Furthermore, recent biblical and liturgical research reveals the need for a reevaluation of the commonly assumed direct relationship between Jewish blessing prayers and Christian anaphoras.[70]

With regard to Eucharistic practice there is the thorny issue of the appropriateness of Eucharistic concelebration[71] specifically when numbers of presbyters can overload a celebration to the detriment of the functioning of other liturgical ministers. What would be fully consonant with the argument already made about liturgical tradition would be to deal with this and other issues of practice in light of an organic development between liturgical origins and contemporary practice that would allow for greater variety in Eucharistic rites[72] respecting the varying ecclesial settings for worship. This is to suggest that the concelebration issue needs to be addressed in light of an ecclesiology rooted in both the tradition and the teachings of Vatican II which emphasizes the liturgical roles of a variety of persons, both baptized and ordained. Part of the research into liturgical tradition here would concern noneucharistic as well as Eucharistic concelebration, the ritual gestures and words presbyters were engaged in, and how various ecclesial settings experienced concelebration (for example, the fact that concelebration of the chrism Mass is well attested). The concelebration question also needs to be addressed in light of theological reality of the particular Eucharistic community. Thus, concelebration at a daily conventual Eucharist in a monastery or religious house[73] or at the occasion of an ordination or the funeral of a priest would be less problematic than it might be in other situations precisely because of the nature of the liturgical community.

Another example of our approach to critical liturgical theology concerns the question of the adequacy of the present rite for the ordination of a priest for non-diocesan clergy. The explicit ecclesiology of the rite is local Church understood in terms of diocese. What about the particularization of priestly ordination that arises from other ecclesiological settings? For example, how adequate is this rite when used for ordaining missionary priests when the ordination takes place in their native diocese and not their diocese of missionary assignment? Or what is the theological adequacy of this rite when used in a community of mendicants, e.g., Franciscans or Dominicans, whose ministry explicitly transcends any local diocese? Or what is the theological adequacy of this ordination rite for a monk priest whose ministry is largely determined by the needs of his monastery and at the will of his abbot? Monastic priesthood is in some way allied with, but it is certainly not determined by the local diocese and bishop.[74] Within the rite itself these questions are reflected in two places: the call to ordination and the promise of obedience to the bishop. The assertion that the candidate is called "after inquiry among the people of Christ" (Rite no. 12) is certainly helpful since it implies reference to the role of the whole Church in calling one to ordination. However, such inquiry is less the case (if it functions at all) in the formation of mendicants and certainly not the case for Benedictine monks (who are called for ordination by the abbot).[75]

The second instance concerns the promise of obedience. It is quite appropriate for a diocesan bishop to ask ordination candidates for that diocese "do you promise respect and obedience to me" or (as the rubrics read "if the bishop is not the candidate's own Ordinary") "to your Ordinary" (Rite, no. 16). However, who is the rightful "Ordinary" for missionaries, mendicants, and monks? If one answers that it is the bishop, then what is the role of religious superiors vis-a-vis the ordained in terms of the liturgical theology of ordination and in terms of ministerial assignment?

If one answers that a monk's Ordinary is the abbot of the monastery then the question has deeper ramifications.[76] On the basis of variety yet complementarily of rites in liturgical tradition could not one legitimately argue for some adjustment in these parts of the ordination rite to reflect more adequately the theological reality of distinctions among the ordained and that provision ought to be provided for them in rites which would not eclipse the ordaining bishop but which would take cognizance of differences among ordained priests, and in particular the difference between diocesan and other clergy? In what follows, where it is appropriate, reference will be made in like manner to critical liturgical theology as a constitutive factor that needs to be considered in establishing and applying a method for liturgical theology.

Our thesis about *context is text* is necessarily open ended in this third part because of the nature of the criteria (noted above) for liturgical indigenization: contemporary theology, liturgical tradition, and pastoral practice. Especially because research in all three fields is ongoing, liturgical indigenization must be regarded as an ongoing task. In addition, indigenization can only be done in light of specific ecclesial groups and in light of specific liturgical needs. This makes the determination of specific cultural *contexts* crucial in the process of establishing new liturgical *texts* (that is, rites).

At the same time with regard to critical liturgical theology one needs to retain a certain reserve when questioning the adequacy of the present liturgical reforms in the sense that we ought not delude ourselves into thinking that we can achieve "the perfect rite." Even after having determined an appropriate criteria for this investigation, all that we can really hope for is to establish the least inadequate liturgical forms, forms which by their nature are meant to support the experience of God in worship, initiated and sustained by the Trinity itself.

In the chapters that follow we shall not be concerned principally with liturgical indigenization, largely because of the ongoing nature of this task, the continuing search for its own method at present and the fact that it is best done *in context*, not in general. Rather our concern will be to address how critical liturgical theology needs to be kept in mind as we develop and apply a method for liturgical theology.

The chief aim of this chapter has been to establish working definitions of "liturgy" and "liturgical theology" and to present the core of our contribution to a method for doing liturgical theology in light of the present revision of the Roman liturgy. Our main focus has been how liturgical theology can be drawn from liturgy as an event and as a theological act. By their nature enacted liturgical rites are somewhat elusive because they involve more than texts on paper. In our perspective they involve texts used in contexts to the extent that *context is text*. Concomitant with interpreting the act of liturgy itself is an exploration of the *constitutive implications* of liturgical engagement. In our perspective this means that *text shapes context* both theologically and spiritually. The balance of this book concerns applying our thesis.

Notes

1. Among others, see Aidan Kavanagh, *On Liturgical Theology* 74–77 and passim. Kavanagh will give his own interpretation to this distinction when he states "the theology which we most readily recognize and practice is in fact neither primary nor seminal but secondary and derivative: *theologia secunda*. It is also to argue that doing liturgical theology comes closer to doing *theologia prima* than *theologia secunda* or a "theology of the liturgy" and that doing primary theology places a whole set of requirements on the theologian which are not quite the same as those placed on a theologian who does only secondary theology" (75).

2. Gerard Lukken, "The Unique Expression of Faith in the Liturgy," *Liturgical Expression of Faith*, Concilium 82, eds. H. Schmidt and D. Power, and trans. David Smith (New York: Herder and Herder, 1973) 16. Also see, G. Lukken, "La liturgie comme lieu théologique irremplacable," *Questions Liturgiques* 56 (1975) 102.

3. G. Lukken, "The Unique Expression," 20.

4. David N. Power, "Two Expressions of Faith: Worship and Theology," *The Liturgical Experience of Faith*, 95.

5. As was already noted ("Preface" p. xi–xii) "liturgical theology" as *theologia secunda* will be argued in Chapters 3–7 and *theologia tertia* will be argued in Chapter 8.

6. Various approaches to making appropriate distinctions about what can be understood by this general term can be found in the following, among others, Hans B. Meyer, "Liturgische Theologie oder Theologie des Gottesdienstes," *Zeitschrift für katholische Theologie* 86 (1964) 327–331, Francois Vandenbroucke, "Sur la théologie de la liturgie," *Nouvelle Revue Theologique* 92 (1970) 135–164, Geoffrey Wainwright, "Der Gottesdienst als 'Locus Theologicus,' oder: Der Gottesdienst als Quelle und Thema der Theologie," *Kerygma und Dogma* 28 (1982) 248–258. Parts of this section rely on the work of Salvatore Marsili, especially the following four articles, "Liturgia," *Nuovo Dizionario di Liturgia*, 725–742, "Teologia Liturgica," *Nuovo Dizionario di Liturgia* 1508–1525, "Liturgia," *Dizionario del Concilio Vaticano II* 1294–1342, and "Liturgia," *Dizionario Enc. di Teologia Morale* 574–582. Among Achille M. Triacca's many articles related to this topic note especially, "La sens théologique de la liturgie et/ou le sens liturgique de la théologie. Esquisse initiale pour une synthèse," in *La liturgie, son sens, son esprit, sa méthode*, 321–337.

7. This important distinction is based on the key insight of Robert Taft in "Toward a Theology of the Christian Feast," *Beyond East and West*: Problems in Liturgical Understanding (Washington: Pastoral Press, 1984) 1–13.

8. See, Chapter 1, p. 10–15.

9. *Hodie Christus natus est: hodie in terra canunt Angeli, laetantur Archangeli: hodie exsultant justi, dicentes: Gloria in excelsis Deo, alleluia.*

10. *Christus natus est nobis: Venite adoremus.*

11. *Haec dies, quam fecit Dominus: exsultemus, et laetemur in ea.*

12. For a succinct feminist critique and proposal about the power involved in the act of blessing see, Janet Walton, "Ecclesiastical and Feminist Blessing: Women as Objects and Subjects of the Power of Blessing," in *Blessing and Power*, Concilium vol. 178, eds. David Power and Mary Collins (Edinburgh: T. & T. Clark, 1985) 73–80.

13. The comment of Karl Rahner in this connection is well known: the church "is most manifest and in the most intensive form, she attains the highest actuality of her own nature, when she celebrates the eucharist" (from *The Church and the Sacraments* trans. W. J. O'Hara [New York: Herder and Herder,

1963] 84). See, among others, the helpful essay of Gerard Békés, "The Eucharist Makes the Church: The Ecclesial Dimension of Sacrament" in *Vatican II. Assessment and Perspectives* Vol. II, ed. Rene Latourelle (New York/Mahwah: Paulist Press, 1988) 347–363.

14. *DOL* nn. 14, 26.

15. For a more complete explanation of this distinction see, Kevin W. Irwin, "Toward a Theological Anthropology of Sacraments," in *A Promise of Presence. Studies in Honor of David N. Power*, eds. Michael Downey and Richard Fragomini (Washington: The Pastoral Press, 1992) 40–43.

16. See below, Chapter 8, pp. 316–324.

17. Recall the list of theological issues related to the liturgy articulated by Mark Searle noted in the "Preface" p. ix.

18. On the symbolic nature of the Word, see Chapter 3, pp. 86–90, and the dialogic nature of symbol see Chapter 4, pp. 142–152.

19. In fact, even the technical language describing the Eucharist from Scholasticism is analogical.

20. Among others, see Harvey Guthrie, *Theology as Thanksgiving*, esp. 181–216.

21. See, Albert Houssiau, "La liturgie," *Initiation á la pratique de la théologie*, vol. 5 (Paris: Les Editions du Cerf, 1983) 158 and Geoffrey Wainwright, "The Praise of God in the Theological Reflection of the Church," *Interpretation* 39 (1985) 42–43 where he states: "to mention the praise of God as the theologian's motivation runs the risk of provoking dissent from colleagues anxious for academic neutrality. Yet scholars who wish simply to describe the Christian faith had better call themselves historians, although good historical description usually calls for at least a certain empathy with the subject, and very little historiography proves to be ideologically 'value-free.' Again, those who wish to undertake an independent 'search for truth' are better called philosophers, for Christian theology does not start from scratch with every thinker but takes place within a tradition and community of faith and praise."

22. See, Albert Houssiau, "La liturgie, lieu priviligié de la théologie sacramentaire," 11, where he cautions against theology that is too didactic, a tendency that can be addressed if liturgy becomes more central as a theological source.

23. See, among others, Pedro Fernandez, "Liturgia y teología. Una cuestion metodologica."

24. The terms "adaptation," "accommodation" and "inculturation" are variously defined and understood to describe the process we will normally term "inculturation."

25. The work of Gerard Lukken and Albert Houssiau is particularly helpful in showing how these skilled theologians have moved the discussion in liturgical theology from texts, to liturgy as event, to the celebration of the reformed liturgy as the source for liturgical theology. See, Kevin Irwin, *Liturgical Theology* for a summary of their work (29–34) and a bibliography of their recent writing on liturgical theology (75–76). A particularly useful statement of the need for a

new method in liturgical theology based on ritual studies as a relatively new discipline and one that is germane to our argument is in Theodore W. Jennings, "Ritual Studies and Liturgical Theology: An Invitation to Dialogue," *Journal of Ritual Studies* 1 (1987) 35–56.

26. As noted above (Preface, fn. 22) the annual reports of the discussions of the "Liturgy and Social Sciences" and "Liturgy and Ritual Studies" study groups in the *Proceedings* are helpful indicators of these methodological discussions.

27. For a more thorough description of the method used at the Institute and its course of study see Pelagio Visentin, "L'Istituto di Liturgia pastorale di S. Giustina - Padova: dati e prospettive," *Notitiae* 20 (1984) 559–567 and Franco Brovelli "Celebrazione: il mistero si fa esperienza. La maturazione del concetto di liturgia nel cammino dell'ILP," in *Una liturgia per l'uomo.* Caro Salutis Cardo 5, eds. Pelagio Visentin, Aldo N. Terrin, R. Cecolin (Padova: Edizioni Messaggero Padova, 1986) 325–342, plus the other essays in this volume. The course of studies of the Institute is summarized in Pelagio Visentin, *Culmen et fons. Raccolta di studi liturgia e spiritualita,* Vol. I and II, Caro Salutis Cardo 3 and 4 (Padova: Edizioni Messaggero Padova, 1986). For a description of what we have called "reflection on the church's liturgical praxis" see Franco Giulio Brambilla, "Ermeneutica Teologica dell'adattamento liturgico," in *Liturgia e Adattamento.* Dimensioni Cultuale e Teologico-Pastorali, eds., A. Pistoia, A. M. Triacca (Rome: Editiones Liturgicae, 1990) 67 where he cites the need for "theological-practical reflection on the pastoral act itself" of liturgy.

28. See, Franco Brovelli, "Fede e liturgia" 545.

29. For an approach to understanding how component parts of liturgical rites are interrelated see, Robert Taft, "The Structural Analysis of Liturgical Units: An Essay in Methodology," *Worship* 52 (July 1978) 314–329.

30. See, Preface, p. x and fn. 13.

31. This emphasis recalls the work of pioneers in the liturgical movement (notably Lambert Beauduin, Romano Guardini as noted in chapter one, and Cipriano Vagaggini) who argued for an appreciation of liturgy that concerned the renewal of the Church's whole life and of the spiritual lives of those who participate.

32. For a careful analysis of the pivotal evolution of the shape of the liturgy in the first three centuries and the thesis that this period saw immense variety in forms, see, Robert Taft, "Historicism Revisited," in *Beyond East and West* 15–30.

33. See, Herman Wegman, *Christian Worship in East and West.* A Study Guide to Liturgical History, trans. Gordon Lathrop (New York: Pueblo Publishing Co., 1986) xiv, where he describes "investigation of worship by historical periods because in this way the evolution of celebration in the church becomes clearer and one can show that a difference exists between essential rites and incidental rites, between what is structural and what is decorative."

34. Robert Taft, "The Structural Analysis of Liturgical Units" 317–318. In a

significant footnote Taft states: "Of course we must not expect history to tell us what present practice or doctrine should be. That would be to confuse history with theology. But history can free us from the temptation to absolutize past or present by opening up to us the changing patterns—and hence relativity—of much in our practice and doctrine" (318, fn. 9).

35. Robert Taft, "Response to the Berakah Award: Anamnesis," 315.

36. Robert Taft, "Liturgy as Theology," 116.

37. Robert Taft, "Response," 313.

38. Ibid., 314.

39. Ibid.

40. G. G. Willis, "The Variable Prayers of the Roman Mass," *Further Essays in Early Roman Liturgy* (London: SPCK, 1968) 116.

41. This is specified and exemplified in Chapter 6, pp. 235-246.

42. See, "The Frequency of the Eucharist Throughout History," in *Can We Always Celebrate the Eucharist?*, Concilium, Vol. 152, eds. Mary Collins and David Power (New York: Seabury, 1982) 13-24.

43. See, Louis Bouyer, *Eucharist. Theology and Spirituality of the Eucharistic Prayer*, trans., Charles U. Quinn (Notre Dame: University of Notre Dame Press, 1968) esp. 1-14 for the methodological premises of the book.

44. See, Nathan Mitchell, *Cult and Controversy: The Worship of the Eucharist Outside Mass* (New York: Pueblo Publishing Co., 1982).

45. For example, John Bossy will argue that in the Middle Ages even though communities did not vocalize liturgical responses or prayers, they did, in fact, "participate" in the liturgy in significant, but nonverbal ways. See, J. Bossy, "The Mass as Social Institution, 1200-1700," *Past and Present* 100 (1983) 29-61; also see his *Christianity in the West 1400-1700* (New York: Oxford University Press, 1985).

46. Liturgy Constitution, n. 13.

47. A useful introduction to this literature is provided in *Liturgy: A Creative Tradition*. Concilium Vol. 162, eds. Mary Collins and David Power (New York: Seabury, 1983).

48. These texts state (from *DOL* nn. 14, 21): "In the restoration and promotion of the sacred liturgy the full and active participation by all the people is the aim to be considered before all else, for it is the primary and indispensable source from which the faithful are to derive the true Christian spirit" (n. 14). "In this restoration both texts and rites should be drawn up so as to express more clearly the holy things which they signify. The Christian people, as far as possible, should be able to understand them with ease and take part in them fully, actively, and as a community" (n. 21).

49. It should be pointed out here that there is some debate about the adequacy of the aim stated by the Council of intelligibility or comprehension of liturgical rites. The issue in liturgy is less verbal understanding and mental

comprehension by the mind and more the shaping of attitudes and allowing one's imagination to be engaged in symbolic acts which by their nature are not oriented to intellectual comprehension alone.

50. This is treated more fully in Chapter 6, pp. 224-229, 235-249.

51. One could also muse about the meaning of these phrases in light of the evolution of the "private mass" (i.e. as opposed to the individual priest celebrating alone) where it is likely that small groups gathered at altars of secondary importance (when compared with the main altar of a shrine or monastery) for a rite experienced as much simpler than that conducted at a main altar during a conventual Mass.

52. See, *The Order of Mass Study: A Report* (Washington: Federation of Diocesan Liturgical Commissions, 1985).

53. Already noted, Preface, fn. 22.

54. The crucial importance of preaching in the reformed liturgy and in developing both an adequate theology of liturgy and spirituality derived from the liturgy will be addressed in Chapter 3.

55. See, among others, the helpful study on the implementation of the rite of infant baptism by Jean Orianne, "Baptism. An Enquiry on the Evocative Force of the Symbolism of the Baptismal Rites," *Lumen Vitae* 26 (1971) 623-648.

56. *Rite of Christian Initiation of Adults* n. 226 and *Rite of Baptism for Children* n. 60.

57. See, Mark Searle, "New Tasks, New Methods: The Emergence of Pastoral Liturgical Studies," *Worship* 57 (July 1983) 291-308 where he deals with "actual liturgical performance" as the locus for pastoral liturgical study.

58. See, Anscar J. Chupungco, *Cultural Adaptation of the Liturgy* New York/Mahwah: Paulist Press, 1982) passim.

59. See the recent work of D. S. Amalorpavadass, "Theological Reflection on Inculturation," *Studia Liturgica* 20 (1990) 36-54 and 116-136.

60. See the particularly helpful approach to this issue in Gail Ramshaw-Schmidt, *Christ in Sacred Speech. The Meaning of Liturgical Language* (Philadelphia: Fortress Press, 1986).

61. Yves Congar's useful term "christomonism" has been used by Edward Kilmartin and others in describing how Western euchology lacks adequate emphasis on the Holy Spirit. Kilmartin's own work *Christian Liturgy* is a useful example of how to develop a theology of liturgy from the perspective of an economic Trinitarian theology. Also see, Edward Kilmartin's insightful comments on this in "A Modern Approach to the Word of God and Sacraments of Christ," in *The Sacraments: God's Love and Mercy Actualized,* ed. Francis A. Eigio (Villanova, Pa.: Villanova University Press, 1979) 59-109 and "Theology of the Sacraments: Toward a New Understanding of the Chief Rites of the Church of Jesus Christ," in *Alternative Futures For Worship* Vol. One (Collegeville: The Liturgical Press, 1987) 123-175.

62. Among the numerous studies on the meaning of the epiclesis in contemporary eucharistic prayers see, John McKenna, "The Epiclesis Revisited: A Look at Modern Eucharistic Prayers," *Ephemerides Liturgicae* 99 (1985) 314–336;" for a review of the meaning of the epiclesis in liturgical history see Achille M. Triacca, "Teología y liturgia de la epiclesis en la tradición oriental y occidental," *Phase* 25 (1985) 379–424.

63. See, L. Mpongo, "Le Rite Zairois de la Messe," *Spiritus* 19 (1978) 436–441, E. Mveng, "Christ, Liturgie et Culture," *Bulletin of African Theology* 2 (1980) 247–255, Anselme Sanon, "Cultural Rooting of the Liturgy in Africa since Vatican II," in *Liturgy: A Creative Tradition*, 61–70.

64. This is discussed below, Chapter 5, pp. 203–207.

65. See, among others, Joseph Keenan, "The Importance of the Creation Motif in a Eucharistic Prayer," *Worship* 53 (July 1979) 341–356 and our discussion in Chapter Four, passim., particularly 163–165.

66. The use of more numerous acclamations in the eucharistic prayers for children is significant both because it reflects a slight modification in the anaphora structure and because composers have written music for the whole of these texts including acclamations. One example of such music is Richard Proulx, *Eucharistic Prayer For Children II* (Chicago: G.I.A. Publications, 1982).

67. See, R. Kevin Seasoltz, "Non-Verbal Symbols and the Eucharistic Prayer," in *New Eucharistic Prayers*. An Ecumenical Study of their Development and Structure. (New York/Mahwah: Paulist Press, 1987) 214–234.

68. See the first part of Jan Michael Joncas, *Hymnum Tuae Gloriae Canimus*. Toward an Analysis of the Vocal and Musical Expression of the Eucharistic Prayer in the Roman Rite: Tradition, Principles, Method. (Rome: Pont. Athenaeum S. Anslemo, Thesis ad Lauream n. 168, 1991) 5–157.

69. See, David N. Power, "The Eucharistic Prayer: Another Look," in *New Eucharistic Prayers* 239–250.

70. Particularly influential studies are those of Cesare Giraudo, *La struttura letteraria della Preghiera Eucaristia*. Analecta Biblica 92 (Rome: Biblical Institute Press, 1981), its sequel *Eucaristia per la Chiesa*. Prospettive teologiche sull'eucaristia a partire dalla "lex orandi" (Brescia: Editrice Morcelliana, 1989) and Thomas Talley, "From *Berakah* to *Eucharistia*: A Reopening Question," in *Living Bread, Saving Cup*, ed. R. Kevin Seasoltz, 80–101. This is discussed more fully below, Chapter 5, 179–180, 203–204.

71. Among the more useful studies of this question in English are Robert Taft, "Ex Oriente Lux? Some Reflections on Eucharistic Concelebration," *Worship* 54 (July 1980) 308–325, Marcel Rooney, "Eucharistic Concelebration, Twenty-Five Years of Development," *Ecclesia Orans* 6 (1989) 117–129 and Gil Osdiek, "Concelebration Revisited," in *Shaping English Liturgy*, eds. Peter Finn and James Schellman (Washington: The Pastoral Press, 1990) 139–171.

72. A related issue in eucharistic practice is the question of using the same eucharistic rite for both weekdays and Sundays. With regard to the structure

of the eucharistic rite it would be legitimate in light of liturgical tradition to argue that the ritual for weekday Eucharist should be simplified and different in terms of ritual structure (e.g., number of processions) and quantity of texts as compared with the Sunday rite.

73. In the light of the evolution of the private mass and its subsequent abuse, eucharistic concelebration for presbyters in such settings would be a decided advance. See, among others, Cyrille Vogel, "Une mutation cultuelle inexpliquée: le passage de l'Eucharistie communitaire à la messe privée," *Revue des sceinces religieuses* 54 (1980) 231–250, and Angelus Häussling, *Mönchskonvent und Eucharistiefeier: Eine Studie über die Messe in der abendlandischen Klosterliturgie des frühen Mittelalters und zur Geschichte der Messhaufigkeit* Liturgiewissenschaftliche Quellen und Forschungen 58 (Münster-Westfsalen: Aschendorff, 1972).

74. See, Kevin W. Irwin, "On Monastic Priesthood," *The American Benedictine Review* 41 (September 1990) 225–262.

75. Ibid., plus *Rule of St. Benedict*, ch. 62:1.

76. The *Rule of St. Benedict* has some cautions on separating monastery from diocese and the bishop of the place. However our question concerns the issue of legitimate authority over the ordained, one aspect of which is ministerial assignment. This surfaces today in terms of the commitment of religious orders or monasteries to staff parishes, and to the role of provincials of orders and abbots of monasteries in making ministerial assignments.

Part 2

Context is Text: Theology of Liturgy

Chapter 3: **Word**

The first part of the thesis *context is text* is applied to the liturgical proclamation of the Scriptures, including examples and implications for celebration.

Chapter 4: **Symbol**

The thesis is applied to the liturgical use of symbol, understanding that ''symbol'' means elements from creation and elements which are the result of human productivity.

Chapter 5: **Euchology**

The thesis is applied to the particular form of liturgical prayers known as blessing prayers (e.g., prefaces and eucharistic prayers), consecratory prayers (e.g., at ordinations) and other variable prayers (e.g., presidential prayers at the eucharist).

Chapter 6: **Liturgical Arts**

The thesis is applied to the use of music, architecture, artifacts and pictorial art as these are intrinsic to liturgy and complement word, symbol and euchology.

Chapter 3

Word

This chapter introduces the first part of our thesis *context is text* by considering how the event of liturgy provides a key to interpreting and preaching the proclaimed Scriptures. Its aim is to delineate the factors derived from the act of liturgy that can influence and shape a theological understanding of the liturgical proclamation of the Scriptures. Liturgists rightly emphasize the theological and liturgical value of the proclaimed Word as that which reveals the mystery of salvation, and in revealing it makes that mystery operative for contemporary communities that hear it in the liturgical assembly.[1] Key issues here concern the hearing, experience and appropriation of a scriptural text as it is proclaimed and enacted in liturgy and how the event of liturgy itself shapes how the Scriptures are heard, interpreted, preached and appropriated.

The Word is treated before other constitutive elements of liturgy (symbol, euchology, and the arts to follow) because it has traditionally been and remains a foundational element experienced in all liturgy. This suggests that the Word has influenced the shape of forms of Christian liturgy (e.g., how the Passover influenced the shape of Christian Eucharist[2]), that the events, symbols and images derived from salvation history continue to exert direct influence on the metaphors and imagery of liturgical euchology and because in the reformed liturgy the proclamation and preaching of the Scriptures is central to every act of liturgy. Some may well argue that symbol ought to be treated before Word because of the symbolic nature of all liturgy[3] (which treatment would necessarily include persons as participants in symbol making and symbolic communication). In fact, our argument about *the symbolic nature of the word* will be argued in a way that lessens the need to choose between Word and symbol.[4] In the liturgy both Word and objects/elements used in worship are intrinsically dialogical, both are best interpreted in relation to each other. In our view sacrament is the highest expression of the inherently symbolic Word.[5]

The four parts of this chapter deal with: (1) the intrinsically dialogical nature of hearing the Word at worship which hearing recreates and shapes the believing assembly in the image of God, (2) how the act of liturgy is the appropriate *context* within which the Scriptures are proclaimed arguing in particular how the various liturgical contexts where the same texts are used influence how they are understood and how these understandings influence the theory and practice of the liturgical homily (among other things) (3) how the Lectionary assignment of biblical texts influences their hearing as well as how liturgical euchology is intrinsically related to the Scriptures, and (4) a theological explanation of what occurs in the hearing of the Word in liturgy and attitudes which should characterize the assembly as it is engaged in a liturgical experience of the Word.

I. Dialogical Hearing

Just as persons are needed for language to be language, that is, for meanings to be comprehended and appropriated through the utterance of words, so persons are needed if language as address achieves its purpose as a medium for communication that is heard and responded to. Truly communicative language requires that persons be in a relationship wherein the words they use reflect familiar patterns of meaning since speech that is address forges, presupposes or deepens communication of values, principles, learning and insight.

In something of the same way the ritual action of hearing the Word presupposes the relationship of faith between speaker and hearers. The act of liturgical proclaiming and hearing the Scriptures invites an assembly into a relationship of ever deepening faith in God. This faith relationship is necessary in order for the religious language of the Bible to function as mediating meaning and for the ritual hearing of the Word to have its effect of deepening the faith of those who share in the event of speaking and hearing the Word. The twofold movement is from God to the community of believers and from the community of believers at worship to God. In light of our argument in chapter 2 this is to say that liturgical proclamation is intrinsically soteriological and ecclesiological.

This is to suggest that the proclamation of the Scriptures invites contemporary communities into the same saving relationship which formed Israel into the holy people of God and the followers of Christ into an *ecclesia*. Only in this framework of speaking and hearing, proclaiming and listening, speaking and being spoken to, can the Scriptures be called the book of the assembly.[6] The action of proclaiming the Word invites and effects conversion for willing hearers; it invites and effects a deepened relationship with God in faith for the already converted.

As an act of address, the Word demands a response.[7] As an act of communication it demands a dialogue partner.[8] To engage in liturgy is *to enact a word and to remember a relationship*. In the liturgy the Bible is proclaimed as address for the assembly in the act of which it is enacted, it is made real as an event of salvation. Its genre as properly liturgical proclamation requires that it be spoken again and again to a community gathered for its hearing and who become more fully God's own assembly because of this proclamation. Thus priority is always given to the Church assembled for hearing the Word in faith in order to deepen their shared faith through the liturgy and to express that faith in ritual prayer.

The effectiveness of God's Word is concretized in the paradigm of the call to the chosen ones and their response in faith, which paradigm characterizes both Old and New Testaments. From Abraham, Sarah and their descendants in Genesis (Gen 15ff.), to the call to Moses and his fellow Israelites throughout Exodus (for example, Exod 3–4), to the promulgation of the law by Ezra and the confession of Israel (Neh 8–9), to the repentance of the chosen people to renew their covenant relationship with God by means of the prophets' invitation (see, for example, Joel 2), through the incarnation of Jesus as the Word now become flesh (John 1:14) whose ministry began with the proclamation of the words of Isaiah (Isa 61:1f.) and his assertion that these words were ''fulfilled in [their] hearing'' (Luke 4:21) it is the dynamic of Word addressed and responded to that characterizes the Judaeo-Christian religion as born by and in the Word. The whole biblical corpus is constituted above all as a function of proclamation and communal listening leading to response and deepened communal conversion. This ecclesial nature of the Word is paramount for it to be interpreted accurately. The true point of departure for interpreting a biblical text proclaimed at liturgy is the celebrating assembly in its present experience of hearing that Word. In and through the liturgy, the Word is always contemporary. To recount founding events at the liturgy means that these primordial and paradigmatic events are actualized for contemporary communities through a medium which invites them to respond to that proclaimed Word and in this way to deepen their conversion and to nourish their faith.[9] When the biblical accounts of such foundational faith events as creation, the call of Israel, the incarnation etc. are proclaimed in liturgy these past events are experienced anew through the medium of the proclaimed Word.

The liturgical assembly thus enters into the same faith relationship with God offered to and forged in Israel and the primitive Christian Church. Such a relationship presupposes a shared vision of life in faith and a relatedness with one another on the most profound level, now based on our common rootedness in Christ. By hearing the Word again and again in the liturgy salvation is experienced anew in ever new ways, which experience requires a response of faith in community.[10] Thus the liturgy of the Word is best understood as a dialogue of call and response experienced through the Scriptures whose repeated reading is a *symbolic rehearsal of salvation*.

The use of the phrase "symbolic rehearsal of salvation" implies that the Word, at its most profound level, is "symbolic." It is true to the literal meaning of the Greek term *symballein* (to "throw together") and *symbolon* (that which is placed together or in a relationship). The purpose of the scriptural Word at liturgy is to place in relationship, to encounter another (the Other and others) and to *re*unite relationships forged and to deepen them.[11] Our understanding of *symballein* implies that symbols require a response from one or all those already in a relationship of shared meaning; in liturgy this is shared faith. The notion of "symbolic language" is therefore redundant in the sense that the language of the Word implies a speaking to and a response by those addressed. It is of the nature of such a "symbolic word" that what is offered in address requires acceptance, encounter and appropriation—a response.

This dialogic notion of the Word helps to explain what contemporary liturgical communities experience in the Liturgy of the Word. Every Liturgy of the Word "rehearses" salvation in the sense that believing communities hear the Word again and again and through this hearing, experience salvation again and again.

The act of recounting the Word requires a dialogue in which the response is shaped by the Word proclaimed, offering the assembled Church images and likenesses of God, of a God ever faithful to the chosen and elected people of God who gather for liturgy.[12] By repeatedly articulating the variety of images of God from the Scriptures, the liturgy invites present hearers to experience God as the one who calls us into relationship and to new life in the very mystery of the living God. Thus in Christian liturgy our relationship in faith with Christ is reciprocal (but obviously not mutual) always being forged more and more deeply in the liturgical experience of hearing this saving Word again and again.

The original (and for our purposes "primary") language of spoken or sung *address* on which the biblical narratives are based and from which the biblical narratives derive, then cedes to written texts in the Bible for the sake of repeated proclamation for successive generations of believers. These written texts are then proclaimed so that the faith community may preserve its tradition and engage in an act of liturgy with its origins actualized for succeeding generations through an act of memory, central to which is the hearing of the Word. This is to say that the distance in time and space between the original acts of salvation in revelation give rise to the written text as codification and preservation of an original saving event.[13] However, the written Word of the Bible returns to its native genre when it is proclaimed liturgically in the hearing of believers. When the medium of the message of sacred speech is unleashed in new Christian liturgical settings, the fullness of Christ's saving grace is experienced and actualized anew among the gathered assembly.[14] It is a "rehearsed" and yet ever new event of salvation.

At the same time that the liturgical celebration actualizes the Word of God it is also equally true theologically that the Word convokes the assembly, the Church, which evokes the *mirabilia Dei* through the Word.[15] Through the liturgy the Word of God gives birth to the Church where the Church is concentrated in the celebration of the liturgy which celebration leads the Church to attain the ends of actualizing that Word in its life of faith.[16] Conversely, the Church gives birth to the Word in the sense that ever new ecclesial settings make the Word come alive in new and varying ways, largely in light of present Church needs and the particular assembly at worship.

Thus the Liturgy of the Word is an event of salvation through which the community of the redeemed is born anew, which birth is mediated through the act of proclaiming the Word. As an event of salvation it is a holy *happening* as opposed to a holy *reading* (*lectio divina*). In our view priority must always be given to the Word as event, which event is contextualized and appropriately prepared for by holy reading in *lectio divina*. The Liturgy of the Word is itself an occurrence of salvation. As is true in all of liturgy, the role of the Word in Church life is to edify, renew and sanctify the Church in and through the Holy Spirit in the present liturgical community of the redeemed, which community yearns for the final fulfillment of this experienced redemption. Liturgy that is thus biblically based serves: as a reminder of an act of God's grace in the past, as the means of actualizing that experience in the present in the expectation that this Word will be incarnated in believers' living according to that Word and as that which turns the attention of believers to the final act of God in history, bringing to completion what the foundational historical act of grace inaugurated in Christ.[17] What is essential in the liturgy is the continual rediscovery of the meaning of the scriptural Word for the present world, as the contemporary community is called to engage in communal self-transcendence leading to a still unknown future in God.

Since the proclaimed Word constitutes and actualizes the Church, the liturgical proclamation of the Word has priority over any devotional reading or meditation. By its very nature the Word proclaimed in liturgy both invites and structures a faith response to that Word. The act of liturgy also preserves the essentially communal nature of hearing and responding to the Scriptures. Exercises of personal devotion based on the Scriptures, *lectio divina* in particular, can help in the appropriation of what happens in the liturgical hearing of the Word.[18] However, they cannot replace the centrality of the liturgical proclamation of the Word where *texts* are restored to their native *context* in proclamation and where proclaimed texts give life to the Church.

II. Liturgy as Context for Text

The dialogic structure of the Liturgy of the Word reflects how the hearing of the Word consists of address and response. In the liturgy, proclamation invites conscious and vocal response. Hence important theological meanings are attached to the responsorial psalms, acclamations and intercessions which follow Scripture readings at Liturgies of the Word (especially in the present revised sacramental rites) and responsories that follow readings at the Liturgy of the Hours (especially at the office of readings). This vocal response to the proclaimed Word reflects the call and response dynamic of biblical religion. The Church that is called into being by the Word responds in faith by giving prayerful voice to the psalms, acclamations and intercessions.

The proclamation of the Word also leads to effecting the Word in sacraments. In our understanding Karl Rahner's assertion that a theology of the Word can "serve as a very adequate basis for a sacramental theology in which the sacrament is conceived as the highest human and ecclesial expression of the word spoken in the church . . ."[19] is important within Roman Catholicism for the integrity of liturgical celebration and for developing systematic theologies of sacraments both within Catholicism and for ecumenical purposes. It is an important foundational principle for our understanding of the theological meaning of liturgy and (sacramental) theology derived from liturgy.[20]

That the Word culminates in the sacramental sign is a given in much contemporary writing and magisterial statements on the theological value of the Word.[21] However, the conventional distinction which asserts that Word leads to sacrament needs to be nuanced since in effect the Word and sacrament are so essentially joined that they form one act of worship (see, Liturgy Constitution n. 56).[22] The recent restoration of the Liturgy of the Word as *constitutive* of the sacramental act is an important ground for theologizing about the proclaimed Word. The famous dictum of St. Augustine "one joins the word to the material element and behold the sacrament, that is, a kind of visible word" has recently been revived as an example of the profound unity between word and sacrament.

Louis-Marie Chauvet comments that the use of the term "word" in this Augustinian text is three-fold since it can mean Christ himself, the proclaimed Scriptures and the sacramental formula,[23] with the last two meanings as experienced in sacramental liturgy derived immediately from the first. Thus the efficacy of the sacraments can only be understood as a means of communication of the Word Incarnate through the Scriptural Word.[24] This is to suggest an anamnetic understanding of Word and sacrament in liturgy through which salvation events are operative for contemporary believers. Among other things, such an approach clearly has important ramifications for ecumenical understandings about sacraments (as will be discussed in chapter seven).

The Liturgy of the Word recalls foundation events (e.g., creation, Exodus) teachings and prophecies. It also contains exhortations and acts of praise, thanks and lament originally uttered or sung at specific times and places in salvation history. In proclaiming these texts now the liturgy enables foundational events to occur still (as opposed to occur again), the teachings and prophecies to be received in ever new and varying ecclesial settings and the acts of praise, thanks, and lament which originated in specific times and places to shape or to put into perspective ever new situations in which believers hear or use them in the present. The repetition and new recounting in the liturgy of these texts enables them to break out of time-bound or time-conditioned parameters; they become salvation experiences for contemporary believers.[25]

Liturgical tradition offers many precedents for recontextualizing scriptural texts in the liturgy. This is to say that scriptural texts are taken out of their native contexts in the Scriptures and are then used liturgically as proclaimed from the Lectionary or used as chants, responses, or acclamations to the Word proclaimed. Contemporary Lectionaries most often give priority to gospels arranged according to a *lectio continua* (principle of continuous reading from beginning to end) or as chosen to fit a given season or feast (principle of harmony), and then arranges Old Testament readings and responsorial psalms (with varying amounts of success and, for some, by doing violence to the value of the Hebrew Scriptures on their own) to reflect those gospel texts.[26] Furthermore, the assignment of specific psalms for morning and evening prayer most usually reflects the time of day of the act of liturgical prayer (the classic examples are Ps 63 for morning prayer and Ps 141 for evening prayer) and responsories to follow the readings at the office of readings reflect a free joining of OT and NT as well as non-biblical texts. Additional examples of moving texts from their original biblical settings and placing them in new settings in the liturgy in order to specify how the scriptural Word pertains to ever new situations of liturgical prayer include the assignment of antiphons and captions in psalters that provide a Christological interpretation of the psalms and canticles at the hours,[27] texts for entrance and communion antiphons at the Eucharist and the *asperges me* or *vidi aquam* antiphons to accompany the rite of holy water sprinkling at Sunday Eucharist. The assignment of primordial (e.g., creation) or historical texts (e.g., Exodus) in the Lectionary implies that their meanings cannot be relegated to what happened once in history. In fact the notion of *in illo tempore* that operates here is that these events happen still *hic et nunc*.[28] In the Liturgy of the Word the event and its announcement coincide. The *in illo tempore* of saving history becomes, in the *hodie* of the liturgical celebration, the *quotidie* of the experience of salvation, as an *et in saecula* and already anticipated experience of salvation celebrated in the *hic et nunc* of the liturgy.[29] Or, in the terminology of Karl Barth, the *illud et tunc* of the Scriptures becomes the *hic et nunc* of revelation for the contemporary Church. If the basis of liturgical commemoration is that "today" saving events are con-temporized so that the mysteries of salvation are communicated to the present Church,[30] it is essential to view the Word as constitu-tive of the act of liturgy understood as an act of memory.

One example of liturgical usage which can hinder the full ap-preciation of this highly anamnetic character of the proclaimed Word is the fact that conventionally the *incipit* for the gospels proclaimed from the Lectionary is most usually "at that time." This difficulty has been lessened in some vernacular Lectionaries in light of the option noted in the General Instruction on the Lec-tionary for Mass that while the customary introductions (e.g., *in illo tempore, fratres* etc.) are given in the revised Latin Lectionary, "for individual languages, such phrases may be dropped by de-cree of the competent authorities" (n. 124).[31] S. P. J. Van Dijk suggests that such introductions and clauses developed quite late in the Western liturgy and that they are classically omitted in the most ancient liturgies, e.g., Good Friday and Easter Vigil.[32] A re-turn to the more primitive usage helps reinforce the "here and now" nature of the liturgical proclamation of the Word. It under-scores how a continuous reading of a given gospel book (with its accompanying other lessons, responses etc.) is the announcement of saving events which are perennially operative and which con-tinually occur in the liturgical assembly.

This is to argue that the vitality and life sustaining meaning of a scriptural text is at once influenced by and independent of its setting within a biblical book. Thus it is important to interpret it not only in relation to its original audience but also in light of where and how it is used in liturgy today.[33] This is to argue that the *liturgical context* affects the interpretation of scriptural texts and that the proclamation of the same scriptural text in differing contemporary contexts requires interpreting that text in light of the differing liturgical settings in which it is used. Such a methodological principle raises important questions, such as what is the relationship between the normativity of scriptural revelation and the varying liturgical contexts which influence its meaning, and how to respect the intention of the author in relation to shifts in context and the notion of an independent life of a text? The methodological approach argued here does not intend to mitigate careful, scientific exegesis. In our understanding, the interpretation of Scripture as used liturgically ought never veer from the intention of the Scriptures as a whole or from meanings uncovered through exegesis. At the same time the liturgical context in which Scripture readings are proclaimed needs to be factored into their interpretation and application to contemporary liturgical assemblies, in particular through the homily. Such an approach leads to enhanced emphasis on the relationship between the proclaimed Word and the liturgical community as well as between Word and sacrament. The liturgical influences which come to bear on the Scriptures proclaimed include the feast celebrated, the season of the Church year, the sacramental action which accompanies the Word, euchological texts of the liturgy, and any contemporary social or cultural situations of the assembly.[34]

The very fact of having a Lectionary insures that the dialogic character of the Word is maintained, in particular by the use of acclamations before ("alleluia") and after readings ("thanks be to God") and the responses after them (responsorial psalms after readings, short responsories after readings at the hours). The Lectionary also implies a structuring of how the Word is to be received in contemporary liturgical assemblies. Thus it is important to determine patterns for the assignment of texts in past Lectionaries and to understand operating principles which govern present Lectionary systems.[35]

Alexander Schmemann asserts that the liturgy is the "ontological condition of theology, of the proper understanding of *kerygma*, of the Word of God, because it is in the Church, of which the *leitourgia* is the expression and the life" that the sources of theology function precisely as sources.[36] The biblical tradition functions as a source for theology especially when interpreted against the background which the liturgy provides for it.

The very fact that a Lectionary tradition exists in a given Church asserts that priority has been and is given to hearing certain texts at certain feasts and seasons, and that the interpretation of these texts implies taking those liturgical contexts seriously. This is also to suggest that establishing the Lectionary as a norm for liturgical proclamation (even one with a wide range of options for texts) admits that "a canon within a canon" of the Scriptures exists in practice since certain texts are chosen for special use (e.g., on feast days) some are used repeatedly (e.g., at sacramental celebrations)[37] some texts will not be emphasized (and some not even used) which results in attendant questions about the nature of canonicity and the role of the Old Testament revelation given the Christological orientation of Lectionaries determined for Christian usage.[38]

The critical function of liturgical theology enters when assessing the value of the present Roman order of readings for the Eucharist. These include the serious flaw in the lack of longer passages from the OT, especially the foundational Adam-Eve, Abraham-Sarah, and Exodus narratives as well as longer selections from the prophetic books. For example, the Abraham/Sarah cycle from Genesis 15-23 is assigned to weekdays in "Year One" from Monday of the twelfth week of the year through Friday of the thirteenth week, but the only parts of this cycle found on Sundays are Genesis 14:18-20 (as the first reading on the Solemnity of Corpus Christi "C" cycle), Genesis 15:5-12, 17-18 (on the Second Sunday of Lent "C" cycle) and Genesis 22 (the sacrifice of Isaac) at the Easter Vigil (which text is optional despite its traditional application to the sacrifice of Jesus and rich theological meaning in Christian liturgy). The following options are also found in votive and ritual masses. Genesis 12:1-4 is assigned to the Common of Saints, the Mass for the Beginning of the Catechumenate, and for the Consecration of Virgins and Religious Profession. Genesis 12:1-7 is assigned to the Common of the Virgin Mary. Genesis 15:1-6, 18 is assigned to Christian Initiation celebrated apart from the Easter Vigil. A wider use of the Abraham/Sarah cycle would invite contemporary believers to dialogue with these models from salvation history whose faith journeys can be illuminative of the faith struggles of contemporary believers. The same criticism could be made of the lack of emphasis on readings from the books of Exodus and Isaiah. While these are assigned to Lent and Advent respectively in the office of readings in the Liturgy of the Hours, they are left largely unheard by the majority of the Church which does not celebrate these hours as liturgy.

The assertion of our methodological principle, simply stated as *context is text*, needs to be set in direct relation to the repetition of scripture readings prescribed in the Lectionary according to a predetermined cycle (e.g., three-year, one-year). The notion of *context* operative here implies that liturgical tradition is implicitly acknowledged as a factor in interpreting scriptural texts in that certain texts have been linked traditionally with given feasts—for example the prologue to the Gospel of John at Christmas. In addition, the very use of a text on a Sunday gives it obvious emphasis as opposed to its proclamation on a weekday. Its use at a Eucharist differentiates it from use at another sacrament as does its use at the Eucharist on a solemnity differentiate it from the office of readings for that day. In addition, while people *hear* gospel texts in the liturgical assembly as proclaimed in succession (day after day and Sunday after Sunday) and hence have a sense of the *lectio continua*, they also hear these same gospel texts in relation to the other readings (responsorial psalm included) at a given celebration.[39] This suggests that the *context* established for the hearing of the gospel by a first reading, psalm, second reading and gospel acclamation influences how that gospel is heard and how it ought to be interpreted. The very fact of having a Lectionary places readings in relation with each other. In fact, this interrelatedness of Scripture texts at a given Sunday liturgy shifts attention away from the *lectio continua* principle to giving attention to how the specific liturgy shapes how a gospel is heard. With the interrelationship of Scripture readings as a given it is essential to develop appropriate tools for interpretation. Thus the notion of the Sunday cycles as revealing "a year of Matthew," or Mark, or Luke is only half true.[40] All Scripture texts proclaimed at a liturgy, taken out of their context in the Bible and placed in relation to each other in the liturgy, influence how we hear them and how we ought to interpret them.

An additional issue concerns the fact that the circumstances of culture, time and place in which the liturgy takes place are never repeated. Thus there is an irrepeatability to the proclamation of the Word in the sense that there will never be another *hic et nunc* celebration to occur the same way, even though the same Scripture texts may be used.[41] While on the one hand the repetition of some Scripture texts means that they will become better and better known by the assembly, the several factors just outlined that help fill out the liturgical context of the Word means that there is no such thing as a liturgy happening twice. The very act of repeating certain texts invites a pluriformity of meanings to be derived from a text interpreted in relation to the changing circumstances of the liturgical community. Therefore this interplay requires attention to the act of liturgy in which texts are heard.

Christian ritual is never the same although it is repeated. In fact, liturgy's ritual structure and repeated use of some texts enables us to enter into the liturgical action more fully and deeply. But the uniqueness of even a "repeated" liturgy derives from the fact that the situation of the Church and world are always new and that our personal and communal histories are always new. This itself sets up a dynamic for the proclamation of the same scriptural Word. Strictly speaking a Liturgy of the Word is never repeated. The same texts may be used again and again, the same music sung, and even the same homily preached (regrettably, considering the dynamism of the Liturgy of the Word already argued) but the interaction of this assembly here and now in their personal and communal histories with these texts interacting with each other in ever new and different ways is always new. *Contexts* always differ; thus the Liturgy of the Word that is experienced is always different. This is to assert the existence of a plurality of meanings for individual Scripture texts (like those disclosed by a tensive symbol) as well as for texts proclaimed at a given liturgy, understanding that the notion of a "plurality of meanings" implies a certain stability of meaning, lest plurality seem to indicate that content is totally fluid or elastic.[42]

In addition, the Bible itself contains a number of texts which themselves contain a plurality of meanings. Particular examples of biblical texts with a plurality of meanings are the highly charged, poetically inspired texts of the Canticles of Zechariah and the Blessed Virgin and the Isaiah Suffering Servant Songs. The surplus of meanings implicit in such texts cannot be exhausted by one act of proclamation; their repetition in varying contexts actually serve to help uncover their many meanings. One could well argue this is why the Canticles of Zechariah and Mary at morning and evening prayer contain antiphons from those texts precisely to highlight one or another aspect of a text so filled with meanings.

This emphasis on new contexts enabling texts to be understood differently derives from the Scriptures themselves. The appropriation of the stories from the Abraham/Sarah cycle in Genesis as classic texts to mark the journey of faith and used in the letters to the Romans and to the Hebrews indicates how different shades of meaning derive from new settings in which traditional stories of faith are placed. The contribution of liturgy here is to allow the contexts in which the proclamation of the Word takes place to become an important factor in the interpretation of scriptural texts. This approach emphasizes the relative importance of how accurately the author portrays the actual historical occurrence reflected in the text, the intent of the author who preserved foundational and saving events by means of a text, or even the understanding of that intent by the text's original audience.

This is to argue that when read at liturgy, Scripture texts should be dealt with (1) as multivalent pericopes taken from their settings in the Scriptures (2) that are proclaimed for a faith community, which proclamation implies that texts are enacted and effective in that community, and (3) that these texts receive their fullest expression as testimonies and witnesses of faith at liturgical celebrations which are particularly disclosive of the presence and action of God. Hence texts taken "out of context" now become texts in a new context, namely the communal act of memory that is liturgy. Here the Bible is the instrument of the *memoria Christi.* The proclamation of the Word continues to establish the foundation of the Church.[43] The historicity of the Bible is not prejudiced here. Rather paradigmatic ways of God's dealing with the chosen and with the Church continue here and now through the proclaimed and enacted ritual Word of God.

Given the varying settings for the proclamation of the Word and the variety in ways of interpreting that Word, it is important also to note that personal and communal histories inform how we hear and appropriate scriptural texts. This is to say that the Scriptures impact on us in terms of these histories. They form part of a continuity in the life of faith. They are not discrete and distinct experiences in themselves. The repertoire of liturgical experiences is thus put in juxtaposition with the element of personal and communal history to form the tapestry that is faith experienced and deepened through the scriptural Word. It is into that context of the vicissitudes of the faith journey of individuals and communities that the assignment of scriptural texts in the Lectionary needs to be placed.

Both the preacher and the homily are crucial if the Liturgy of the Word is to be the kind of experience of salvation presumed here. Through the homily the preacher articulates aspects of salvation enacted in the Word proclaimed that day as these relate to the given liturgical and ecclesial context in which the Scriptures are heard. At times the "breaking open of the Word" can include laying bare infidelities and weakness in faith. At other times it can include discovering new ways of comprehending and experiencing the living God. The two-edged sword of the Word can both cut through well worn habits of vice and foster new habits of virtue. At all times, however, the Liturgy of the Word is an experience of salvation for the contemporary Church since through it Christ once more accomplishes salvation "for us and for our salvation."

Our understanding of the interpretation of scriptural texts implies a fundamentally ecclesial and eschatological reading of the Word. The kingdom breaks in on the liturgical assembly through the Word by means of the presence and action of the Spirit. If in fact liturgy is our present experience of the eternal liturgy where the Father is adored in spirit and truth,[44] then Christian worship is different from synagogue liturgy since the Spirit is active among the baptized to bring it to all truth in Christ through the Scriptures. The Spirit abiding in the Church enlivens the liturgical assembly always to hear and experience the Scriptures anew. Thus the *synaxis* of the Word is itself an eschatological experience—of salvation experienced here and now and of the fullness of salvation to be realized in the eternal kingdom.[45] Thus all liturgy can be understood as a privileged, though provisional, encounter with saving events of the past experienced anew through the liturgy. The strengths and weaknesses of contemporary liturgical assemblies contextualize how the Word is received; they also indicate the inherent provisionality of such communities as they continually plead for the full realization of the kingdom. The Liturgy of the Word, which manifests and is an epiphany of the kingdom, moves the Church toward the time of its completion and fulfillment in the eschaton.

III. Lectionary and Euchology

Because of their highly charged, poetic nature the suffering servant songs from Isaiah afford a most useful example of the various ways such texts are used in Christian liturgy and how their liturgical use necessarily influences how they are interpreted and preached. These servant songs include Isaiah 42:1-7, 49:1-7, 50:4-9 (or 11) and 52:13–53:12. In general it may be asserted that these texts have been understood to refer to Israel (whether historical or ideal) to an Old Testament historical character before or during Isaiah's lifetime or to the prophet himself.[46] For our purposes here, however, the Christian liturgical usage of these texts as referring to (the fulfillment of these prophecies in) Jesus is of particular interest, especially how their use during the course of the liturgical year or at sacramental celebrations casts a particular Christological light on them.

Isaiah 42:1-7. In the proper of seasons in the Lectionary for Mass this first servant song (vv. 1-4, 6-7) is assigned as the first reading on the feast of the Baptism of the Lord[47] and as the first reading (vv. 1-7) on Monday of Holy Week. It is also assigned (vv. 1-3) as an option for the first reading at a Eucharist when confirmation is celebrated. In addition in the office of readings in the Liturgy of the Hours this text is assigned as the first reading on the Friday between January 2 and Epiphany as well as on the feast of the Baptism of the Lord (42:1-9 combined with 49:11-19). Clearly the placement of this text at both the office of readings and at the Eucharist on the feast of the Baptism of the Lord indicates its importance as a Christologically rich text used on the day when the Church commemorates the inauguration of Jesus' earthly ministry. Its placement at a confirmation liturgy would also seem to underscore a similar mission interpretation. On the other hand another dimension of the text is brought out when it is used as the first reading at Eucharist on Monday of Holy Week. This placement reflects the statement in the Lectionary introduction that "in the first half of Holy Week the readings are about the mystery of Christ's passion."[48]

These varied Christological interpretations of the same servant song when used in Christian liturgy would seem to be upheld by the responsorial psalms which follow them. The psalm on the feast of the Baptism of the Lord is Psalm 29 with the refrain "The

Lord will bless his people with peace."[49] The response to the text on Monday of Holy Week is Psalm 27 with the refrain "The Lord is my light and my salvation."

Isaiah 49:1-7. Major parts of this text are assigned as a first reading at the Eucharist (vv. 1-6) on Tuesday of Holy Week and on the second Sunday of the year (vv. 3, 5-6) in cycle A. This song is also assigned as a first reading at the Eucharist on the solemnity of the Birth of St. John the Baptist, June 24 (day Mass). On this same day it is broken up to form the short scripture readings at midmorning (49:1), noon (49:5-6), and midafternoon prayer (49:7b). On the feast of the Beheading of John the Baptist, August 29, Isaiah 49:1b-2 is used as the short reading at morning prayer. The obvious role which this text plays in the liturgical commemorations in honor of John the Baptist should not be missed (although it is interesting that this text does not play a role in the readings assigned during Advent when John's role as the one who prepared for the Messiah is emphasized). Evidently the reference in two places in this text that the Lord called him from his mother's womb (vv. 1 and 5) makes it an obvious choice for commemorations of the birth and even the beheading of John.

The use of the text during holy week corresponds to the use of 42:1-7 above. The assignment of Isaiah 49:3, 5-6 on the second Sunday of the year is notable since it was likely chosen to coincide with the Messianic overtones reflected in the gospel for the A cycle, John 1:29-34, which recounts John's acclaiming Jesus as "the Lamb of God" (1:29), which acclamation is repeated in v. 36, a verse that is part of the gospel assigned to the B cycle for this Sunday, which same acclamation is used at the breaking of the bread at the Eucharist. This gospel also states that Jesus is the one on whom the Spirit descended "like a dove from the sky" (v. 32). Such references are the more significant because in the liturgical calendar this Sunday follows the feast of the Baptism of the Lord at which the gospels recount the beginning of Jesus' ministry with the bestowal of the Spirit in the form of a dove (Mark 1:10 and par.).

Isaiah 50:4-11. This third servant song is assigned in the Lectionary for Mass to Passion (Palm) Sunday (vv. 4-7), to Wednesday of Holy Week (vv. 4-9), to the twenty-fourth Sunday of the year B cycle (vv. 4-9), and to one of the Old Testament readings for votive masses for the triumph of the holy cross (vv. 4-9). Isaiah 50:5-7 is assigned as the short Scripture reading at morning prayer from Monday through Thursday of Holy Week. The assignment of this text to the twenty-fourth Sunday of the Year cycle B offers an Old Testament precedent of suffering and rejection (especially v. 6) and of the servant's complete faith in God, for the gospel from Mark 8:27-35 containing the Messianic confession of Peter at Caesarea Philippi (vv. 27-29) and the instruction that the Son of Man would suffer much, be rejected, undergo death, and rise three days later to come into his glory (vv. 31-32). This connection is underscored by the verses of the responsorial psalm from Psalm 116 referring to distress, sorrow, and death (vv. 3-4), the Lord's rescuing the faithful from death (v. 8) and the confident refrain "I will walk in the presence of the Lord, in the land of the living" (v. 9).

The paschal context and overtones of this text, however, are obviously paramount in the present Lectionary assignments. In all the situations where this text (comprising at least vv. 4-9) is to be proclaimed it is the servant himself who speaks words of instruction, crafted by God who gave him "a well-trained tongue . . . to speak to the weary a word that will rouse them" (v. 4). References to offering his back to those who beat him and "cheeks to those who plucked my beard" (v. 6) illustrate graphically the sufferings of the servant. Yet the attitude of confident trust before the Lord is also exemplified in the servant's words:

"The Lord God is my help,
    therefore I am not disgraced;
I have set my face like flint,
    knowing that I shall not be put to shame" (v. 7).

The twin focus in this text on the actual suffering of God's servant and on his quiet confidence in God is also reflected in the structure of the Liturgy of the Word on Passion Sunday where it is used. After this text is read the assembly uses verses of Psalm 22 and the refrain from the same psalm (v. 2) "My God, my God, why have you abandoned me?" as the responsorial psalm. The second reading that follows is the Christ hymn from Philippians 2:6-11 whose pivotal verse noting Christ's obedience and God's exalting him (vv. 8-9) is used as the gospel acclamation preceding the passion proclamation. This juxtaposition of texts points up the irony of this day which commemorates both Jesus' messianic entrance into Jerusalem and his humiliation in obediently accepting the crucifixion.

Isaiah 52:13–53:12. This last of the servant songs is proclaimed in its entirety at the afternoon liturgy of Good Friday and is offered as an option for votive Masses of the Triumph of the Holy Cross. Parts of it are assigned to the twenty-ninth Sunday of the year B cycle (53:10-11) and as an option at Masses for the sick (53:1-5, 10-11). Verses of this song are also used in the Liturgy of the Hours on Good Friday where it is broken up to form the short Scripture readings at midmorning (53:2-3), at noon (53:4-5) and midafternoon prayer (53:6-7).

The trust of the servant in the Isaiah text is drawn out in the responsorial psalm for Good Friday from Psalm 31 with the confident refrain from Luke 23:46 "Father, I put my life in your hands." The plea that the Lord's face might "shine upon your servant" (v. 17) and the servant's acclamation of faith:

"But my trust is in you, O Lord;
  I say, 'You are my God.'
In your hands is my destiny; rescue me
  from the clutches of my enemies and
  my persecutors" (vv. 15-16)

clearly point to the ultimate triumph of the servant, a triumph clearly disclosed in the proclamation of the Johannine passion account to follow on Good Friday. In fact the helpful combination of the three readings at the liturgy on Good Friday is hinted at in the Lectionary introduction which states that "on Good Friday the liturgical service has as its center John's narrative of the passion of him who was portrayed in Isaiah as the Servant of Yahweh and who became the one High Priest by offering himself to the Father."[50]

That the suffering of the sick can be redemptive when looked upon as the present Church's participation in the suffering of the servant of the Lord is hinted at in the use of sections of this text for Masses for the sick. The last section of this text is particularly hopeful for those who see their suffering in light of suffering servant (and by extension) with Christ.

"Because of his affliction
  he shall see the light in fullness of days:
Through his suffering, my servant shall justify many,
  and their guilt he shall bear" (53:10-11).

The assignment of this text to the twenty-ninth Sunday imitates the use of the third song on the twenty-fourth Sunday noted above. Here the gospel from Mark 10:35-45 concerns the request of James and John that they share now in the fullness of Jesus' glory, a request that causes Jesus to discourse about real authority and the central description of the disciple as one who serves the needs of all (v. 44) because "the Son of Man has come not to be served but to serve—to give his life in ransom for the many" (v. 45).

This review of the Lectionary assignment of texts serves to illustrate the thesis that the proclamation of the same Isaiah servant songs during the time of Epiphany, on feasts of John the Baptist, on the days of the paschal triduum, on selected Sundays of the year, at votive masses, or at celebrations of sacraments implies that these texts need to be interpreted in light of their liturgical contexts. The thesis that *context is text* is thus illustrated since the Lectionary assignment of Scripture readings implicitly respects the varied meanings of Scripture texts whose full range of meanings and implications are brought out through their being proclaimed over time at varied liturgies. This implies that the Scriptures are understood differently because of how the texts relate to the other scriptural readings in the liturgical act, because of the differences among the feasts themselves (some of which are disclosed in the euchology of the day), and because of the variety of the communities at worship. This is particularly true of texts such as the servant songs. Such "classics" are overloaded with meaning; they can literally exhaust their hearers because of their many meanings. The liturgical act itself helps to focus the many directionalities of such texts and enables the worshiping communities to appropriate something of their rich meaning.

A key factor in explicating a focus for the many shades of meaning inherent in such texts is the homily. While repeatedly insisted upon as a constitutive element of the liturgy, the homily should be considered as part of the word itself.[51] This is to suggest that the homily is not delivered after the proclamation of the Word. It is part of the proclamation itself. It serves to enable the Bible to come to rebirth anew in the liturgical assembly. Preaching is literally a sacramental act[52] in the sense that it actualizes the Word and explores implications of that proclaimed Word for the believing Church. The homily is a continual reactualization of the Lord who explained the Scriptures on the road to Emmaus (Luke 24:27) and of the anointed one of God who affirmed that the scriptural word of Isaiah is fulfilled in their hearing (Luke 4:16ff.).[53] Scriptural exegesis provides important background for the preacher as does a study of saving history. This leads to an understanding of the text's central importance as a theological event here and now in the Church as well as for what these texts "say" to contemporary situations in human life. Here both the preacher and liturgical community are transformed because through the proclaimed (and preached) word[54] each comes to new possibilities of existence now and of appropriate responsibilities for the future.

The thesis argued here implies that a proper interpretation of the Scriptures demands a liturgical component whereby the *context* established by the liturgical proclamation of the Scriptures figures into how the texts are understood in terms of the contemporary usage of such texts. In addition, homilists need to understand that this *dynamic hermeneutic of liturgical context* implies that the strengths and weaknesses of the given assembly are taken seriously and that the particular history of a given congregation influences and helps to shape the text of the homily. Part of the *context* intrinsic to a liturgical hermeneutic is the given assembly and the given occasion for the proclamation of the Word. The communal history of the assembly is brought into contact with the Scriptures through the Liturgy of the Word in the following five-fold act.

1. *Story recalled and retold.* To assert that we are dealing with a *story* that must be told implies that Scripture is composed not of eyewitness accounts or accounts that aim for eyewitness accuracy, but of texts/stories crafted out of retelling (admitting, however, that one test of kerygmatic authenticity in the Lukan corpus is "eyewitnesses" such as Matthias in Acts 1:15-26). Texts that have emerged from acts of storytelling are thus restored to their native context when proclaimed liturgically.

2. *Response to the proclamation.* The dialogical nature of this event is reflected in the community's response to the reading of the

Scriptures in silence, responsorial psalm, and acclamation. The observance of generous silence after acclaiming "the word of the Lord" enables contemporary communities to ruminate on the Word just heard, allowing it to take deep root in their hearts.

The very selection of specific psalms to complement the readings discloses how the Lectionary assignment of texts is explicated by the assignment of psalm verses to follow the reading. Theologically this also means that proclamation presumes dialogue and that the liturgical assembly is engaged in the Liturgy of the Word as a dialogue partner.

3. *Homily.* To our way of thinking, there is no single theology of preaching. Rather theologies of preaching that facilitate the naming of grace and of the holy in human life (as derived from theologians such as Edward Schillebeeckx[55]) and that facilitate the reception of grace through the Word (as derived from Karl Barth, among others) are most helpful in appreciating the central importance of preaching. To our way of thinking, the homily continues the act of liturgical hearing in that it focuses on an aspect of the proclaimed texts for the appropriation of a given congregation. The homily is an interpretation of the Scriptures in order that their anamnetic character can be unleashed in contemporary ecclesial settings. The homily is intrinsic to the Word event because through it the Word of God becomes the mystery of salvation enacted in the particularity of diverse celebrations.[56]

The homily also serves primarily as worship. Gerald Sloyan states:

"the homily . . . is primarily worship or praise which is also thanksgiving and petition, like the total liturgical act. Commentary on the word does not stand apart from the remainder of the divine service; it is not different from it in kind. The eucharistic act praises God for the deed done on our behalf in Jesus Christ through the power of the Holy Spirit. The homily must do that as much as the biblical readings, the eucharistic prayer . . . and the communion rite."[57]

In addition it serves as an important link between what is enacted through the Scriptures and what is enacted in what follows their proclamation in the given liturgy, especially when thus includes a sacrament. Since all liturgy is the actualization of the work of our redemption, *opus nostrae redemptionis,*[58] the Word stands as an intrinsic part of that actualization. It also leads to the community's response in intercessions and/or the celebration of sacraments. The move from Word to sacrament is established theologically and liturgically as more of a bridge than a leap because of their similarity as disclosive of the paschal mystery.

4. *Intercessions.* These are part of the Word event to the extent that they carry through on what has been heard as applied to the contemporary life and world situation of the assembly. These essentially ecclesial prayers link individual celebrating communities with each other in giving voice to the needs of the Church and all the world.

5. *Euchology.* The Liturgy of the Word is itself contextualized within a wider act of liturgy, seen especially clearly in the liturgy of sacraments where rites containing symbolic actions and prayers can set up the hearing of the Word (e.g., introductory rites at baptism) and in particular how liturgical euchology complements the announcement of the Word (e.g., blessing prayer for water at baptism). Liturgical evidence suggests how the Word influences euchology and how the celebration of a sacrament specifies what is proclaimed in the Word. Basic to this relationship of common imagery, language and theme is the theological truth (already enunciated) that Word necessarily leads to the rest of the liturgy, especially sacramental liturgy,[59] and that liturgy should be understood as an act of memory comprised of both Word and sacrament.[60] This is to suggest that the language referring to the Word and sacrament as "two tables" from which the liturgical assembly is fed, is really theologically imprecise. The one source for the Church's sustenance is the paschal mystery of Christ actualized through the action of the Spirit in the liturgical proclamation of the Scriptures and the sacramentalization of this announcement in sacraments.

The understanding that sacraments are ecclesial acts of speech[61] is exemplified in the way that the euchology is influenced by the Scriptures of the day or from the Scriptures as a whole as they come to bear on the particular act of sacramental liturgy. In light of the treatment of the servant songs above the following euchological references are of particular import.

The preface for feasts of John the Baptist contains a reference to the second servant song, Isaiah 49:1 when it states:

"his birth brought great rejoicing:
even in the womb he leapt for joy."[62]

This same preface contains a reference to the Baptist's acclaiming Jesus as the Lamb of God from John 1:29, the gospel proclaimed on the Second Sunday of the Year cycle A, when the second servant song is proclaimed.

"You chose John the Baptist from all the prophets
to show the world its redeemer,
the lamb of sacrifice."[63]

As already noted, on Passion (Palm) Sunday the third servant song is followed by the proclamation of the Christ hymn from Philippians 2:6-11 and one of the synoptic accounts of the passion. These readings obviously influence the references to suffering (first reading) and obedience (second reading) in the opening prayer for this day:

"Almighty, ever-living God,
you have given the human race Jesus Christ our Savior
as a model of humility.
He fulfilled your will
by becoming [one like us] and giving his life on the cross.
Help us to bear witness to you
by following his example of suffering
and make us worthy to share in his resurrection."[64]

In a more general way at the Easter Vigil (itself a most significant context for the Liturgy of the Word containing important texts of saving history) the responsorial psalms and prayers which follow each reading establish directionalities for the hearing of such central texts in salvation history as the act of creation from Genesis 1:1–2:2 and the passage of Israel through the Red Sea from Exodus 14:15–15:1. In addition the proclamation of the *Exsultet* itself aids in setting up this act of proclamation.

For example, the Genesis myth (understanding that here "myth" means a story whose truth is so important that it must be told by means of a story whose recounting actualizes salvation)[65] is followed by Psalm 104 and the prayer

"Almighty and eternal God,
you created all things in wonderful beauty and order.
Help us now to perceive
how still more wonderful is the new creation
by which in the fullness of time
you redeemed your people
through the sacrifice of our passover, Jesus Christ
who lives and reigns forever and ever."[66]

The text of Exodus is followed by the song of Miriam from the
verses which follow upon the reading (Exod 15:1-6, 17-18) with
the refrain from the last line of the reading:

"Let us sing to the Lord;
he has covered himself in glory."

The prayer which follows reads:

"Father,
even today we see the wonders
of the miracles you worked long ago.
You once saved a single nation from slavery,
and now you offer that salvation to all through baptism.
May the peoples of the world become
    true [children] of Abraham
and prove worthy of the heritage of Israel."[67]

The *Exsultet* contains references both to creation and the Red Sea,
again giving these texts a particular slant and interpretation:

"Rejoice, heavenly powers! Sing choirs of angels!
    Exult, all creation around God's throne!
Rejoice, O earth, in shining splendor,
    radiant in the brightness of your King!
    Christ has conquered! Glory fills you!
    Darkness vanishes for ever!
This is the night when first you saved our fathers:
    you freed the people of Israel from their slavery
    and led them dry-shod through the sea.
This is the night when Christians everywhere,
    washed clean of sin

and freed from all defilement,
are restored to grace and grow together in holiness."[68]

What is clearly disclosed in such euchological texts is the fact
that at liturgy the Church interprets Scripture in light of the
"work of our redemption" wrought by Christ experienced
through the liturgy. Such texts help indicate how the Scriptures
are used in light of the Christian liturgical context. Among other
things, the issue at stake at the Easter Vigil is describing how the
world is recreated by the proclamation of such cosmogonic myths
as Genesis 1:1–2:2, how the enlightened are initiated by the use of
Word and water (both polyvalent symbols which are directly related to baptism in the Church's euchology) and how the already
baptized are themselves recreated and their baptism renewed by
Word, water and table. The cosmic context established by the
Spring season (in the northern hemisphere)[69] should not be lost
here. At the very moment when the earth is about to burst forth
in new life, the Church celebrates its newness in the risen Christ.
From the many directionalities inherent in the Scriptures
proclaimed this evening, a Christological focus and cast is given
them through the liturgical euchology.[70]
It was argued above that the Liturgy of the Word was intrinsically ecclesial and eschatological. The eschatological aspect of the
Easter Vigil liturgy is crucial for its interpretation. Here, at the
very moment when the Church comes to rebirth in Christ's resurrection, the Church is also aware that while the sin of Adam has
been undone in Christ the second Adam, it is also painfully true
that the Church has not yet come to "full stature" and that
redemption is still in the process of being completely accomplished
and experienced even in the believing Church. An eschatological
reading of Genesis 1, for example, would heighten the Church's
awareness of how it is still on the way to fully realizing and experiencing the paschal mystery. On the one hand creation has
been redeemed in Christ; on the other it "groans and is in agony
even until now" (Rom 8:22). At the Easter Vigil the Church is
brought to new birth; yet even that rebirth awaits a "new heavens
and a new earth" in the kingdom. The every fact that the initiated
approach the Eucharist at the conclusion to the vigil liturgy is itself an example of redemption's incompleteness. The Church
needs to continue to gather at the Lord's table to share more fully

110

and deeply until it is called to the "Supper of the Lamb" (Rev 19:9).

At every Eucharist the choice of greeting, words of introduction, penitential rite, intercessions, and the introduction to the Lord's Prayer all offer possibilities for a judicious choice of texts which can enhance the Scriptures proclaimed that day. In addition, on most days the choice of such euchological texts as the preface, Eucharistic prayer, blessing or prayer over the people could be done in order to offer something of an echo in the euchology of what was proclaimed in the Scriptures that day. On some occasions (e.g., weekdays of the year) the choice of the Mass formula could also be done to enhance the Scriptures proclaimed that day. Such a selection of options and composition of comments ought not be construed as establishing a "theme" for a given liturgy whereby the many meanings inherent in the Scriptures and in the symbolic engagement in sacrament are eclipsed and centered only on one. Rather the hope here is to surround the proclamation of the Scriptures in such a way that their impact and power can be unleashed in ever new ways at the liturgy.[71]

IV. Theology of the Word Event

The purpose of this section is to offer some theological perspectives on what occurs in the liturgical proclamation of the Word and observations about attitudes which believers can bring to the Liturgy of the Word so that the proclaimed Word can achieve its requisite effect.

1. *Act of Creation.* Scriptural texts about saving events that happened once in history (e.g., Exodus, passion, death, resurrection of Jesus) recount for contemporary liturgical assemblies what cannot be relegated to the past. Such saving acts are, by their nature, transtemporal and metahistorical. They occur still and have effects upon believing communities here and now. It is in the liturgy that these texts achieve their proper significance as recounting saving events from a primordial or historical time, which events are still effective here and now. Paradigmatic of this understanding of the effectiveness of the proclaimed Word is the story of creation from Genesis 1:1–2:2 proclaimed at the Easter Vigil. The annual proclamation of this text (which is allied with other such texts called

"cosmogonic myths"[72]) underscores the theological reality that when the Scriptures are proclaimed they are effective and actualize what they recount. The introductory words "in the beginning" are understood to mark one beginning in history as well as the annual new beginning celebrated in nature in the spring and the Church's annual new beginning in redemption at Easter. Recounting such texts gives them life. They are as truly creative now as the event they describe. Similarly, the event of the Liturgy of the Word itself can be understood as an act of creation that effects what it recounts.

The account of creation proclaimed at Easter is particularly instructive in that it describes how God brought an orderly creation out of primordial chaos. In a similar way we can say that the Liturgy of the Word is a creative act through which God orders the chaos of our preexisting communal and personal lives, and through the proclamation of the Word recreates us ever anew. We are not created *ex nihilo* each time we celebrate the liturgy. Rather our lives are once again set in proper order; we are always being refashioned as the baptized who are becoming more fully the holy ones of God. The scriptural Word is always effective in the sense that it accomplishes what it was sent to accomplish (see, Isa 55:10-11). It is living and active among us as fully as was God's act of speaking in Genesis that caused chaos to be ordered aright.

Not coincidental is the fact that the classic gospel text for Christmas, the prologue of John's Gospel (1:1-14), recounts the incarnation of the Word made flesh beginning with the words "In the beginning was the Word . . ." (1:1) which phrase imitates the opening of Genesis "In the beginning . . . God said . . ." (Gen 1:1). Theologically we can say that the Liturgy of the Word is always a new beginning, a fresh start, a time to order the chaos of our personal and communal lives according to the designs of creation and the purpose of Christ's redemption, according to the image and likeness of God (see, Gen 1:26).

The second story of creation in Genesis (2:4b-25) is also illustrative here in the sense that in this older creation story "the Lord God formed man out of the clay of the ground and blew into his nostrils the breath of life" (Gen 2:7). This can apply to the Liturgy of the Word in the sense that what was creative breath in Genesis becomes the Holy Spirit, the very life breath of the Christian assembly. It is through God's very Spirit that we engage in any act of liturgy. It is this same sustaining Spirit who regenerates us through the Word to be truly begotten of God. The spirit which Jesus delivered up at his death on the cross (John 19:30) can be understood as the Spirit that continues to enliven us at the liturgy to receive his Word and in receiving it, to be refashioned as God's holy people. The proclamation of the Word may thus be understood as occurring for the sake of our ongoing recreation and renewal.

That the Liturgy of the Word is a continual means for the Church's progressive recreation into the more perfect body of Christ on earth is supported in the way the Bible itself deals with creation. The accounts in Genesis are related to Romans 8:18-25 about the whole creation waiting to be set free from "its bondage to decay and obtain the glorious liberty of the children of God. We know that the whole creation has been groaning in travail together until now. . . ." (vv. 21-22). The limitations humanity and all of creation experiences here and now leads to yearning for the fullness of what is promised in Revelation 21. That is, to a time and place—the kingdom—when the limits of creation will be overturned and there will be "a new heavens and a new earth" (Rev 21:1). Creation will be restored, and even more, it will become what God intended it to be. In the meantime, the Liturgy of the Word is always an act of recreation and hope until the new heavens and earth are fulfilled.

That the Word is effective and enacts what it proclaims is noted in the cure of the centurion's servant (Matt 8:5-11) the gospel assigned to Monday of the First Week of Advent. The centurion's reliance on Jesus' "word" is central: "Lord, I am not worthy to have you come under my roof; but only say the word, and my servant will be healed" (v. 8, RSV trans.). Hence its appropriateness as a text with which to begin Advent, a time of patient listening to the Word of God. Also notable is the use of this text (in an adjusted form) at the invitation to the reception of the Eucharist "Lord, I am not worthy to receive you, but only say the word and I shall be healed."

God's Word is thus ever creative and recreative. Just as the Lord's speaking has a demonstrable effect in the biblical record of creation and of the incarnation, so when we read biblical stories of faith at liturgy God works among us to form and shape us into his chosen ones.

113

2. Act of Transfiguration. The synoptic accounts of the transfiguration are proclaimed on the Second Sunday of Lent. This event is unique in the gospel accounts of the life and ministry of Jesus; its privileged eyewitnesses are Peter, James, and John. One of its purposes in the gospels is to offer the disciples a share in what is experienced by all believers after the resurrection—the full realization of Christ's glory. The privilege of witnessing to the glory of Christ is now extended through the liturgy to all who come to worship. The placement of this account in the Lenten liturgy offers contemporary believers a glimpse during Lent of the resurrection glory to be shared in at Easter. Yet even through the liturgy of Easter we are reminded again of its provisionality until the second coming. As the prayer after Communion on this Sunday states:

"Lord,
we give thanks for these holy mysteries
which bring to us here on earth
a share in the life to come."[73]

In the meantime of the Church the transfiguration can stand as an example of how the liturgy itself is a unique, though provisional, experience of God's glory. Like the transfiguration, the liturgy cedes to (and leads to) the final realization of the kingdom in eternity.

The event is marked by the divine declaration "This is my Son, my beloved. Listen to him" (Mark 9:10 and par.).[74] This indicates that attentive listening to God's Word should mark contemporary believers who, in imitation of the three witnesses to the transfiguration, are charged to listen and obey the divine Word. It is fitting that the temptation account of the First Sunday of Lent in which Jesus asserts that we live "not on bread alone but on every word that comes from the mouth of God" (Matt 4:4, Luke 4:4, derived from Deut 8:3, which text is also used as gospel acclamation in all three Lectionary cycles) is followed by this divine assertion of the importance of faithful and attentive listening to the Word.

The Liturgy of the Word can be understood as a moment of transfiguration in the sense that it provides us with unique, though provisional, experiences of God's glory which divine actions draw us into a new experience of the mystery of God. One central way this is accomplished is through the medium of the message of salvation—the scriptural and incarnate word of God. Attentive listening to the Word in the liturgical assembly can be an effective experience of repeated transfiguration for the Church. Such moments of *transfiguration* are also moments of *transformation* whereby God graces the Church directly and endows it with his life-giving Spirit so that the body of Christ can appropriate more fully the life of grace and live its life consonant with that grace.[75] The Word at liturgy can thus be appropriately described as a Word of epiphany, manifestation, and transfiguration[76] whose purpose is to enable believers to experience in the liturgy moments of their progressive transformation into the very mystery of God.

3. *Acts of the Kingdom.* A major part of the instructive preaching of Jesus is through parables. This genre of literature teaches principally through stories which, while set in ordinary life, most often illustrate the confounding nature of God's kingdom by overturning normalcy and disclosing through them paradoxical and confounding surprises. The proclamation of these parables is not primarily to gain instruction about the kingdom. They are proclaimed in the liturgy to allow the contemporary assembly of believers to experience the surprises of the kingdom here and now. The paradoxical happenings of parabolic speech occur at the speech act of liturgy. Thus the faith which suffices is the size of a mustard seed, not the size of the Cedars of Lebanon. The last to come to faith will share in the kingdom as equally as those who labored all day. And it is the foreigner, the Samaritan, who shows compassion on the injured man, not the man's kinsfolk in Israel. Again, the medium of the message is listening, in this case to parables, and in listening to them to experience their overwhelming and paradoxical result.

Three cases in point derive from Luke 15, a chapter unique to the Lukan corpus. The first parable concerns the lost sheep (Luke 15:4-7), the second concerns the lost coin (vv. 8-10), and the third recounts the story of the prodigal son (vv. 11-32). This latter is appropriately assigned in the present Lectionary to the Fourth Sunday of Lent C cycle. The stories are familiar but that very familiarity may prohibit their parabolic point from being appreciated. Certainly no shepherd would leave the ninety-nine to seek one lost sheep for fear that other sheep would be lost in the process. No woman would spend all that time searching her house for a single (almost valueless) coin and in the process lose a day's wage from work. While we can understand fatherly compassion on a "prodigal son," the extent of the father's generosity in the parable is astounding when we realize that half the father's estate has been squandered. Despite that, a party is called in the son's honor. All three texts point to the overturning of expected behaviors. They enact the biblical insight that what may be bad economics is really good theology. This insight, along with many others about God's forgiving and reconciling love, is offered in phrases from the Eucharistic prayers for reconciliation:[77]

"When we were lost
and could not find the way to you,
you loved us more than ever. . . ."
(First Eucharistic Prayer for Reconciliation)

"God of power and might,
we praise you through your Son, Jesus Christ,
who comes in your name.
He is the Word that brings salvation.
He is the hand you stretch out to sinners.
He is the way that leads to your peace.
God our Father,
we had wandered far from you,
but through your Son you have brought us back."
(Second Eucharistic Prayer for Reconciliation)

Such parables of the kingdom as those from Luke 15 are thus enacted in the liturgy. Through hearing them, contemporary liturgical communities share in the same salvation offered to those who were lost—the sheep, the coin, and the son.

4. *Obedient Listening.* The classic psalm that begins the Liturgy of the Hours, Psalm 94, contains the poignant exhortation:

"Oh, that today you would hear his voice:
Harden not your hearts as at Meribah,
as in the day of Massah in the desert,
Where your fathers tempted me;
they tested me though they had seen my works.

116

Forty years I loathed that generation,
and I said: 'They are a people of erring heart,
and they know not my ways.
Therefore I swore in my anger:
They shall not enter into my rest'." (vv. 7-11).

This text is most appropriately placed as the invitatory for the
hours since believers cannot come to the Liturgy of the Word
throughout the day with "erring" or "hardened" hearts lest the
Word not effect among them what it signifies. An attitude of obedient listening marks the liturgical assembly. An example of the
importance of obedient listening to the Word can be found in
Jesus' own battle against Satan in the desert.

The account of Jesus' temptation is proclaimed in all three Lectionary cycles for the First Sunday of Lent, an appropriate over-
ture to the season. Central to the temptation account is the
reminder that we live "on every word that comes from the mouth
of God" (Matt 4:4) which text forms the gospel acclamation and
the Communion antiphon for this day. Thus Lent begins with the
example of Jesus who resolutely rejected Satan's temptations in
order to do the will of his Father.

An attitude of obedience is also central to the Philippians 2
hymn, proclaimed on Passion (Palm) Sunday which text emphasizes how Christ *obediently* accepted death for our salvation (vs. 8).
(As already noted) this attitude is reflected in the opening prayer
of this liturgy with the phrase

"you have given the human race
Jesus Christ our Savior
as a model of humility.
He fulfilled your will
by [coming among us] and giving his life
upon the cross."

It is also reiterated throughout the paschal triduum when this
verse is used as the responsory to the short Scripture reading at
morning and evening prayer on Good Friday and Holy Saturday.
Recalling our comment about the interrelationship of text and
music in liturgy it is appropriate to note that the Gregorian chant
musical setting of this text emphasizes the word *obediens* in such a

way as to make it the central phrase musically.[78] Such an emphasis coincides well with the theological meaning of the text influenced by its liturgical context.

This same attitude of obedience to the Lord's Word is noted in the second reading at the Easter Vigil (Gen 22:1-18) recounting Abraham and Sarah's sacrifice of Isaac. It was because of this act of obedience that Abraham's name has come into the Roman Canon as "Abraham our father in faith." This same attitude is reflected in the way the Advent liturgy portrays Mary. On the Fourth Sunday of Advent in the B cycle, Mary's words that conclude the reading are: "I am the servant of the Lord. Let it be done to me as you say" (Luke 1:38).[79]

The theological point made in such texts is that a central hallmark of believers should be their obedient listening to and then responding to the Word of God. The second Eucharistic prayer reiterates this at its conclusion:

"Have mercy on us all;
make us worthy to share eternal life
with Mary, the virgin Mother of God,
with the apostles, and with all the saints
who have done your will throughout the ages."

For the word of creation to be creative, for the transfiguring word to transform us, and for the parabolic message of the gospel to become a reality among us requires an openness to the Word proclaimed in the liturgical assembly and an appreciation that it can and should have its requisite impact on and among us. At its base such openness is an attitude of obedience.[80]

The thesis argued here that *context is text* asserts that the most appropriate theological setting for the appreciation and interpretation of the Scriptures is the act of liturgical proclamation. Such a *context* requires that communities of faith appreciate the origins of these texts as derived from similar assemblies who were called into being by God, which gatherings resulted in collecting stories of faith for their use in posterity. At the liturgy the Bible comes to new life; when the Bible is thus enlivened the Church comes to rebirth.

The context of the Church assembled in faith establishes the most appropriate setting for the Word to be truly heard. Such a context yields a scriptural text with many layers of meaning. The very variety of liturgical settings in which the Word is heard allows much of its richness to be disclosed. Concomitant with our emphasis on the liturgical assembly is the importance of other constitutive elements of liturgy—specifically symbol and euchology—(to be treated in the next two chapters) which help to support and draw out the meaning and implications of the Liturgy of the Word. Our thesis *context is text* is operative in these discussions.

However, the full meaning of the Word, symbol, and euchology will not be disclosed until the elect are called from the earthly liturgy to the supper of the Lamb. It is there and then that believers will abide in eternal communion in the living God. The final medium for the message will be the love that draws believers into experiencing the mystery of God finally and fully. Until that time believers stand in need of sacred texts and liturgical contexts. When combined they afford the believing Church a unique (but not exclusive) and a privileged (but always provisional) experience of the living God.

Notes

1. See, for example, I. Dalmais, "La liturgie celebration du mystere salut," *L'Église en prière*, Vol. I, 262–281.

2. This comment prescinds from the question of whether or not the Last Supper was a Passover meal, with most scholars today arguing that it was not.

3. See the method by Gordon Lathrop in *Holy Things. An Ecumenical Liturgical Theology* (Minneapolis: Fortress Press, 1993) which sets "sacred objects" before the "sacred word." It may be a paradoxical sign of the times ecumenically that he, a Lutheran, writes so much of symbols/objects and our approach (Roman Catholic) stresses words.

4. See below, this chapter, 88–89.

5. On the ecumenical implications of this see, Gerard Békés, "Parola e Sacramento. Il rapporto tra due fattori nella partecipazione alla salvezza," *Ecclesia Orans* 8 (1991) 261–276.

6. See, Philippe Beguerie, "La Bible née de la liturgie, *La Maison Dieu* 126 (1976) 109–111.

7. Ibid., 111–112.

8. Ibid., 113 and Innocenzo Gargano, "L'uso della Bibbia nella Liturgia: L'esegesi 'Spirituale' Oggi," in *La Bibbia nella Liturgia* (Genova: Marietti, 1987)

86–87. The author goes on to argue the insufficiency of the "literal sense" of the Scriptures since by its very nature the Word at worship is meant to engage participants in an encounter, not to describe a past event enshrined in the Bible or merely to explain what biblical events have meant or can mean.

9. Louis-Marie Chauvet, *Symbole et sacrement*. Une relecture sacramentelle de l'existence chrétienne (Paris: Les Editions du Cerf, 1987) 197–199. Chauvet here acknowledges his reliance on I. H. Dalmais in "La Bible vivant dans l'Église," *La Maison Dieu* 126 (1976) 7–23.

10. See, Clark Hyde, "The Bible in the Church: The Lectionary as Paradigm" *Worship* 61 (July 1987) 326 where he speaks of the Bible as having been compiled from a believing community whose proper interpretation derives from the faith community.

11. See, Louis-Marie Chauvet, *Symbole et sacrement* 120–131, part of which utilizes the work of E. Ortigues.

12. Beguerie, "La bible" 114.

13. See, Chauvet, *Symbole et sacrement,* 206–218 for an analysis of how the written Bible came to be produced and especially the role of the assembly in this process. He argues that the liturgy set parameters for biblical canonicity before the Bible was formally compiled. He insists that the Bible is always the boo‘ in the hands of the community.

14. See, Dalmais "La bible vivant dans l'Église" 7, who argues that the entire function of the Bible is for the proclamation of the Word and for communal listening to the Word. Thus the Bible is *the* book of the assembly/synagogue/church that is convoked; the Word is normative for the hearing and identity of the faith community.

15. See, among others, Achille M. Triacca, "Bibbia e Liturgia" in *Nuovo Dizionario di Liturgia* 179.

16. Ibid., 180.

17. See, B. Agourides, "The Bible in the Orthodox Church: the biblical substance and vision of Orthodox worship and spirituality," *Scripture Bulletin* 10 (Summer, 1979) 12.

18. That *lectio divina* is a most important part of monastic prayer is reflected in the *Rule* of St. Benedict, chap. 48. See, for example, 48:1 "Idleness is the enemy of the soul. Therefore, the brothers should have specified periods for manual labor as well as for prayerful reading" (*lectione divina*); vs. 10 "the brothers ought to devote themselves to reading until the end of the second hour" (*lectioni*); vs. 14 "during the days of Lent, they should be free in the morning to read until the third hour" (*vacent lectionibus suis*); vs. 17 "while the brothers are reading" (*vacant fratres lectioni*); vs. 18 ". . . to see that no brother is so apathetic as to waste time or engage in idle talk to the neglect of his reading" (*et non est intentus lectioni*); vs. 22 "on Sunday all are to be engaged in reading except those who have been assigned various duties" (*Dominico item die lectioni vacent omnes*). All texts from *RB 1980. The Rule of St.*

Benedict. In Latin and English With Notes, ed., Timothy Fry, et.al. (Collegeville: The Liturgical Press, 1981) 248–251. For an indication of how meditative reading can be useful for non monks, especially for preachers, see Caroline Walker Bynum, *Docere Verbo et Exemplo. An Aspect of Twelfth Century Spirituality*. Harvard Theological Studies No. 31 (Missoula/Ann Arbor: Scholars Press, 1979) who shows how the medieval debates between these groups often centered on the observation that the monk's meditation on the Word is basically internal (*lectio divina*) while the canon's meditation ultimately has an external goal in preaching.

19. Karl Rahner, "What is a Sacrament?" *Worship* 47 (May 1973) 275–76.

20. See below, Chapter Seven, 295–303.

21. See, Luigi Della Torre, "La predicazione nella Liturgia" in *Nelle Vostre Assemblee Vol. I*, Teologia pastorale delle celebrazioni liturgiche, second edition (Brescia: Queriniana, 1975) 250.

22. It is noteworthy that conciliar and postconciliar magisterial statements about the Eucharist seek to remove any divorce between the Liturgy of the Word and the Liturgy of the Eucharist in order to emphasize their combined importance to comprise one act of liturgy which itself is appropriately understood as an act of memory. "The two parts that, in a certain sense, go to make up the Mass, namely the liturgy of the word and the liturgy of the eucharist, are so closely connected with each other that they form but one single act of worship" (*Sacrosanctum Concilium* n. 56), "Pastors should, therefore, 'insistently teach the faithful to take their part in the entire Mass,' by showing the close connection that exists between the liturgy of the word and the celebration of the Lord's Supper, so that they may clearly perceive how the two constitute a single act of worship" (*Eucharisticum Mysterium* n. 10) and "The Mass is made up as it were of the liturgy of the word and the liturgy of the eucharist, two parts so closely connected that they form but one single act of worship. For in the Mass the table of the God's word and of Christ's body is laid for the people of God to receive from it instruction and food" (GIRM n. 8). All translations from *DOL*, nn. 56, 1239 and 1398. See, Gaston Fontaine, "Commentarium ad Ordinem Lectionum Missae," *Notitiae* 5 (1969) 258, as well as Clark Hyde, "The Bible in the Church," 334, J. P. Jossua, "Parole de Dieu et liturgie," in *La liturgie après Vatican II* (Paris: Les Editions du Cerf, 1967) 142, and Antonio Maragon, "Bibbia e liturgia: dall'esegesi all'ermeneutica attraverso la celebrazione," in *Una Liturgia per l'uomo* 251.

23. L.-M. Chauvet, *Symbole et Sacrement*, 227.

24. Ibid., 232. Significantly Thomas Aquinas introduces his treatment of sacraments as follows: "Now that we have completed our consideration of the mysteries of the Incarnate Word, our next field of investigation is the sacraments of the Church, seeing that it is from this same Incarnate Word that these derive their efficacy" (*Summa Theologiae* IIIa, q. 60, Blackfriars translation, *The Sacraments* 3).

25. See, Ildephonse Herwegen, "L'Ecriture sainte dans la Liturgie," *La Maison Dieu* 5 (1946) 9, where he states that the phrase *dicit Jesus discipulis suis* which

introduces the parables of Jesus in the liturgy is used as a way to address the believing assembly directly and immediately.

26. Clearly the intention of trying to find Old Testament precedents for gospel events has not been uniformly successful in the present Lectionary and can have the unfortunate result of fostering a contemporary kind of Marcionism in that the Hebrew Scriptures are only read in relation to the light they can shed on the New Testament. For a succinct indication of the many problems associated with this approach to the Lectionary assignment of the Old Testament see, Gerard Sloyan, "Some Suggestions for a Three-Year Lectionary," *Worship* 63 (November 1989) 521–535.

27. As an example of how this has functioned in the liturgy of the hours see, Pierre Salmon, "De l'interpretation des psaumes dans la liturgie aux origines de l'office divin," *La Maison Dieu* 33 (1953) 21–55, Andre Rose, "La repartition des psaumes dans le cycle liturgique," *La Maison Dieu* 105 (1971) 66–102, and Balthasar Fischer, "Les titres chretiens des psaumes dans le nouvel office divin," *La Maison Dieu* 135 (1978) 148–157.

28. See, Gaston Westphal, "La prédication, présence du Seigneur," in *La Parole dans la Liturgie* Lex Orandi 48 (Paris: Les Editions du Cerf, 1975) 145–146.

29. See, for example, A. M. Triacca, "Bibbia e liturgia," 187.

30. See, I. H. Dalmais, "Rites et prières accompagnant les lectures dans la liturgie eucharistique," in *La Parole dans la liturgie* 107.

31. See, *Ordo Lectionum Missae.* Editio Typica Altera (Vatican City: Libreria Editrice Vaticana, 1981) xlix. Thus the citation of the gospel for the First Sunday of Advent cycle A is noted by the *incipit* "In illo tempore: Dixit Iesus discipulis suis dies Noe. . . ." (p. 5). This is sustained in the second edition of the Italian Missal as in *Messale di Ogni Giorno* (Milano: Ancora, 1984) "In quel tempo, Gesu disse ai suoi discepoli: 'Come fu ai giorni di Noè. . . .'" (6). The present American Lectionaries do not include these introductions, e.g., "Jesus said to his disciples: 'The coming of the Son of Man. . . ." from, *Lectionary for Mass* (New York; Catholic Book Publishing Co., 1970) 17.

32. For an overview of the place of such textual additions to scriptural readings see, S. J. P. Van Dijk, "The Bible in Liturgical Use," *Cambridge History of the Bible Vol. II* (New York: Cambridge University Press, 1970) 226. It would be interesting to trace the origins of the use of *in illo tempore* to determine whether it is connected in any way with the kind of historicization which influenced some elaborations found in the liturgy and popular piety surrounding Holy Week.

33. Adrien Nocent, "La lettura della Sacra Scrittura," *Nelle Vostre Assemblee* Vol. I, 232.

34. See, Luigi Della Torre, "La predicazione nella Liturgia," *Nell Vostre Assemblee*, 252.

35. Hence the advantage of having a General Instruction on the Lectionary to accompany the publication of the revised Roman Lectionary for Mass.

36. See, Alexander Schmemann, "Theology and Liturgical Tradition" 175.

37. See, Gerard S. Sloyan, "The Lectionary as a Context for Interpretation," *Interpretation* 31 (1977) 131.

38. In "L'Ecriture sainte dans la Liturgie" (9) I. Herwegen will argue the primacy of a Christological reading of the Scriptures at liturgy by stating that only the presence and action of Christ in the liturgy makes us worthy of opening the Scripture. It is only in Christ the Lamb of sacrifice that we can receive the most profound meaning of the Scriptures. On the question of a Christological reading of the Old Testament see, A. Rose, "La parole vivante de Dieu dans la liturgie," *La Maison Dieu* 82 (1965) 49ff.

39. See, A. Nocent, "La lettura della sacra scrittura," 232.

40. See, J. A. Lamb "The Place of the Bible in the Liturgy," in *Cambridge History of the Bible, Volume I,* 572 who argues that the words used to introduce the gospel (*sequentia sancti evangelii*) provide a significant indication of the importance which the liturgy attaches to the *lectio continua.*

41. A. Triacca, "Bibbia e Liturgia," 181.

42. Carlo Martini will argue that the plurality of meanings of a given text is disclosed in relation to the unity of the Scriptures which is the paschal mystery. See, "The School of the Word," *Worship* 61 (May 1987) 196.

43. Tullio Citrini, "Come e dove si ascolta Dio che parla. Problemi dell' ermeneutica," in *La Bibbia nella Liturgia,* 33.

44. See, Jean Corbon, "L'economie du Verbe et la liturgie de la Parole," in *La Parole dans la liturgie* 162.

45. Ibid., 159ff.

46. For an indication of the issues involved in interpreting these songs see, for example, Carroll Stuhlmueller, "Deutero-Isaiah and Trito-Isaiah," in *The New Jerome Biblical Commentary,* eds. Raymond E. Brown, Joseph A. Fitzmyer, and Roland E. Murphy (Englewood Cliffs: Prentice Hall, 1989) 330–331, and John J. Collins, "Isaiah," in *The Collegeville Biblical Commentary,* eds., Dianne Bergant and Robert J. Karris (Collegeville: Liturgical Press, 1989) 414–416.

47. This assignment is for all three cycles of the Sunday lectionary according to the 1969 *Ordo Lectionum Missae.* In the second edition of the *Ordo* this assignment remains for the A cycle but other texts are offered as options for the other cycles, i.e., Isa 55:1-11 for "B" and Isa 40:1-5, 9-11 for "C."

48. See, *Lectionary for Mass. Introduction.* Liturgy Documentary Series One (Washington: USCC 1982) n. 98.

49. It should be noted that not all verses of the psalm are used for the responsorial psalm. Where germane to our argument those verses having particular relevance to our argument will be indicated. Otherwise only the number of the psalm will be noted.

50. Lectionary "Introduction," n. 99.

51. For a useful comment on how the homily is constitutive of the liturgy see, Albert Houssiau, "Le service de la Parole," *Questions Liturgiques* 65 (1984) 209.

52. See, J. A. Goenaga, "La homilia: acto sacramental y de magistero," *Phase* 95 (1976) 345.

53. Ibid., 351.

54. See, Gargano, "L'uso della Bibbia," 87.

55. Among others, see the work of Mary Catherine Hilkert, in particular "Theology of Preaching," *New Dictionary of Sacramental Worship*, 996–1003, plus bibliography.

56. See, A. M. Triacca, "Bibbia e Liturgia," 185.

57. See, Gerard Sloyan, "Is Church Teaching Neglected When The Lectionary Is Preached?" *Worship* 61 (March 1987) 131.

58. See, A. M. Triacca, "Bibbia e Liturgia," 181 who cites the Latin phrase from the prayer over the gifts from the Evening Mass of the Lord's Supper (which text was formerly assigned in the Roman Missal to the Ninth Sunday after Pentecost). It is also assigned to the Second Sunday of the Year.

59. See, Gordon Lathrop, "A Rebirth of Images: On the Use of the Bible in Liturgy," *Worship* 58 (July 1984) 295–296 where he asserts that Scripture is set in relation to font and table and that Sunday readings are not fully understood unless they lead the assembly to the Supper. Also, see, Antonio Marangon, "Bibbia e liturgia" 250–251. This article is especially helpful since it summarizes the way that the relationship between the Bible and liturgy is taught in the S. Giustina Institute of pastoral liturgical studies in Padua.

60. A rubrical direction from the General Instruction on the Roman Missal, n. 42 that "the homily should ordinarily be given by the priest celebrant" can be understood as a way of underscoring the theological link between Word and table, which link is rather completely described in the preceding paragraph when it states: "the homily is an integral part of the liturgy and is strongly recommended; it is necessary for the nurturing of the Christian life. It should develop some point of the readings or another text from the Ordinary or from the Proper of the Mass of the day, and take into account the mystery being celebrated and the needs proper to the listeners" (n. 41).

61. See, .L.-M. Chauvet, *Symbole et sacrement*, 218–232.

62. Present ICEL translation of Latin text:
"Qui cum nascendo multa gaudia praestitisset,
et nondum editus exsultasset ad humanae salutis adventum. . . ."

63. Present ICEL translation of Latin text:
"ipse solus omnium prophetarum
Agnum redemptionis ostendit."

64. Present ICEL translation of Latin text:
"Omnipotens sempiterne Deus,
qui humano generi, ad imitandum humilitatis exemplum,

Salvatorem nostrum carnem sumere,
et crucem subire fecisti,
concede propitius,
ut et patientiae ipsius habere documenta
et resurrectionis consortia mereamur."

65. See, Lawrence Hoffman, *Beyond the Text: A Holistic Approach to Liturgy* (Bloomington/Indianapolis: Indiana University Press, 1987) 75–144 for a helpful treatment of the liturgical use of sacred myths.

66. Present ICEL translation of the Latin:

"Omnipotens sempiterne Deus,
qui es in omnium operum tuorum dispensatione mirabilis,
intellegant redempti tui, non fuisse excellentius,
quod initio factus est mundus,
quam quod in fine saeculorum
Pascha nostrum immolatus est Christus.
Qui vivit et regnat in saecula saeculorum."

67. Present ICEL translation of the Latin:

"Deus, cuius antiqua miracula
etiam nostris temporibus coruscare sentimus,
dum, quod uni populo a persecutione Pharaonis liberando
dexterae tuae potentia contulisti,
id in salutem gentium per aquam regenerationis operaris,
praesta, ut in Abrahae filios et in Israeliticam dignitatem
totius mundi transeat plenitudo.
Per Christum Dominum nostrum."

68. Present ICEL translation of the Latin:

"Exsultet iam angelica turba caelorum:
exsultent divina mysteria:
et pro tanti Regis victoria tuba insonet salutaris.
Gaudeat et tellus tantis irradiata fulguribus:
et, aeterni Regis splendore illustrata,
totius orbis se sentiat amisisse caliginem.

Haec nox est,
in qua primum patres nostros, filios Israel
eductos de Aegypto,
Mare Rubrum sicco vestigio transire fecisti.
Haec igitur nox est,
quae peccatorum tenebras columnae illuminatione purgavit.
Haec nox est,
quae hodie per universum mundum in Christo credentes,
a vitiis saeculi at caligine peccatorum segregatos,
reddit gratiae, sociat sanctitati."

69. The specification of the northern hemisphere here is essential since the southern hemisphere does not experience spring at Easter. This issue will be taken up more fully in Chapter 5.

70. An important issue in the contemporary ongoing reform of the Eucharistic liturgy concerns whether or not it would be useful if each Sunday's prayer formulas (especially the opening prayers) reflected the Scriptures proclaimed that day. While the historical and theological precedent for such a move is somewhat slim, nevertheless some liturgists at present argue for the usefulness of such an adjustment in future editions of the Sacramentary. The second edition of the Italian *Messale di Ogni Giorno* reflects this approach where for Sundays of the year three texts are offered for the opening prayer (in addition to the one prayer established in the *Missale Romanum*) based on readings of each year of the three year Lectionary cycle. This is discussed in more detail in Chapter 5.

71. See, for example, Kevin W. Irwin, *Sunday Worship*. A Planning Guide (New York: Pueblo Publishing Co., 1983), *Lent*. A Guide to the Eucharist and Hours (New York: Pueblo, 1985) and *Advent-Christmas*. A Guide to the Eucharist and Hours (New York: Pueblo, 1986) and *Easter*. A Guide to Eucharist and Hours. A Pueblo Book (Collegeville: The Liturgical Press, 1991).

72. On this term in the history of religions and why it was repeated annually, most usually in the Spring see, Mircea Eliade, *Cosmos and Myth*, trans., Willard Trask (New York: Harper Torchbooks, 1959).

73. Present ICEL translation of the Latin:
"Percipientes, Domine, gloriosa mysteria,
gratias tibi referre satagimus,
quod, in terrra positos,
iam caelestium praestas esse participes."

74. It is notable that the communion antiphon in the Roman Missal for the Second Sunday of Lent states "This is my Son, my beloved, in whom is all my delight: listen to him" (Matt 17:5).

75. See below, Chapter 8 where this theme is elaborated with regard to what can be called spirituality derived from the liturgy.

76. See, J. Corbon, "L'economie" 161.

77. A particularly acute instance of the deficiencies in the present euchology in the Roman Missal is that the mass formulas for the third, fourth and fifth Lenten Sundays reflect the gospel readings of the A cycle only. Hence additional mass formulas for the B and C cycles would enable the prayers of the liturgy to enhance the reading of the word that day. The mass formula for the fourth Sunday "C" cycle when the prodigal son parable from Luke: 15:1-3, 11-32 is read is at issue here. An example of how the second edition of the Italian missal offers new prayers is in the opening prayer for the "C" cycle:
"O Dio, Padre buono e grande nel perdono,
accogli nell'abbraccio del tuo amore,
tutti i figli che tornano a te con animo pentito;
ricoprili delle splendide vesti di salvezza,
perché possano gustare la tua gioia
nella cena pasaquale dell'Agnello."

78. This is described in more detail below, Chapter 6.

79. The only echo of this attitude in the euchology for this day is in the alternative opening prayer which states:

"Father, all-powerful God,
your eternal Word took flesh on our earth
when the Virgin Mary placed her life
at the service of your plan."

It is noted indirectly in the second edition of the Italian version of the Roman Missal when it states:

"Dio grande e misericordioso,
che tra gli umili scegli i tuoi servi
per portare a compimento il disegno di salvezza,
concedi alla tua Chiesa la fecondità dello Spirito,
perché sull'esempio di Maria
accolga il Verbo della vita e si rallegri
come madre di una stirpe santa e incorruttibile."

The text offered for the "C" cycle is more direct:

"O Dio, che hai scelto l'umile figlia di Israele
per farne la tua dimora.
dona alla Chiesa una totale adesione al tuo volere,
perché imitando l'obbedienza del Verbo
venuto al mondo per servire,
esulti con Maria per la tua salvezza
e si offra a te in perenne cantico di lode."

80. It is not coincidental that the Latin word *audire* when followed by the dative case means "to obey."

Chapter 4

Symbol

This discussion of symbol is placed after our consideration of the Word in liturgy because the liturgical use of symbol (meaning elements from creation or the product of "the work of human hands") shares some of the characteristics of symbolic engagement described in the previous chapter. Just as we argued that human persons are necessary for language to be language and human interaction in liturgy is required for liturgical language to be regarded as *symbolic*,[1] so our interpretation of symbol, which includes creation (e.g., sun, water) and "manufactured" symbols (e.g., bread and wine), requires that we emphasize how the liturgical community engages in symbolic interaction in worship. Just as the liturgical *use* of and *context* for the Word was our concern in chapter 3, so here our concern will be with the liturgical *use* of symbol and how the liturgical act provides the required *context* for its interpretation.[2]

Throughout this discussion (in particular) the role of imagination in liturgy will be presumed in the sense that multivalent liturgical rites unleash many and varied meanings, often appropriated only in prereflective ways, especially in the imagination. By their nature, symbols invite one to such rumination. Their accompanying texts in liturgy tether one's imagination (but do not control it) most usually by recalling paradigmatic moments of saving history in whose retelling liturgical communities experience salvation once more. The mediation of meaning through symbols often enough relies as much (if not more) on imagination as it does on intellectual understanding. Thus the importance of underscoring imagination's role in liturgy in general and in this discussion of symbol. One of the key values in appreciating varying contexts for the celebration of the same liturgy is that each offers fresh insight on the whole, the way the various angles of a cut diamond all reflect differently both the gem and the light reflected by the gem. Imagination is a crucial factor in unleashing the varied meanings offered through the symbol system of the liturgy.

This discussion presumes ideas discussed in chapter 3 on the importance of the dialogical character of symbol, that the liturgy can be understood as a "symbolic rehearsal of salvation," that enacting liturgy is for the sake of "remembering a relationship" (with God and with others in the Church), and that varying contexts contribute to the interpretation of symbols used in worship. The location of this discussion after the Word also underscores that the theology of announcement of the Word, based on symbolic hearing and communal appropriation, has its parallel in the way both the things of the earth and the "work of human hands" are used symbolically in worship. Symbol is the appropriate specification of and complement to the announcement in the symbolic Word with the two realities of Word and symbol together comprising the liturgical enactment and experience of the paschal mystery.[3]

The fact that symbol is treated separately from our major discussion of euchology (to follow in chapter 5) needs to be explained because euchology and symbols normally function together in liturgy, and even here we will use euchological texts to exemplify our discussion of symbol. The purpose of separating symbol from euchological texts is both for emphasis and for (what might be termed) remedial purposes. First, the emphasis placed on liturgical *texts* as the chief meaning of the *lex orandi* in much liturgical writing in general (some of which was noted in chapter 1) is appropriately contextualized and, in our opinion, only correctly understood when texts are appreciated in light of the way they are used in liturgical settings especially when they accompany the use of symbols. This requires at least a concomitant, if not a preliminary, discussion of the liturgical use of symbol. We will treat symbol first. Second, the contemporary rediscovery of the role of creation and symbol in worship[4] is particularly germane to the Roman Catholic tradition (but clearly not exclusively so) which has continually sustained the use of creation and symbol in its liturgy. This usage is especially notable in light of the comparative lack of emphasis placed on symbolic interaction in liturgy in many non-Catholic Christian Churches after the Reformation. For example the infrequent celebrations of the Eucharist and more common celebrations of the Word, even on Sundays.

However, it is to be admitted that at certain times in history Roman Catholicism also downplayed creation and symbol in worship in order to emphasize other truths. For example the post-Tridentine apologetic emphasis placed on the Eucharistic species as containing the real presence of Christ had unfortunately eclipsed appropriate emphasis on the liturgical assembly partaking of the symbolic elements of consecrated bread and wine to complete their participation in the sacrificial sacrament of the Eucharist.[5] In addition even when Catholicism retained symbolic usage in liturgy, too often this has meant a minimalistic understanding that emphasized only "matter" and "form" as requisites for valid and licit sacramental celebration. Hence placing due emphasis on symbol in a separate chapter seems appropriate.

This discussion of symbol fits our overall scheme in four ways, which four elements comprise the subdivisions of this chapter. (1) Since God's self-revelation through creation and an incarnational emphasis in theology are hallmarks of Roman Catholicism, the first part of our treatment of symbol is a consideration of the sacramentality of all of creation. (2) Our discussion will then focus on how enacted rites presume *symbolic engagement*, namely, how the liturgical community interacts with symbols and how symbolic interaction needs to be regarded as an essential part of a theology of liturgy. (3) Our thesis *context is text* is particularly operative in our discussion of the interpretation of some primary liturgical symbols in varying contexts to indicate their pluriform meanings. (4) The chapter concludes with some observations on the relative (in)adequacy with which the present reformed liturgy deals with creation and symbol both in liturgical enactment as well as in liturgical texts.

I. Sacramentality of Creation

The purpose of this section is to indicate how the liturgy notes, relies upon and emphasizes the sacramentality of all of creation. It is a tenet of much Christian philosophy that creation express God's creative idea and reveals the divine intention to manifest God's power and goodness (sometimes called the formal cause and final cause respectively). Creation, therefore, besides its ontological reality, constituted by the effective divine causality, is also a sign that indicates that the creator is able to communicate the creator's knowledge and love. Based on this mediating function of the knowledge and love of God seen through creation, we can talk of the symbolic-sacramental significance of creation in liturgy.

This is to assert that according to divine revelation and theology based on revelation, creation, besides its ontological reality, holds a symbolic-sacramental significance: it is a mediating *sign* of God's creative idea and action, and for that reason is able to communicate God's knowledge and love. Consequently it can function as a means of mediating the divine between God and human beings, as a means of communication about the divine and as a means of salvation (experience of the divine) for humanity. Hence we can say that a chief characteristic that undergirds the practice and understanding of worship is its reverence for and use of creation.

What can be termed the *integrative* function of the liturgy derived from this kind of usage would emphasize how the liturgy itself is the privileged and traditional means to relate "the world's problems, hopes and difficulties to the sacramental experience. . . . [which by its very nature is intended] to indicate the cosmic and catholic, i.e., the all-embracing, all-assuming and all-transforming nature and scope of Christian *leitourgia*."[6]

Because the human person is the pinnacle of God's creation and in virtue of the Christian's baptismal consecration, the vocation of Christians is to be *priests* who stand

"in the center of the world and [unify any dichotomy between the natural and supernatural, between the secular and the sacred in their] act of blessing God, [that is] of both receiving the world from God and offering it to God—and by filling the world with this eucharist, [they transform their very lives] into life in God, into communion."[7]

A contemporary statement of this classic understanding of the role of human activity in liturgy from the Orthodox perspective states that

"just as the priest at the Eucharist offers the fullness of creation and receives it back as the blessing of Grace in the form of the consecrated bread and wine, to share with others, so we must be the channel through which God's grace and deliverance is shared with all creation. The human being is simply yet gloriously the means for the expression of creation in its fullness and the coming of God's deliverance for all creation."[8]

Alexander Schmemann summarizes the importance of the use of material creation in the Church's act of liturgy by stating:

"the Church is the sacrament of the Kingdom—not because it possesses divinely instituted acts called 'sacrament,' but because first of all, it is the possibility given to [humanity] to see in and through this world the 'world to come,' to see and to 'live' it in Christ. It is only when, in the darkness of *this world*, we discern that Christ has *already* 'filled all things with Himself,' that these *things*, whatever they may be, are revealed and given to us as full of meaning and beauty. A Christian is the one who, wherever he [or she] looks, finds everywhere Christ, and rejoices in Him. And this joy *transforms* all his [or her] human plans and programs, decisions and moves, makes all his [or her] mission the sacraments of the world's return to Him, who is the life of the world."[9]

With regard to sacramental worship specifically, representative Roman Catholic thought would assert that

"a sacrament is not a stand-in for something else, a visible sign for some other invisible reality. The essence of a sacrament is the capacity to reveal grace, the agapic self-gift of God, by being what it is. By being thoroughly itself, a sacrament bodies forth the absolute self-donative love of God that undergirds both it and the entirety of creation. By its nature a sacrament requires that it be appreciated for what it is and not as a tool to an end; in Buber's terms, a sacrament is always 'thou.' "[10]

These texts serve to indicate that part of the fundamental anthropological and theological foundation upon which the act of liturgy is based—in our terminology this is part of liturgy's *context*—is the use of creation and symbolic interaction through which means the divine is disclosed and faith in the divine is shaped and renewed. The following discussion of two characteristics of the use of creation in worship help to exemplify this premise and to specify part of the *context* for liturgy: times for celebration and motivation for celebration. In the discussion on the times for celebration our presumptions are based on the rhythm of the cosmos as perceived in the northern hemisphere. Certainly the increasing literature on inculturation has pointed out the difficulties (not to mention a certain cultural imperialism) associated with applying this uncritically to the southern hemisphere. Even though our concern here does not concern inculturation specifically (largely because of the specificity of other local cultures and needs) at times we will note the limitations of assuming that our argument here should be universalized. Recalling that our principal concern here is with a theology of the liturgy, it is necessary, in our opinion, to articulate how the rhythm of the cosmos has influenced the evolution of so many aspects of the Church calendar.

1. *Times for Celebration.* The determination of times for the celebration of the daily rhythm of the Liturgy of the Hours, the seasons of the Church year and some feast days is derived from the rhythm of the cosmos. The determination of dawn for morning prayer and dusk for evening prayer is underscored in the General Instruction on the Hours which states that morning prayer is "celebrated . . . as the light of a new day is dawning" (n. 38). It is appropriate that Zechariah's canticle is always used at this hour with the text:

"the dawn from on high shall break upon us,
to shine on those who dwell in darkness
    and the shadow of death. . . ." (Luke 1:79).

It is not a coincidence that this same text is used as the communion antiphon for the Solemnity of the Birth of John the Baptist since the date of this feast, June 24, was deliberately chosen in accord with the length of the sun's rays. Just as the daylight begins to diminish after June 21, (often called "the longest day of the year") the Church commemorates the birth of the Baptist whose saying "Jesus must increase, but I must decrease" (John 3:30) determined the date for this commemoration. The sign of diminishing daylight in the cosmos has determined the feast of him whose self-effacement ("decrease") led his followers and other people to put their faith in Christ ("the dawn from on high"). That this feast has a rich tradition of liturgical importance is attested to by the fact that the only other births commemorated in the calendar are those of Jesus and the Blessed Virgin Mary, that there are a number of Mass formulas honoring the Baptist in the Verona collection of presidential prayers[11] and the fact that in the present Sacramentary the only saints who have their own preface besides

John the Baptist are the Blessed Virgin Mary, St. Joseph (March 19) and Sts. Peter and Paul (June 29).

With regard to evening prayer the same Instruction states that "when evening approaches and the day is already far spent, evening prayer is celebrated . . . [when] we join the Churches of the East in calling upon the 'joy-giving light of holy glory' . . . now that we have come to the setting of the sun and seen the evening star. . . ." (n. 39). The Jewish tradition of lamplighting in the Temple at evening prayer (called the *lucernarium*) is also part of the liturgical ritual traditionally attached to this hour of prayer.[12]

The phases of the moon and its location determine the date for our celebration of Easter.[13] The diminishing of the intensity of the sun (in the northern hemisphere) is reflected in the Lectionary and euchology of Advent and Christmas, which texts become the more compelling when this natural phenomenon is recalled. Part of the Johannine Prologue, the traditional gospel on Christmas morning states:

"The light shines on in darkness
a darkness that did not overcome it" (John 1:5).

The following euchological texts now used at Christmas and Epiphany are the more notable for this reason.

"Father,
you make this holy night radiant
with the splendor of Jesus Christ our light."
(Opening Prayer, Mass at Midnight)[14]

"Father,
we are filled with new light
by the coming of your Word among us."
(Opening Prayer, Mass at Dawn)[15]

"In the wonder of the incarnation
your eternal Word has brought to the eyes of faith
a new and radiant vision of your glory."
(Christmas Preface I)[16]

"Today in him a new light has dawned upon the world:"
(Christmas Preface III)[17]

134

"Today you revealed in Christ your eternal plan of salvation
and showed him as the light of all peoples."
(Epiphany Preface)[18]

The addition of the Old Testament reading of Isaiah 9:1-6 ("a
people who walked in darkness have seen a great light" v. 1) to
the traditional Scripture readings for Midnight Mass (Titus 2:11-14
and Luke 2:10-11) also underscores the light symbolism of
Christmas.

It is commonly agreed that a preexisting (pagan) feast of ingathering the first fruits of the Fall harvest influenced Judaism's
practice of celebrating *sukkoth* ("tabernacles" or "booths") as a
Fall festival of covenant renewal.[19] This same idea is congenial in
Christianity with celebrations commemorating the "first fruits of
creation" in the apocalyptic and eschatological themes reflected in
the Lectionary for Mass prior to and on the First Sunday of Advent, one example of which, from the second reading on the
Solemnity of Christ the King (the Last Sunday of the Year B cycle)
even states "Jesus Christ is the faithful witness, the first-born
from the dead and ruler of the kings of earth" (Rev 1:5).[20] That
the Johannine prologue (used on Christmas day) uses a variation
on the word "boots" or "tabernacles" is significant when it acclaims that "the Word . . . made his dwelling among us" (John
1:14) which verb form in Greek is literally "he set up his tent" or
"he tabernacled" among us. (While not part of the historical
rationale why the commemoration of All Saints and All Souls occurred at this time of year, our present celebration of All Saints
and All Souls is not unconnected with the theme of "first fruits
of creation.")

2. *Motivation for Celebration.* In light of our thesis it is appropriate
now to highlight how creation repeatedly serves as both *context*
and *text* in liturgical prayer. It is *context* in the sense that praise to
God the creator, acclaimed in the Creed as the maker of heaven
and earth, of all that is seen and unseen,[21] is constitutive of the
theology of the Liturgy of the Hours. For example, a hymn of
praise for the days of creation was assigned to ferial vespers for
each day (except First Vespers of Sunday) in the former breviary.
This usage is retained in the *editio typica* of the present revision
(ferial office weeks 1 and 3). These texts, likely from the same au-

thor (perhaps Gregory the Great) devote four stanzas to the work of each day of creation. Sunday's vesper hymn *Lucis creator optime*, itself reflecting the light/darkness motif of evening prayer, begins with the following two verses:

"O blest Creator of the light,
Who mak'st the day with radiance bright,
And o'er the forming world didst call
The light from chaos first of all;
Whose wisdom joined in meet array
The morn and eve, and named them Day:
Night comes with all its darkling fears;
Regard Thy people's prayers and tears."[22]

The rest of the Vesper hymns reflecting praise for the days of creation are *Immense coeli Conditor*, "O great Creator of the sky" (Monday),[23] *Telluris alme Conditor*, "Earth's mighty maker, whose command/Raised from the sea the solid land" (Tuesday), *Caeli Deus sanctissime*, "O God whose hand hath spread the sky, And all its shining hosts on high" (Wednesday), *Magnae Deus potentiae*, "O Sovereign Lord of nature's might, Who bad'st the water's birth divide; Part in the heavens to take their flight, And part in ocean's deep to hide" (Thursday) and *Hominis supernae Conditor*, "Maker of man, who from Thy throne,/Dost order all things, God alone" (Friday). The hymn for First Vespers of Sunday, *Iam sol recedit igneus* is by a different author (perhaps St. Ambrose) and refers to the Trinity and to praising God in the morning and evening:

"As fades the glowing orb of day,
To Thee, great source of light, we pray;
Blest Three in One, to every heart
Thy beams of life and love impart.
At early dawn, at close of day,
To Thee our vows we humbly pay;
May we, mid joys that never end,
With Thy bright Saints in homage bend."[24]

What makes the retention of these hymns in the *editio typica* of the revised breviary of particular note is that in the present structure for evening prayer the third "psalm" is actually a Christological hymn from the New Testament, two of which (Col 1:12-20 and Eph 1:3-10) deal specifically with praise for creation. One could make a case for the appropriate juxtaposition at this hour of praise for the days of creation and for our recreation in Christ. Because these hymns specify Christ in connection with praise for creation any "generic deism" associating the Christian God with creation is avoided.

The text of Colossians 1:12-20 is particularly notable acclaiming Christ as

"the image of the invisible God,
    the first-born of all creatures.
In him everything in heaven and on earth was created,
    things visible and invisible,
    whether thrones or dominations, principalities or powers;
All were created through him, and for him" (vv. 16-17).

The text from Ephesians 1:3-10 is also notable since it contains the verses:

"Praised be the God and Father of our Lord Jesus Christ
    who has bestowed on us in Christ
    every spiritual blessing in the heavens!" (v. 3).

"God has given us the wisdom to understand fully the mystery,
    the plan he was pleased to decree in Christ,
    to be carried out in the fullness of time: namely,
To bring all things in the heavens and on earth
    into one under Christ's headship" (vv. 9-10).

At Sunday morning prayer the use of the canticle from Daniel 3 (vv. 57-88, 56 are used Sunday week 1 and vv. 52-57 are used Sunday weeks 2 and 4) is significant in this connection. The opening verse

"Bless the Lord, all you works of the Lord
    praise and exalt him above all forever" (v 57)

is followed by a series of acclamations citing various facets of creation and redemption as motives for praising God. These include verses about praise for creation.

"Sun and moon, bless the Lord;
  stars of heaven, bless the Lord.
Every shower and dew, bless the Lord;
  all you winds, bless the Lord" (vv. 62-64).

and for redemption

"Blessed are you, and praiseworthy,
  O Lord, the God of our Fathers,
  and glorious forever is your name.
For you are just in all you have done;
  all your deeds are faultless,
  all your ways right" (vv. 26-27).

Praise for redemption ends the canticle:

"Hananiah, Azariah, Mishael,
  bless the Lord;
  praise and exalt him above all forever.
For he has delivered us from the nether world,
  and saved us from the power of death;
he has freed us from the raging flame
  and delivered us from the fire.
Give thanks to the Lord, for he is good,
  for his mercy endures forever.
Bless the God of gods,
  all you who fear the Lord;
praise him and give him thanks,
  because his mercy endures forever" (vv. 88-90).

These same motives for praising God are found in much of the
psalter, and in the present arrangement of the Hours a "praise
psalm" is used as the third psalm at morning prayer many of
which contain explicit praise of God for creation (e.g., Pss 19, 29,
65, 147, 148, 150).[25]

Two phrases from the *Te Deum* (used at the conclusion of the office of readings on most Sundays and solemnities) capture and
summarize this theology:

"All creation worships you. . . .
Holy, holy, holy, Lord, God of power and might,
heaven and earth are full of your glory."

Fittingly, these last two lines are repeated in the preface acclamation (*Sanctus*) in the present Eucharistic prayers which prayers themselves reflect the theme of praising God for creation and redemption derived from the *berakah* and *todah* traditions of Jewish prayer.[26] That this acclamation combines praise for creation with praise for redemption, specifying the obedient life, death, and resurrection of Jesus, is notable since this combination of themes is part of the "classical" shape of Eucharistic anaphoras.[27] It also appears in the present prefaces and Eucharistic prayers in the Roman liturgy (even though this is sometimes all too brief).[28]

The theology operative in the fourth Eucharistic prayer in the present Sacramentary[29] concerns praising God who has made all things and who is the source of all life.

"The creation motif [in the fourth eucharistic prayer] brings out the universal need for the paschal mystery, and the universal effects which are intended to flow from the paschal mystery [and it] gives cosmic dimensions to the ritual of the eucharist both in regard to its meaning and its intended effects. The cosmic meaning is brought out in the cosmic praise of the preface; the cosmic effects are seen in the petitions and eschatological conclusion of the prayer after the institution narrative."[30]

The preface to this prayer refers to the entire creation and to the Father as the ultimate source of creation and the one who is manifested in creation. The purpose of creation and how human beings can fulfill that purpose is by joining in the praise that is voiced in the Eucharistic liturgy. It is a worldview in a capsule form. "Because of the goodness of the Father, the Church joins in the hymn of the angels. All other creatures on earth are enabled to express their praise through the voices of those in the Church who speak for the mute creatures. Thus the praise takes on cosmic proportions."[31]

An important example in a classical Eastern Eucharistic prayer of how praising God for creation functions as a motive for giving thanks and recounting the fall establishes why humanity needed a savior, is found in the *Apostolic Constitutions* Book VIII.[32] It is significant that the breadth of this prayer concerns praising God for creation, for sustaining in life all that God has created, for the history of salvation and for sending Jesus as our redeemer. This

Christological section capitalizes on a number of paradoxes notably the statement that he who was present at creation is acclaimed as "the firstborn of all creation."

The value of creation in reflecting the power of God and as the arena where divine salvation overturns universal estrangement from God as used liturgically is exemplified (as already noted) by the selection of the first creation account, Genesis 1:1–2:2 as the first reading at the Easter Vigil. Its annual proclamation at Easter underscores the notion that creation happens still among us through Christ, even as we yearn for the "new heavens and a new earth." The texts of both prayers that follow this reading at the Easter Vigil are significant in this regard:

"Almighty and eternal God,
you created all things in wonderful beauty and order.
Help us now to perceive
how still more wonderful is the new creation
by which in the fullness of time
you redeemed your people
through the sacrifice of our passover, Jesus Christ.[33]

"Lord God,
the creation of man was a wonderful work,
his redemption still more wonderful.
May we persevere in right reason
against all that entices to sin
and so attain to everlasting joy."[34]

The Roman Catholic principle and doctrine of the sacramentality of creation is closely linked with the principle of Incarnation—that God is revealed through created means, including the human, and that salvation for the human race came through the Incarnation of God's Son. The sacramentality of creation and of the Incarnation underscores the discoverability of God in human life and explains why created things are used both as a motivation and a means to praise and worship God.

The mediating function of creation is exemplified in its specific *Christological* sense in the liturgical use of such Scripture texts (as already noted) as the Johannine prologue (John 1:1-14) used on Christmas day and in the Christological hymn in the letter to the Colossians (1:15-20, specifically verses 15-18). According to the

Johannine prologue God's creative idea is the Logos, the second divine person. The "high" Christology of the pre-existent Logos in the prologue and the introductory words of the prologue "in the beginning" combine to underscore how Christ was present and active at the creation of the world. Verse 3 summarizes this by stating "through him all things came into being, and apart from him nothing came to be." The recreation of the world was accomplished through the same Christ, cited at the prologue's end as "the Word [who] became flesh, and made his dwelling among us, and we have seen his glory, filled with enduring love" (v. 14).

This emphasis on the Christological axis of liturgy, specifically the paschal mystery, has recently been appropriately supplemented by a pneumatologically informed emphasis on liturgy and sacraments as experiences through and in which the Church is drawn into the life of the triune God. All liturgy incorporates the Church into the triune God. It is the triune God who makes liturgy occur. Just as Jürgen Moltmann can rightly argue that creation is the result of the power and life of the Spirit, thus ending what perhaps can be regarded as too Christological an approach to how God creates,[35] so we can emphasize how the liturgy is dependent on the dynamism of the Trinity (particularly when understood both immanently and economically).[36] The renewed emphasis on the theological meaning of the epiclesis in the Eucharistic anaphoras added to the Roman rite in the present reform and in all other blessing prayers (e.g., to bless water at initiation, etc.) gives added stimulus to the theological elaboration of the role of the Trinity, and particularly of the Spirit, in all liturgy. It is the triune God who gathers the assembly into the praying Church ("the family you have gathered here before you").[37] In addition to the use of the indicative mood in verbs in the anaphora, the use of the subjunctive characterizes the epiclesis. When the text of the second Eucharistic prayer reads:

"Let your Spirit come upon these gifts to make them holy,
so that they may become for us
the body and blood of our Lord, Jesus Christ. . . .
May all of us who share in the body and blood of Christ
be brought together in the unity of the Holy Spirit"[38]

The *lex orandi* of the Roman rite overcomes the weakness of the lack of an explicit epiclesis in the Roman canon and draws on a wider euchological tradition to substantiate the addition of such texts which explicitly invoke the Spirit with the deferential verb form the subjunctive.[39] Such usages illustrate the central importance of understanding liturgy as initiated by, sustained in and reaching its perfection in the Trinity.

Explicit faith in the Trinity is also illustrated in the creed:[40]

"Credo in unum Deum,
Patrem omnipotentem, factorem caeli et terrae
visibilium omnium et invisibilium.
Et in unum Dominum Iesum Christum . . .
per quem omnia facta sunt. . . .
Et in Spiritum Sanctum, Dominum et vivificantem."

Thus, the act of creation is not limited to the Father; it is equally Christological and pneumatological. Further, the intrinsic link between praise of God for creation and the triune God substantiates both a central motive for liturgy and means of praising God, creation, and the experience of the triune God in creation and in worship.

II. Symbolic Engagement

In this section symbol is understood to be both *text* and *context*. It is *text* because it is a constitutive element of liturgy. It is *context* because the use of symbol and gesture in liturgy (symbolic engagement) is constitutive of the act of liturgy with the use of symbols most often accompanied by (principally euchological) liturgical texts.[41]

When interpreted together, symbols and the texts of blessing prayers comprise what conventional sacramental theology has called the "matter" and "form" of sacramental action. One contribution of Roman Catholicism to the tradition of liturgy and sacraments has been the retention, albeit minimal at times, of symbolic engagement in liturgy. That the present reformed liturgy calls for enhanced emphasis on symbol is really to restore and to emphasize what liturgical tradition has presumed and what Roman Catholicism has retained. In this discussion of symbol in liturgy, which discussion presumes and deepens the previous discussion of the importance of creation in worship, a distinction is made between the use of things "of the earth" and things "made by human hands." Thus a proper liturgical theology rests on the importance attached to the use of creation in worship as well as to things manufactured through human ingenuity.

A basic premise of this section is that symbolic elements used in worship: earth, air, fire, water, oil, bread and wine etc., ground the complementary symbolic gestures of movement, bathing, baking bread, pouring wine, dining, touching, and salving with oil. These symbolic gestures comprise an essential part of the anthropological foundation of liturgical rites. Symbols and symbolic gestures used in liturgy reflect and are derived from actions performed in human life. In the words of David Power these actions are "daily and domestic things."[42] This is to say, for example, that water as a symbol is important for the act of bathing, that bread and wine are important for the act of dining and the embrace is important as a sign of relatedness and reconciliation. This means that "gestural speech" and "symbolic action" are essential to and constitutive of liturgy and liturgical theology.[43]

Thus what is central here is the *use* of symbols and *symbolic engagement* in worship, as opposed to *objectification* of symbols or their reduction to being *signs* since (customarily today) both objectification and signs convey *one* meaning and have a one-to-one correspondence with what they signify. Symbols and symbolic gestures, on the other hand, by their nature are polyvalent and have many meanings. The polyvalent meanings intrinsically attached to symbolic engagement are all unleashed in liturgy by the very fact that symbols and symbolic actions are used. These meanings, both positive or negative, are many. Gordon Lathrop's comment about Eucharist is helpful in this connection. "The meal is both the thanksgiving and the eating and drinking. The thanksgiving prayer gives words to what happens in communion. The eating and drinking is always more than the prayer can say."[44]

In the celebration of sacraments some of these meanings are articulated in the blessing prayers that accompany symbolic usage. Hence the theological value of euchology. Generally these meanings are derived from salvation history as these events are paradigmatic or applicable in the present experience of salvation through liturgy. These meanings from salvation history most often articulate obvious positive meanings or they give a positive dimension to what could be understood as a negative meaning. (For example, in the following discussion about the use of water in baptism the Genesis account of Noah's ark is treated as a victory: "the waters of the great flood you made a sign of the waters of baptism that make an end to sin and a new beginning of goodness.") The variety of meanings present in such texts, when appropriated into a liturgical theology of what is celebrated, give direction to the polyvalent meanings inherent in the use of water. One can receive new life from water to slake one's thirst; one can also drown in it.

In addition, the use of symbols has the effect of expressing what is really inexpressible, that liturgy is the act of being drawn into the mystery of God in ways that invite believers into an ever deepening relationship with God in the manifold ways that salvation is imaged and reflected in such texts. Hence the use of water in initiation is meant to evoke its pluriform meanings, to draw those bathed in it into a relationship with God, through Christ's paschal mystery in the power of the Spirit enacted in the Church.

In our argument, therefore, priority is always given to symbolic engagement and liturgical participation through symbol as these means are used to draw the community to share more fully in the mystery that is God, which communion is imaged in a number of ways and experienced through the use of symbol. This is to suggest that the objectification of given symbolic elements used in liturgy, for example bread and wine for the Eucharist, can paradoxically diminish the *reality content* of the symbols upon which sacramental liturgy and liturgical theology is based for at least two reasons. First, because symbolic elements complement the symbolic Word as essentially dialogical realities, to emphasize symbols as objects reduces the essentially dialogic character of consecrated bread and wine as a specification of having shared in the proclaimed Word, which itself is inherently dialogical. This is to assert that the act of Communion signifies the ratification on the participant's part of the offer of Christ through these symbolic means. Bread and wine have been consecrated in order to be eaten by those who participate. That this is a traditional tenet of Roman Catholic theology and practice is seen in the canons of the Council of Trent which note that the Eucharist, by its nature, is "to be received" (*ut sumatur [cf. Mt 26, 26ss] insitiutum*, DS 1643). "To put it another way: the first truth of the eucharistic doctrine is, 'this is my body,' not 'here I am present'."[45] Second, because the presumed ecclesial community, for whom symbols function in

144

liturgy, is normally left out of the theology based on objectified symbols (e.g., real presence) there is a diminished ecclesiological aspect to Eucharistic theology. This is all the more jarring when most Eucharistic prayers now contain explicit epicleses about drawing the Church community into greater unity, which prayers are legitimately used to illustrate the (often termed "Augustinian") emphasis on Church unity as illustrated through Eucharistic sharing and as specified in other euchological texts such as the prayers over the gifts and prayers after Communion.[46] It is also jarring in light of the conciliar and postconciliar texts about Christ's presence in the Church, the Word, the person of the minister, and in the Eucharistic species.[47] Thus in our understanding the operative notion of symbol in the liturgy is dynamic, involving and ultimately transformative of the community. Consequently the liturgical theology derived from symbols used in the *context* of the whole liturgy simply cannot concern "objects" alone.

From another perspective it is important to view *active participation* and *symbolic engagement* as essential aspects of the *ecclesial enactment* of liturgy. This emphasis is far different from understandings of the liturgy drawn from the theater, for example, which would separate "actors" and "spectators" and which would leave the assembly quite passive. The restored emphasis on the community's active participation in the doing of liturgy necessarily has its complement theologically in the reality that through its liturgical participation, specifically by its sharing more and more fully in the high priesthood of Christ made available through the liturgy, the community is progressively transformed into the body of Christ.

This is to suggest that "active participation" means more than *doing something* in the liturgy. On a more fundamental level it means that *God does something among us* at liturgy, namely, to allow us *to take part in* and to become *partakers* and *sharers in* the priesthood of Christ. Hence liturgical activity is to be understood as a way of responding to God's initiative in the act of worship, the major component of which is to draw us into, and to enable us to share more and more fully in, the high priesthood of Christ. Hence there are no "spectators" or "only hearers" at liturgy. One advantage of the present reformed rites is that they presume the active participation in the rites through word, song, gesture, and movement.[48] A helpful derivative theologically is exploring the meaning of participation in terms of *taking part in* the mystery of the living God.

We turn now to the present *lex orandi* in order to exemplify the importance attached to the use of symbol in liturgy and the theological meanings derived from it.

Water: Symbolic Use and Theological Meanings. Our methodological concern in this section is merely to illustrate the importance of the *use* of symbols in liturgy as derived from the General Instruction of a given rite and from the liturgical ritual itself. The specific example chosen is *water* as described and used in the present Rite of the Christian Initiation of Adults.[49] In line with our thesis the theological point illustrated here is that the combined use of symbol and text discloses part of the *context* that provides the *text* from which to develop the theology of liturgy of a given rite and the theology of a given symbol.

1. Symbolic Use. The General Instruction on Christian Initiation[50] states that "the water used in baptism should be true water and, both for the sake of authentic sacramental symbolism and for hygienic reasons, [it] should be pure and clean" (n. 8). "The baptismal font . . . should be spotlessly clean and of pleasing design" (n. 9). These texts overturn centuries of usage (from Trent on) when the baptismal water blessed at the Easter Vigil was stored in baptisteries to be used for a whole year. Water's freshness and life-giving properties are underscored in this rubrical change. Now, the water blessed at Easter is used only during the Easter season in which case a "thanksgiving" prayer for water already blessed is used when baptisms occur.

The Instruction goes on to explain how the water will be used in the act of water baptism: "either immersion, which is more suitable as a symbol of participation in the death and resurrection of Christ, or pouring may lawfully be used" (n. 22). By its very nature as symbol, water is polyvalent expressing both positive and negative associations. It evokes washing, cleansing, refreshment, purification, and an end of thirst (hence the continuance of life). It also evokes images of the uncontrollable force of storms, torrents, the realm of demons, and the place of drowning (hence the loss of life). In using water, the act of baptism carries with it these (and many other) associations. The fact that such a symbol can be ambivalent lends support to the need for texts to direct its appropriation in liturgy. Water's positive directionality at baptism comes from its use in association with the combination of Scripture texts, blessing prayers as well as other references in the rite to its lifegiving character. The very fact that water can signify both sustaining life and the destruction of life makes it all the more poignant as the symbol used in baptism to signify Christ's triumph over sin and death and the means through which believers are initiated into the faith community that stands against sin and death.

The rite for adult initiation offers three texts for blessing the water and two for offering thanksgiving for the blessed water. The rubrics for the first of these prayers state that toward the end of the prayer (after recounting a host of images about the use of water in salvation history) the celebrant "touches the water with his right hand." This simple rubric suggests that the freshness and life-giving properties of water are to be noted by hearing and seeing the water move; it thus becomes "living" water. The text that accompanies this gesture derives from Romans 6:3-11, a correlation that is particularly important when this passage and this blessing are used together at the Easter Vigil:

"We ask you, Father, with your Son
to send the Holy Spirit upon the waters of this font.
May all who are buried with Christ in the death of baptism
rise also with him to newness of life" (222 A).

The rite for adult initiation also states that the celebration of baptism takes place at "the baptismal font, if this is in view of the faithful; otherwise in the sanctuary, where a vessel of water for the rite should be prepared beforehand" (218). These explicit directions indicate the value of communal participation in the use of water in the liturgy of baptism. That pluriform meanings attend to the liturgical use of symbol is exemplified in the discussion to follow on water as used in the rite of adult initiation.

2. Theological Meanings. After the rubrics to the RCIA state that "water is God's creation" it immediately describes the "sacramental use of water" as important for the "unfolding of the paschal mystery" in water baptism and in remembering "God's wonderful works in the history of salvation" (210). It then invokes "the Holy Trinity at the very outset of the celebration of baptism" calling to

147

"mind the mystery of God's love from the beginning of the world and the creation of the human race." "By invoking the Holy Spirit and proclaiming Christ's death and resurrection, [the use of water] impresses on the mind the newness of Christian baptism, by which we share in his own death and resurrection and receive the holiness of God himself" (210). The importance of water is cited in the introduction to the Litany of the Saints which states: "may [God] give them the new life of the Holy Spirit, whom we are about to call down on this water" (220). In both thanksgiving prayers the term "consecrated water" leads to the designation of the effects to be derived from it:

"by the mystery of this consecrated water
lead them to a new and spiritual birth" (222 D, E).

The act of baptizing in water is described in no fewer than five places as *washing*. In light of our thesis it is important to point out that this designation is set within a ritual of *bathing* in water, which symbolic act is most notable through immersion. The rite states clearly that "the celebration of baptism has as its center and high point the baptismal washing and the invocation of the Holy Trinity. Beforehand there are rites that have an inherent relationship to the baptismal washing . . ." (209). At the conclusion of the preparatory rites on Holy Saturday the final blessing of the elect draws on the example of the "holy prophets" who proclaimed to all who draw near to God "wash and be cleansed." The result of this washing is "rebirth in the Spirit," being "reborn as [God's] children" and entering "the community of [God's] church" (203). During the rite, immediately after the profession of faith, the elect experience Christ's paschal mystery "as expressed in the washing with water" (212). The rubrics state that "the washing with water should take on its full importance as the sign of that mystical sharing in Christ's death and resurrection through which those who believe in his name die to sin and rise to eternal life." It then places immersion before infusion as the way to administer the baptismal washing (as stated also in 226) which usages are to be understood not as a mere "purification rite but the sacrament of being joined to Christ" (213). The second form of the blessing prayer also capitalizes on the notion of washing by asking God to

148

"make holy this water which you have created,
so that all who are baptized in it may be washed clean of sin
and born again to live as your children" (222 B).

The allied usage of baptismal *cleansing* also finds a prominent
place in four of the blessing prayers. In one text God is praised
for having "created water to cleanse and give life" (222 B). Three
others end with the same phrase

"you have called your children . . .
to this cleansing water and new birth . . ." (222 C, D, E).

Both options for the exorcism to be prayed over the elect at the
first scrutiny capitalize on the gospel of the Samaritan woman
(John 4:5-42) proclaimed that day:

"Grant that these catechumens,
who, like the woman of Samaria, thirst for living water . . ."
   (154 A).

"Now, by your power,
free these elect from the cunning of Satan,
as they draw near to the fountain of living water" (154 B).

The prayer over the elect at the presentation of the Lord's Prayer
adapts the "living water" image by stating:

"Deepen the faith and understanding
of these elect, chosen for baptism.
Give them new birth in your living waters,
so that they may be numbered among your adopted children"
   (182).

The scriptural allusion to Jesus' crucifixion in John 19:34 "and immediately blood and water poured out" (and, at least indirectly
for what some regard as more direct sacramental symbolism, 1
John 5:8 "there are three witnesses, the Spirit, the water, and the
blood"[51]) is incorporated into two of the three blessing prayers for
water and in one of the two thanksgiving prayers for water already blessed. The texts state:

"Your Son willed that water and blood should flow from his side as he hung upon the cross" (222 A).

"Praise to you, Lord Jesus Christ, the Father's only Son, for you offered yourself on the cross, that in the blood and water flowing from your side and through your death and resurrection the Church might be born" (222 B; repeated in 222 D).

It is also used in the prayer accompanying the anointing after baptism when confirmation is separated from baptism. The text states:

"The God of power and Father of Our Lord Jesus Christ has freed you from sin and brought you to new life through water and the Holy Spirit. He now anoints you with the chrism of salvation, so that, united with his people, you may remain for ever a member of Christ who is Priest, Prophet and King" (228).[52]

The description of what results from the use of water at baptism is stated in the General Instruction on Christian Initiation: "this first sacrament pardons all our sins, rescues us from the power of darkness, and brings us to the dignity of adopted children, a new creation through water and the Holy Spirit" (n. 2).[53] The rite itself cites "life," "new life," "new birth" and "rebirth" resulting from baptism as seen in the texts:

"May he give them the new life of the Holy Spirit whom we are about to call down upon this water" (220).

"Praise to you, almighty God and Father, for you have created water to cleanse and to give life" (222 D).

". . . by water and the Holy Spirit you freed your sons and daughters from sin and gave them new life" (234).

"By the power of the Holy Spirit give to this water the grace of your Son, so that in the sacrament of baptism all those whom you have created in your likeness

150

may be cleansed from sin
and rise to a new birth of innocence . . ." (222 A).

"You have called your children, N. and N.,
to this cleansing water and new birth . . ." (222 C, D, E).

"We pray for these your servants,
who eagerly approach the waters of new birth
and hunger for the banquet of life" (175 B).

"Let us pray for these elect, that God in his mercy may make them responsive to his love, so that through the waters of rebirth they may receive pardon for their sins and have life in Christ Jesus our Lord" (182).

"Give them new birth in your living waters,
so that they may be numbered among your adopted children"
(182).

"As proclaimed in the prayers for the blessing of the water, baptism is a cleansing water of rebirth that makes us God's children born from on high" (GI, CI, 5).

It is clear from this methodological example about only one aspect of the *lex orandi* for adult initiation that the revised rites offer a wealth of material from which to develop a liturgical theology of baptism. The value placed on creation is implicit throughout the rite for its purifying properties. The theological meaning of sharing in the paschal mystery is reiterated throughout the rite; it is particularly clear when water baptism is done by immersion. Thus we have exemplified the crucial role that symbolic usage plays in the doing of sacraments and in theological reflection about through this mining this example of the Church's *lex orandi*.

III. Symbols in Context

The purpose of this section is to consider two of the more important and frequently used symbols of the liturgy—light and bread and wine (treated together)—as examples of how their use in different settings—*contexts*—helps to draw out the meaning of these intrinsically polyvalent realities. Our thesis *context is text* is operative here in two ways. First, the way *light* is used liturgically in its *varying contexts* helps toward developing a liturgical theology of light as symbol. Second, the consideration of bread and wine at the Eucharist derives both from how these elements came into existence as the result of "the work of human hands" and from how they are used in liturgy.

1. *"Natural" Symbol—Light.* In this section two facets of the light symbolism are discussed. The first concerns the light in creation and how it is referred to in the liturgy. The second concerns the use of candles in worship.

a. LIGHT IN NATURE. It was argued in the first section of this chapter that one of the determining factors for the times of celebrating hours of prayer as well as some feasts and seasons is the location of the sun and moon. Hence light and darkness form part of the cosmic symbolism intrinsic to the liturgy, the appreciation of which helps to draw out the complete meaning of a feast or season and the place of each in the liturgical year. (Recall the comment already made about the presumption of the northern hemisphere here.)

The phenomenon of diminishing daylight and heat in the winter establishes the cosmic context for the references to light in the Advent liturgy. "Light" is used to offer hope at the very moment when natural light and heat diminish. To pray "O Radiant Dawn, splendor of eternal light, sun of justice: come, shine on those who dwell in darkness and the shadow of death" (ICEL translation) as the antiphon to the Canticle of the Blessed Virgin Mary at evening prayer on December 21 is particularly poignant since this is the day of daylight's shortest duration. This and all the other "O" antiphons (used from December 17 through 23) give shape to the kind of savior whom we await in Advent: *O sapientia,* "wisdom of our God Most High," *O Adonai,* "leader of ancient Israel," *O radix Jesse,* "flower of Jesse's stem," *O Clavis David,* "key of David," *O Oriens, splendor lucis aeternae, et sol justitia* "radiant dawn splendor of eternal light, sun of justice," *O Rex gentium,* "king of all nations" and *O Emmanuel,* "Emmanuel" in the antiphons to Mary's canticle on these Advent evenings helps to focus on the kind Messiah whom we await in this season.[54]

However, in addition to the meanings of these antiphons from salvation history[55] other meanings derive from their *context* in the liturgy, both past and present. Thus the use of the antiphon welcoming the "radiant dawn" at evening prayer on December 21 in the present (and immediately past) Liturgy of the Hours draws on the cosmic symbolism of early sunset and the hope of a slightly later sunset the next day.[56]

The importance of *context* is also evident in the fact that in the present Lectionary for Mass the same seven "O" antiphons are now offered for use as the alleluia verse before the gospel from December 17 through the morning of the 24th. In this case they can be used in succession to complement their usage the same evening, or the verses can be chosen to coincide with the gospel of the day they introduce. In this case one could choose the text "Come, Emmanuel" (from the antiphon used at evening prayer on December 23) as the alleluia verse on December 18 when the gospel at Mass is Matt 1:18-24 containing the text "and they shall call him 'Emmanuel' (Matt 1:23)." Alternatively the *O Oriens* antiphon could be the alleluia verse on the morning of December 24 when the gospel is Zechariah's canticle from Luke 1:67-79 with the text "the dawn from on high shall break upon us."

Still another level of meaning for these texts derives from the musical notation to which they were set. In the *Liber Usualis* all the "O" antiphons were accompanied by impressive chant settings. (Guéranger calls them chants "replete with melodious gravity"[57]). To interpret these antiphons as fully as possibly as liturgical texts would require attention to the musical settings for these texts, specifically whether such chant settings are used and whether the same (or any) music is used when the texts function as antiphons at vespers and as alleluia verses preceding the gospel at Mass. Our thesis *context is text* is thus clearly applicable, and to our way of thinking, necessary to interpret these texts.

b. CANDLE/LIGHT. Two of the most prominent examples of light symbolism attached to the liturgical use of candles are the feast of the Presentation of the Lord and the Easter Vigil.[58] On the Presentation the rubrics state that everyone present carries candles which are lighted before the liturgy begins. The very use of candles is significant. These are commodities whose purpose is to shed light and, by their nature to be totally consumed in the act of being burnt. The purpose of the candle is to be burned, consumed. It is a complete oblation. Sacrificial overtones of complete self-offering are thus operative because of the nature of the candle as symbol.[59] Other themes expressed in the euchology about hope, the universality of salvation and the splendor of Christ's light overcoming the darkness of sin (coinciding with increasing daylight in the northern hemisphere at this time of year) are all set against the symbolic use of lighted candles.

The antiphon sung when the assembly has gathered outside the church acclaiming the "Lord [who] will come with mighty power and give light to the eyes of all who serve him" sets the stage for what is to follow. The introduction to the blessing of the candles (which can be adapted in accord with the rubric "in these or similar words") refers to the feast of Christmas forty days prior, to the presentation of Jesus in the Temple in the presence of Simeon and Anna and (in themes reminiscent of Advent) to recognizing the Lord "in the house of God . . . [until Christ the Lord] comes again in his glory." The blessing prayer itself acclaims God as "source of all light" and recalls that on this day Simeon welcomed the "light of revelation to all nations." In it we pray:

"May we who carry them to praise your glory
walk in the path of goodness
and come to the light that shines for ever."[60]

The alternative text touches on these same themes. Of particular note in both is the strong eschatological note of coming to share eternal joy and the light of God's glory. The lighted candles are then carried in procession into the church while verses of the Canticle of Simeon (Luke 2:29-32) are sung (the same canticle sung daily at night prayer) with the important phrase:

"A light to reveal you to the nations
and the glory of your people Israel" (v. 32).

The central part of the proper preface for the Presentation is a succinct summary of the themes of this feast:

"Today your Son,
who shares your eternal splendor
was presented in the temple,
and revealed by the Spirit
as the glory of Israel
and the light of all peoples."[61]

During the spring light symbolism is capitalized on during Lent and Easter, particularized through the Easter season in the paschal candle. In fact, the only required addition to the liturgical environment over and above that normally used for the celebration of the Eucharist that is ever required is the placing of the paschal candle in a prominent location from after the Easter Vigil through Pentecost. The gospel proclamation of the curing of the man born blind (John 9) on the fourth Sunday of Lent A cycle, and the complementary exorcism texts at the scrutiny of the elect this day (RCIA 168 A, B) are traditional elements of the Roman liturgy recently restored for contemporary use. These references set up the symbolism of light at the Easter Vigil which is celebrated "at night." (Even the title of the celebration in the Sacramentary states: "Easter Sunday, During the Night, The Easter Vigil".)

The very first part of the liturgy is called the "service of light" with the community gathered outside the church building. The Sacramentary states that "candles should be prepared for all who take part in the vigil." These are lighted for the first time during the procession with the Easter candle. They are then relighted for the renewal of baptismal promises during the liturgy of baptism.

The first prayer of this liturgy is the blessing of the fire outside the church, which text capitalizes on the darkness experienced at night and the hope deriving from Christ "the light of the world."

"Father,
we share in the light of your glory
through your Son, the light of the world.
Make this new fire holy, and inflame us with new hope.
Purify our minds by this Easter celebration
and bring us one day to the feast of eternal light."[62]

The references in this succinct prayer deriving from the light symbolism are most notable. When these images are expressed with the assembly gathered outdoors in darkness around the new fire—context—images such as "light of the world," "new fire," "inflame us," "purify" and "feast of eternal light" are all the more poignant.

As he lights the Easter candle from the new fire the priest says:

"May the light of Christ, rising in glory,
dispel the darkness of our hearts and minds."

The sung acclamation "Christ our light," repeated three times, accompanies and articulates the meaning of the procession into the church. During the procession everyone lights individual candles, the experience of which shows how single candles when combined radiate enormous light. The fact that candles are used leads to an experience that stimulates both emotions and imagination as this light is at the same time enticing and warming as well as clarifying of the path the assembly walks into the church. The experience of the Easter candle and the candlelight from everyone's individual candles in a darkened church is provocative and draws on the assembly's emotions and imagination.

This procession ends with the assembly in place and to the deacon's singing of the *Exsultet*, salient phrases of which refer to the light symbolism. Again our understanding of *context* enters here since the *Exsultet* has traditionally been sung to a chant melody that has been considered particularly beautiful.[63] A proper interpretation of this *text* requires attention to its *context* in terms of the way it is sung today, specifically whether this reflects the beauty of the traditional chant or whether new settings enhance themes not emphasized in the former setting.

Most verses of the proclamation refer to or capitalize on the darkness/light theme which references are all the more striking when heard in a church illuminated only by candlelight. Among these are the phrases:

"Rejoice, O earth, in shining splendor,
    radiant in the brightness of your King! . . .
The risen Savior shines upon you! . . .
[My dearest friends, standing with me in this holy light. . . .]
This is the night
    when first you saved our fathers. . . .
    when the pillar of fire
        destroyed the darkness of sin! . . .
    when Christians everywhere, washed clean of sin. . . .
    when Jesus Christ broke the chains of death. . . .
Most blessed of all nights, chosen by God
    to see Christ rising from the dead!
    Of this night scripture says:
        'The night will be as clear as day:
        it will become my light, my joy.' . . .
The power of this holy night
    dispels all evil, washes guilt away. . . .

Night truly blessed when heaven is wedded to earth. . . .
Therefore, heavenly Father, in the joy of this night. . . .
Accept this Easter candle,
  a flame divided but not undimmed,
  a pillar of fire that glows to the honor of God.
Let it mingle with the lights of heaven . . .
  to dispel the darkness of this night!
May the Morning Star which never sets find this flame still
    burning:
  Christ, the Morning Star, who came back from the dead,
  and shed his peaceful light on all mankind. . . .''

It should also be recalled that in the first reading of the Easter
Vigil (Gen 1:1-2:2) God's act of creating begins with the command
''Let there be light.'' Hence the value of underscoring the light
symbolism of the opening prayer of this vigil liturgy as contextualized by the night vigil's being held in darkness, by the striking of
the new fire, by the lighting of the Easter candle, by the dissemi-
nation of candlelight to individual candles and to the creation account beginning with its reference to light. The prayer states:

''Lord God,
you have brightened this night
with the radiance of the risen Christ.
Quicken the spirit of sonship in your Church;
renew us in mind and body
to give you whole-hearted service.''[64]

2. ''Manufactured'' symbols—Bread and Wine. In addition to symbols from creation, the liturgy uses symbols which are the result
of the ''work of human hands,'' among which are bread and
wine. In accord with our thesis about context the argument in this
section concerns how the human manufacture of bread and wine
is understood to be a part of the context for these symbols. What
is argued here is not meant to ignore the indigenization issue concerning whether bread and wine ought not be replaced by other
foods—making the phrase ''substantial food and festive drink''
more suitable in such discussions.

In a very helpful study Philippe Rouillard has argued that the
institution of the Eucharist during the course of a meal ''is deeply

rooted in a human action indispensable to life and . . . rich in human and sacred symbolism: eating and drinking and having a meal."[65] In treating the "symbolism of bread and wine" Rouillard asserts that these "fundamental elements of the nourishment of people in the Mediterranean basin . . . are rich in symbolism"[66] and that their manufacture relies on the cycle of "dying and rising" in nature,[67] which symbolism is most fitting to symbolize the dying and rising of Jesus. These elements rely on the agrarian cycle and the cosmic symbolism of planting seed, which then "die" in the earth to mature in stalks of wheat and bunches of grapes. At their harvesting they "die" once again by being picked and then crushed to produce the raw material of wheat flour and grape juice. Other ingredients are then added to the flour, especially yeast, to make the dough which rises (at least once) and after baking becomes bread. The liquid derived from crushing the grapes is preserved in casks to mature and thus to become wine. These "produced" elements are then taken as the most apt symbols to use to commemorate the death and resurrection of Jesus in the Eucharistic meal. These elements of nourishment are then consecrated as the Eucharistic food to nourish the Church.

The key to interpreting these elements is human ingenuity and productivity. In other words, the cycle of dying and rising and the "work" of human labor, because they are intrinsic to the bread and wine used for the Eucharist, form part of the *context* for Christian Eucharist. The General Instruction on the Roman Missal states that "following the example of Christ, the Church has always used bread and wine with water to celebrate the Lord's Supper" (n. 281). It then states that

"the nature of the sign demands that the material for the eucharistic celebration truly have the appearance of food. [E]ven though unleavened and baked in the traditional shape, the eucharistic bread should be made in such a way that . . . the priest is able actually to break the host into parts and distribute them to at least some of the faithful. . . . The action of the breaking of the bread, the simple term for the eucharist in apostolic times, will more clearly bring out the force and meaning of the sign of the unity of all in the one bread and of their charity, since the one bread is being distributed among the members of one family." (n. 283)

Hence we can argue that both our overall thesis about *context* and our thesis about *symbolic usage* are borne out in the Eucharistic species in two ways. First, the *context* for the celebration of the Eucharist requires that cycles of nature and human manufacture together form the source for the Eucharistic symbols. Second, the consecrated bread and wine are designated for *symbolic usage* in the liturgy in such a way that the symbolism of breaking and sharing from the one bread and one cup in the Church assembly (as found in 1 Cor 11 and repeated in numberless patristic and subsequent descriptions of the Eucharist)[68] is the focal point toward which consecration and transformation leads.

In addition the *use* of the Eucharist in varying settings draws out different theological emphases. For example, the celebration of the Eucharist as part of the Easter Vigil is the clearest symbolic usage of the "first-fruits" of the new creation. The rubrics state that the Eucharist is only given as viaticum on Holy Saturday and that the bread and wine to be used at the vigil are "brought forward by the newly baptized." Behind these rubrical guidelines is the understanding of the end of the "old leaven" (signifying our former way of life) and the beginning of the new leaven with new Eucharistic breads (signifying new life in the risen Christ). Just as the feast of unleavened bread in pre-existing rituals was historicized by Judaism into the Passover feast, so the Jewish practice of unleavened bread was historicized and spiritualized by Christianity to refer to the "unleavened bread of sincerity and truth" (1 Cor 5:8). This symbolism is sustained by the use of this same verse as part of one of the options for the second reading on Easter Sunday from 1 Corinthians 5:6-8 (part of which is the Communion antiphon for the vigil, 1 Cor 5:7-8).

Other contexts for the celebration of the Eucharist draw out other theological meanings. These include the motif of the renewal of the covenant of baptism since the cup-word at the institution narrative speaks about "the new and everlasting covenant." Sunday Eucharist is particularly noteworthy in this regard when the rite of blessing and sprinkling with holy water is used. The Eucharist as a rite of passage is clearly specified when the Eucharist is given outside of Mass to the dying. The special prayers for the rite of administering viaticum are most helpful to draw out this somewhat neglected aspect of Eucharistic theology.[69] Of special interest is the direction that in the homily "the priest explains the meaning and importance of viaticum" (n. 189), that one alternative to the customary invitation to Communion says "Jesus Christ is the food for our journey; he calls us to the heavenly table," and that two of the prayers after the reception of Communion refer to this as a rite of passage, specifically of being led "safely into the kingdom of light" and of entering "your kingdom in peace" (n. 209).[70]

IV. Symbolic (In)adequacy

The critical function of liturgical theology in general, and a Roman Catholic approach to liturgy and sacraments specifically, raises concerns about the symbolic substratum of the present liturgy based on a theology of creation and of human productivity. Regrettably the all too frequent practice of a comparatively long Liturgy of the Word and a less than robust experience of symbolic engagement in the rites of the Eucharist, including texts and distribution of bread and wine, and especially when only one species is given in Communion, has often led to a heavily didactic experience of Eucharistic worship. Similarly, in the liturgy of baptism the preference given to sustaining the former usage of infusion over immersion also minimizes the kind of symbolic engagement presumed in the revised rite. Theologically such practices raise the important question about how or whether the liturgy actually evidences a reverence for creation and of the gifts and talents implicit in human ingenuity in manufacturing these (and other) liturgical symbols.

Another related and rather acute instance concerns the diminution in the "primal-ness" of liturgy in terms of exploring its "earthy" aspects. In the Roman rite, the Easter Vigil still stands as the chief example of a liturgy whose primal basis in symbolic expression is clear. However, even this liturgy can tend to be less "earthy" and more antiseptic because of a certain self-consciousness in celebrating rituals which concern cosmic regeneration and which depend for their symbolic integrity on cosmic and symbolic foundations. Abbreviated processions, or those which concern only some of the assembly, or (even worse) which involve only liturgical ministers, miss the point of this liturgical rite of passage, exemplified by the processing of the assembly from outdoors to indoors and especially since the first part of the rite (outdoors) draws on the cosmic symbolism of the earth coming to rebirth in nature in the spring. Subsequent processions involve the assembly's movement to the lectern bathed in the light of the Easter candle and from which the Word is proclaimed, to the baptismal font for the baptismal washing, to the altar for the rite's Eucharistic conclusion.

While the clearest euchological example of praising God for creation in the present liturgy of the Eucharist is in the fourth Eucharistic prayer, the fact remains that this emphasis is minimal especially when compared with the Eastern anaphoras cited above, in particular Book VIII of the Apostolic Constitutions. One wonders whether the dangers of pantheism or companation have mitigated against a freer development of a creation motif in these prayers. In addition to the valuable symbolic substratum contained in the very use of bread and wine, more emphasis on the symbolism of creation and the use of manufactured goods would be welcomed in new Eucharistic prayer texts.

In the contemporary debate about the Eucharist the issues we have discussed here about natural symbolism and human productivity need to be respected. This is to say that to raise the question of "which foods" other than wheat bread and grape wine are suitable for the Eucharist is incomplete without clear and constant reference to their symbolic origins and meaning. Important symbolic questions concern whether the "paschal cycle" of dying and rising so clearly demonstrated in the manufacture of bread and wine is inherent in any foods proposed as substitutes.[71]

A precedent for the use of an oil other than olive oil for the anointing of the sick has been established in the revised rite. This is clearly a positive aspect of ritual adaptation in places where olive oil is hard to find or where it is simply not customarily used. However, one can legitimately critique this same revised rite in its reduction of the number of anointings from five (in the previous rite) to two (or even one)[72] and ask whether this is pastorally useful. Despite the stated possibility of increasing the number of anointings,[73] unfortunately the conventional practice of minimalism in the prior sacramental practice can easily lead in practice to making the act of anointing itself minimal. The principle of maximizing sacramental symbolism would seem to require the retention of the former five anointings (except in case of emergency, for example when a person is in surgery).

Another example concerns the liturgical year. Many of its

premises (often reflected in euchology) are based on the northern hemisphere and the seasons of nature when liturgical feasts and seasons occur. The difficulty concerns what happens when spring renewal is presumed and capitalized upon for the paschal celebrations ("new life" at Easter) when these take place during winter in the southern hemisphere. Given the fact that both the northern and southern hemispheres have traditionally celebrated and continue to celebrate the liturgical feasts and seasons at the same time, would it not be appropriate to adjust the euchology to reflect the seasons that are actually occurring in nature. For example, this would mean changing the euchology of Easter for the southern hemisphere to fit a winter season, not the spring. In effect this would mean doing for Easter what was done for Christmas. That is, the Christmas euchology draws on the symbolism of light even though the same symbolism is more fully used at Easter when the symbolic usage includes the use of a fire, Easter candle and individual candles. At Christmas "light" is referred to in the euchology as a sign of hope and no special use of candles is prescribed. In addition, attention needs to be given to liturgical contexts where the seasons are called "rainy" or "dry." Here the euchology could speak less of light/darkness and more of abundant water for life and the yearning for God predicated on the psalmists's imagery "like a dry . . . land without water (Ps 63:2)."

In addition, with regard to the present calendar, it is regrettable that scant attention is given to rogation days or days of lesser litanies, at which times the agrarian foundation of symbolic liturgical usage can be emphasized. The tradition of annual processions around fields emphasizing the value of symbols "which earth has given and human hands have made" is largely lost today. The present option in the General Norms for the Liturgical Calendar (nn. 47–49) for the development of local rituals for these occasions has gone largely undeveloped.[74]

Our repeated assertion about varying contexts for liturgical celebration can help toward redirecting attention to creation symbolism as operative and truly central to the liturgy of the Easter Vigil. The success of the adult catechumenate and adult initiation at Easter in the United States attests to the retrieval of important aspects of how Christians are made, as well as to aspects of the Easter Vigil liturgy which had gone unemphasized (especially before the Holy Week reforms in the 1950s when the vigil was held during the day). However, the paradoxical result of emphasizing the initiation of new believers into the Church at the vigil can mean mitigating the theology of cosmic regeneration intrinsic to this night celebration, which theology was itself important as a foundation as to why Christians are initiated on this night.

That we celebrate Christ's regeneration to new existence through the resurrection at the very time when creation is regenerated in the spring calls for our communal reappropriation of both through the Easter Vigil. These understandings stand side-by-side at the Easter Vigil and ought to be appropriated together annually. This is sacramentalized at the liturgy when all sacramental symbols start anew, i.e., light struck for the first time, the singing of the *Exsultet* as an overview of what this feast is about, the reading of the Genesis creation story, the reading of Romans 6 about our identification in Christ, the blessing of water, immersion in water, anointing with newly blessed oils, and the new leaven of the paschal Communion. To over identify with the person of Christ without reference to the cosmic underpinnings intrinsic to the Easter Vigil can diminish the creation centered foundation for our celebration of these mysteries in Christ. To overemphasize initiation as identification with Christ's paschal mystery without an appreciation of the fittingness of celebrating paschal victory at the very time when creation is renewed in the spring is to do a disservice to liturgy—to both its *context* and *text* at Easter.

An example of the broadening perspective gained from celebrating the same feasts in different contexts would be that of an Easter Vigil celebrated in a monastery. Here there are no catechumens and no one making profession of faith in the Catholic Church. Hence the vigil's cosmic symbolism would be all the clearer in such a setting, especially if the monastery earns its livelihood from farming or a farming related occupation. The theology of monastic profession as a second baptism could suitably be underscored in such a setting on this night, which theology would coincide well with the renewal of baptismal vows of all the baptized at this liturgy.

A final critique concerns the contribution which concern for creation and the environment can make to the theology of the presentation of the gifts at the Eucharist. Several recent studies in English have summarized the debate about the theological adequacy of these rites in the present reform and avenues for their further refinement in the Roman rite.[75] Most authors agree that the simplification of these rites from the Tridentine Missal was long overdue and that the present reform at least eliminates any kind of proleptic Eucharistic prayer which had unfortunately burdened the former rite. The reform calls these rites the "preparation of the gifts" or the "preparation of the altar and the gifts"—not the "offertory."

The simplified rites are a distinct improvement. The parallel texts "blessed are you, Lord God of all creation. . . ." are unfortunately problematic in that they reiterate what is explicitly and traditionally a central theological theme of the Eucharistic prayer: to praise, bless and thank God for the *mirabilia Dei*, especially as these continue to be experienced here and now through the Eucharist. What emerges from an examination of the present rites of the presentation is too exclusive focus on the particular gifts of bread and wine, whereas reference to God's providence in providing all the goods of the earth for nourishment and sustenance would be helpful. In addition, and more theologically pertinent, is the absence of explicit reference to the contribution of human ingenuity, industry, and productivity in the manufacture of the elements of bread and wine. This is not to argue for a Pelagian-like theology of earning the gifts of salvation by work. It is to argue for some clear statement that the gifts presented represent a wealth of human productivity, including planting, harvesting, refining, making flour, pressing grapes, baking loaves of bread, and aging the fruit of the vine to become wine.

Put somewhat differently, the theology reflected in this rite should take some cognizance of the fact that these polyvalent symbols, bread and wine, reflect the contribution of human productivity to the liturgy, as opposed to the use of symbols taken from nature such as water. In this connection it is significant that the recently revised *Lutheran Book of Worship*[76] contains the following rubric concerning what occurs as "the Offering is received as the Lord's table is prepared" (n. 24). "The appointed Offertory may be sung by the choir as the gifts are presented, or the congregation may sing one of the following offertories, or an appropriate hymn or psalm may be sung" (n. 25). The text of the Offertory that follows is:

"Let the vineyards be fruitful, Lord,
and fill to the brim our cup of blessing.
Gather a harvest from the seeds that were sown,
that we may be fed with the bread of life.
Gather the hopes and dreams of all;
unite them with the prayers we offer now.
Grace our table with your presence,
and give us a foretaste of the feast to come."[77]

In these days of ecumenical convergence and mutual enrichment
(which terms will be explored more fully in chapter 7) it is significant that this text says far more theologically than do our double
"blessed are you" presentation prayers. This text is far more ex-
pansive in terms of evoking images of harvest and of human
productivity. It also offers an explicit eschatological reference at
this point of the rite which without such a reference could be
limited in its focus on the presentation of this particular bread and
wine. While the adoption of this text in the Roman rite would
have its own set of problems, nevertheless, this example of Lutheran *lex orandi* affords a significant example of how ecumenical
cooperation can afford insight and guidance in continuing liturgical revision and in developing the theological implications of that
revision.

Should Roman Catholicism continue to avoid correcting these
and other examples of diminished emphasis on symbol, it will sur-
render what, paradoxically, has traditionally been one of its major
contributions to the theology and experience of worship—the use
of creation and symbolic engagement in liturgy. In fact the Roman
Catholic implicit respect for symbolism in liturgy should be a chief
arguing point for a theology of the environment (more fully
argued in chapter 8). This is clearly a case of turning the critical
function of liturgical theology to critical communal self-reflection
and critique. Such an approach to sacramental theology and practice is contained in this Orthodox statement:

"But, when we look today at our world, we see a very different
picture. Humanity's rebellion, poise and greed has shattered the
primordial relationship of Adam. It has ignored or discarded the
Church's understanding of our role as priests of creation. For now
we behave like the exploiters and robbers of creation. By doing so,

we have brought not just species but entire eco-systems to destruction. Our world is facing a crisis of death and corruption to a degree never before experienced. The Fathers of the Church—while being able to recognize this basic cause—sin—never at their time had to experience such all-embracing and life-threatening consequences of sin to creation as we do today."[78]

Notes

1. See above, Chapter 3, p. 85.

2. The recent literature on symbol in general and symbols used in worship is vast. Even though the limits of our discussion of symbol have been set in the context of liturgy it is appropriate to note some of the sources that have been influential on the developing of our thesis. These include, Charles André Bernard, *Théologie symbolique* (Paris: Téqui, 1980), José Maria Castillo, *Simbolos de Libertad*. Teologia de los sacramentos. (Salamanca: Ediciones Sigueme, 1981), Louis-Marie Chauvet, *Symbole et sacrement*, idem. *Du sybolique au symbole. Essai sur les sacrements* (Paris: Les Editions du Cerf, 1979), Jean Corbon, *The Wellspring of Worship*, trans., M. J. O'Connell (New York/Ramsey: Paulist Press, 1988), Stephen Happel, "Symbol," *The New Dictionary of Theology*, ed. J. Komonchak. et. al. (Collegeville: The Liturgical Press, 1987) 993–1002, idem. "Symbol," *The New Dictionary of Sacramental Worship* 1237–45, Francois Isambert, *Rite et efficacité symbolique* (Paris: Editions du Cerf, 1979), David N. Power, *Unsearchable Riches:* The Symbolic Nature of Liturgy (New York: Pueblo, 1984) and Theodor Schneider *Zeichen der Nähe Gottes.* Grundriss der Sakramententheologie (Mainz: Matthias-Gruenwald Verlag, 1979).

3. See above, Chapter 3, p. 91 and fn. 22.

4. Two papers written in preparation for discussion of the Faith and Order Commission of the World Council of Churches which touch on this subject are P. Prenter, (then chairman of the European section of the Faith and Order Theological Commission on Worship) "Worship and Creation," *Studia Liturgica* 2 (1963) 82–95 and V. Vajta, (then Director of the department of theology of the Lutheran World Federation) "Creation and Worship," *Studia Liturgica* 2 (1963) 29–46. See also, Cinette Ferriere, "A propos de 'Dieu-potier' createur," *Paroisse et Liturgie* 48 (1966) 533–548 and Pelagio Visentin, "Creazione—Storia della salvezza—Liturgia," *Rivista Liturgica* 77 (1990) 252–268.

5. I am indebted to Edward Kilmartin for the term "sacrificial sacrament" as a description of how to express how the Eucharist is a sacrifice.

6. This statement from the Orthodox theologian Alexander Schmemann is a particularly useful description of liturgy. See, Alexander Schmemann, *Sacraments and Orthodoxy* (New York: Herder and Herder, 1965) 7.

7. Ibid., 16.

8. *Orthodoxy and the Ecological Crisis* booklet from The Ecumenical Patriarchate, World Wide Fund for Nature International, 1990, 8.

9. A. Schmemann, *Sacraments and Orthodoxy* 142. A recent Roman Catholic articulation of this same notion asserts "essential to our sacramental system and liturgical prayer is the practice of using material elements—water, oil, bread, wine etc.—as sacred signs, sacraments of God's presence and power among us. Catholic sacramental practice embraces the gifts of creation and uses them for praise and thanksgiving. Fundamental to that practice is the conviction that creation is itself holy and is appropriately used for worship" (Pastoral Letter of Bishop) Anthony Pilla, "Christian Faith and the Environment," *Origins* 20 (November 1, 1990) 333–338.

10. Michael J. Himes and Kenneth R. Himes, "The Sacrament of Creation," *Commonweal* 117 (January 26, 1990) 44–45.

11. There are five mass formulas for "VII Kalens Iulias Natale Sancti Iohannis Baptistae" in the *Sacramentarium Veronense*, ed., L. Cunibert Mohlberg et. al., Rerum Ecclesiasticarum Documenta 1 (Rome: Herder, 1954, 1978) nn. 232–256.

12. Recent descriptions of the *lucernarium* and its influence on Christian vespers are found in Paul Bradshaw, *Daily Prayer in the Early Church* (New York: Oxford University Press, 1982) 22, 51, 57, 75–77, 80, 116, 119, 135, George Guiver, *Company of Voices*. Daily Prayer and the People of God (New York: Pueblo, 1988) 62–66, 202–203 and Robert Taft, *The Liturgy of the Hours in East and West* (Collegeville: The Liturgical Press, 1986) 26–28, 36–38, 55–56, 211–212, 355–356.

13. One of the disadvantages to the proposal to establish a "fixed date" for Easter (largely for ecumenical purposes) is the fact that this would mitigate the sense of relying on cosmic rhythms to establish its dating.

14. Present ICEL translation of this prayer from the former Roman usage. Interestingly, the *Missale Romanum* designates this mass formula as *Ad Missam in nocte*. See, Pierre Bruylants, *Les Oraisons du Missel Romain* (Louvain: Mont Cesar, 1952) n. 347. The Latin text reads:
"Deus, qui hanc sacratissimam noctem
veri luminis fecisti illustratione clarescere,
da, quaesumus, ut, cuius in terra mysteria lucis agnovimus,
eius quoque gaudiis perfruamur in caelo."

15. Present ICEL translation of text from former Roman usage, P. Bruylants, *Les Oraisons* n. 176. The Latin reads:
"Da, quaesumus, omnipotens Deus,
ut dum nova incarnati Verbi tui luce perfundimur,
hoc in nostro resplendeat opere,
quod per fidem fulget in mente."

16. From former Roman usage, originally from the Hadrianum. See, Jean Deshusses, *Le Sacramentaire Grégorien* (Fribourg: Ed. Universitaires, 1979) n. 51. The Latin reads:

"Quia per incarnati Verbi mysterium
nova mentis nostrae oculis lux tuae claritatis infulsit:
ut, dum visibiliter Deum cognoscimus,
per hunc in invisibilium amorem rapiamur."

17. Present ICEL translation of original from *Sacramentarium Veronense* n. 1260. The Latin text reads: "Per quem hodie commercium nostrae reparationis effulsit. . . .''

18. From former Roman usage, from a combination of two original sources, see, *Sacramentarium Veronense* n. 1247 and the old Gelasian sacramentary, *Liber sacramentorum Romanae ecclesiae ordinis anni circuli*, Rerum Ecclesiasticarum Documenta IV, ed., L. C. Mohlberg (Rome: Herder, 1960) n. 59. The Latin text reads:

"Quia ipsum in Christo salutis nostrae mysterium
hodie ad lumen gentium revelasti,
et, cum in substantia nostrae mortalitatis apparuit,
nova nos immortalitatis eius gloria reparasti."

19. See, among others, John Bright, *A History of Israel* (Philadelphia: Westminster, 1959) who states that "Unleavened Bread (and Passover), Weeks, and Ingathering . . . were far older than Israel and, save for Passover, were agricultural in origin. Israel borrowed them [and] gave them a new rationale by imparting to them a historical content. They ceased to be mere nature festivals and became occasions when the mighty acts of Yahweh toward Israel were celebrated. Presumably these feasts were for practical reasons celebrated at local shrines as well as at Shiloh. But there is evidence of a great annual feast at Shiloh to which godly Israelites repaired (Judg 21:19; 1 Sam 1:3, 21). Though we are not told, this was probably the autumn feast of Ingathering and the turn of the year. It is exceedingly probable, too, and very likely in connection with this annual feast, that there was a regular ceremony of covenant renewal (Deut 31:9-13). . . .'' (148). Also see, Gerhard von Rad, *Old Testament Theology.* Volume One, trans., D.M.G. Stalker (New York: Harper and Row, 1962) 15–35.

20. It is not coincidental that the continuous reading from Revelation occurs in the office of readings in the Liturgy of the Hours from Monday of the Second Week of Easter through Saturday of the Fifth Week of Easter and as the second reading at Sunday Mass during the Easter season C cycle indicating how Easter is a season of rebirth and sharing the first fruits of the resurrection.

21. How creation can serve the mediating function of coming to know God is also explicitly confirmed through the NT. A classic text used to support how creation can lead to knowledge of God is Rom 1:19-20: "in fact, whatever can be known about God is clear to them; he himself made it so. Since the creation of the world invisible realities, God's eternal power and divinity, have become visible, recognizable through the things he has made." Notably, Rom 1:25 ("the Creator . . . is blessed forever") is printed in the present text of the liturgy of the hours as the phrase that can be meditated on when praying the canticle of Dan 3:52-57 at morning prayer.

22. All English translations are from Matthew Britt, *The Hymns of the Breviary and Missal* (New York: Benziger Brothers, 1922) 74.

23. Each of these hymns is discussed in succession in Britt, *The Hymns*, 73–85 with Latin and English texts, notes on authorship and a theological commentary.

24. Translation from Britt, *The Hymns* 84. Additional hymn texts from the former breviary that concern praise for creation include: *Audi benigne Conditor* (Lenten Vespers), *Quem terra, pontus, sidera* (Matins of the Blessed Virgin Mary), *Rerum Creator optime* (Wed. matins), *Rerum Deus tenax vigor* (None, throughout the year), *Salutis humanae Sator* (Vespers, Ascension to Pentecost), *Aeterne rerum Conditor* (Sunday, Lauds), *Ecce jam noctis* (Sunday Lauds), *Splendor paternae gloriae* (Monday Lauds), *Primo die, quo Trinitas* (Sunday, Matins), *O Sol salutis, intimis* (Lauds, Lent), *Rex sempiterne coelitum* (Matins, Eastertide) *Veni Creator Spiritus* (Vespers and Terce on Pentecost and through octave). See, *The Hymnal for the Hours* (Chicago: GIA, 1989) nn. 148–157 and *The Summit Choirbook* (Summit: Monastery of Our Lady of the Rosary, 1983) nn. 179–186 for Vesper hymns translated into English and set to various metrical settings. Some of additional Matins and Lauds hymns noted here are also in *The Hymnal for the Hours* e.g., nn. 175, 191, 198 etc., and in *The Summit Choirbook* nn. 168–178.

25. The General Instruction on the Liturgy of the Hours, n. 43 states: "the psalmody of morning prayer consists of one morning psalm, then a canticle from the Old Testament, and finally a second psalm of praise, following the tradition of the Church."

26. Significant examples of how contemporary liturgical scholarship has rediscovered and appropriated the Jewish cultic terms *berakah* and *todah* as central to understanding the eucharistic prayer are in Louis Bouyer, *Eucharist*, 15–135 and Cesare Giraudo, *La struttura letteraria della preghiera eucaristica*. Saggio sullagenesi letteraria di una forma. *Toda* veterotestamentaria *Berakah* giudaica, Anafora cristiana (Rome: Biblical Institute Press, 1981) and C. Giraudo, *Eucaristia per la Chiesa*. Prospettive teologiche sulla l'eucaristia a partire della "lex orandi" (Rome: Gregorian University Press, 1989).

27. The use of "classic" here is meant to indicate those elements which are most generally found in eucharistic prayers in the tradition. It is not meant to suggest that there is but one model for Eucharistic praying. If fact, a review of such prayers discloses much variation within the commonly agreed upon anaphoral structure as is noted in Chapter 1 fnn. 27–28.

28. See below, section four of this chapter for a critique of the present liturgy in this regard.

29. Louis Bouyer (*Eucharist* 448) argues that the sources for this prayer are Eastern and include the *Apostolic Constitutions*, the Liturgy of St. James and of St. Basil.

30. Joseph Keenan, "The Importance of the Creation Motif in the Eucharistic Prayer," *Worship* 53 (July 1979) 355.

31. Ibid., 349.

32. The full text is found in Anton Hanggi and Irmgard Pahl, eds., *Prex Eucharistica* Textus e variis liturgiis antiquioribus selecti (Fribourg: Editions Universitaires, 1968) 82–95 and translated in *Prayers of the Eucharist* 104–113.

33. The source for both these prayers is the previous Roman Missal, see, P. Bruylants, *Les Oraisons* nn. 786 and 385. The Latin text reads:

"Omnipotens sempiterne Deus,
qui es in omnium operum tuorum dispensatione mirabilis,
intellegant redempti tui, non fuisse excellentius,
quod initio factus est mundus,
quam quod in fine saeculorum
Pascha nostrum immolatus est Christus."

34. The Latin text of this second prayer yields something of the balance customarily found in Latin collects, which text is from the former Roman Missal.

"Deus, qui mirabiliter creasti hominem
et mirabilius redemisti,
da nobis, quaesumus,
contrea oblectamenta peccati mentis ratione presistere,
ut mereamur ad aeterna gaudia prevenire.
Per Christum Dominum nostrum."

35. Jürgen Moltmann, *God in Creation*. A New Theology of Creation and the Spirit of God (San Francisco: Harper and Row, 1985) 9–13.

36. See, Edward J. Kilmartin, *Christian Liturgy* esp. 100–199 and Jean Corbon *The Wellspring of Worship*.

37. Because of the weaknesses in the present ICEL translation the Latin text is particularly illustrative:

"Vere sanctus es, Domine,
et merito te laudat omnis a te condita creatura,
quia per Filium tuum,
Dominum nostrum Iesum Christum,
Spiritus Sancti operante virtute,
vivificas et sanctificas universa,
et populum tibi congregare non desinis,
ut a solis ortu usque ad occasum
oblatio munda offeratur nomini tuo."

38. The Latin reads:

"Haec ergo dona, quaesumus,
Spiritus tui ruore sanctifica,
ut nobis Corpus et Sanguinis fiant
Domine nostri Iesu Christi.

"Et supplices deprecamur
ut Corporis et Sanguinis Christi participes
a Spiritu Sancto congregemur in unum."

39. This assertion is not to ignore the difficulty some liturgists have with the present "split epiclesis," that is, the now separate invocations for the transformation of the gifts and the intercession for the church. Among others, see Richard Albertine. "The Problem of the (double) Epiclesis in the Roman Eucharistic Prayers," *Ephemerides Liturgicae* 91 (1977) 193–202.

40. See, Cinette Ferriere, "A propos de 'Dieu-potier' Images de la création et foi chrétienne en Dieu créateur," *Paroisse et Liturgie* 48 (1966) 533–548.

41. Examples of euchology accompanying symbolic action include the blessing of water at initiation, of oil at the anointing of the sick, the Eucharistic prayer at the Eucharist. An example of a non euchological text accompanying a symbolic action is the *Agnus Dei* chant at the breaking of the bread.

42. D. N. Power, *Unsearchable Riches* 96.

43. These phrases are from Edward Kilmartin, "Liturgical Theology," *Worship* 50 (July, 1976) 313.

44. Gordon Lathrop, "Holy Things. Foundations for Liturgical Theology" *Institute of Liturgical Studies* Number 7 (Valparaiso: Valparaiso Institute, 1991) 35.

45. See, Karl Rahner, "The Presence of Christ in the Sacrament of the Lord's Supper," *Theological Investigations, Vol. IV* trans., Kevin Smyth (Baltimore: Helicon Press, 1966) 309.

46. A helpful summary of the importance of the epiclesis in both contemporary Roman Catholic and other Christian churches' Eucharistic prayers see, Edward J. McKenna, "The Epiclesis Revisited," in Frank C. Senn, ed., *New Eucharistic Prayers*, 169–194.

47. See, *Sacrosanctum Concilium* n. 7, *Mysterium Fidei* nn. 34–51, *Eucharisticum Mysterium* n. 9, and GIRM n. 7. It is significant that in *Mysterium Fidei* Paul VI adds that "Christ is present in his Church when it prays . . . where two or three are gathered . . . and as it performs works of mercy" (n. 35).

48. In fact one of the unfortunate legacies of some initial attempts at the reform of the liturgy has been that while presiders, readers, cantors, Eucharistic ministers, musicians, etc. have received some measure of training and their ministry is an assumed part of liturgy, it is regrettable that more often than not liturgical assemblies have not been taught to participate in such a way that their active participation is understood to be an essential component of the liturgical event. The legacy of "actants" in the sanctuary area and passive assemblies is all too real. A similar comment is made below in Chapter 6 as a critique of the phrase in *Music in Catholic Worship* that singles out the qualities of the presider as affecting the experience of worship, rather than citing how these same characteristics in the whole assembly and in the other liturgical ministers affect worship.

49. See, Jordi Gilbert Tarruell, "Los formularios de la Benedicion del Agua," *Ephemerides Liturgicae* 88 (1974) 275–309, and the recent studies in English by Mark Searle, "*Fons Vitae*: A Case Study in the Use of Liturgy as a Theological Source," in Gerard Austin, ed., *Fountain of Life* (Washington: Pastoral Press,

1991) 217–242, which essay is also important methodologically regarding liturgical theology, and Dominic E. Serra, "The Blessing of Baptismal Water at the Paschal Vigil in the Post Vatican II Rite," *Ecclesia Orans* 7 (1990) 343–368.

50. The General Instructions and Rites of Christian Initiation for Adults and for Children are introduced by another document called the General Instruction [on] Christian Initiation, the source for this reference. In what follows it is cited as "GICI." All quotations from GICI and from the adult rite of initiation (RCIA) are from the International Committee on English in the Liturgy translation of 1988. The numbering cited is that used in the *Study Edition* (Chicago: Liturgy Training Publications, 1988).

51. Among others, see Sebastian P. Brock, "The Consecration of Water in the Oldest Manuscripts of the Syrian Orthodox Baptismal Liturgy," *Orientalia Christiana Periodica* 37 (1971) 317–332.

52. This prayer refers to the important notions of remaining "a member of Christ who is Priest, Prophet and King" which references are absent if confirmation follows immediately. In our judgment the inclusion of this statement into the sequence of water baptism-confirmation-first Eucharist at the Easter Vigil would be a helpful adjustment to this rite.

53. The footnote to this text cites Rom 8:15, Gal 4:5, Trent Denz. 796 (1524). Our concern here is not to describe in full all the results of baptism, as, for example, those listed in GICI 5, but merely to indicate the results of using the symbol of water or in tests that refer to the use of water.

54. For a succinct commentary see, M. Britt, *The Hymns*, 91–94.

55. For a very useful discussion of the way these antiphons use the Old and New Testaments see, Adrien Nocent, *The Liturgical Year* Vol. 1, trans., Matthew O'Connell (Collegeville: The Liturgical Press, (1977) 162–168; for a more elaborate description (and somewhat hortatory in style) see, Pius Parsch, *The Church's Year of Grace* Vol. 1, trans., William Heidt (Collegeville: The Liturgical Press, 1957) 176–191.

56. However, if these "O" antiphons are prayed at morning prayer to accompany Zechariah's canticle on the days preceding Christmas as happened in some places in the Middle Ages they would convey other levels of meaning. In this particular case the welcoming of the sun at dawn at about the time the *O Oriens, splendor lucis aeternae, et sol justitiae*, "splendor of eternal light and the sun of justice" is sung would be all the more striking because of this temporal coincidence and because of the verse of Zechariah's canticle about light following the antiphon: "the dawn from on high shall dwell upon us." In fact the understandable sense of dread at the cosmic darkness and the waiting for the hoped for Messiah are reflected in the present antiphon to Zechariah's canticle on December 21: "there is no need to be afraid; in five days our Lord will come to us."

57. See, Prosper Guéranger, *The Liturgical Year, Advent*, vol. 1, trans., Laurence Shepherd (Westminster: Newman Press, 1952) 484.

58. Helpful recent studies of these feasts include Kenneth Stevenson, "The

Ceremonies of Light—Their Shape and Function in the Paschal Vigil Liturgy," *Ephemerides Liturgicae* 99 (1985) 170-185, *idem.* "The Origins and Development of Candlemas: A Struggle for Identity and Coherence?" *Ephemerides Liturgicae* 102 (1988) 316-346, and Eileen Roberts, "The *Exsultet* in Twelfth Century Sicily as an Indicator of Manuscript Provenance," *Ecclesia Orans* 5 (1988) 157-164.

59. It is not coincidental that this feast has conventionally been important in Rome for a papal liturgy at which superiors of religious communities make an offering of rather large candles to the pope whose homilies are specifically addressed to the value which religious offer by their religious consecration and vows.

60. The (whole) blessing is taken from three texts in the former Roman Missal. See, P. Bruylants, *Les Oraisons* nn. 513a, 781a, 492c. The Latin text of the section we are emphasizing reads:

"quae ad tui moninis laudem eos gestatura concurrit,
quatenus per virtutum semitam
ad lucem indeficientem pervenire mereatur."

61. Antoine Dumas (In "Les prefaces du nouveau missel," *Ephemerides Liturgicae* 85 (1971) 25 cites the present Presentation preface as derived largely from the Supplement to the Hadrianum: Jean Deshusses, ed., *Le Sacramentaire Grégorien: Ses principales formes, d'après les plus anciens manuscrits.* Spicilegium Friburgense 16. Fribourg: Editions Universitaires, 1971) n. 1745. The Latin text reads:

"Quia coaeternus hodie in templo tuus Filius praesentatus
gloria Israel et lumen gentium a Spiritu declaratur."

62. The text is from the previous Roman Missal, see P. Bruylants, *Les oraisons* n. 423. The Latin text reads:

"Deus, qui per Filium tuum
claritatis tuae ignem fidelibus contulisti,
novum hunc ignem sanctifica,
et concede nobis,
ita per haec festa paschalia caelistibus desideriis inflammari,
ut ad perpetuae claritatis
puris mentibus valeamus festa pertingere."

63. The use of the singular here ("chant") is not intended to mean that the *Exsultet* had only one setting. The fact that certain religious communities to this day preserve their own settings indicates pluriformity here. Our point concerns the combination of hymn text with musical setting, a theme more fully discussed below, Chapter 6, 239-246.

64. The proposed ICEL translation of this traditional prayer in the Roman rite (see, P. Bruylants, *Les Oraisons* n. 346) for the new edition of the Sacramentary is:

"O God,
you brighten this most holy night
with the radiance of the risen Christ.

Quicken within your children the spirit of adoption,
so that, renewed in mind and body,
we may dedicate our lives wholeheartedly to your service."

The Latin is:

"Deus, qui hanc sacratissimam noctem
gloria dominicae resurrectionis illustras,
excita in Ecclesia tua adoptionis spiritum,
ut, corpore et mente renovati,
puram tibi exhibeamus servitutem."

65. Philippe Rouillard, "From Human Meal to Christian Eucharist," in R. Kevin Seasoltz, ed., *Living Bread, Saving Cup*. Readings on the Eucharist (Collegeville, Minn.: The Liturgical Press, 1982) 126; this article appeared originally in *Notitiae* 131–132 (1977).

66. Ibid.

67. These verbs are placed in quotation marks because in the winter nature does not "die," rather it is "fallow" or "dormant." Hence this cycle is more accurately described as "lying in dormancy" and "bursting forth to new life."

68. See, Jerome Murphy O'Connor, "Eucharist and Community in First Corinthians," *Living Bread*, 1–30 and for some important patristic sources, W. Rordorf, et. al., *The Eucharist of the Early Christians* trans., Matthew O'Connell (New York: Pueblo, 1978) for descriptions of the Eucharist from the *Didache* through the *Apostolic Constitutions* and helpful commentaries.

69. See, 1983 edition of *Pastoral Care of the Sick: Rites of Anointing and Viaticum*, noting in particular the distinction between rites for the sick and those for the dying as well as the new Mass formula in the Sacramentary if either the rite of anointing, or viaticum, or both, take place during Mass.

70. It is notable that the rite presumes the Communion under the forms of both bread and wine even when viaticum is given outside of Mass (n. 193, 207).

71. This, however, is not meant to be the only determinative factor in arguing for a change of these elements. Another major concern is the fact that bread (whether barley or wheat) and wine were used by Jesus and that the Church's practice has traditionally sanctioned both on the basis of dominical practice, not just that they were the customary foodstuffs of the Judaism of his time.

72. See, *Rite of Anointing* n. 23.

73. Ibid., n. 24.

74. See the short commentary, Kevin W. Irwin, "Overview of *General Norms for the Liturgical Year and the Calendar*," in *The Liturgy Documents: A Parish Resource*, Third edition (Chicago: Liturgy Training Publications, 1991) 170.

75. See, Annibale Bugnini, *The Reform of the Liturgy, 1948–1975*, trans. Matthew J. O'Connell (Collegeville: The Liturgical Press, 1990) 337–392, Frederick

R. McManus, "The Roman order of Mass from 1964-1969: The Preparation of the Gifts," *Shaping English Liturgy* 107-138, Thomas A. Krosnicki, "Preparing the Gifts: Clarifying the Rite," *Worship* 65 (1991) 149-159, and Edward Foley, Kathleen Hughes and Gilbert Ostdiek, "The Preparatory Rites: A case study in Liturgical Ecology," *Worship* 67 (January 1993) 17-38.

76. *Lutheran Book of Worship* prepared by the churches participating in the Inter-Lutheran Commission on Worship (Minneapolis: Augsburg Publishing House, 1978).

77. Ibid., 66.

78. *Orthodoxy and the Ecological Crisis*, 9, and, more fully, 9-14.

Chapter 5

Euchology

A major contribution to the development of contemporary liturgical method, especially in light of Anton Baumstark's *Comparative Liturgy*,[1] has been the amassing, critical editing, publication, and historical critical study of the many textual sources used over the centuries in the celebration of liturgy.[2] Most notable in this regard are sacramentaries, rituals, and pontificals because they contain *euchological texts.* The four parts of this chapter concern method for and about the study of liturgical euchology. The first section deals with defining what is commonly called "euchology" and distinguishing among the various kinds of euchological texts. The second part deals with a method concerning the contents and use of euchological texts (past and present) to help disclose the theology of a given liturgical rite. The third section deals with some of the issues that surround the contemporary task of translating prayers from Latin to the vernacular and of composing additional new euchological texts. The fourth section delineates some unfinished agenda that remain in contemporary Eucharistic euchology.

This chapter is linked to chapter three on the Word in that often enough euchological texts contain collections of scriptural images, allusions, and metaphors in prayers whose meaning, especially when accompanying symbolic engagement, is more fully understood as a complement to the Word proclaimed in liturgy. It is also linked to chapter 4 about symbol (especially the example about baptismal bathing and washing) because euchological texts give direction to the symbolic usage in the liturgy by offering a number of meanings to accompany the act of unleashing the power of a symbol used liturgically.

I. Genre, Definitions, Examples

A proper interpretation of euchological *texts* for their theological meaning requires that, like other liturgical texts, their *proper genre* be understood and respected. Euchological texts are essentially poetic, metaphorical, and image-filled. They are among the chief means intrinsic to the liturgy that describes one or another aspect of the divine action occurring in liturgy or of the theology of the liturgy being celebrated. They offer glimpses and insights rather than exact definitions.

The word *euchology* derives from the Greek *euche* meaning "prayer" and *logos* meaning "discourse about." Matias Augé asserts that "euchology" includes the study of liturgical prayer texts in general, the study of (what some call) the laws that regulate their formulation and the contents of the liturgical prayers contained in ritual books (e.g., sacramentary, missal, ritual).[3] In our understanding euchology includes, in the first place, prefaces and Eucharistic prayers, solemn blessings (e.g., over water at baptism) and consecratory prayers (e.g., over chrism, at ordination etc.). In the second place it includes "the presidential prayers" (so termed in GIRM n. 10) such as the collect, prayer over the gifts, prayer after Communion, prayer over the people, and psalm prayers.[4] (Because the use of psalm prayers is optional in the present reform of the hours, psalm prayers should be regarded as a less important example of this second set of euchological texts. However, their restoration, and for our purposes particularly *how* they are prayed, is important because most often they refer back to the psalm or canticle just sung and thus provide a kind of summary prayer,[5] proclaimed by the celebrant as a way of summing up the silent prayer of the assembly after the text of the psalm is prayed.[6] More will be said below on the importance of these components, especially how the silent prayer of the assembly preceding an oration or collect is articulated by the one presiding.)

The historical and comparative study of euchological texts yields rich theological insight both about what occurs in the rite being studied (theology of liturgy) and about naming and describing God and God's actions in the liturgy on behalf of the Church (liturgical theology) in particular how the liturgy is (among other things) a soteriological, ecclesial and Trinitarian act.

It should be noted that some authors would include scriptural readings and biblical chants under "euchology" and a good case can be made for this inclusion. However, since we have treated the Word separately (in chapter 3) noting especially the theological meaning of the *proclaimed* Word and the theological meaning of the use of psalms in responsories, etc. our understanding of euchology in this chapter is more restrictive. At the same time, recalling this relationship between the scriptural Word and euchology is important since many euchological and other liturgical texts are composed in light of the Scriptures in general[7] (e.g., blessing prayer over water at initiation) or the particular texts proclaimed at a given feast or season (e.g., euchology for the solemnity of the birth of John the Baptist). In addition to the blessing, Eucharistic, and consecratory prayers, other chief examples of poetic texts composed in light of the Scriptures in the present revised liturgy are the *Exsultet* (in pride of place) as well as the sequences for Easter (*Victimae paschali laudes*), Pentecost (*Veni, Sancte Spiritus*),[8] the solemnity of the Body and Blood of Christ[9] (*Lauda, Sion*) and the Memorial of Our Lady of Sorrows (*Stabat Mater*).[10]

These different kinds of texts are found (traditionally and in the present reform) in the Sacramentary for Mass, the Roman Pontifical, and the Roman Ritual. The grammar (meaning the structure of these books and the sentence structure of the prayers they contain) of these sources is an essential key to interpreting and appreciating euchology. Among the things which liturgical euchology expresses are the following. First, euchology articulates how the mystery of Christ's redemption is enacted in a specific act of liturgy and how specific aspects of redemption are enacted at a particular liturgy or during a specific season (often by way of emphasis). For example, while all liturgy enacts the paschal mystery in such a way as to draw believers into it more and more deeply (customarily by the use of "our" and "us" in euchology) the euchology of Advent emphasizes (usually in a subtle way) how all liturgical memorial is also eschatological and hopeful. For example, the opening prayer on the First Monday of Advent states:

"Lord our God,
help us to prepare
for the coming of Christ your Son.
May he find us waiting,
eager in joyful prayer."[11]

Or the Christmas euchology can underscore how the annual liturgical journey of commemorating the redemption Jesus accomplished by his death and resurrection begins by commemorating the incarnation. The prayer over the gifts at the Christmas Vigil specifies this by stating:

"Lord,
as we keep tonight the vigil of Christmas,
may we celebrate this eucharist
with greater joy than ever
since it marks the beginning of our redemption."[12]

Liturgical euchology articulates what the Church believes to happen through the doing of liturgy in a genre of prayer whose language is intended to reflect more directly the socio-cultural conditions and language expressions of the assembly especially when compared with the various language genres in the Bible. Therefore euchological texts can be regarded as the most characteristic way a liturgical community has to acclaim and describe the divine mysteries actualized in the liturgy. Matias Augé cites approvingly the statement that "the study of liturgy is principally a euchological study."[13]

The following two examples describe and illustrate liturgical euchology: the Eucharistic prayer and the presidential prayers of the Eucharist. The purpose in describing their structure in some detail is to invite an appreciation of the theological meaning conveyed through these means.

1. Eucharistic Prayer. The Eucharistic prayer is of central importance because its origins, structure, and style reach back to the important *berakah* and *todah* traditions in Judaism and is rightly regarded as the "center and high point of the entire [Eucharistic] celebration" (GIRM n. 54).[14] The introductory dialogue sets up the anaphora as pivotal. The parallel established by this dialogue and the dialogue preceding the gospel is notable as both introduce proclamations of central importance. In addition the preface and memorial acclamations mark it as a prayer that the assembly participates in by sung (or spoken) acclamations, as well as by listening and watching what occurs at the altar.[15] Through these prayers the *magnalia Dei* are articulated. Through this articulation contemporary faith communities share in the very same saving deeds of God in such a way that a new event of grace occurs. Of all euchological prayers, this prayer is the medium through which the Church is drawn into and made real partakers in God's acts of salvation, presaged and realized in Israel, fulfilled and accomplished once for all in Christ, experienced in a unique way in the liturgy and to be completed in the kingdom.

Similarly, other blessing and consecratory prayers, for example, that used to bless water or chrism at (or for) initiation, perform the same function. Their recital of salient events in saving history, emphasizing especially scriptural images to describe what is now accomplished in the liturgy, actualizes those same saving events here and now and leads to a new experience of salvation through the liturgy. This new reality of salvation occurs because it is intrinsically anamnesis—memorial—"not of a past history, but of the present reality of our lives" in Christ.[16] In liturgy, what is present is *our* being born anew in Christ, *our* entrance into new life through this coming of God to us *now*. For as St. Leo says in his famous aphorism that is an entire liturgical theology, what Christ did visibly during his earthly ministry has now passed over into sacrament.[17] In the words of Jean Daniélou:

"The whole of Christian culture consists in grasping the links that exist between Bible and liturgy, Gospel and eschatology, mysticism and liturgy. The application of this method to scripture is called exegesis; applied to liturgy it is called mystagogy. This consists in reading in the rites the mystery of Christ and in contemplating beneath the symbols the invisible reality."[18]

Thus the Eucharistic prayer is the Church's central proclamation of how what happened once for all is actualized here and now in an ever new experience of grace through the paschal mystery. Thus, the issue in euchology is not to describe God in generic terms, or describe a generic God. Rather, it is to proclaim the *mirabilia Dei* and to specify how saving deeds are experienced through liturgy.

The structure of the Eucharistic prayer specifically as found in the present reform is summarized in the General Instruction of the Roman Missal (n. 55) as containing: thanksgiving, acclamation, epiclesis, institution narrative, anamnesis, offering, intercessions, and final doxology. The prayer begins by naming and/or addressing God, sometimes based on a divine attribute. For example the "classic" introduction to the Western Eucharistic prayer is: "Father, all powerful and ever living God" (*Domine sancte Pater, omnipotens et aeternae Deus*).[19] This first section is an extended prayer of praise and thanks for creation and redemption. In the Roman rite this was traditionally done by proclaiming one of a number of varied prefaces.[20] In the present reform some new prefaces are intrinsically connected in thought pattern and inherent logic with the rest of the Eucharistic prayer that follows, e.g., the preface to the fourth Eucharistic prayer, prefaces to Eucharistic prayers for reconciliation and those for children.[21]

The addition of an explicit epiclesis in the new Eucharistic prayers for the transformation of bread and wine into the body and blood of Christ marks a transition in the prayer that explicitly links past and present deeds of salvation. Theologically the Church's partaking in the paschal mystery is possible only through the power and work of the Holy Spirit, which Spirit is explicitly invoked in this (first) epiclesis (of two) to transform the elements of bread and wine. A second epiclesis (or the second part of what is sometimes called the "split epiclesis"[22]) is used to invoke the Spirit on the Church, especially to bring the Church into greater unity. The central section of the Eucharistic prayer recalls the Last Supper through the words of institution and the gestures made with and over the Eucharistic bread and cup. The explicitly paschal nature and paschal theology of this prayer is articulated in particular in the anamnetic sections of the prayer, namely, through the memorial prayers and memorial acclamations that now follow.[23]

Among the present translations of the explicit anamnetic sections of this prayer, the text from the fourth Eucharistic prayer "we now celebrate this memorial of our redemption" is preferable to the phrase "calling to mind"[24] of the third prayer which translation does not convey the sense that anamnesis is an action and is not limited to mental recollection. Liturgical remembering is always in the *doing* not the *thinking*. It is also theologically significant that some of the new Eucharistic prayers contain explicit eschatological references in their anamneses which were not found in the Roman Canon.[25] Examples include "and ready to greet him when he comes again" (*sed et praestolantes alterum eius adventum*) in prayer 3 and "looking forward to his coming in glory" (*et, exspectantes ipsius adventum in gloria*) in prayer 4.[26]

The second explicit invocation of the Spirit for the whole Church, leads to an intercessory section that explicitly denotes the communion of local Churches by naming the pope, bishops, clergy, and all the baptized. The intercessory section of this prayer corresponds with the Jewish origins of this prayer where praise of God's saving acts leads, logically and theologically, to asking that God continue this saving action for the assembly, the wider community of believers and for the world. This is an important moment of communal self-transcendence and active intercession by the assembled Church for the whole Church extending (in the fourth Eucharistic prayer) as far as "those who seek you with a sincere heart" (*et circumstantium, et cuncti populi tui, et omnium, qui te quaerunt corde sincero*).

The concluding doxology recalls the first part of the prayer ("thanks and praise") and functions as a kind of résumé. This Trinitarian doxology is significant for many reasons, not the least of which is the theological statement that the Christological emphasis of this prayer is focused within a prayer that is also explicitly Trinitarian and (in part just by being Trinitarian) is also ecclesial. Historical research reveals that the phrase in the concluding doxology "in the unity of the Holy Spirit" (*in unitate Spiritus sancti*) is intrinsically both ecclesial and Trinitarian at the same time. This concluding doxology refers to the Church as the subject engaged in praising the triune God.[27]

2. Variable Presidential Prayers. The structure and theological meaning of the three variable prayers used at the Eucharist[28] are important, even though they are less significant theologically than the Eucharistic prayer. The common Roman usage employs *oratio* for these prayers with the second termed *oratio super oblata* ("over the gifts") and the third termed *oration ad complendum* ("prayer at the conclusion").[29] These prayers express the mystery of salvation accomplished in Christ as presently experienced through the liturgy, which characteristic has caused them to be regarded as intrinsically anamnetic[30] and as prayers asking God to continue to make known his salvation here and now. There is some debate concerning the nature of the liturgical and theological meaning of the "opening prayer" or "collect." The title *oratio* precedes this prayer in the ancient Sacramentary Mass formulas, which title perdures up to and including the Tridentine Missal. In the present reform it is entitled *collecta,* a term which expresses part of its theology as a prayer that summarizes the (silent) prayer of the assembly at the beginning of the Eucharist,[31] which theology is sustained in the text of the General Instruction on the new Roman Missal n. 32: "the priest invites the people to pray and together with him they observe a brief silence so that they may realize they are in God's presence and may call their petitions to mind."

The debate about the nature of this prayer concerns whether it ought to be considered the conclusion to the beginning of the Eucharist (i.e., procession of ministers and/or the introductory rites) or whether it looks to the readings of the day or whether it articulates a theology of the feast being celebrated (including the theology of Sunday).[32] Under the heading "Opening Prayer or Collect" the GIRM n. 32 states that "the opening prayer, which custom has named the 'collect' . . . expresses the theme of the celebration and the priest's words address a petition to God the Father through Christ in the Holy Spirit." That the introductory period of silence is important here is asserted in GIRM n. 88: "With his hands joined, the priest invites the people to pray. All pray silently with the priest for a while. Then the priest extends his hands and says the opening prayer, at the end of which the people respond: Amen." Less controverted in the tradition and the present reform is the (rather brief) description of the theological meaning of the other two prayers. Under the title *prayer over the gifts,* the GIRM n. 53 states:

"Once the gifts have been placed on the altar and the accompanying rites completed, the preparation of the gifts comes to an end through the invitation to pray with the priest and the prayer over the gifts, which are a preparation for the eucharistic prayer."

Under the title *prayer after communion* the GIRM n. 56k states that "in the prayer after communion, the priest petitions for the effects of the mystery just celebrated and by their acclamation, Amen the people make the prayer their own."

Unlike the comparative effusiveness of the language and style of the Eucharistic prayer (especially as exemplified in Eastern anaphoras)[33] these variable prayers are "more terse . . . well balanced, economical of words, and direct."[34] In particular, the collect (both traditionally and in the present reform) "pays careful attention to the rules of the *cursus* of Latin prose,"[35] that is, to a style requiring an economy of words,[36] and that is succinct and abstract.[37]

Like the Eucharistic prayer, these texts begin by naming and addressing God, more often than not (especially in the opening prayer and the prayer after Communion) by acclaiming a divine attribute (e.g., "all-powerful," *omnipotens*[38]) or one of God's saving acts linked to our present need. An example of the latter that also captures the succinctness of the Latin *cursus* is the traditional collect from the Christmas day Eucharist, which prayer itself is most important as reflecting the theology of the feast of Christmas:

"Lord God,
we praise you for creating man,
and still more for restoring him in Christ.
Your Son shared our weakness:
may we share his glory,
for he lives and reigns. . . ."[39]

M. Augé argues that anamnetic motifs in these prayers include the word(s) used to address and describe God (e.g., *omnipotens*) on which basis the Church offers its prayer and the explicit naming of our Lord at the end of the prayer through whom we presume to offer it (e.g., *per Dominum nostrum*).[40] The use of the plural in the subjunctive verb form *quaesumus* ("we ask") reflects (in an exemplary succinct way) the ecclesial and petitionary nature of this prayer. Liturgical prayer is always made through the risen Christ for the sake of the Church.[41] This prayer ending articulates the fact that all Christian liturgical prayer is paschal, which theological statement and truth sets an essential part of the *context* of liturgical prayer. This paschal context and reference is notably explicit, for example, in the collect at the Vigil Mass for Christmas which text demonstrates how collect prayers can combine the particular feast being celebrated (the Incarnation) with the paschal mystery, always acclaimed as *the* way that God mediates salvation to us.

"God our Father,
every year we rejoice

as we look forward to this feast of our salvation (*redemptionis nostrae*).
May we welcome Christ as our Redeemer (*suscipimus Redemptorem*), and meet him with confidence when he comes to be our judge. . . ."[42]

In addition to distinguishing among kinds of euchological texts, it is important to differentiate among other kinds of texts of the Eucharist found in the tradition: liturgical greetings, litanies, intercessions and hymns (e g , Glory to God) and in the present reform: the Christological acclamations (or *tropes*) in the third form of the penitential rite[43] and in an extended (sung) Lamb of God as well as the ("Blessed are you, Lord God of all creation") prayers that now accompany the presentation of bread and wine. Other texts, such as those expressing the priest's unworthiness at receiving the Eucharist and which are designated as "private preparation of the priest" before Communion, are to be "said softly" (GIRM 56f.) while the assembly prays silently. Hence they may be said to be of only relative importance theologically.[44]

The present Eucharistic liturgy contains two new elements in its structure that are important to distinguish from euchology: optional comments (at the penitential rite, before the readings, before the preface and at the dismissal) and sample texts introduced by the phrase "in these or similar words" (such as the introduction to the blessing of palm and palm procession on Passion Sunday or the introduction to the blessing of candles and procession on the Presentation of the Lord). Strictly speaking these are not euchological, although they do contain important hints about the theology of the feast being celebrated. When "other words" are chosen one needs to respect the genre of these comments as preparatory indications of what is to come; they are not intended to be full explanations, explicitly didactic, or too long. In addition, their genre is that of informative comments, not stylized liturgical prayers.

II. Euchology: Texts in Context
In light of our argument thus far euchology cannot be interpreted properly apart its *context* in liturgical rites. The liturgical use of euchology—texts in specific contexts and texts which themselves help frame the liturgical context—discloses its genre an appreciation of which is essential for proper interpretation. The

185

proclaimed Scriptures, as the biblical Word of God, and euchology, as (what may be called) the word of the Church, classically formed the essential spoken parts of the ancient liturgy. They comprise two essential parts of the present revised liturgy. In addition, in sacramental liturgy euchological texts combine with engagement in symbolic (inter)action to complement and provide a demonstrative parallel to the scriptural Word. Essentially, euchological texts describe how in liturgy "the work of our redemption is accomplished."[45]

Given the contemporary revolution in hermeneutics for interpreting texts it is helpful to insist that liturgical texts are not neutral. Our concern now is to articulate some methodological principles that should be brought to bear on the correct interpretation of euchological texts and which accord with our thesis *context is text*.

1. Euchology: Evolution and Present Use. The first part of this method concerns the *historical evolution, historical critical and comparative study* of euchological texts both East and West. This phase includes contextualizing euchological texts within the social and ecclesial settings in which they were originally found then tracking their evolution up to its present version and contemporary use. Useful tools here include the (already cited) monumental compendium of texts and indices used up until the present reform by Placide Bruylants in *Les Oraisons du Missel Romain* and for the present euchology in *Concordantia verbalia Missalis Romani.*

Evidence from this study yields much insight about the normativity and longevity of some texts and the situation of the Church's life that influenced the style and content of these prayers.[46] For example, this kind of euchological study for Christmas discloses the central role of humanity's divinization through Jesus' incarnation and how the incarnation points to the paschal mystery as the purpose for Christ's coming in the flesh. To say that these texts for Christmas are normative is to underscore (among other things) the way liturgical euchology both East and West directs attention to the divine/human interchange and the centrality of the paschal mystery. Prayer texts do not remain on the level of historical description or merely retell the story of the birth, life, death and resurrection. They always specify how in the liturgy the community shares in the same salvation won for us, which once for all experience is now a new reality of salvation. The fact that all euchological texts in the present Sacramentary for Christmas are taken from already existing euchological sources underscores the theological value that has been ascribed to them.[47] To suggest that these texts are *normative* does not mean that they have not or cannot be changed. In fact, it may well be that the terseness of the (*cursus*) style of speech in the variable prayers for Christmas needs to be adjusted to suit a contemporary situation in which another style of speech is needed (for example, some repetition, a more elaborate style of speaking or which speak more directly to the heart). What remains normative, however, is the *theology* of the way euchology underscores the reality of divine/human interchange leading to identification of and more importantly (through the liturgy) *with* the paschal mystery as *the* mystery of faith.[48]

Another example that illustrates this facet of our methodological concern builds on the observations in chapter 2 regarding the present liturgy, the liturgical theology of ordination derived from it and questions about the adequacy of these rites in the present.[49] The historical study of consecratory prayers of the ordination rite beginning with that of Hippolytus needs to be done in light of prevailing Church order and Church structures and the subsequent evolution and changes these prayers underwent through the history of the Western liturgy. Part of the ecclesial context in which this text functioned included a Church polity whose ministers and ministries were certainly pluriform and which included both ordained and non ordained.[50] For example, Chupungco will state that

"[t]he effect of inculturation on theology and the liturgy has not always been exactly positive or edifying. The ordination prayers of the Sacramentary of Verona reflect a Constantinian situation that framed priestly ministry in the context of promotion, rank, dignity, and honor, although in this book these socio-political categories have been methodologically entrenched in biblical typology and Christian outlook."[51]

The value of tracking the historical evolution of such a text can help determine significant shifts in the liturgical theology of ordination in light of prevailing Church polity and structures. This background can lead to both an informed appreciation of when, how and (on the basis of this evidence) why the rite has changed over time.

In our method, to develop a liturgical theology of ordination it would be crucial to interpret the euchological texts used in the rites along with the Scriptures proclaimed and symbolic engagement entered into by the participants in the rite, including all liturgical ministers, those from the assembly engaged in particular aspects of the rite and the ordinand(s).[52] Of particular note would be indicating clashes of theology articulated in the rite, for example where a Scripture reading might speak of humility and service and a euchological text speak of rank and order.

Another very significant factor that deserves to be factored into this discussion is the fact that in the revised ritual ordinations take place on a Sunday in the community of the Church assembled for worship.[53] These factors speak compellingly of the fact that one is ordained from within the community of the baptized and that service for the Church is one of the root metaphors for the liturgical theology of ordination. Similarly, a liturgical theology of ordination requires that the varied charisms functioning in the Church community—and experienced at the ordination rite itself—be part of the context brought to bear on it. In our opinion, only in light of these several factors can liturgical theology be said to be developed.[54]

2. Present Euchology in Contemporary Contexts. The method outlined here would also lead to an informed analysis of the *present* euchology including an analysis of the other texts, especially the Scriptures, and the symbolic engagement used in the rite (e.g., oil used at the anointing of the sick, water for initiation etc.). This aspect of euchological study would also be undertaken in light of the General Instruction to the particular rite and any other documentation relating to the revisions of that rite after Vatican II. The attempt to determine the theological adequacy of a given rite means studying all the euchology for a given sacrament or for a given season, not just an individual text. Then any individual prayer or text can be interpreted as to its liturgical and theological adequacy. Hence the season of the liturgical year when texts are prayed, at what sacrament and at what part of the Liturgy of the Hours (e.g., morning and evening) are examples of the necessary contextual questions that need to be raised to interpret these texts. In addition it is essential to ask what Scriptures are read and what symbols are used along with euchological texts to comprise the act of liturgy.

A related issue concerns how a particular text is emphasized in celebration, important examples of which concern the singing of blessing or consecratory prayers. For example, the fact that consecratory prayers at ordination are set to music in both the Latin and the ICEL (English) text of the *Pontifical* certainly highlights them in celebration and makes a statement about their genre as sung prayer.[55] The fact that traditionally the Sacramentary presents prefaces to the Eucharistic prayer with musical notation underscores this prayer's importance. Similarly, the fact that the Sacramentary contains sample notation for singing the variable prayers of the Mass also indicates their importance. Furthermore, to determine the adequacy of a particular rite means asking to what extent the presumed priority given to a text in the ceremonial books is sustained in celebration and how these texts are heard and understood.

A working premise here is that the fullness of symbolic interaction in liturgy is achieved over time and in a number of settings where euchology helps disclose the meaning of the symbolic word and gestural speech that is liturgy. Reviewing texts in the course of the liturgical year presents the fullness of the ways in which the "work of our (accomplished) redemption" is experienced in liturgy: i.e., euchology of the entire liturgical cycle of feasts, seasons, sacraments, Hours etc. Because liturgical prayers address the pluriformity of life's circumstances, in light of which various aspects of salvation are imaged in these texts, only a theology derived from a cross section of prayers can represent what can be termed a liturgical theology of a given sacrament or a liturgical theology of the triune God.

For example, a liturgical theology of Eucharist derived from the Eucharistic prayer sustains images of God as one who feeds, heals, strengthens, reconciles, and transforms his chosen people through the Eucharist. It also sustains images of thanksgiving, memorial, invocation of the Spirit, intercession and sacrifice (among other things). Again, when the Eucharistic prayers are used as sources for Eucharistic theology, these prayers in their totality need to be probed to articulate the variety and complementarily of images of God, for redemption and of the sacrament of the Eucharist inherent in the Eucharistic prayers. This is to say that, when placed in the *context* of liturgical celebration, the Eucharistic prayers offer a host of traditional (although often neglected) avenues for developing Eucharistic theology. A theology derived from the Eucharistic prayer would include (among other things) notions of the *actualization* of the paschal mystery, God's inviting and involving the Church in the act of making Eucharist, the centrality of the *memorial* of the paschal mystery in Eucharist, a pneumatological cast to Eucharistic theology derived from the epiclesis and the work of the Spirit in the transformation of the species, the importance of personal (communal and individual) appropriation of the Eucharistic presence of Christ as concomitant with the liturgical understanding of Eucharist, the reality of Eucharist as a *sacrificial sacrament* with categories of sacrifice derived from the liturgy and the eschatological nature of Eucharistic participation as the actual, involving and dynamic presence of Christ which looks to its fulfillment in the eternal banquet of heaven.

With regard to texts in context more specifically, this means that the proclamation of the Eucharistic prayer in a variety of settings (not just the texts themselves) opens up important avenues for Eucharistic theology and the prayer for blessing water at initiation opens up important avenues for initiation theology. Different yet complementary aspects of Eucharistic theology derive from the Eucharist celebrated at initiation, weddings, ordinations, and profession rites. These include the intimate bond of God's covenant love as expressed at a wedding or the theological motif that the Eucharist is always a renewal of the baptismal covenant, notably when this occurs at rites of profession and ordination, which rites are intrinsically related to specifying the covenant of baptism.

In addition, the use of the same prayer for blessing water at both adult and infant baptism requires that it should be interpreted differently precisely because of these differing *contexts*. It is "heard" differently because of these differing settings. This can imply that images of divine initiative in initiation and the free endowment of grace through initiation would predominate at infant baptism. At adult baptism other images of response to God's invitation and the requisite response to initiation in ethical living would likely predominate.

Similarly with regard to the liturgical year this means that varying aspects of Eucharistic theology come to the fore when a Eucharist is celebrated during different seasons or on different feasts. During Advent, for example, when the eschatological aspects of the Christian faith are articulated through the Scriptures and euchological texts, these texts help to establish the *context* within which the inherently eschatological aspects of the Eucharistic celebration are emphasized.[56] The judicious use of additional tropes at the (third form of the penitential rite), the phrasing of the general intercessions and additional Christological acclamations at the Lamb of God can also draw out the eschatological aspect of the Eucharist.

Helpful examples of such usage are found in the second edition of the postconciliar Italian Missal which contains a number of additional tropes for the third form of the penitential rite listed according to season. Nine additional tropes are offered for Advent, six for Christmas, nine for Lent and nine for Easter. Those for Advent acclaim "Lord, you have come into the world to save us," "Christ, you continue to visit us with the grace of your Spirit," "Lord, you will come one day to judge us according to our works," "Lord, you came to defend the poor," "Christ, you are the refuge of the infirm," "Lord, you are the hope of sinners," "Lord, you come to visit your people in peace," "Christ, you come to save that which was lost," "Lord, you come to create a new world."[57]

The second edition of the postconciliar Spanish Missal contains additional options for the introductory greeting at Mass depending on the season and some additional tropes for the penitential rite (although fewer than the Italian edition). The Advent greeting is "The Lord who came to save us be with you."[58] The intrinsically eschatological aspect of Eucharistic theology is also implied when the Eucharist is celebrated in conjunction with the rites of anointing of the sick and, even more directly, in the rites of viaticum and commendation of the dying.

Another example concerns the celebration of the Eucharist during the Easter season when the inherently resurrection and feeding overtones of the Eucharist are brought to the fore. For example, when the accounts of the resurrection are proclaimed during the Easter octave and the Emmaus text is proclaimed on Easter night and on the third Sunday, these very readings draw out the inherently resurrection and meal sharing themes of Eucharistic theology. The use of the varying Easter prefaces indicates some of this as does the use of the variable parts of the Roman Canon proclaimed during Easter octave. The use of alternate greetings, tropes and, most directly during Easter, Christological acclamations for the Lamb of God would also underscore this aspect of Eucharistic theology.

When initiation is celebrated at a Eucharist, the understanding of Eucharist itself as the term of the initiation process and as a sacrament of initiation renewal is emphasized. These themes are seen specifically on Sunday when the rite of blessing and sprinkling with holy water is used. Also the cup-word about "the new and everlasting covenant" is seen as underscoring this theology. With all that is said about confirmation, when it is celebrated at a Eucharist what is clear is the close conjunction of confirmation with baptism and Eucharist as together forming the rites of initiation. That confirmation is a reaffirmation and renewal of baptism can be argued from the rite of confirmation itself, especially when it is celebrated at the Eucharist.

It is also important to allow the varying contexts inherent in different liturgical seasons to shed varying shades of color on the Eucharist itself. It would seem that the very singing of the Eucharistic prayer during Easter would underscore the priority of Easter as a Eucharistic season. The celebration of the Eucharist during a season like Lent, especially when accompanied by the use of the Eucharistic prayers for reconciliation, indicates how the Eucharist itself is necessarily to be seen as *a* sacrament of reconciliation. It could be argued that it is *the* sacrament signifying reconciliation begun in the sacrament of penance including the confession of sins which follows theologically upon the hearing of the Word, ratified personally in the act of absolution, expressed in acts of penance undertaken as a consequence of individual confession as an antidote to the sins committed. The original meaning of reconciliation to Eucharistic sharing would thus be restored to a central place in Eucharistic theology and personal spirituality.

The notion of covenant renewal is underscored when the rite of Christian marriage is celebrated at a nuptial Eucharist. This Eucharistic celebration says a great deal about the sacramentality of marriage in the first place which needs to be developed for a liturgical theology of marriage, as opposed to consent only. Equally important at such a Eucharist would be an emphasis on nuptial imagery emphasizing how deeply intimate and personal is the relationship of the Lord with the liturgical assembly gathered at such a Eucharist.

III. Roman Missal: New Translations, New Compositions

Among the host of unfinished tasks in which the contemporary Church is engaged because of the reform of the liturgy at least three concern euchology—determining the nature of the contents of the present *Missale Romanum*, translating the euchology of the Latin Missal into the vernacular and composing new euchological texts in vernacular languages.

1. Roman Missal: Old and New. In Pope Paul VI's Apostolic Constitution introducing the publication of the new Roman Missal in 1969, he states that, compared with the former Missal, the new Missal has

"corrected and considerably modified . . . the Proper of the Seasons, the Proper of the Saints, the Common of Saints, ritual Masses, and votive Masses. In all of these changes, particular care has been taken with the prayers. Their number has been increased, so that the new forms might better correspond to new needs, and the text of older prayers has been restored on the basis of the ancient sources. As a result, each weekday of the principal liturgical seasons, Advent, Christmas, Lent and Easter, now has its own distinct prayer."[59]

A. Bugnini succinctly summarizes the work of the Consilium's study group on the Missal drawing special attention to the new Missal's "euchological riches." He writes that the new Missal contains some sixteen hundred prayers—twice the number found in the old Missal. Almost all the prayers of the former Missal are used in the new edition, "revised if need be to harmonize them with the reform and teaching of Vatican II."[60] The additional texts are from the manuscript collections, the liturgies of East and West and, "where there were no new models to follow in meeting new needs (for example, the prayer for nonbelievers on Good Friday or some Masses for various needs and situations), the experts employed their own talents and charism."[61]

Bugnini's phrasing that some prayers from the former Missal were "revised if need be to harmonize them with the reform and teaching of Vatican II" is at least intriguing in that it substantiates the interrelationship of *lex orandi/lex credendi* and gives weight to the Church's theology as being influential on the Church's prayer. The Consilium itself stated that the prayers and rites surrounding the "offertory" were most in need of a revision that removes any expression that anticipates ideas proper to the Eucharistic prayer itself.[62] A. Dumas himself states that the revisers of the prayers over the gifts sought to avoid any such anticipatory expressions, and that certain turns of phrase remaining from ancient sources should be translated in their "weaker" sense as designating the gifts of the assembly or in a way that makes clear that the expression refers to the Eucharist about to be celebrated.[63] While one may want to debate the value of this kind of *a priori* insistence on the meaning of this prayer, it certainly illustrates how theology influenced some of the work of the Missal's revisers.

From the point of view of theology derived from the liturgy, the revised Latin edition of the Roman Missal is unprecedented in that it contains a number of structural and textual elements that are new to the Church's euchology and that had to be translated into a host of vernacular languages. The Consilium decree on translating the Missal states that

"these texts, whether ancient or modern, have a precise and studied theological elaboration. If the text is ancient, certain Latin terms present difficulties of interpretation because of their use and meaning, which are much different from their corresponding terms in modern language. The translation will therefore demand an astute handling and sometimes a paraphrasing, in order to render accurately the original pregnant meaning. If the text is a more recent one, the difficulty will be reduced considerably, given the use of terms and a style of language which are closer to modern concepts."[64]

In this connection the kind of background work evident in the three ICEL *Progress Reports* (indicating the shape and scope related to the second ICEL translation of the Missal) is significant.[65]

2. *New Translations*. As has already been noted, the Concilium pointed out that the translation of the succinct and, at times, ab-

stract prayers of the Missal taken from the ancient Roman tradition "may need to be rendered somewhat more freely while conserving the original ideas. This can be done by moderately amplifying them or, if necessary, paraphrasing expressions in order to concretize them for the celebration and the needs of today."[66] An example from the first ICEL *Progress Report* can illustrate this point.

The *collecta* (term used in the Latin Missale) for the solemnity of Epiphany is:

"Deus, qui hodierna die Unigenitum tuum
gentibus stella duce revelasti,
concede propitius, ut qui iam te ex fide cognovimus,
usque ad contemplandam speciem tuae celsitudinis perducamur."

In Bruylants' *Les Oraisons* this text is well attested in liturgical tradition (found in fifteen of his source texts) contains only the slightest variation (*celsitudines* instead of *celsitudinis* in one manuscript source) and was used in this place on Epiphany in the former Missal.[67] The text is in classic Roman collect form: naming God (*Deus*) followed by the relative clause (*qui . . . revelasti*) and a transition (*concede*) to a tersely worded request (*ut . . . perducamur*). Bruylants cites Matthew 2:2-9, the visit of Magi (the present Lectionary uses Matthew 2:2-12 as the Epiphany gospel) and 2 Corinthians 5:7 as the Scripture texts related to the prayer. The *gentibus stella duce revelasti* refers to the Gospel and *ut qui iam te fide congovimus* is almost directly from St. Paul "we walk by faith, not by sight" (2 Cor 5:7). The present *opening prayer* (term used in the ICEL English translation) reads:

"Father,
you revealed your Son to the nations
by the guidance of a star.
Lead us to your glory in heaven
by the light of faith."

The naming of God as "Father" instead of "God" in this ICEL translation is not unique in the first edition of the English Sacramentary. It is, however, problematic. The Latin *Missale Romanum* uses *Pater* in collect prayers only twenty-one times. However, some 560 translations use *Father*.[68] Three reasons are advanced for this usage. First, the senior members of ICEL's Advisory Committee explained that *Father* was used so frequently in order "to make clear to the hearer that Roman euchological presidential prayers are addressed to the First Person, a point which in some cases might otherwise not be evident until the conclusion." Second, euphony was a consideration; *Father* sounds better than *God* at the beginning of a prayer. (Related to this reason is the fact that the title *Lord* is often joined with *God* in order to avoid this euphony problem.) Third, the use of *Father* may also show greater appreciation that God is personal, and immanent as well as transcendent.[69]

This collect has undergone important revisions (four to date) in preparation for the second ICEL Missal translation. The latest text "reworked for the Advisory Committee" reads:

"God of mystery,
on this day you revealed your only Son to the nations
by the guidance of a star.
We know you now by faith;
lead us into that presence
where we shall behold your glory face to face."[70]

Interestingly, in the third proposed translation (immediately preceding this text) the second half of the prayer read:

"Lead us who know you here by faith
into that presence
where we shall behold your glory face to face."

Obviously this example of an ICEL translation raises a host of issues, many unforeseen even a few years ago. The translators obviously made adjustments from the concise Latin original, e.g., from *Deus* to *God of mystery*. The translation of *hodierna die* to *on this day* is a most useful change. Here the significant liturgical terminology of *hodie* and *haec dies* can be restored to its rightful place as privileged liturgical vocabulary. The movement from "by the guidance of a star. We know you now by faith" is at least awkward in English, especially when compared with the succinct *concede, propitius, ut qui iam te ex fide congovimus* and as placed in a subordinate clause. The sense of *usque ad contemplandam speciem* is admittedly difficult to translate. The latest English text leaves something to be desired in this connection. The fact that the pre-ferred ICEL prayer conclusion will likely change from "who lives and reigns with you and the Holy Spirit" to "who lives and reigns with you in the unity of the Holy Spirit" is decidedly a theological improvement because *in the unity of the Holy Spirit* re-stores an ecclesial sense to the ending of liturgical prayer.

Another English rendering of the Latin Epiphany collect, from the *St. Michael's Daily Missal*, reads:

"O God, on this day you led the gentiles by a star and revealed to them your Son. We know you now by faith: lead us on to the sight of your heavenly glory."[71]

This translation raises the question of style in translating from the Latin; more precisely, the advisability of a single English transla-tion of the Missal with a uniform style. It is at least arguable that to try to achieve a uniform translation of the Sacramentary for all English-speaking ecclesial situations is not wise. The variety exem-plified in, for example, a Trappist monastic community, or a former Episcopalian parish now able to use some of its former Prayer Book usages as Roman Catholics, or an inner-city African-American parish or a suburban or rural congregation exemplifies at least something of the complex nature of the audience for whom the translated Missal is intended. Further, if the desire for a more formal style in celebration can be satisfied in some mea-sure by the use of the Revised Standard Version of the Scriptures, is there not something to be said in favor of a more formal Eng-lish translation of the Sacramentary? If a more formal style is desired, a more suitable translation of the Epiphany collect for such purposes might well read:

"Almighty God,
who this day revealed your only-begotten Son
to the Gentiles;
grant that we who know you now by faith,
may be brought to the everlasting vision
of your glory.
Through Jesus Christ our Lord,
who lives and reigns with you,
in the unity of the Holy Spirit, forever and ever."

Such a translation would attend to a number of difficulties already raised. It would avoid the overuse of naming God as *Father*. It would sustain more clearly the Latin collect style by its use of *who . . . grant . . . may*. It would use the arguably more literal (and familiar) theological term "everlasting vision" than the more immediately involving style in the proposed "we shall behold your glory face to face." The elimination of "we ask this" is more trustful of the integrity of the prayer as a unit, ending it with "through Jesus Christ our Lord. . . ."

3. Translation, Adaptation, Inculturation. The same Concilium document on translations from the Roman Missal states that

"texts translated from another language are clearly not sufficient for the celebration of a fully renewed liturgy. The creation of new texts will be necessary. But translation of texts transmitted through the tradition of the Church is the best school and discipline for the creation of new texts so 'that any new forms adopted should in some way grow organically from forms already in existence' (quoting the Liturgy Constitution, n. 23)."[72]

A related issue here concerns the normativity of the euchological texts in the Roman Missal. Does the fact that a euchological text has been chosen for a specific feast necessarily imply that a particular text is normative and must be used? If, in fact, the language of a prayer is too terse as to be too foreign in style or language and thus be nearly unintelligible, should not the text be expanded, or adjusted, or another composition replace it? In this connection recall the distinction (noted above)[73] which Anscar Chupungco makes between texts and the expression of texts when he argues that a text may be considered normative but may be expressed through words and an idiom more congenial to the language and thought patterns of contemporary congregations.

Again, a precedent in this connection is the fact that the present ICEL Sacramentary contains new compositions in the Sunday Mass formulas termed the *alternative opening prayer*. In addition, the second edition of the Italian Sacramentary contains three additional collect (opening) prayers for each Sunday reflecting the specific Lectionary readings of that particular (A, B, or C) cycle. This same arrangement will likely be used in the second ICEL edition with the texts composed in English.[74]

198

There are, however, major theological implications concerning the addition of original prayers for each Lectionary cycle. First, the very fact of preparing texts so closely tied with the Scriptures strongly implies that the purpose of the opening collect is to set up the Liturgy of the Word. Our review of historical and theological perspectives on the variable prayers of the Missal above indicates that the exact purpose of these texts has not been determined. The exclusive use of opening prayers directly related to the day's Lectionary readings, for example, could mitigate the theological value of having these prayers articulate a theology of Sunday Eucharist as the Church's ongoing participation in the paschal mystery. Second, the fact that the new compositions are so intrinsically related to the readings invites a word of caution lest the rites surrounding the Liturgy of the Word and the proclamation of the Word itself be considered as didactic in nature.

Put another way, the fact that these prayers correspond so closely to the Scriptures can be salutary in the way they offer a prayer quality to what will be proclaimed. The negative side of this, however, is that the introductory rites of the Eucharist can be too concerned with the Liturgy of the Word only. Furthermore, the introductory rites themselves, especially if the third form of the penitential rite and the optional original prayers are chosen, can lead to a diminished appreciation of the highly symbolic and multi-directional meanings expressed and experienced through the Eucharist as a whole and not just through the proclaimed Word. Introductory comments that begin the Eucharist should not be restricted to comprehending the Scripture readings, or even to appreciating how the texts are enacted when proclaimed liturgically.

In effect, over time, these comments should refer to the whole of the Eucharistic liturgy that is presently occurring. With regard to the unity of Word and table, the precedent of Communion antiphons reprising a phrase or verse from the day's Scripture readings is an important indication of the intrinsic link between word and sacrament. Whatever options are chosen for the introductory rites of the Eucharist, we would argue for a more anamnetic and less didactic theology of the Word as constitutive of the liturgical theology of the Eucharist.

In light of our thesis about interpreting elements of the liturgy in relation to each other, specifically Scripture readings in relation to euchology, the establishment of a three year cycle of collects to coincide with Sunday Lectionary would certainly contribute positively to how the Scriptures ought to be interpreted. For example the *Second Progress Report on the Revision of the Roman Missal* gives the following as the optional opening prayer for the First Sunday of Lent, B cycle when the Scriptures are: Genesis 9:8-15, Psalm 25, 1 Peter 3:18-22, Mark 1:12-15:

"God of the covenant,
as the forty days of deluge
swept away the world's corruption
and watered new beginnings
of righteousness and life,
so in the saving flood of baptism
we are washed clean and born again.
Throughout these forty days, we beg you,
unseal within us the wellspring of your grace,
cleanse our hearts of all that is not holy,
and cause your gift of new life to flourish once again.
Grant this through our Lord Jesus Christ, your Son,
who lives and reigns with you in the unity of the Holy Spirit
God forever and ever."

In a number of ways this text is a very helpful opening prayer. This text is admittedly longer and departs somewhat from the traditional Roman collect structure. However, on this Sunday when the Gospel account of Jesus' temptation for forty days dominates all three Lectionary cycles, and in the Markan account to be read today the number "forty," the location of the "wilderness" and the ministering "angels" are specified, it is at least curious that these motifs are absent in this prayer. Admittedly, the references to "covenant" and "baptism" go a long way toward reinstating a baptismal consciousness to Lent.

However, Catholic piety has also traditionally been nurtured by images of identifying with Jesus as he was tempted in the desert, that the forty days of penitence invites deep identification with Jesus and that Lent as a "desert experience" reflects the desert as a unique location—a place where one cannot hide from anyone or anything, where one is exposed (to the elements and because of one's sins) and where one meets God. Some reference to the desert as a place of no protections except protection received from

200

Jesus and his ministering angels would at least be equally useful images in this text.[75] In other words, could the use of these collects imply that there is *one* way to interpret these texts when proclaimed together? Does the prayer's use solve the question about what these texts ought to say?

Because of the precedent established in the second Italian Missal with these three optional prayers, some have found it useful to translate these optional texts and to use them as the concluding prayer of the general intercessions on the appropriate Sunday. This is indeed a creative use of these prayers and one that allows these texts to inspire the composition of intercessions to reflect their metaphors, applications and turns of phrase. However, it should at least be pointed out that the concluding prayers to the sample formulas for the general intercessions in the Sacramentary Appendix are far more general in theme (and are not connected with specific Scripture readings) and most usually conclude the spoken intercessions by referring to the offering of these prayers. In addition, one could make a legitimate case for the fact that once the Scriptures are proclaimed and the homily delivered, the assembly has already moved beyond the literal Scriptures to implications and contemporary applications of these texts. Thus it is at least debatable whether concluding collects to the prayer of the faithful should be taken from prayers which are intended to introduce the day's readings. The other side of the debate, however, could maintain that the very use of this kind of collect would prevent the intercessions from becoming too focused on one or another Lenten theme.

4. Language: Familiar and Formative. One of the legacies of the fixity and comparative rigidity of the Roman rite from Trent through to Vatican II was that liturgical assemblies could become quite familiar with the rites in such a way that (among many other things) the use of proscribed chant melodies (sung by the congregation and/or the schola), of ceremonial conducted according to specified rubrics and the color and style of vesture worn could become so familiar as to be presumed and almost "second nature." The use of a particular chant, for example, could signal a particular feast or season without any explanation. In more recent decades leading to the present reform of the liturgy, the use of hand missals in the vernacular deepened this sense of familiarity for even if people did not know Latin they most usually were able to hear enough of it to know what they should be reading along in these missals. For example, the singing of the Roman collect as dictated by a chant melody that varied only according to the length of the collect was familiar. The reading of a vernacular translation was guided by hearing this intonation.

This kind of ritual familiarity enabled people to participate in liturgy in such a way that the non-variability of the rite led to the distinct, very desirable prospect that the communion with God experienced through the liturgy was *supported* by familiar rites, not *dominated* by them. The kind of prayer experienced rested on but also transcended rubric, symbol, or text. Liturgy was not self-conscious since the rites were proscribed. Diligent care was to be expended in executing them. By contrast, the present liturgy can lead to ritual self-consciousness because the legitimate variety now invited by the present reform can allow "liturgical performance" (admittedly a poor phrase)—how gestures are executed, how symbols are used, and what words are used in the prayers—to become almost too important.

The legacy of the former Roman rite invited a level of liturgical participation that transcended the particular rites and words in order to draw participants into an experience of the divine that is almost a contemplative stance before and in God. In this case language becomes merely a prop that discloses and unleashes meanings both verbally and nonverbally. Prayer language should always be oriented to such description and disclosure of the mystery that is God as God is experienced through the liturgy. If it becomes too important then the *means* to this end of being drawn ever more fully into the mystery of God can become the *end* in itself. In short, language should be a vehicle that supports an experience of God on a number of different affective and spiritual levels.

Among the problems with euchological language at present are the naming of God and the elimination of language that is non-inclusive. Our argument is that as far as possible the work toward a second edition of the ICEL Sacramentary translations should be expedited so that inadequate names for God and unnecessarily exclusive language be replaced by idioms that are biblically normative and appropriately inclusive. A related issue concerns comprehending liturgical language. Some have argued that trying to pay attention to every word in a prayer that is filled with biblical images and metaphors is very difficult because no one can really hear and retain them all. Our argument is that one ought not try to "retain" all of them; one ought to allow one's imagination to ruminate on a few, perhaps even one, in order that the act of God recalled through a particular metaphor can be appreciated as being experienced here and now.

Since most euchological metaphors are from the Scriptures, it would be highly desirable for participants to react to the vernacular language used in the liturgy as very familiar and as articulating one or another biblical event on which this particular enactment of the liturgy is grounded. (When hearing euchological language, one should be able to say to oneself "oh yes" rather than "oh my.") The precedent for this is described above when the silent prayer of the assembly would be summed up in the vocal "collect" prayers. In collect prayers the structure to allow for silence is a theological statement as much as it is a rubric. The use of silence invites the personal prayer of all the assembled. The collect is a resume, not necessarily of individual silent prayers but of the fact that everyone prayed silently at the allotted times in the liturgy provided by pauses.

IV. Euchological Unfinished Business

Because of the emphasis placed in this chapter on the Eucharistic prayer and on the variable prayers of the Eucharist our focus in this section will be on these kinds of euchological prayers.[76] Methodologically this critique is based on elements which are constitutive of the prayers used at the Eucharistic liturgy (Eucharistic prayer and variable prayers) and to what extent these elements are or ought to be reflected in contemporary Eucharistic euchology which data in turn would be the basis for a liturgical theology of the Eucharist.

The first critique concerns the texts of the Eucharistic prayer. The Eucharistic prayer, particularly its introductory section, is a classic *locus* for explicit reference to praise and thanks for creation.[77] Theologically this leads to praising God for redemption, which section is highly Christological. Regrettably in the present euchology, only the preface to the fourth Eucharistic prayer contains any notable reference to praise for creation. While it is true that a highly Christological emphasis has classically marked the

Roman prefaces, it is certainly regrettable that the inroads in this direction evident in recent liturgical scholarship (the *berakah* and *todah* genres of Jewish prayer)[78] and signalled by the introduction of the fourth Eucharistic prayer were not more deeply made in the rest of the present euchology.

Allied with this criticism is the debate often engaged in by liturgical theologians about what ought to be in the text of a Eucharistic prayer text and whether or not the anaphora should reflect general themes or whether it should reflect a particular need. This is to say that some argued against the publication of Eucharistic prayers for reconciliation and a preface for Masses when the anointing of the sick takes place because such prayers were thought to focus too directly on a single theme. An obvious loss to the structure and contents of the Eucharistic prayer could most likely be this motif of praise for creation when prefaces and Eucharistic prayers for particular needs are developed.

A second critique (with some corollaries) concerns the present structure of all the Eucharistic prayers added to the Roman rite in the present reform. For example, the suitability of separating the newly added explicit invocation of the Holy Spirit in the epiclesis is at least debated.[79] Additional new Eucharistic prayers could well reflect what some would argue is the more common structure of a single epiclesis, not two or a split epiclesis.

Another critique concerning structure is evident in the debate that has ensued over the ICEL sponsored "original eucharistic prayer" in English. Among the issues debated was the use of the phrase "death would hunt him down" as referring to Jesus' passion and death. The criticism is that this text does not comply with the phrase from the second Eucharistic prayer "before he was given up to death, a death he freely accepted" (present ICEL translation). It would seem that one might well argue that such an alternative phrasing underscores aspects of Jesus' passion not cited in the second anaphora. These include the fact that in the Synoptic accounts Jesus endured an agony in Gethsemane before acknowledging "thy will be done" and that it is only in the Gospel of John that Jesus is so resolutely set on accepting death on the cross. It would seem legitimate to have both these scriptural approaches to passion and death reflected in Eucharistic prayers.

Another critique about structure concerns the way "praise and thanks" are so positively presented in the present texts. Here, a more realistic appraisal of Eucharistic praying would call for adding a section to the Eucharistic prayers that is explicitly in the form of lament.[80] To acknowledge betrayal, doubt, even despair in the human condition in such texts, particularly as a result of incomprehensible inhumanity like the Holocaust, would reflect a particularly strong aspect of lament derived from the Psalms tradition. In this case, at least part of Eucharistic praying would concern hope amid such agonizing doubt and despair. From a slightly different point of view one could argue that the prevalence of suffering in contemporary human life and the apparently hopeless situations in which many people find themselves in terms of personal oppression, terminal illness, prejudice, etc. almost requires that Eucharistic prayers speak much more realistically about strength and hope amid turmoil rather than the assurance that suffering will end. This could lead to greater appropriateness in terms of actual needs named in liturgical prayer, which would likely result in more appreciation for the "not-yet-ness" of the Christian life while at the same time offering hope and support in the midst of such trials.

Another structural critique regarding the Eucharistic prayer concerns placing the memorial acclamation *before* the anamnesis prayer itself; its location *after* the anamnesis prayer in the Eucharistic prayers for children is illustrative. The move from institution narrative directly to memorial acclamation followed by the memorial prayer does seem to break up the flow of the prayer. Hence the Eucharistic prayers for children would reflect the more suitable structure.

The next critique is more general. With regard to the structure of the present order of Mass, it can be argued that there are comparatively few references to the eschatological aspect of liturgy expressed in the Eucharistic liturgy. One is the prayer after the rite of sprinkling with holy water:

"may almighty God cleanse us of our sins,
and through the eucharist we celebrate
make us worthy to sit at his table
in his heavenly kingdom."

Another is one of the sample introductions to the Lord's Prayer:

"Let us pray for the coming of the kingdom
as Jesus taught us."

A third is the invitation to Communion:

"This is the Lamb of God
who takes away the sins of the world.
Happy are those who are called to his supper" (from Rev 19:9).

Both liturgical tradition in general and the experience of the Eastern liturgies more particularly indicate how such references are central to the celebration of liturgy. They ought be expressed more directly in the reformed Roman rite to sustain the pluriform aspects of Eucharistic theology that are drawn from the traditional structure of anaphoras and from the present Eucharistic prayers, which sources ground the pluriform aspects of a liturgical theology of the Eucharist.

An additional welcome adjustment would be the inclusion of additional prefaces to the Eucharistic prayer that reflect more fittingly the saint being commemorated. The precedent established in the present Dominican Sacramentary, with two prefaces for St. Dominic, could lead to a richer set of prefaces to reflect more specifically (rather than so generally) the saints honored in the liturgical year.[81]

A final critique reiterates the material already argued about the fact that the present euchology and calendar reflect the northern hemisphere and ignore the experience of liturgical praying and feasting in the southern hemisphere. The argument in favor of composing a new euchology for the major seasons of Advent-Christmas-Epiphany and Lent-Easter-Pentecost rests on viewing the many traditional and time-honored euchological texts used at this time of year as *paradigmatic* of the theology of these feasts and seasons, not as literal norms. In fact, because this euchology would not be predicated on the notions of the passing of the longest nights of the year (Christmas) or the renewal of the earth in spring (Easter) it could break ground in articulating the kind of hope believers have in view of redemption still to be completed. Eschatological yearning and hope in the process from such euchology could serve the renewal of euchology for the Church in both hemispheres by emphasizing the fact that the redemption celebrated in liturgy is still incompletely experienced in the rest of life.

It is highly doubtful that the debates about a truly adequate and theologically rich liturgical euchology will ever cease. What is attempted here is to express some indication of the lines along which a more adequate euchology could be constructed. As in efforts in naming God and in theologizing about God more generally, the task here is to argue for less and less inadequate formulations in liturgical euchology. The provisionality of all liturgy should be recalled here. At issue in liturgical euchology (and liturgical ritual more generally) is allowing theologically informed texts to contribute to the experience that allows the powerful presence and action of God to be unleashed within and for the liturgical assembly in ever new ways. Ways not defined by euchology at all, but through words, symbols, gestures, and silences that evoke and invite assemblies to experience the mystery that is God.

We noted above (in this chapter) that it is important to be attentive to the grammar of liturgical praying. The fact that the vast majority of euchological texts use the *subjunctive* mood is indicative that liturgical prayers articulate *our* need for God, always addressed as *thou/you*, a need that will not come to an end until life on this earth has ended. In the meantime euchological prayers function the most adequately when they name our need, place it within the sweep of saving history, express that need in direct address to God and, in this way, give voice to the silent groanings of our hearts. Such texts are less concerned with providing answers than they are with providing an experience of ecclesial hope in the midst of our need. Such is one of the strengths gained from liturgical *texts* prayed in their proper ecclesial *context*. In terms of our thesis, *ecclesial context is text*.

Notes

1. See above, Chapter 1, 23–24.

2. The translation into English and the enhancement by significant additions of Cyrille Vogel's *Introduction aux sources de l'histoire du culte chrétien au Moyen-Age* (Spoleto: Centro Italiano di Studi sull'Alto Medioevo, 1981) as *Medieval Liturgy: An Introduction to the Sources* (Washington: Pastoral Press, 1986) has made this an even more important tool for euchological study. Also important in this connection (among others) are the essays and bibliographies in: Jose Aldazábal, "El libro liturgico como pédagogía de la celebracion," *Phase* 116 (1980) 111–124, Matias Augé, "Principi di interpretazione dei testi liturgici,"

in *Anamnesis I* (Torino: Marietti, 1974) 151–179, *idem.*, "Eucologia," in *Nuovo Dizionario di Liturgia*, 509–519, Annibale Bugnini, *The Reform of the Liturgy* 396–405, Ildebrando Scicolone, "Libri Liturgici," in *Nuovo Dizionario di Liturgia* 701–713, Achille M. Triacca and Burkhard Neunheuser, "Il libro liturgico e la celebrazione: ieri e oggi," *Rivista Liturgica* 63 (1976) 57–76, and Herman Wegman, *Christian Worship in East and West*, 71–76, 150–203.

3. M. Augé, "Eucologia," 509, as well as the definition in the *Nuovo Dizionario*, 1622. For stylistic reasons (to avoid constant repetition of "sacramentary") throughout the chapter the terms "sacramentary" and "missal" will be used interchangeably.

4. As distinguished from hymns, antiphons, responsories, etc.

5. The General Instruction on the Liturgy of the Hours (n. 112) states "Psalm-prayers for each psalm are given in the supplement to *The Liturgy of the Hours* as an aid to understanding them in a predominantly Christian way. An ancient tradition provides a model for their use: after the psalm a period of silence is observed, then the prayer gives a resume and resolution of the thoughts and aspirations of those praying the psalms."

6. The reason for noting this definition here is that some authors argue that the opening prayer at the Eucharist still has this same function, about which more will be said below. It is commonly asserted that the function of psalm prayers is to "collect" the silent prayers of the assembly formulated after the psalm ends (which assembly may well not have recited or sung the psalms at the Liturgy of the Hours). For an insight into this important aspect of liturgical prayer see, among others, Adalbert DeVogué, ed. and comment., *La Règle de saint Benoit*, in *Sources Chrétiennes 185* (Paris: Les Editions du Cerf, 1972) 582–585, *idem.*, "Le sens de l'office divin," *Revue d'Ascétique et de Mystique* 42 (1966) 391–404, 43 (1967) 21–33.

7. This wording is deliberately vague since assigning authorship of euchological prayers is difficult. In trying to determine authorship critical scholarship repeatedly goes beyond the names associated with ancient sacramentaries (e.g., "Leonine," Gelasian and Gregorian) and names associated with the editing of these sacramentaries (e.g., Benedict of Anianne for the *Hucusque* Supplement to the Gregorian) to internal textual evidence, verbal correspondences and similarity of phrasing between Sacramentary texts and other writings (notably homilies) of possible authors. In addition, even when there is a verbal or logical correspondence linking Scriptures, euchology, catecheses and homilies it is nonetheless often still very difficult to determine which of these texts came first and was thereby influential on the other(s).

8. GIRM n. 40.

9. The addition *et sanguinis* to the conventional title *Corpus Christi* in the present Sacramentary, Lectionary and the revised *Graduale Romanum* is notable. The new Code of Canon Law adds *et sanguinis* in the two places it refers to the feast: canons 944 and 1246. The conventional title *Corpus Christi* is retained in the 1968 Declaration of the Sacred Congregation of Rites *Cum recen-*

tioribus temporibus (on the transfer of Epiphany, Ascension, and Corpus Christi to Sunday), Paul VI's *Mysterium Fidei* (1965) n. 63, GIRM n. 3, the General Norms for the Liturgical Year and the Calendar (1969) n. 102 and the General Instruction on the Worship of the Eucharist Outside of Mass (1973) n. 7.

10. The present *Graduale* also contains the sequence *Laeta dies* for the Solemnity of St. Benedict on July 11.

11. The Latin text of the original from the *Sacramentarium Gelasianum Vetus* n. 1128 is

"Fac nos, quaesumus, Domine Deus noster,
adventum Christi Filii tui sollicitos exspectare,
ut, dum venerit pulsans, orationibus vigilantes,
et in suis inveniat laudibus exsulantes."

All cited sources are according to the indices provided by Antoine Dumas, "Les sources du nouveau missel romain," *Notitiae* 7 (1971) 37–42, 74–77, 94–95, 134–136, 276–280, 409–410. Other helpful tools for euchological research on the present Roman Sacramentary are: A, Dumas, "Les préfaces du nouveau Missel," *Ephemerides Liturgicae* 85 (1971) 16–28; *idem.*, "Pour mieux comprendre les textes liturgiques du Missel Romain," *Notitiae* 6 (1970) 194–213, Pierre Jounel, "Les collectes du sanctoral au missel romain," in *Lex Orandi, Lex Credendi*, eds. Gerard Békés and Giustino Farnedi (Rome: Editrice Anselmiana, 1980) 347–377. The index and compilation of prayer texts from the present Missal is most helpful in Thaddaus A. Schnitker and Wolfgang A. Slaby, *Concordantia verbalia Missalis Romani* (Westfalen: Aschendorff, 1983). The index and collection of texts of the prior Roman Missal still remains very helpful in this regard, Pierre Bruylants, *Les Oraisons du Missel Romain*.

12. The Latin text of the original from the *Sacramentarium Veronense* n. 1254 is

"Tanto nos, Domine, quaesumus,
prompitiore servitio haec praecurrere concede sollemnia,
quanto in his constare principium
nostrae redemptionis ostendis."

13. M. Augé, "Eucologia," 509, from Pio Alfonso, *L'eucologia romana antica. Lineamenti stilistici e storici* (Subiaco, 1931) 7.

14. That the spoken articulation of the Eucharistic prayer and the variable prayers is a presidential function is reflected in GIRM 10: "Among the parts assigned to the priest, the Eucharistic prayer has precedence; it is the high point of the whole celebration. Next are the prayers: the opening prayer or collect, the prayer over the gifts, and the prayer after Communion. The priest, presiding in the person of Christ, addresses the prayers to God in the name of the entire assembly of God's people and of all present, and thus they are called presidential prayers."

15. The notion of watching as an important aspect of liturgical participation is explored in John Bossy, "The Mass as Social Institution."

16. Robert Taft, "Toward a Theology of the Christian Feast," in *Beyond East and West*, 10.

17. Ibid., "Quod itaque Redemptoris nostri conspicuum fuit, in sacramenta transivit."

18. Quoted in R. Taft, ibid., 11, from "Le symbolisme des rites baptismaux," *Dieu vivant* 1 (1945) 17.

19. As of this writing ICEL has proposed additional translations of this classic Latin text: "God of majesty and loving kindness" and "God of holiness and might." See Gail Ramshaw-Schmidt, *Christ in Sacred Speech* (Philadelphia: Fortress Press, 1986) 27–34 for a brief discussion about this cluster of names for God. Other introductions to the Eucharistic prayer presently proposed for the revised ICEL edition of the Sacramentary include: "O God of hope and promise" (for Advent), "almighty God, king of endless glory" (for Christmas) and "merciful and faithful God" (for Lent). Ramshaw-Schmidt states: "Thus at the beginning of the Great Thanksgiving, we pray along with Abraham who obeyed the call (Gen 12:4), with Moses, who received the Torah (Exod 19:20), and with Jesus, who was the Word (John 1:1). As we eat bread and wine, we recall Abraham, who shared his food with three mysterious visitors (Gen 18:8), Moses, who ate and drank with God on Sinai and did not die (Exod 24:11), and Jesus, who breaking bread on Sunday evening, showed forth his wounds (Luke 24:31)" (30).

20. This number changed over time. G. G. Willis (in "The Variable Prayers of the Roman Mass" 94) asserts that while the Verona Sacramentary contained 269 proper prefaces, there was a tendency in the sixth and seventh centuries to reduce the number. Hence the Gregorian (Hadrianum) had fourteen; by the eleventh century there were only nine.

21. The American translation and adaptation of the first edition (1969) of the revised Sacramentary contained eighty-one prefaces. The present edition (1975) contains prefaces intrinsically connected to their proper Eucharistic prayers, e.g., for children and reconciliation as well as one preface for masses at which the anointing of the sick takes place, two additional prefaces for the dedication of a Church and one for Mary, Mother of the Church. Not all of the additions to the American Sacramentary have been found euchologically successful or theologically sound. A particularly striking example is the preface for Thanksgiving Day where the "founding fathers" of the United States are likened to Israel as the chosen ones to share in God's covenant. The parallelism is at least forced, if not theologically naive, when the saving event of the Exodus is followed by:
"It happened to our fathers,
who came to this land as if out of the desert
into a place of promise and hope."

22. Section 4 of this chapter will contain some criticisms of the structure of these new prayers, one of which concerns the problematic nature of this "split epiclesis."

23. Again, see below, section 4 of this chapter for a critique of the present sequence of memorial acclamation—memorial prayer.

24. Regrettably, as of this writing, the proposed ICEL revision retains this same wording despite the fact that the Latin reads "Memores igitur, Domine." By way of contrast it is interesting that the present ICEL translation of "memores igitur mortis et resurrectionis eius" of the second Eucharistic prayer is "in memory of his death and resurrection" and that the proposed change reads "remembering, therefore, his death and resurrection." It would seem preferable for the translation of the memorial prayer in the third prayer to be equally dynamic as an action, not merely as a mental recollection.

25. The present translation of the first part of the memorial prayer in the Roman Canon states:

"Father, we celebrate the memory of Christ, your Son.
We, your people and your ministers,
recall his passion,
his resurrection from the dead,
and his ascension into glory. . . ."

26. The new ICEL proposal for this phrase in the third Eucharistic prayer is "and eagerly awaiting the day of his return"; the proposal for the phrase in the fourth Eucharistic prayer remains the same.

27. The fact that the opening collect always ends with a Trinitarian formula *in unitate Spiritus sancti* underscores the significant Trinitarian and ecclesial meanings inherent in this expression.

28. This limitation to three texts is intended to simplify this discussion of method. The revival of the "prayer over the people" at the conclusion of the Eucharist is notable and certainly fits within the category of "variable prayers." In addition, while some Mass formulas in the Veronense have a single prayer (oration) before the prayer over the gifts, others have two. Two orations are also found in most of the formularies in the Gelasian Sacramentary. Scholars have asked whether the second oration may not represent a conclusion for the General Intercessions. See, Bernard Capelle, "Messes du pape S. Gélase dans le Sacramentaire de Vérone," *Travaux liturgiques de doctrine et d'histoire* (Louvain, 1955–67) 2:70-105, and "L'oeuvre liturgique de saint Gélase," *ibid.*, 146–60; A. Chavasse, "L'oratio 'super sindonem' dans la liturgie romaine," *Revue Bénédictine* 70 (1960) 313–23.

29. G. G. Willis, "The Variable Prayers of the Roman Mass," 105.

30. M. Augé, "Eucologia," 511.

31. G. G. Willis, "Variable Prayers," 108.

32. G. G. Willis asserts that the collect in the Roman rite originally was like that from Syria and Egypt as a prayer related to the lessons that followed it ("The Variable Prayers" 93). By the time of Leo the Great, however, it had clearly become "a variable prayer related to the day or feast rather than to the attentive hearing of the lessons, and it has so continued ever since" (116). In the same essay he notes that Jungmann asserted that it concludes the entrance of the ministers (ibid., 109). M. Augé ("Eulogia" 517) argues that this prayer can be considered the end of the entrance rites or simply the opening

payer of the liturgy. Its specific function is to create a spiritual ambience in which the assembly sets about the hearing of the Word of God and celebrating the Eucharist. The opening prayer gives a very synthetic thought about the feastday or of the liturgical season. Robert Cabie (in "La collecte," *L'Eglise en prière. Vol. II,* 212–213) argues that the oration or collect which followed the Kyrie or Glory to God marked the end of the initial rites of the Eucharist. A. M. Martimort (in "Les collectes," *L'Eglise en prière, Vol. I,* 166) argues that it was the prayer spoken by the celebrant after the people had prayed; thus it concluded either a diaconal litany or a time of silent prayer. When the prayer had been a silent one, the faithful already formulated their praise and petitions in their hearts . . . the purpose of the celebrant's prayer was to gather up these supplications . . . to give them public expression, and to reduce them to unity; whence the names *collectio* and *collecta.*

33. The introductory section of the Liturgy of St. James is instructive (translation from Jasper-Cuming, *Prayers of the Eucharist,* 90, see Hanggi-Pahl, *Prex Eucharistica* 269)

"It is truly fitting and right, suitable and profitable, to praise you, [to hymn you,] to bless you, to worship you, to glorify you, to give thanks to you, the creator of all creation, visible and invisible, [the treasure of eternal good things, the fountain of life and immortality, the God and Master of all.] You are hymned by [the heavens and] the heaven of heavens and all their powers; the sun and moon and all the choir of stars; earth, sea, and all that is in them; the heavenly Jerusalem. . . ."

34. G. G. Willis, "Variable Prayers," 117.

35. Ibid., 113: "which [style] did not appear in liturgical use until the last quarter of the fourth century, and of which there is scarcely a trace in the Roman Canon given by St. Ambrose in *De sacramentis* about 390."

36. G. G. Willis, "Cursus in the Roman Canon," in *Essays in Early Roman Liturgy* 113–117, at 113. He notes that the "Roman liturgical composition, like the work of the papal chancery, conformed to the principles of the *cursus* from some time in the fourth century until the middle of the seventh"; "the *cursus* became the rule in the papal chancery from the time of Siricius (384–98) and disappeared after St. Gregory the Great (604). As a liturgical composition it prevailed roughly from 350 or a little later till about 650." The collects of the three ancient Roman Sacramentaries abound in rhythmic endings. In comparison the Canon of the Mass contrasts sharply with the collects of the ancient Sacramentaries in its comparative lack of rhythmic endings.

37. From the Consilium Instruction, *Comme le prévoit* on the translation of liturgical texts, 25 January, 1969, *Notitiae* 5 (1969) 3–12, n. 34. The full text (DOL n. 871) states: "[t]he prayers (opening prayer, prayer over the gifts, prayer after Communion, and prayer over the people) from the ancient Roman tradition are succinct and abstract. In translation they may need to be rendered somewhat more freely while conserving the original ideas. This can be done by moderately amplifying them or, if necessary, paraphrasing expressions in order to concretize them for the celebration and the needs of today."

38. By far the most frequent divine attribute expressed in these prayers is *omnipotens*, used in the present Roman Missal 277 times. While most of these uses are in collect-type prayers, 19 are found in blessing prayers, 6 in Eucharistic prayers, and 4 in antiphons. Scattered other uses are in the *Exsultet*, the introductions to various rites (e.g., sacramental initiation), petitions in the sample general intercessions and the priest's preparation for Mass. The majority of the rest are found in the variable prayers. For the summary of the use of *omnipotens* see, T. Schnitker, *Concordantia verbalia Missalis Romani* col. 1704–1716.

39. The source of this prayer is the Veronense 1239:

"Deus, qui substantiae dignitatem
et mirabiliter condidisti, et mirabilius reformasti,
da, quaesumus, nobis eius divinitatis esse consortes,
qui humanitatis nostrae fieri dignatus est particeps.
Qui tecum vivit."

40. Augé, 513.

41. Hence the problematic nature of the individualism in the Mass formula in the present Sacramentary "For the Priest Himself" whose opening prayer states:

"you have given me charge of your family
not because I am worthy
but because of your infinite love. . . ."

"sed sola ineffabilis gratiae tuae largitate,
me familiae tuae praesse voluisti
tribue me tibi digne persolvere. . . ."

42. Among the reasons why the citation of the Latin phrases here is important is the fact that the parallelism in the Latin original is not reflected in the present ICEL translation. The prayer is from the former Roman Missal (see, P. Bruylants, *Les oraisons* n. 410). The Latin text reads:

"Deus, qui nos redemptionis nostrae
annua exspectatione laetificas,
praesta, ut Unigenitum tuum,
quem laeti suscipimus Redemptorem,
venientem quoque Iudicem securi videre mereamur."

43. GIRM n. 30 states "each [Kyrie, Christe eleison] acclamation is normally made twice, but, because of the nature of the language, the music, or other circumstances, the number may be greater or a short verse (trope) may be inserted. If the Kyrie is not sung, it is to be recited." *Music in Catholic Worship* n. 65 states: "This short [Kyrie] litany was traditionally a prayer of praise to the risen Christ. He has been raised and made 'Lord' and we beg him to show his loving kindness. The sixfold Kyrie of the new Order of Mass may be sung in other ways, for example, as a ninefold chant. It may also be incorporated in the penitential rite, with invocations addressed to Christ. When sung, the setting should be brief and simple so as not to give undue importance to the introductory rites."

44. Known as *apologiae*, these prayers were "expressions of unworthiness, confessions, statements of sinfulness and guilt" said by the priest celebrant before the beginning of the liturgy, during the walk to the altar (the Confiteor together with Ps 43 is the best known example), as preparation for the proclamation of the gospel (*munda cor meum et labia mea*), the prayers during the offertory (in the former Missal at the preparation of bread and cup and during the hand washing), before Communion, and before the final blessing (see, H. Wegman, *Christian Worship*, 189). See, Adrien Nocent, "Les apologies dans la célébration eucharistiques," in *Liturgie et rémission des péchés* (Rome: Edizione Liturgiche, 1975) 179–196.

45. The prayer over the gifts from the present Holy Thursday evening liturgy (and the Second Sunday of the Year) from which this phrase is taken, was used in the former Roman Missal as the secret prayer for the Ninth Sunday after Pentecost. The phrase *opus nostrae redemptionis exercetur* is often referred to in the literature on liturgical theology to sum up the theology of liturgy. See, for example, the important seminal allusion to this prayer's "liturgical theology" in Odo Casel, "Beitrage zu römischen Orationen. Die Sekret vom 9. Sonntag nach Pfingsten im romischen Messbuch," *Jahrbuch für Liturgiewissenschaft* 11 (1931) 35–36. The crucial role which translations play in the reformed vernacular liturgy is exemplified in this phrase. When used on Holy Thursday the present ICEL translation reads "the work of our redemption is accomplished." When used on the Second Sunday of the Year the very same text reads "[for when we proclaim the death of the Lord] you continue the work of his redemption." More will be said about translations below.

46. That some of these texts as still used are found wanting will be reflected in observations in section four of this chapter.

47. See, for example, Franco Brovelli, "Le orazioni del Tempo di Avvento e di Natale," in *Il Messale Romano del Vaticano II. Orazionale e Lezionario*. Vol. I. La celebrazione del Mistero di Cristo nell'anno liturgico (Torino: Elle Di Ci, 1984) 114. This collection of essays is a very significant contribution to euchological study. However, the method adopted in most of these essays is restricted to either Lectionary or euchology, not both together or both in context of the whole liturgical event.

48. See, Anscar Chupungco, *Liturgies of the Future*, 85.

49. See above, Chapter 2, 72–73.

50. Helpful indications of how women functioned ministerially in this context are in Roger Gryson, *The Ministry of Women in the Early Church*, trans., Jean Leporte and Mary Louise Hall (Collegeville: The Liturgical Press, 1976) passim., but especially 22–24 for the discussion of Hippolytus.

51. *Liturgies of the Future*, 33.

52. See, Albert Houssiau, "The Theological Value of the New Ordination Rite," *Louvain Studies* 3 (Spring, 1970) 31–40. A particularly useful example of deriving the theology of orders from liturgical euchology is some of Herve

Legrand's work. Also helpful in this connection is David N. Power's *Ministers of Christ and His Church* (London: G. Chapman, 1969).

53. The introduction and revised rites for the ordination of a deacon, priest and bishop all state the following: (n. 1) "the ordination of a deacon/priest should take place on a Sunday or holyday, when a large number of the faithful can attend, unless pastoral reasons suggest another day." And (n. 7) "the readings may be taken in whole or in part from the Mass of the day or from the texts listed in Chapter VI" (i.e., Texts for Use in Ordination). The Introduction to the Ordination of a Bishop adds to n. 1 "unless pastoral reasons suggest another day, such as the feast of an apostle." Interestingly, the Introduction to the rite of Blessing of an Abbot states (n. 1) "the blessing of an abbot should take place in the presence of a gathering of religious and, if circumstances permit, of the faithful. The blessing should take place on a Sunday or feast day; for pastoral reasons another day may be chosen."

54. In this connection see my critique of Mary Collins' article "The Public Language of Ministry," in *Liturgical Theology. A Primer*, 56–57. This article breaks significant new ground in liturgical theology while offering a critique of the present language for ordained ministers. However, some methodological questions remain. Unfortunately when Collins speaks of the rites of ordination she usually is speaking of the texts used and not the context of the rite taking place in the midst of the baptized. This living setting of the ritual might well (and in our opinion, should) contextualize some of her concerns and underscore that one is ordained in and among the people who are to be served. In addition, Collins does not treat the Lectionary texts for ordinations, the variety of which in the present reform is a significant factor concerning a contemporary liturgical theology of orders. Images from those texts about service and love for the Church should also be part of the context for interpreting the euchological texts. Collins correctly notes that Hippolytus' rite for episcopal ordination must be understood in relation to other charisms functioning in the community, specifically those of confessor and healer over whom the bishop had no authority. One could raise the same issue with regard to the use of Hippolytus' text today; the very pluriformity of ministers in the Church today witnesses to the functioning of a variety of charisms whose authority derives primarily from the Spirit, not institutional designation.

55. See, *Pontificale Romanum De Ordinatione Diaconi, Presbyteri, et Episcopi*. (Vatican City: Typiis Polyglottis Vaticanis, 1968) for deacons 20–26, for presbyters 38–43 and for bishops 70–74. Also see *The Roman Pontifical* (Washington: ICEL, 1978) 165–168 and 196–197.

56. See the helpful collection of eschatologically rich Eucharistic texts and the exposition on them and on eschatology as constitutive of Eucharistic theology in Geoffrey Wainright, *Eucharist and Eschatology* (London: Epworth Press, 1971).

57. See, *Messale di Ogni Giorno* (Roma/Milano: Editoriale Consortium, 1984) 632–635 with Advent tropes, 633.

58. See, *Nuevo Misal del Vaticano II*, eds. Jaime Sancho y Gabril (Ramis/Bilbao:

Ediciones Mensajero/Editorial Desclée de Brouwer, 1989) 1033–1035: other greetings for seasons: Advent, Christmas, Lent, Easter season. The text for Advent is "El Senor, que viene a salvarnos, esté con vosotros."

59. Paul VI, Apostolic Constitution, *Missale Romanum*, DOL, n. 1363.

60. See, *The Reform of the Liturgy*, 396–405, esp. 396.

61. Ibid., 396–397. The task at hand was found "to require so much research, harmonization of texts, and creativity [that it] could only be brought to completion by a group of careful, sensitive specialists with a good knowledge of the Church's euchological sources, both Eastern and Western" (397). The study group's director was Placide Bruylants. His untimely death in 1966 caused Carlo Braga to be pressed into service and to lead the committee's work to completion.

62. Consilium for the Implementation of the Constitution on the Liturgy, Study Section 10, Schemata n. 9 (30 September 1964), "Report on the Prayer over the Gifts," nn. 57–58, as quoted in *Second Progress Report on the Revision of the Roman Missal* (Washington: ICEL, 1990) 12.

63. See, A. Dumas, "Pour mieux comprendre," 194–213; see also *Second Progress Report*, 12.

64. Consilium, *Instruction, Comme le prévoit* n. 33; DOL n. 870.

65. The sections of *A Lexicon of Terms of the Missale Romanum* (privately printed "in house" ICEL project) in the *Progress Report on the Revision of the Roman Missal* (Washington: ICEL, 1988) 34–44 are particularly instructive, especially in describing the meaning of such terms as *devotio, munus,* and *oblatio*. By way of contrast and comprehensiveness a comparison of the *Lexicon* with the work of Mary Pierre Ellebracht is very instructive. See, *Remarks on the Vocabulary of the Ancient Orations in the Missale Romanum* (Nijmegen/Utrecht: Dekker and Van De Vegt, 1966) in particular 97–100 for *devotio*, 163–168 for *munus* and 80–83 for *oblatio*.

66. Ibid., n. 34; DOL 871.

67. P. Bruylants, *Les Oraisons* II, n. 351.

68. See, J. Frank Henderson, "ICEL and Inclusive Language," in *Shaping English Liturgy: Studies in Honor of Archbishop Denis Hurley*, eds. Peter C. Finn and James M. Schellman (Washington: The Pastoral Press, 1990) 274.

69. Ibid.

70. *Progress Report* 57. A footnote about 1. 4 states: "the change from 'already' to 'here' in the second and subsequent versions reflects an annotation on the first revision: the force of lines 3-4 of the Latin would be better rendered by translating *iam* as 'now' not 'already,' i.e., so that the text corresponds to 2 Corinthians 5:7: 'We walk by faith, not by sight,' and 1 Cor 13:12: 'Now we see in a mirror dimly, but then face to face.'"

71. *Saint Michael's Daily Missal*. English translation of the Missale Romanum. Authorised for public use by the Hierarchy of England and Wales. (Alcester

and Dublin: Goodliffe Neale, 1973) 39. The "Foreword" (5*) to this edition, signed by Wm. Gordon Wheler, Bishop of Leeds, Chairman of the National Liturgical Commission of England and Wales, states that this publication marks the end of a first phase of postconciliar revision of the English liturgy when publishers were allowed to use "any authorised translations of their choice for the proper of the Mass." The new directive for this second stage allows publishers to choose from only three translations: "1) The text known as that of the National Liturgical Commission (N.L.C.), 2) The text prepared by the International Committee for English in the Liturgy (ICEL), 3) The text known as Glenstall-Headingley, when it became available." The Chairman also observed that he presumed that this *St. Michael's* text would only be in use for a few years, in anticipation of "the right final version."

72. *Comme le prevoit* n. 34: DOL 871.

73. See, this chapter, 186–187 and fn. 48.

74. This project is nearing completion and as of this writing, critiques and comments on these proposed prayers are being received and evaluated by the ICEL advisory committee.

75. This argument takes account of the fact that the present Sacramentary translation of the Preface for the First Sunday of Lent speaks of "this . . . holy season of self-denial," the "devil's temptations," the "hidden corruption of evil" and "purity of heart." This prescribed preface for all three Lectionary cycles exemplifies what is lacking in this proposed collect.

76. This is not to ignore possible adjustments to other rites, for example the location of the nuptial blessing in the marriage rite. An analysis of the theology of the liturgy reflected in the marriage rite concerns the very *context* in the rite when the nuptial blessing is pronounced. It would seem more appropriate to have such a prayer follow the consent of the couple instead of after the Lord's Prayer. Such a rearrangement would seem to be much more faithful to Christian liturgical tradition where the proclamation of the nuptial blessing is closely tied to the specific notion of the sacramentality of Christian marriage.

77. For important background for our critique arguing that in reforming the liturgy liturgical scholars had not concerned themselves with creation despite the fact that it was present so strongly in patristic writings about Sunday and also in oriental liturgies, see Yves M. Congar, "Le Thème de Dieu-Créateur et les explications de l'hexamèrons dans la tradition chrétienne," *L'Homme devant Dieu* (Lyons: Editions Montaigne Aubiere, 1963) Vol. I, 189–215. It is also true that the variable prayers of the Missal could benefit from more frequent reference to God as creator. An example of the first part of a collect from an Advent weekday, Dec. 17, is *Deus, humanae conditor et redemptor naturae* (the present ICEL translation is "Father, creator and redeemer of mankind").

78. Recall comments above Chapter 2, 71 (with fn. 65) and Chapter 4, 163–165.

79. Chief among the structural problems in the anaphoras published after the Council is the "split epiclesis." See, Richard Albertine, "The Problem of the

(double) Epiclesis in the Roman Eucharistic Prayers." For a more general assessment and call for additional Eucharistic prayers see the essays edited in Frank Senn, *New Eucharistic Prayers*.

80. David Power's work in this area, reflected in several of his writings, is particularly notable.

81. See, *Dominican Sacramentary*, A draft translation of the Missale et Lectionarium, O.P. (1985). (Chicago: Dominican Liturgical Commission U.S.A., 1986) 126–127: Preface of St. Dominic I:
"Father all-powerful . . .
We praise and bless you today
because you called our Father Dominic
to enrich the church by renewing the apostolic way of life.
Disciple of Christ,
the very Christ who became poor for our sake,
Dominic called the lost and the wandering home
by preaching the Good News.
He gathered a band of preachers together.
Nourished by the light of sacred study
they gave themselves without reservation
to the proclamation that Jesus Christ is Lord."

Also, *Dominican Sacramentary*, 140: Preface of St. Dominic II:
"Father, all-powerful . . .
We praise and bless you today
because you called our Father Dominic to proclaim your truth.
He drew that truth from the deep springs of the Savior,
water for a thirsty world.
Supported by the prayers of Mary, the mother of your Son,
and compelled by a concern for the salvation of all,
Dominic accepted the ministry of the Word for his family.
Speaking always with you or about you, O God,
beginning all his actions in contemplation,
he advanced in wisdom.
he brought many to Christ by his life and teaching,
he devoted himself without reserve
to the building up of the Church, the body of Jesus Christ."

Chapter 6

Liturgical Arts

Our methodological interest continues but shifts slightly in this chapter. It concerns what we regard as *complementary elements* of the experience of liturgy and as *complementary sources* for liturgical theology, which presume and enhance our approach to interpreting Scripture, symbol, and euchology in the *context* of liturgical celebration. To our way of thinking, *liturgical arts* include the music, architecture, artifacts, and pictorial art used in or reflected in the act of liturgy.[1] We will argue that these elements and forms of art are *intrinsic* to the liturgy and that their use is required for the *integrity* of the act of worship.[2] They are intrinsically connected with Word, symbol, and euchology in that music is normatively the medium through which Word and euchology are communicated,[3] and the architectural space provides the setting for symbolic interaction in liturgy, in particular when artifacts and vessels hold elements of creation or objects manufactured for use in liturgy.

The fact that these artistic elements are constitutive of the act of liturgy and of the theology of liturgy indicates, once again, the importance of human ingenuity and creativity in liturgy's symbolic expression and in any theology of the liturgy derived from liturgical enactment. The various arts that collaborate in the celebration of liturgy include architecture, painting, sculpture, music, choreography. What participants see: lights and colors, harmony of the space; what they hear: voice, song, playing instruments; what they smell: incense, perfumed oils; what they taste: bread and wine; what they touch: offering the sign of peace, kissing the gospel book, exchanging a wedding ring and what movement they are engaged in: stational Masses, processions on Palm Sunday, Candlemas and Rogation days are all part of the experience of worship and require our methodological attention.[4]

Our methodological interest here emphasizes the *lex agendi* of liturgical enactment in such a way that the liturgical arts, which have often been relegated to secondary importance (if not relative unimportance)[5] in delineating a theology of liturgy are emphasized as being intrinsic to liturgy and as requiring attention alongside discussions of Word, symbol, and euchology. Understood as *intrinsic* aspects of enacted liturgy, the arts have shaped and, to our way of thinking especially in the present reform, shape in very forceful ways, how the enacted liturgy is experienced, appreciated, and appropriated. Our particular discussion of the music, architecture, and artifacts of the liturgy concerns the theological meaning of these art forms as intrinsically related to and complementary to Word, symbol, and euchology. Theologically, what is presupposed throughout this discussion, and what is of central importance for the theology of liturgy, derives from the *fact* that the arts are used in worship and the *fact* that they are the result of human creativity, whether of human ingenuity, as in architectural design or musical composition, or human manufacture as in the execution of an architectural design or the performance of a musical piece or the manufacture of symbolic elements of the liturgy (e.g., bread and wine).[6] That they are the result of the work of human hands indicates how a theology of work and of human labor is intrinsic to the very doing of liturgy.

To speak of liturgical arts is to speak at the same time of beauty and aesthetics. In using liturgical arts the believing Church is attempting to manifest and to make present the depth of God's self-communication (understanding liturgy as the privileged locus where God's self-communication is experienced). That this self-communication is accomplished through aesthetically pleasing and beautiful liturgical arts fits the anthropological foundation for and inherent framework of Christian worship. This is to say that liturgy is the most fitting of human expressions because it relies on humanity's means of self-communication—including (especially) words, gestures, and symbols. In what follows aesthetics[7] and human labor ("no labor, no liturgy") converge in the filling out the theology of liturgy argued here.[8]

Our methodological concern is uppermost in the contents and divisions of this chapter. The first part considers a contemporary vision of the appropriate use of the liturgical arts in the liturgy, noting especially how musical and artistic variety and flexibility are emphasized in the contemporary conciliar and postconciliar documents of the liturgical reform. The second part explicates our thesis *context is text* by offering an historical interlude about church construction and the pictorial arts as these influenced (and still influence) how liturgical texts are experienced and appropriated. In both discussions the ecclesiology operative in liturgical enactment will be emphasized. The third section offers some reflections on contemporary liturgical celebration as guided by contemporary renewal documents. The final section offers some critique of the *agendi* of the implementation of the reformed liturgy, paying particular attention to the American documents guiding the implementation of the liturgy. It concludes with some comments about ongoing indigenization in various settings because, in our understanding, the arts are always culturally and concretely conditioned and the evolution of the arts is itself a clear example of ongoing liturgical indigenization.

I. Liturgical Arts: Contemporary Renewal

1. Liturgical Arts and Liturgical Aesthetics. To highlight the value of liturgical arts is to highlight at the same time the importance of liturgical aesthetics, understanding aesthetics as a centrally important criterion about the adequacy of the artistic and expression that is intrinsic to liturgy. In the words of Don Saliers, "Liturgical aesthetics studies the perceptual elements and the art of ritual enactment which render [the] human activities [used in liturgy] alive with significant form." Furthermore, "liturgical aesthetics must address the question of how the *style* (emphasis added) of celebration opens access to understanding and participation in that which theology can explain but can only comprehend in wonder and adoration" namely, "an epiphany of the mystery of the divine self-communication."[9] Our discussion of aesthetics is essential for and intrinsic to appreciating liturgy as a unique phenomenon. "Liturgical action does not simply use art, it IS art—dialogue with God in symbolic form."[10]

To our way of thinking, to say that the liturgical arts are *complementary elements of liturgy* and *complementary sources for liturgical theology* suggests that music, architecture, pictorial art, and artifacts support and enhance how Word, symbol, and euchology are expressed and experienced in the act of liturgy. This is to say that

221

the arts are not to be regarded as either unnecessary to or as substitutes for the liturgical assembly's active engagement in Word, symbol, and euchology. On the one hand, that which should be the *essential, artistic means through which* Word, symbol, and euchology are expressed and experienced should not in effect become substitutes for them. On the other hand, the use of the arts in worship should not be considered as merely utilitarian or functional. The expressive power and emotional force of music, architecture, pictorial art, and artifacts are such that liturgy's use of the arts supports these characteristics, relies on them and unleashes them in an act of divine communion. Liturgy's use of the arts implies that they are respected as the result of human creativity (both in imagination and in execution) and are to be enjoyed precisely as art in worship. Thus the arts are not to be subjugated to preconceived ends, especially intellectual understandings.

Part of our argument thus far on the variety of meanings unleashed through Word, symbol, and euchology—*context is text*—should be applied both to the use of the arts as conveyors of meaning in themselves and as complementary means to express the meaning of rites—especially texts and symbols—in liturgy. When the arts are used in liturgy, these media both support the message of liturgy and they become a major part of the message of the liturgy.

To attend in this chapter to the traditional use of the arts in Roman Catholic worship is to support a liturgical aesthetic in which the good, the true, and the beautiful serve as essential components of the criteria for evaluating the soundness of worship. In terms more closely linked to our overall thesis we will argue that liturgical arts comprise a major part of the *context* for worship in the sense that the arts facilitate how Word, symbol, and euchology are experienced and the arts invite worshipers into a privileged experience of the transcendent and immanent God through the arts. At the same time the arts serve as important nonverbal demonstrations of how the human experience of worship necessarily includes that which is artistically satisfying, that which has deep emotional resonances and that which fosters a degree of communion with God that is only possible through artistic means. Effective worship is only possible through what is affective.

The last two chapters of the Constitution on the Sacred Liturgy deal (respectively) with "sacred music" (chapter 6) and "sacred art and furnishings" (chapter 7). Of particular note is the way these paragraphs emphasize the importance of the creative arts in worship, especially in the way they support how the Church has emphasized the arts as reflective of the theology of the incarnation whereby the divine is mediated through and experienced in the human. (Recall here our discussion of symbol above in Chapter 4.) The Liturgy Constitution's treatment of music begins with the assertion that "the musical tradition of the universal Church is a treasure of inestimable value, greater than that of any other art" (n. 112). The chapter on sacred art and furnishings begins with the assertion

"[t]he fine arts are deservedly ranked among the noblest activities of human genius and this applies especially to religious art and to its highest achievement, sacred art. These arts, by their very nature, are oriented toward the infinite beauty of God, which they attempt in some way to portray by the work of human hands. They are dedicated to advancing God's praise and glory to the degree that they center on the single aim of turning the human spirit devoutly toward God" (n. 122).

With regard to the theology of liturgy it is important to note how these chapters of the Constitution balance criteria of beauty with (what we shall call) liturgical suitableness about participation through music and about building churches that foster active participation. In this connection the Constitution acknowledges how the Church has "been the friend of the arts, has ever sought their noble help, and has trained artists with the special aim that all things set apart for use in divine worship are truly worthy, becoming, and beautiful. . . ." (n. 122). Notable here as well is the balance maintained between preserving what is truly dignified and beautiful for liturgical use from the riches of the past and the document's encouragement about creativity in the liturgical arts reflective of local needs and contemporary culture (e.g., nn. 116 and 119).

The assertion in the Liturgy Constitution that "the Church has not adopted any particular style of art as its very own but has admitted styles from every period" (n. 123) reiterates a traditional Catholic value about artistic style and reflects the way the liturgical arts have developed in history. Thus it keeps open the door for artists in our day to be truly creative, not imitative, in artistic expression and in the creation and use of contemporary art forms in and for worship.

2. *Documents of Implementation*. That the rather general proscriptions in the Liturgy Constitution were intended to be followed by subsequent documents to guide implementation is exemplified in the publication of the Roman document, *Musicam Sacram* (1967)[11] and the subsequent documents of local bishops' conferences on the arts, specifically music and architecture. In the United States these latter documents (up to now) are *Music in Catholic Worship* (1972), *Environment and Art in Catholic Worship* (1978) and *Liturgical Music Today* (1982).[12] These documents attest to the seriousness with which the implementation of the Liturgy Constitution's directives on the arts were taken, linking together (in remarkable though admittedly different ways and from varying perspectives) aesthetics, theology and liturgical practice.[13]

The present reformed liturgy, true to its nature when compared with the Tridentine Liturgy, allows for great flexibility in the use of the arts, in particular with regard to style. With regard to the amount and style of music specifically, the careful wording of the Liturgy Constitution is informative though modest and deliberately open-ended.[14] It retains Gregorian chant in "pride of place" and yet balances this assertion with openness to "other kinds of sacred music . . . provided they accord with the spirit of the liturgical service" (n. 116). The leap to the assertion of *Musicam Sacram* (1967) in this connection is notable, if not startling: "the term 'sacred music' here includes: Gregorian chant, the several styles of polyphony, both ancient and modern, sacred music for organ and for other permitted instruments, and the sacred, i.e., liturgical or religious, music of the people" (n. 4b).[15]

In addition, the directive of *Musicam Sacram* in terms of the present experience of flexibility in the amount of singing at liturgy is most significant.[16] Thus the inherited distinctions among "solemn," "high" and "low" Mass are transcended. The documents of local liturgical implementation presume and build upon this movement to enormous musical flexibility. Similarly, with regard to the arts used to design, to build and to worship in appropriate liturgical spaces, the present latitude allows for (the liturgically appropriate and theologically important) indigenization of church buildings and spaces for worship as well as the vesture, vessels and artifacts used in worship. Once again, the question of a uniform *style* has been transcended and pluriformity is presumed in implementation documents.

In stressing the importance of aesthetics in liturgy in this section, we have deliberately set upon an approach to the present and continuing implementation and indigenization of the liturgy that stresses a factor that is often presumed or underemphasized in documents on the implementation of the reformed liturgy. Happily, in the opening section of the American document of implementation *Environment and Art* it states:

"Like the covenant itself, the liturgical celebrations of the faith community (Church) involve the whole person. They are not purely religious or merely rational and intellectual exercises, but also human experiences calling on all human faculties: body, mind, senses, imagination, emotions, memory. Attention to these is one of the urgent needs of contemporary liturgical renewal" (n. 5).

To our way of thinking this statement reflects how this document is an improvement over both *Music in Catholic Worship* and *Liturgical Music Today* which (by comparison) chiefly concern "hands on" implementation of their principles for music in the liturgy.[17]

Of these three documents, the most helpful in emphasizing the theological rationale for its artistic and liturgical principles is *Environment and Art*. The clear assertions that the subject of every liturgical action is the Church understood as the body of believers, that the church building is appropriately termed *domus ecclesiae* and that liturgical participation involves human interaction (nn. 27, 28, 29, 39) are helpful. They are certainly a vast improvement over descriptions of artifacts and buildings not intrinsically joined to the ecclesiology of worship, in particular to the liturgical assembly's active participation in liturgy. This linking of ecclesiology to liturgical participation leads to helpful statements in *Environment and Art* on furnishings (some of which we would call "artifacts") in liturgical celebration, which section most usually combines insights about the theological rationale for specific furnishings, their import in the revised liturgy and then some guidelines for their construction and placement.

The most helpful theological description in this section rightfully concerns the altar (nn. 71-73). The importance of the Liturgy of the Word in the revised liturgy calls for the appropriate emphasis given to it here (n. 74). The latitude in how best to design the baptistery and the Eucharistic chapel is again a welcome development in this document (nn. 76-77, 78-79). The clear separation between the liturgical action and Eucharistic reservation (e.g., in a tabernacle) is also illustrative in this connection (n. 81). The flexibility also evident in comments about a reconciliation chapel and the sacristy is also helpful (nn. 81-82). Specific furnishings given particular emphasis are benches or chairs for the assembly (nn. 68-69) and the chair from which to preside (n. 70). The comparatively brief discussions of the "objects used in liturgical celebration" that follow (noting how their placement itself is important) are very useful: the cross (n. 88), candlesticks and candles (n. 89), books (n. 91), vestments (n. 95), vessels (n. 96) and images (n. 98).

One of the main contributions of *Music in Catholic Worship* to both the American and the wider Church's implementation of the revised liturgy is its articulation of how to evaluate music that is appropriate in celebration. The evaluation that should be made is threefold: musical, liturgical, and pastoral (n. 25). From the perspective of trying to insure that aesthetics enter into the criteria for and the experience of the reformed liturgy, the specification of the "musical" judgment is helpful.

"Is the music technically, aesthetically, and expressively good? This judgment is basic and primary and should be made by competent musicians. Only artistically sound music will be effective in the long run. To admit the cheap, the trite, the musical cliche often found in popular songs on the grounds of instant liturgy is to cheapen the liturgy, to expose it to ridicule, and to invite failure" (n. 26).

This is followed by a helpful assertion that distinguishes "the judgment of music" from "the judgment of musical style [since the document argues that] style and value are two distinct judgments" (n. 28).

After noting that this musical judgment "is basic but not final" (n. 29), the document describes the liturgical and pastoral judgments. "The nature of the liturgy itself will help to determine what kind of music is called for, what parts are to be preferred for singing and who is to sing them" (n. 30). This assertion is most helpful, both by the fact that it is made and by its elasticity. Subsumed under the liturgical judgment are requirements regarding the structure of the liturgy, the texts of the liturgy, and the active participation of the congregation, the cantor, the choir, and the instrumentalists. "Structural requirements" concern "the choice of sung parts, the balance between them and the style of musical setting(s) . . . [which] should reflect the relative importance of the parts of the [liturgy] and the nature of each part" (n. 30.a). "Textual requirements" concern whether the music expresses and interprets the text correctly, keeping in mind the principal classes of liturgical texts: "proclamations, acclamations, psalms and hymns, and prayers" (n. 30.b). "Role differentiation" concerns respecting the theologically and liturgically significant assertion of the Liturgy Constitution that each minister "who has an office to perform, should do all of, but only, those parts which pertain to his office by the nature of the rite and the principles of liturgy" (n. 28).

This section concludes with two especially helpful comments which are germane to our aesthetic concerns. It asserts that "song is not the only kind of music suitable for liturgical celebration. Music performed on the organ and other instruments can stimulate feelings of joy and contemplation at appropriate times" (n. 37). Thus the nature of liturgy as comprised of nonverbal as well as verbal, the emotive as well as the intellectual is here appropriately underscored with especially helpful attention to music. Once again, however, it is appropriate to underscore the breadth of the latitude expressed in such a statement.

The final judgment proposed, the pastoral, is the shortest in description and, appropriately, the most open-ended.

"The pastoral judgment governs the use and function of every element of celebration. Ideally this judgment is made by the planning team or committee. It is the judgment that must be made in this particular situation, in these concrete circumstances. Does music in the celebration enable these people to express their faith, in this place, in this age, in this culture?" (n. 39).

To our way of thinking this statement hints at what we have argued methodologically in this book. The relationship between the one reformed liturgy and the various ecclesial settings in which it is celebrated is crucial in terms of appreciating and determining the adequacy of the liturgy as experienced in particular settings and in the way various contexts draw out shades of theological meaning inherent in the revised liturgy.

This document sets a new standard for liturgical normativity and musical adequacy. These are to be found not in predetermined formulas but in a confluence of musical, liturgical, and pastoral judgments. The rest of the document is to be read in light of these criteria. But even then, and true to its nature as a provisional document for implementing the revised liturgy, *Music in Catholic Worship* was supplemented a decade later with *Liturgical Music Today*. Even though the "Introduction" to *Liturgical Music Today* asserts that it is primarily concerned with matters left unaddressed in the former document, i.e., the revised sacramental rites and the Liturgy of the Hours (n. 3) it also adds additional "General Principles" for liturgical celebration. These concern: the structure of the liturgy (nn. 6–7), the place (n. 8), function (n. 9–10) and form of song (n. 11) within each unit of the liturgy and in the liturgy as a whole (n. 12) a discussion of the principle of progressive solemnity (n. 13),[18] and (the admittedly thorny issues surrounding) language and music idioms (nn. 14–15). Most of these principles are liturgically and theologically sound (e.g., enhancing the Liturgy of the Word with music, under "structure" nn. 6–7). A particularly significant distinction is made regarding "song that is meant to accompany ritual actions" (n. 9) and "sung prayer itself [as] a constituent element of the rite" (n. 10). The clearest enunciation of aesthetic criteria in these principles concerns "mixing different musical idioms and media" (n. 14) in one celebration[19] wherein the pastoral value of musical plurality "should never be employed as a license for including poor music" (n. 15).

The concluding section of *Liturgical Music Today*, entitled "Other Matters," is helpful especially because it articulates the need for contemporary liturgical music that is "as diverse and multi-cultural as the members of the assembly" (n. 55). The invitation to compose "new liturgical music appropriate to various cultures" drawing on "the great musical gifts of the Hispanic, Black, and other ethnic communities in the Church should enrich the whole Church in the United States in a dialogue of cultures" (n. 55) is a most fitting statement in that it deliberately leaves open ended the progress of implementing the reformed liturgy and liturgical indigenization. Its respect for varying cultures coincides with our repeated emphasis on respecting the varying contexts in which worship takes place.

While one might critique these documents for conveying an implicit Western classical bias in terms of musical composition and evaluating music[20] this kind of document and the contribution of additional statements for particular communities within the American Catholic Church such as *Plenty Good Room*[21] for the African American Catholic community, is appropriately invitational and open ended without sacrificing the value of an aesthetical judgment for worship.

To our way of thinking and in accord with our thesis *context is text* this latitude in the liturgical arts *requires* that emphasis be placed on liturgical *agendi* for at least three reasons. First, theologizing from *lex agendi* recognizes that the way the *lex orandi* is experienced depends to a large degree on the way the arts facilitate, enhance, or hinder *how* Scripture, symbols, and euchology are heard, understood, and appreciated in the act of liturgy. Second, the fact that historically there were times when music and the other arts overshadowed the assembly's experience of Word, symbol, and euchology (for example the silent Canon overshadowed by choral performance of polyphonic *Sanctus* and *Benedictus*) requires that the *lex agendi* be critiqued for the way the present experience of liturgy may do that now. Third, the value of liturgical aesthetics in evaluating the liturgical arts requires that liturgical performance be critiqued for the artistic and aesthetic quality of the liturgical arts used in worship.

II. Historical Interlude

As we argued in Chapter 2 about the normative character of the liturgy,[22] to raise the question of the adequacy of liturgical *texts* is to raise the question of the adequacy of the *contexts* in which liturgical rites take place. Specifically, our emphasis on *lex agendi* requires that the relative adequacy of the settings for worship—*contexts*—be evaluated, specifically for whether and how they do or do not facilitate and enhance the experience of worship so that rites and texts can be comprehended and appreciated. Our concern in this section will be illustrative, not exhaustive, of some of the issues regarding *lex agendi* regarding architecture and music.

Concretely, our interest in this brief historical interlude is to raise questions about how *contexts*—specifically as shaped by the liturgical arts of music, architecture, pictorial art and artifacts—might have influenced the appropriation of liturgical texts and rites. To be faithful to our thesis it is crucial to set texts within the context of celebration and to determine whether what the texts *say* was/is actually enacted.

Some initial comments about a liturgical theology of the Eucharist are meant to set up this "historical interlude" by illustrating the factors *in addition to the liturgical arts* that are implied in our understanding of *context is text*. For example, to isolate the Eucharistic prayer from the total act of making Eucharist is to isolate this particular kind of text, the prayer of blessing, from its living context in the whole of the Eucharistic liturgy. The act of making Eucharistic memorial consists (among other things) in sharing in Word and in the Eucharistic supper, understanding that sharing in the supper is an act of communion that follows upon hearing and praying the Eucharistic prayer. To recontextualize the Eucharistic prayer within the rest of the act of making Eucharist for the sake of proper interpretation would be faithful to the kind of liturgical theological method Bouyer desires[23] and more faithful to a unified appreciation of the act of making Eucharist.

In addition, while a study of Eucharistic anaphora texts is essential to glean the theology they reflect, more recent research would correctly emphasize not only the texts themselves, but how they were, or were not, "heard" and how they influenced, or did not influence, contemporary Eucharistic piety. Popular piety combined with the silent Canon in the West made it most unlikely that the text of the anaphora was understood or appreciated during the celebration. As John Jay Hughes has insightfully noted, while the text of the Roman Canon at the time of the Reformation was free from doctrinal error with regard to "earning salvation," nevertheless it is equally clear that, despite this fact, the piety of the time, which helped shape the liturgical *context* of the age, was thoroughly influenced by the abuses of selling indulgences and "buying masses."[24] Popular catechesis and piety were obviously separated from a careful explanation of the text of the Canon, especially because it was silent. Most often such catechesis and piety were the far more influential for understanding the Eucharist than either systematic treatises *on* the Eucharist or careful explanations *of* the Eucharistic prayer (to use a distinction which Louis Bouyer makes in throughout *Eucharist*).

Notable in this connection are Ralph Keifer's observations about the criticisms that Robert Ledogar levelled at Joseph Powers' *Eucharistic Theology* which Ledogar claims gave no place to key issues of liturgical theology such as anamnesis or memorial, anaphora, praise, confession, thanksgiving, etc.,[25] which criticisms would be congenial with the theology proposed and detailed by Bouyer. However, Keifer points out that

"systematic theology may have been more attentive to the actual prayer of the Church than liturgiologists suppose. The categories listed by Ledogar [memorial, epiclesis, doxology] do not play a very important role in the [Roman] Canon. And until recently, that was *the* eucharistic prayer for Roman Catholic theologians. Its text is most aptly described as expressing an oblation for the benefit of the living and the dead."[26]

While this latter point can be debated, it may well be that the practice enshrined by the use of the Roman Canon in the context of a piety emphasizing Mass intentions and stipends could lead one to this conclusion based on a *praxis* kind of liturgical influence on theology.

One concrete application of this kind of argument is that even if a balanced theology of the paschal sacrifice of Jesus is reflected in the *texts* of the (past and present) Roman rite, it may well be that an imbalanced notion of sacrifice emphasizing only the circumstances of Jesus' death is endorsed in the setting in which the liturgy takes place, specifically in architecture, statuary, stained glass, painting, and in the printed books of the liturgy. Given the value which Latin Christianity has placed on cruciform churches, a value which places high priority on Christ's paschal sacrifice and on Christ as the active mediator of all liturgical prayers, this architectural fact raises the question of how such a structure influences the hearing of euchological texts given the canons of their construction, including their being essentially Trinitarian. Given the experience of Western Catholicism, it can be asked to what extent a cruciform church with the crucified Christ as the only sanctuary decor surrounded by stations of the cross throughout the building adequately reflects the sweep of the paschal mystery as stated in

231

the liturgical texts which include references to Jesus's obedient life, experience of rejection, acceptance of death on the cross, and exaltation in the resurrection and ascension.

The proclamation of liturgical prayers, especially those that reflect a balanced approach to paschal mystery, pneumatology, and ecclesiology, in a variety of church buildings offers significant opportunities for textual interpretation and meaning. A particularly striking example is that of San Vitale in Ravenna. Although the church defies brief characterization, it is an octagonally shaped dome-surmounted church dating from the mid-sixth century. Its very shape with eight sides invites a number of avenues for interpretation, all beyond the cruciform. Inside, its mosaics are among the most celebrated of the entire Western world.[27] Covering the apse is a mosaic rendition of a clean-shaven Christ, striding the world flanked by saints and angels. To the right is the mosaic of Empress Theodora and her court, and to the left the man who married the courtesan-actress, Emperor Justinian, and his entourage.

The apse contains the priest's chair in the middle of a marble presbytery facing the free standing altar. The mosaics in the presbytery surround the mystical, paschal lamb of Revelation set over a background of stars. The number and detail of the basilica's mosaics depicting birds (with special symbolism attached to the peacock, pairs of doves and the ibis) and vegetation (vine and doves, cantharis) is most notable. One can only imagine how this kind of setting would help to bring alive the proclamation of the Eucharistic prayer from book 8 of the Apostolic Constitutions, in particular its theology of creation.[28]

Of even greater interest for the Western liturgy is the connection between the depiction in the presbytery mosaics of the Roman Canon's references to Old Testament "types" of the Eucharist and the text itself:

"Look with favor on these offerings
and accept them as once you accepted
the gifts of your servant Abel,
the sacrifice of Abraham, our father in faith,
and the bread and wine offered by your priest Melchisedech."

The scenes above the altar on the left side are of the angels announcing the birth of Isaac, Abraham, and Sarah offering hospitality to the three visitors and Abraham on the verge of sacrificing Isaac. The depictions on the right side are of Abel's and Melchizedek's sacrifices offered at either side of a center altar table.

Another non-cruciform church building that has different facets to its uniqueness is that of San Stefano Rotundo in Rome (including the very *fact* that it stands as singular among the churches of Rome). Originally constructed in the fifth century, restored with new features in the eighth and again restored in the fifteenth, this church also contains mosaics of a Byzantine influence, specifically Christ superimposed rather than crucified on the cross.[29]

From our primary methodological interest of *lex agendi*, the evidence of the shape of such church buildings and their pictorial art necessitates that these factors at least be recognized as formative on how the *lex orandi* is received and ultimately formative of *lex credendi*. Specifically, the theology of redemption imaged in buildings like San Vitale and San Stefano supports a rich biblical and liturgical heritage. While one would not necessarily want to imitate this kind of mosaic superabundance today, nevertheless, the construction of church buildings in octagonal form with this kind of pictorial arts supporting a biblical-liturgical theology of the Eucharist certainly provided a unique *context* for appropriating the liturgy celebrated therein.[30]

Similarly, the theology of baptism imaged in the very placement of the baptistery building close to (but not inside) the cathedral of Florence and the pictorial art both outside (particularly the doors) and inside this baptistery is similarly biblically inspired and liturgically rich. The baptistery alongside the cathedral of Rome, St. John Lateran, is similarly significant, especially its octagonal shape and mammoth size. This very building attests to how baptismal fonts are appropriately described as both "womb and tomb"—the womb of the Church deriving life and begetting new life from the three days Jesus lay in the tomb.

An allied factor (though often not adverted to) from the liturgical arts that bears on the theology of liturgy derived from its *context* concerns the printing and publication of liturgical books. Concretely, the use of calligraphy in manuscripts and the reproduction of religious paintings in missals and sacramentaries themselves influence how a printed text is "heard" and "interpreted." Specifically this is to raise the question about what kind of formative value did the *text* of the Roman Canon have when recited from various ceremonial books. If recited from a manuscript whose calligraphy emphasized the capital "T" of *Te igitur* one would need to look at what is depicted in the calligraphic design to attempt to appreciate how the priest or bishop's thoughts and imagination were likely influenced by the way this text was lettered. A more recent example concerns the printed text of the Tridentine Missal in Latin. The vast majority of printed altar missals contained the Latin canon on the right side of the book with the reproduction on the left side of the page of Guido Reni's painting of Christ's crucifixion, which painting is still located over the main altar in the church of San Lorenzo in Lucina in Rome.[31] Whatever else historical investigation will disclose about the evolution from the caligraphically embellished "T" at the beginning of the Canon, to the "T" symbolizing the crucifixion, to reproducing Reni's crucifixion, it is at least clear that the priest's or bishop's imagination was stimulated to musing about the passion even though the prayer he was saying, the Canon, contained explicit references to the whole paschal mystery—specifically to passion, death, resurrection, and ascension. One application of this would certainly seem to include not underestimating the artistic beauty and theological meaning of liturgical books themselves, specifically their layout and the religious art on their pages.[32]

That church buildings have classically been used for catechesis as well as liturgical celebration is illustrated not only by liturgical artifacts and mosaics, but also through the use of stained glass. Once again from our methodological perspective it is helpful to try to situate (when possible) the celebration of liturgy in spaces whose stained glass and sculpture had an obvious effect on seeing, hearing, and participating in the rite. But even more important is how the worshipers' imaginations can be influenced by such artistic achievement as that in churches like the cathedral "Church of Saint Mary" in Chartres, France.[33] The stained glass windows in this church stand as among the highest achievements of this craft, especially in terms of color (some never reproduced), shapes and style.[34] That the glass and sculpture of Chartres are significant witnesses to the Scriptures as well as to liturgical and theological substance is obvious and remarkable. Only comparatively recently, however, have some studies been undertaken to relate Chartres's sculpture and stained glass with the liturgy.[35]

For our purposes, admitting the relationship between this building and the celebration of the Roman liturgy of the time is supremely important. Once again one's imagination can be fostered by stained glass and sculpture to appreciate and understand the Christian mystery. The Church's *lex orandi* can obviously be significantly influenced by this aspect of the *lex agendi*. Directly related to the Church's *lex agendi* at this historical period, however, is the fact that the Church's liturgy was and is celebrated with or on behalf of specific local Churches. This is to suggest that the liturgy of a cathedral like Chartres was just that—cathedral liturgy with pilgrimages a frequent occurrence.

Alternatively, monastic and mendicant experiences of the daily divine office in the Middle Ages did not always involve or include members of parish churches. In this case and for a number of reasons (literacy being one) books for individual devotions called "books of hours" substituted for the Liturgy of the Hours. In addition to studying the prayer texts of these books, it is equally important to study the layout and pictorial art used in them.[36] A complete appreciation of liturgical and (now) devotional prayer forms requires consideration of the socio-cultural situation of the Black Death in Europe which was highly influential on the development of these prayer books, as is seen in some of the illuminations and calligraphic designs in these books.

The purpose of this historical interlude is not to argue that we reproduce the churches cited here as imitable and apt as they are for contemporary liturgical use,[37] or to suggest a wholesale return to former ways of printing liturgical texts. Rather its purpose is to demonstrate the value classically placed on the liturgical arts in the Catholic tradition which surround the doing of the liturgy. It is also to underscore the value of materials that are authentic and substantial—theologically, liturgically, and artistically. This interlude is illustrative of a part of our main thesis in bringing historical evidence to the fore in interpreting the various elements that comprise the act of liturgy.

III. Renewal Documents and Liturgical Practice

1. Music in the Liturgy. In keeping with our methodological interest, this section is intended to be illustrative of some of the issues surrounding the contemporary and ongoing use of music in the liturgy. As we have already noted in this chapter church music legislation in this century has undergone significant evolution and change. Among the more important liturgical strands of continuity within that evolution, however, are the principles that music has a ministerial function in the liturgy,[38] that active participation in liturgy should include music[39] and that normatively music is an intrinsic part of every liturgy.[40] Underlying these statements from a theological viewpoint is the fact that music at liturgy is meant to support the texts of the liturgy. Henceforth, the fact that music is intrinsic to the liturgy is a factor in appreciating the texts and rites *of* the given liturgy, not texts or musical expressions at variance with or added to the liturgy. The fact that Gregorian chant has received pride of place among the musical idioms of the liturgy from Pius X on is most significant. Once again, one of the chief reasons why chant is so prized is that the antiphons, psalms, *Kyrie, Gloria, Sanctus, Agnus Dei,* and other chants *of* the Eucharistic liturgy, not texts *added to* it (e.g., hymns, as we will argue shortly) are supported by singing this comparatively simple style of music in order to underscore the liturgy itself.

It is significant that there is nothing in the writings of Pius X or in subsequent documents requiring that the *style* of chant *qua* chant be the required music at liturgy. The principles (stated above) about why chant is most useful for liturgical participation are, in our opinion, more compelling theologically and liturgically than they are musically. This is to say that the value of Gregorian chant is that its simplicity, when compared with polyphony, facilitates the assembly's active participation, and its role in enhancing the texts *of* the liturgy, as opposed to texts set to music from sources other than the Bible or the liturgy (e.g., hymn texts) appropriately focuses attention on the texts of the liturgy themselves. To our way of thinking, this makes Gregorian chant a useful *means* to restore liturgical participation to the whole assembly. This is to say that statements about chant in this century are really more important ecclesiologically than they are stylistically. In fact none of the post Pius X legislation exalts the chant *style* over other musical styles. The use of chant, or a similar musical idiom that is (comparatively) simple, matched to the texts of the liturgy, is what is paramount in order to facilitate participation, not this particular musical style (or even the Latin language).

A related issue, however, concerns the appropriateness of the musical forms used in the liturgy. Since we have argued here that music is a *complementary* source, it is important to explore how whatever (style of) music is used in liturgy ought to cohere in style and text with the intended purpose(s) of the rite at issue. For example, this is to raise the question of the adequacy of using hymns in the Eucharistic liturgy. Here the classic understanding of the way hymns function differently in Roman Catholic and Protestant churches comes to the fore.[41] From the perspective of method about *lex orandi, lex credendi* this means, in part, evaluating Geoffrey Wainwright's argument (one might even say insistence) that hymns are a source for liturgical theology.[42] In light of our thesis we wish to inquire about the *context*—historical evolution and liturgical tradition—which caused hymns to evolve into being a major part of contemporary liturgical experience. Specifically we wish to critique at least the overuse of hymns in Roman Catholic Eucharist. Historically, hymns came into many liturgies at the Reformation, precisely because the Roman liturgy's use of Latin made liturgical music inaccessible for the assembly's participation. In our opinion they now need to be evaluated across denominational lines in terms of their legitimacy within the Eucharistic rite itself and then for the value that should be placed on them as theological sources.

This issue is rightly debated today because while they are germane to the Liturgy of the Hours, their use at the entrance, presentation of the gifts, Communion, and recession in the Eucharistic liturgy is not reflective of the traditional Roman rite.[43] Because the post Tridentine liturgy allowed for no textual or rubrical variation or substitution, the movement favoring popular participation (especially from the 1940s on) required that if music other than Gregorian chant was sung, it had to be *added* to the liturgy. Hence the incorporation of the "four-hymn" structure for popular participation in the Eucharistic liturgy. This, in our view, is merely "conventional," not "traditional" in the sense that hymns have only recently come into Catholic Eucharistic practice; liturgically they are germane to and are an intrinsic part of the hours, not the Eucharist.[44]

Hence, it is important to be as precise as we can be regarding contemporary liturgical legislation about music at these places in the Eucharistic liturgy. With regard to the "entrance song," for example, the *General Instruction on the Roman Missal* n. 26 states:

"The entrance song is sung alternately either by the choir and the congregation or by the cantor and the congregation; or it is sung entirely by the congregation or the choir alone. The antiphon and psalm of the *Graduale Romanum* or *The Simple Gradual* may be used, or another song that is suited to this part of the Mass, the day or the season and that has a text approved by the conference of bishops."[45]

The *Appendix to the General Instruction [on the Roman Missal] for the Dioceses of the United States of America* states that

"as a further alternative to the singing of the entrance antiphon and psalm of the *Roman Gradual (Missal)* or of the *Simple Gradual*, the Conference of Bishops has approved the use of other collections of psalms and antiphons in English, as supplements to the Simple Gradual, including psalms arranged in responsorial form, metrical and similar versions of psalms, provided they are used in accordance with the principles of the Simple Gradual and are selected in harmony with the liturgical season, feast or occasion. . . .

"There are thus four options for the entrance song:
1. the entrance antiphon and psalm of the *Roman Gradual;*
2. the entrance antiphon and psalm of the *Simple Gradual;*
3. song from other collections of psalms and antiphons;
4. other sacred song chosen in accord with the above criterion.
The same options exist for the sacred song at the offertory and Communion. . . ."[46]

In this legislation the tradition of the Roman Eucharistic rite is upheld regarding music at the entrance procession. The introit, offertory, and Communion music in the Roman rite traditionally consists of an antiphon, most usually taken from or inspired by the psalms or another verse of Scripture, sung by the assembly, followed by some (usually an open ended number of) verses of a psalm chosen to reflect the text of the antiphon and/or the feast or season being celebrated. The doxology "Glory be to the Father" follows these psalm verses, and it, in turn, is followed by repeating the antiphon with which the music began.

Their structure is a helpful accompaniment to the ritual of a procession, especially the entrance, for a number of reasons. First, the brevity of the antiphon (and also its derivation from the Scriptures) makes it something the assembly can sing without having to read from printed texts. The antiphonal nature of the introit enables the assembly to listen to the psalm verses while they watch the action of the entrance procession. The open ended number of verses enables flexibility so that the amount of singing here is determined by how much music is required to accompany the processional movement. Once the ministers are in their places the introit can conclude. To our way of thinking the *context* established (and establishes) the contours of the liturgical *text* used here.

The introit is an open form (as opposed to the comparatively "closed" metrical hymn form) in the sense that the emphasis is on the text and accompanying music of the antiphon, not a fixed poetic text used in the hymn. It is "open" in the sense that the number of psalm verses can be adjusted during the liturgy itself. A hymn, or other "closed" form would require the singing of the whole poetic text to understand its full (theological) meaning.[47] Hence, from the point of view of *form* we would argue that the hymn is not an appropriate form of music for the entrance.[48] Also with regard to the texts set to music, the deficiency of substituting hymns for these chants is that they replace the biblical text of the psalter. What ought to be a central source for the Christian's liturgical and personal prayer—the psalter—is at least eclipsed if not ignored when hymns are used. The Roman Catholic liturgical *context* in Eucharist does not countenance the use of hymns at entrance, presentation, or Communion.[49]

Another issue concerns the question of what are the appropriate theological themes that ought to be found in the entrance music. For example (in Chapter 5) we cited the theological value from the Liturgy of the Hours of using the traditional vesper hymns of praise for the seven days of creation and the doxological hymns such as the *Te Deum*. However, it is at least problematic, if not quite incorrect, to suggest that praise for creation should be a theme of the entrance music in the Eucharistic liturgy. In fact (as we have argued) this theme is constitutive of the preface and Eucharistic prayer, not an entrance hymn.[50]

Two additional aspects of our thesis *context is text* are appropriate to point out in this discussion of the entrance antiphon: the source for these texts and how they are sung. We argued (in Chapter 3) that one of the uses of Scripture in the liturgy is as sources for the Eucharistic antiphons.[51] Just as we argued regarding the Scripture readings themselves where texts are taken out of context and then placed in the new contexts of liturgical celebration, so verses of Scripture, in being a source for antiphons, are taken out of their native contexts in the Bible and then, often in an accommodated sense, are used as antiphons. Therefore, the antiphon for the common of the dedication of a church (traditional in the Roman rite and presently found in the *Graduale Romanum*) is, not surprisingly, taken from Genesis 22:17, 22. Originally the text referred to (what has come to be called) the "Jacob's ladder" sequence in Genesis. The two verses are separated by five intervening verses in Genesis 22. The interpretation of the composite is clearly influenced by its *context* as the beginning of the dedication liturgy: "how awesome is this place! This is none other than the house of God and the gate of heaven: and it shall be called the house of God."

Closely connected with this text is the following (assigned) verse Psalm 84:1 "how lovely is your dwelling place, O Lord of hosts. My soul longs for the courts of the Lord." Clearly, scriptural accommodation is used to introduce the liturgy of the dedication of a church from sources which have nothing to do in their original context with dedicating buildings. In such a case, texts are taken out of their native locus in the Bible to shape a new liturgical *context*.

The second aspect of establishing the correct *context* for interpreting traditional sung texts in the Roman liturgy extends to the musical, Gregorian chant notation for the various musical elements used in the liturgy. The connection between music and text is assumed in the *Graduale Romanum* and should also be assumed in its interpretation. At least part of interpreting the entrance antiphon must necessarily include the chant melody accompanying it. For the dedication of a church the notation to the text *terribilis est locus iste* ("How awesome is this place . . .) is most significant in being quite low at the beginning, building upwards to *locus iste* and again to *porta caeli* ("the gate of heaven"). The "awesomeness" of the words is matched by the haunting chant melody[52] to emphasize how awesome indeed is the church, "this place," since it is the "gate of heaven."

To answer our question about whether or to what extent hymns are sources for liturgical theology, we would answer that to the extent that their texts reflect the theology of the entrance anti-phons found in the *Graduale Romanum* or *Missale Romanum* it is to this extent that these texts may be so regarded. In light of our thesis we can say that the *context* for the use of hymns as derived from the historical evolution of the Roman rite would indicate that the use of hymns at this part of the liturgy is at least a novelty, if not an inappropriate intrusion into the Catholic Eucharistic rite. Because of the fact that hymns are traditional at the Hours, that four poetic and metrical sequences remain in use in the present Roman Eucharistic liturgy[53] and that some would argue that the Gloria and Sanctus texts are hymnic (admitting that this is clearly debatable) then one can argue that they are sources for liturgical theology. The criterion at work here is the tradition supporting their incorporation into the liturgy in history and their use in the liturgy today. However, we would make a distinction between the "Glory to God" and "Holy, holy, holy" on the one hand, which are required in the Eucharistic liturgy, and the sequences which are not. These latter were judged not essential in the reformed liturgy, one reason being that they were substitutions for the hearing of the gospel and preaching on it. With both proclamation and biblical preaching restored in the reform, such compositions are less necessary.

One might legitimately argue, however, that the use of hymns at Roman Catholic worship is an example of inculturation since hymns continue to nurture the faith of many communities in an idiom that invites easy participation. Such usage can also help to make up for what some regard as the too laconic and elusive quality of Roman euchological and other liturgical texts. However, if hymns are used, one would have to ask to what extent their texts are drawn from the antiphons printed in the present *Graduale* or *Missale*, lest additional, and possibly quite unrelated theological themes are found in them. In addition, we would argue that the entrance antiphons given in the Roman Missal should be understood as providing a model for the content of what is actually sung at the entrance rite of the liturgy. Thus, at the Evening Mass of the Lord's Supper on Holy Thursday, the entrance antiphon given in the Missal adapted from Galatians 6:14: "We should glory in the cross of our Lord Jesus Christ . . ." should be noted with care. This antiphon introduces what is celebrated during the whole Easter triduum because it emphasizes Christ's suffering and death; it does not merely note the institution of the Eucharist or any other allied Eucharistic themes. If a hymn is used here (granting that this would not be our preference) that concerns only the Eucharist then one could argue that the depth of the meaning of the original antiphon is lost.

A related issue concerns how the liturgical practices of the Roman Catholic and Reformation Churches reflect different approaches to hymns during the Liturgy of the Word at sacramental liturgy. A first issue (as already noted) concerns what happens to the psalter when hymns replace them as the introit or response to the readings. Another issue is structural, that is, in many Reformed Eucharistic rites a hymn is sung before or after the sermon. This is to suggest that some "hymns of the day" (to use the contemporary title from the *Lutheran Book of Worship*)[54] from the Reformation tradition may function well in their worship, but that these same hymns ought not be used uncritically in contemporary Roman Catholic worship because other facets of the theology of liturgy are operative. We would argue that part of the reason why Roman Catholic worship does not utilize a hymn before or after the homily is theological. Hymn texts that reprise the gospel of the day[55] are not appropriate in Roman Catholic Eucharistic worship because after the homily attention shifts from the hearing of Scripture texts to appropriating the Word in the rest of the liturgy to follow, especially at the Eucharist. We would also argue that this is traditional in Catholicism because Sunday liturgy always meant the Eucharist and in the Reformation Churches this was not always so. To paraphrase the gospel in a hymn at the presentation of the gifts in the Roman Eucharistic rite is, in our opinion, to skew the inherent logic of how the homily and intercessions really are hinges that move from scriptural Word to altar and the rite of presenting gifts focuses on the gifts themselves, on the Eucharistic anaphora and on the transformation of gifts to come. At this point to return to a retelling of the gospel is to destroy the inherent theological logic of the Eucharistic liturgy.[56]

This issue and our comments throughout about preaching as inherent in the Eucharistic liturgy, call for at least a comment about the service of the dramatic arts in worship, specifically the tradition of passion, miracle, and mystery plays. Recently Anscar Chupungco has argued for the restoration of some form of liturgical service on Easter Sunday in addition to the Masses *in die*. Spe-

cifically he argues for the restoration of the liturgical plays of
Easter Sunday, which dramatic presentations are an anamnesis
through mimesis of Christ's post resurrection appearances.[57]
Whereas the Easter Vigil and a traditional form of Easter Sunday
Vespers concerned anamnesis/"memorial" through the liturgies of
baptism-chrismation-Eucharist, these plays dealt more directly with
the scenes of Christ's resurrection appearances. The difficulty this
raises from the point of view of liturgical theology is whether such
"liturgical plays" are sufficiently "liturgical" in the sense that it is
classically through the texts and rites of the liturgy, specifically
sacramental liturgy, that the Church experiences and appropriates
the paschal mystery anew. Hence one could rightly question
whether a dramatic enactment of a post resurrection appearance is
sufficiently respectful of the meaning of liturgical *memorial* in terms
of *anamnesis* as opposed to a dramatic reenactment of a gospel
event. It would seem preferable, if only as a first stage of the liturgical elaboration of Easter, to emphasize baptismal font, lectern,
and paschal candle as the central symbolic means through which
the contemporary Church experiences the paschal mystery on
Easter.[58]

Similarly, this is to argue against orchestrating a Christmas pageant at the Christmas liturgy at the proclamation of the gospel.
Theologically the inherent logic of the rite is that the proclamation
of the Scriptures leads immediately to homily and intercessions
that draw out its meaning and to sacramental engagement (understood as intrinsically connected with the Word) in order to facilitate its appropriation in the contemporary experience of believers.
To dramatize the Christmas gospel with a pageant would put too
much emphasis on the telling of the gospel story. In liturgy, the
gospel is proclaimed in order that it might be appropriated
through homily, intercessions and experienced most fully in the
sacrament of the Eucharist. Christmas pageants and Easter plays
may well have their place if in fact they are supplementary to the
liturgy. Unfortunately, however, the temptation to historicize liturgical feasts is still with us,[59] even in settings where liturgical inculturation has been attempted.[60] A central contribution of liturgical
memorial over staging (or even reenacting) saving events is that it
is through the liturgical repertoire of words, gestures, and symbols
(among other things) that the whole paschal mystery is commemorated for the Church. By intention this avoids the possibility of

erring on the sides of individual privatizing or historicizing these events of salvation.

To return to hymns during the Eucharist in general, this is to ask whether the *texts* of the hymns generally reflect the theology of what is celebrated in the Eucharist in terms of the contemporary appropriation of the gospel, or whether they refer back to and form a "gospel literalism." Are the images in hymn texts appropriate to the levels of symbolic engagement intrinsic to and inherent in the Eucharist? Are the texts, for example, Christmas carols and Easter hymns, liturgically appropriate? More specifically, do these texts reflect or are they at variance with the Scripture verses chosen for the (past and present) *Graduale Romanum?*

Here our thesis *context is text* comes into play by pointing up how the texts of some music sung at liturgy are really "out of context" with what should be communicated at that time. For example the refrain "O come let us adore him" to the familiar Christmas carol articulates quite a different message from the divine/human interchange that is at the heart of the feast of Christmas euchology or from the polyvalent meanings that derive from the entrance antiphons at the Masses of Christmas, none of which invite the Church to communal adoration. Rather these antiphons point to the urgency of the coming feast (Exod 16:6-7, Vigil Mass), the generation of the Son from the Father (Ps 2:7, at midnight), the coming of a light acclaimed as "wonder counselor, prince of peace" (Isa 9:2, 6, Luke 1:33, at dawn) and the gift of God's son born for us and for our salvation (Isa 9:5, day Mass). The refrain "come let us adore him" would more accurately reflect the invitation to the Liturgy of the Hours in Psalm 94: "come, let us sing joyfully to the Lord, let us acclaim the rock of our salvation." Similarly, with regard to the paschal triduum, it seems imprecise, if not incorrect, to use a hymn that asks "were you there when they crucified my Lord" when, in fact, the Good Friday liturgy commemorates our identification with Jesus's redemptive suffering and death and through these liturgies the Church annually rises to new life in him.

A helpful illustration of the traditional use of an antiphon at both the Eucharist and the Hours during Holy Week is the text from Philippians 2:8-9 "Christ became obedient for us even to death, dying on the cross. Therefore God raised him on high and gave him a name above other names."[61] The full text of the Christ hymn from Philippians 2:6-11 is the second reading on Passion (Palm) Sunday. In both the preconciliar and postconciliar liturgy this antiphon (often termed the *Christus factus est*) precedes the proclamation of the passion on both Passion Sunday and Good Friday. That Philippians 2:8-9 is used to set up the proclamation of the passion is theologically significant in that it emphasizes both Christ's *obedience* and being *raised on high*. This emphasis is made much more clear in its accompanying chant notation.[62] These same two verses were traditionally used just before the conclusion of lauds during the paschal triduum, with different (shorter, then growing to longer) endings. These same verses are used today toward the end of morning prayer on Good Friday and Holy Saturday. In the former hour of lauds on Holy Thursday the text included: "Christ . . . even death on a cross." On Good Friday and Holy Saturday the whole text "Christ . . . a name above every other name" was used. In the present morning prayer on Good Friday the text ends with "death on a cross"; on Holy Saturday the text ends "above other names."

The theological implication here is that a short Scripture text is set to music (chant is merely an example) in order to set up the reading of a Scripture text and to reiterate a major theme of a feast or season. Here the emphasis on Christ's obedience sustains the Church's annual commemoration of the paschal mystery and it offers the Church a characteristic virtue of Christ's to imitate. The chant melody itself emphasizes *obediens*, which text would have been sung in all the settings described in holy week. However, the chant places greatest emphasis on Christ's (*illum*) receiving a name above every other name because of God's exalting him (*nomen*). In this instance, the *context* established by the musical notation is crucial to interpreting properly how the Scripture text is used and interpreted.

The movement in this century toward music that truly supports the liturgy—making music *intrinsic* to liturgy—has placed great emphasis on acclamations, responses, antiphons etc., often called the "service music" *of* the given liturgy. That "hymnals" and other contemporary "worship aids" presently include more and more "service music" and fewer and fewer hymns per se is a sign that the Church legislation has been taken seriously and is taking root. Musical compositions of sung Eucharistic prayers with acclamations in the same musical style and melody interspersed within them (the efforts of Joseph Gelineau with the Eucharistic prayers for Masses with children were particularly ground breaking in this regard) are particularly effective examples of ways of emphasizing liturgical texts in context, where context here is aided by the musical arts.[63] The very singing of the Eucharistic prayer during the whole Easter season can be a forceful demonstration of how Easter is *the* season of the Eucharist. Such a practice supports our thesis in that it enhances a regular part of the Eucharistic liturgy in such a way that its *text* is emphasized merely by singing it.

2. Architecture for Worship. In this section we will be concerned primarily with the ecclesiology of liturgy as expressed in *Environment and Art in Catholic Worship* as complemented by *The Parish Church. Principles of Liturgical Design and Reordering* published by the Bishops' Conference of England and Wales[64] and *Building and Reorganisation of Churches*, Pastoral Directory of the Episcopal Liturgical Commission of Ireland.[65] These latter titles are precise in that these documents disclose what is also the primary (though under-expressed) concern of *Environment and Art*—the space for parish liturgy. To our way of thinking the *context* established by varying "assemblies of believers" requires that the design of adequate spaces for celebrating the reformed liturgy take this variety into consideration. To design a church building for a monastic or a mendicant community for whom the Liturgy of the Hours is a staple of daily liturgical prayer is a very different task from designing a parish church. Furthermore, churches that have been named shrines and basilicas because of certain circumstances which make them important places for pilgrimage have different liturgical needs from those of a parish church. Hence the shrine nature of the Church of the Holy Sepulchre in Jerusalem where for centuries Christians have revered the location of the cross of Jesus and of the empty tomb. An appropriate church design that would enhance the kind of liturgy celebrated here would differ from that of a parish church. In addition (from a uniquely Roman Catholic perspective) the location of many basilicas is dictated by the fact that a saint is buried there. Just as a votive Mass in honor of the saint buried there may be celebrated in that church on (almost) any day, for example, to honor St. Francis of Assisi at the tomb of St. Francis, so particular adjustments are in order for the design of liturgical spaces in such a location. Because pilgrimages are a marked feature in such places, the emphasis in design would necessarily be on adequate space for celebrating Eucharist at the tomb of the revered saint as well as penance, as opposed, for example, to baptism or the Hours. (The issue here is proportion, admitting that baptismal symbolism is important in any liturgical space and that the Hours may well be celebrated in such locations.)

The statement of *Environment and Art* that "among the symbols with which liturgy deals, none is more important than the assembly of believers" (n. 28) is helpful in the sense that it broadens the highly restrictive (clerical) notion espoused in *Music in Catholic Worship* (n. 21) "no other single factor affects the liturgy as much as the attitude, style, and bearing of the celebrant. . . ." But it is also limited. As it stands this statement can be as passive as Eucharistic theologies which center on the presence of the Eucharistic species and do not address the inherently transformative character of Eucharistic engagement. Thus the more precise theology of the assembly in such a document would rather speak of a community gathered for the act of liturgy, principally of the Eucharistic word and sacrament. This kind of statement would support a theology of the Word that is dynamic in its power to move and change hearts and a theology of sacrament that emphasizes continuing communal transformation and self transcendence.[66] Hence any trace of passivity for the assembly is overcome by emphasis on how the assembly is gathered for the sake of liturgical engagement.

Specifically, we would argue that the requirements of locating and constructing a monastic choir within an abbey church call for artistic directives that emphasize the location of stalls or chairs facing each other for the Liturgy of the Hours. Similarly, the theology and liturgy of the mendicant tradition should be reflected in the location of its choir and, among other sanctuary artifacts, the pulpit or lectern, considering the importance of preaching in much of the mendicant (e.g., Dominican) tradition. It would seem that the emphasis on architectural space for baptism in the parish church would not need to be as compelling in monastic or mendicant settings. Our wording here is careful since the contemporary retrieval of one aspect of monastic and religious vows concerns how they deepen baptismal commitment. Therefore "as compelling" means that a baptismal font for the taking of holy water upon entering, ought be located at the entrance to monastic or mendicant liturgical spaces.

Similarly, architectural and liturgical factors combine in "shrine churches" to present a unique challenge to liturgical artists. The fact that shrine churches are erected to commemorate a person, event or aspect of Christ's redemption has frequently led to constructing buildings focused on these persons or events as primary centers of attention. Examples here include the Church of the Holy Sepulchre in Jerusalem or the basilica church at Lourdes. The traditional value of celebrating the Eucharist as close to the location of an event of saving history (e.g., the place of the resurrection or the appearance of Mary to Bernadette) has sometimes required tiny spaces for a few people to celebrate at shrine altars. The key issue concerns balancing the appropriate value placed on "the subject of liturgical action: the church" (in the words of *Environment and Art*) with the subject of the shrine in terms of its being a place of pilgrimage and a "sacred" location, making it the subject of devotional practice. (Linked to this kind of construction is the custom of placing relics in altars erected apart from the locations of such events or the burial places of outstanding saints. Hence relics made this kind of commemoration portable.)

Allied with these concerns derived from the varying *contexts* for liturgy is the question of what kind of liturgy is regularly celebrated in a given space. Examples could include a shrine frequently used for weddings, or charismatic prayer meetings, cursillos, lectures, etc. along with the celebration of Eucharist. Similarly, the demands of the more regular celebration of the anointing of the sick in parish churches would demand that liturgical spaces be designed with this purpose in mind. The fact that one of the stated intentions of the reform of the Liturgy of the Hours is that it become a staple in the liturgical prayer of all communities requires that these celebrations be facilitated by the liturgical space. This does not mean that parish churches should imitate monastic or mendicant settings, especially since much recent research distinguishes the "monastic" from "cathedral" or "parish" celebration of the Hours. The use of responsorial psalmody in the cathedral tradition would not require the construction of facing choir stalls in parish churches. In fact, the presence of facing choir stalls in many medieval churches still in use today is problematic since the altar is frequently at the far end of the stalls away from the congregations' pews. The flexibility that is highly prized in *Environment and Art* would apply here to allow for appropriate (and greater) flexibility in the spaces used for the Eucharist and the Hours.

Among the criteria for adequate liturgical spaces for worship, the following four would seem to be paramount.

(1) The reiteration of the value of "active participation" in the reformed liturgy from the Liturgy Constitution through to documents of implementation makes this a chief value in planning and constructing spaces for worship.

(2) The flexibility built into each of reformed liturgical rites and the flexibility required when individual communities celebrate various liturgies (e.g., marriages, ordinations on occasion, Hours more regularly, communal penance services, etc.) would require that worship spaces be constructed to facilitate such flexibility.

(3) The fact that we are dealing with sights, sounds and bodily involvement in liturgy would call for spaces that facilitate the assembly's seeing all that is occurring liturgically. For example, the celebration of marriage, ordination, and confirmation would be enormously enhanced if the assembly did not have to look only at the backs of the heads of those involved. Enabling the assembly to actually see the faces, gestures, and expressions of those involved in such sacraments would add to the intrinsic human dynamic in the act of liturgy. Allied with this is the requirement of adequate lighting and flexibility in the lighting that allows for wide areas to be illuminated and thus used for such sacraments.

(4) A criterion touched upon in the *Environment and Art* documents concerns audibility (n. 51). A lasting legacy from churches that housed the Tridentine liturgy is the lack of adequate provision for actually hearing the (musical and recited) texts of the liturgy. This may be compounded even in newly constructed churches containing sound-absorbing carpeting, ceiling tiles, and the like.[67] In addition to audibility of texts, however, is audibility of symbolic engagement such as breaking of bread, pouring wine, immersing in water etc. That these are audible as well as visible requires that appropriate sound systems be in use.

IV. Critical Liturgical Theology

This last section deals in succession with what we have argued throughout comprises liturgical arts—music, architecture, artifacts, and pictorial art—especially in light of the American documents of liturgical implementation. At the outset it is important to underscore that these documents are, by intention, provisional and that what is offered here be taken into consideration in drafting subsequent texts.

The first issue is rather general and argues that more work is needed on what we have termed liturgical "aesthetics." This theoretical framework would emphasize how that which is aesthetically pleasing reflects the glory of God and how aesthetically-pleasing arts and artifacts are intrinsic to the experience of liturgy and to the theology of liturgy. Just as the categories of the good, true, and beautiful are being revived as crucial for contemporary ethics, the theology developed from the reformed liturgy necessarily includes them and gives them shape. To agree that liturgy ought to be aesthetically pleasing and that its component elements should be qualitatively beautiful would not be difficult. A legitimate challenge to this statement, however, could rightly be mounted when aesthetics is equated with ostentation and beauty merely with expense. Nuance and precision of argument is clearly necessary. It is also difficult to program how aesthetics and beauty should be intrinsic parts of the liturgical experience. But the lack of these qualities in the conduct of worship (despite the money spent) and in the construction of houses for worship requires that these matters be raised.

Too often the contemporary liturgy is criticized for a lack of beauty that can raise the human heart to God and a lack of artistic depth and integrity in church buildings, art, music, artifacts, vesture, and decorum in enactment. That these might be prized for their own sake and when used in worship derogate from the celebration of the liturgy are obvious dangers. However, that the category of aesthetics or the category of beauty be relegated to relative non-importance in planning and constructing churches or in the planning and celebration of liturgy would be (and unfortunately is) equally dangerous. Theologically, liturgy presumes the contribution of the "work of human hands." Aesthetics requires that these reflect high artistic standards in continuity with the premises on which the theology of liturgy is based. It would also reflect the breadth of the Catholic tradition in terms of the use of art and architecture for worship.

Second, in light of our thesis it would be very important to view the use of liturgical arts in historical and liturgical context. Thus what has been regarded as helpful church architecture for Cistercian monasteries or medieval European cathedrals (such as Chartres) should be appreciated for their particular *contexts*. At the same time that they might not serve well as models for contemporary parish church construction they also should not be criticized for containing what is necessary for the celebration of the reformed liturgy. Many of them still stand as significant testaments to faith and as witness to the variety of settings in which liturgy takes place.

That some contemporary church buildings and liturgical spaces are regarded as "empty" or "cold" should be viewed in light of the fact that these are built to house *the Church at worship*. As such, the house for the Church will logically seem cold without the Church which it is designed to house. The contemporary emphasis on "ourselves—we who are the Church, the baptized, the initiated" (*Environment and Art* n. 27) is most helpful when understood as offering a theological support for active liturgical participation. Yet, the statement is somewhat limited and limiting. A more complete understanding of the Church requires attention to belonging to a wider membership beyond a given local Church and to a vocation to communal and personal self-transcendence beyond a specific liturgical community. In this connection our emphasis on *context* could serve as a reminder that a study of the history of both church art and architecture can help to fill out the helpful, dynamic directions of this part of *Environment and Art*.[68] That the liturgical space is a place "for human interaction and active participation" (*Environment and Art* n. 39) is certainly true. At the same time, however, it is somewhat limited with regard to ecclesiological and liturgical depth and breadth and certainly not inclusive of devotional needs of worshipers. In all likelihood some location near (or) the liturgical space (itself) is a place for personal prayer, which location could be enhanced by pictorial arts and artifacts which, while conforming to the principles of the liturgy, could foster other kinds of payer. More attention to criteria for designing theologically appropriate pictorial art (paintings, glass, statues) would be appropriate. The comments made above about existing works of art from the Catholic tradition serve to recall the deep and rich merging of the theological and the artistic in the Catholic tradition—which merging we would wish were not lost in the present reform. The pictorial arts comprise a good part of this tradition.

Third, one of the contributions which monastic Eucharistic liturgy can make to the present evolution of appropriate music for the liturgy is in the area of antiphonal and responsorial psalmody at the entrance, presentation and communion processions. It would seem that the (former) monastic experience of using the *Liber Usualis* (or a variation on it) for both Eucharist and Hours could well serve in the move away from the (over)use of hymns in the present Eucharistic liturgy. This is to say that monastic communities might serve the wider Church by offering a variety of musical compositions for the vernacular translations of the antiphons as they presently exist in the *Graduale Romanum* and the Sacramentary for Mass. To offer antiphons to be sung by all, structured in accord with the tradition of the Roman introit, "offertory," and Communion would go a long way toward dealing with the inadequacy of using hymns so commonly at the Eucharist.

A fourth issue concerns the design and use of liturgical artifacts that reflect varying cultural needs. This is to suggest that liturgical vesture and vessels could be developed more freely with local cultures in mind. For example, the fullness of vesture worn at the Eucharist celebrated near the Equator would obviously be best designed for material lighter in weight than that used farther north or south with their change of seasons. Similarly, the design of liturgical artifacts should not be determined by Eurocentric models.

To our way of thinking the helpful phrase "form follows function" recalls in a pithy way the value of liturgical engagement as a central criterion for the liturgical arts. It should not, however, be read as artistic minimalism. "Function" should not mean pragmatically functional, especially where this phrase can mean without artistic merit. Admittedly, the contemporary liturgical arts are still in their comparative infancy. What still needs to be worked out are criteria that combine aesthetics with the demands of the reformed liturgy. The value of the true, the good and the beautiful should be intrinsic parts of such an aesthetic, understanding that these criteria are also adaptable depending on local culture and ecclesiological circumstances.

Our thesis *context is text* has been advanced and illustrated in this chapter in a number of ways. The liturgical arts are both central and complementary to the experience of worship. They shape the *context* of engagement in the present reformed liturgy in a number of verbal and nonverbal ways. They also complement Word, symbol, and euchology, so much so that the way these central elements—*texts*—of liturgy are appreciated often derive from the way they are or are not enhanced by the liturgical arts—*context*. While we have argued that varying ecclesial contexts require variety in liturgical arts, at the same time the experience of this variety can help varying contexts explore and develop more adequate aspects of the arts used in and developed for worship (e.g., music used at monastic liturgy of the Eucharist). That the arts are among the more dynamic and highly influential aspects of liturgical engagement is clear. The concern of this chapter has been to underscore this dynamism, to support ongoing creativity in their regard and to suggest some aspects of theological depth implicit in liturgical engagement that should help to shape ongoing creativity in the liturgical arts.

Notes

1. The phrase "the music, architecture, artifacts and pictorial art" is admittedly and deliberately a general description of this chapter's concerns. For example, the term "pictorial art" and what it signifies is comparatively foreign to the experience of Western liturgy whereas the use of icons is intrinsic to much Eastern liturgy. See, for example, Peter Galadza, "The Role of Icons in Byzantine Worship," *Studia Liturgica* 21 (1991) 113–135 and Constantin Kalokyris, "The Content of Eastern Iconography," *Symbol and Art in Worship.* Concilium 132 (New York: Seabury, 1980) 9–18. In comparison, in the West (our principal concern) music, architecture and artifacts are more obviously used and recognizable in the act of liturgy. Also, by way of distinction and explanation, the term "environment" is used in many contemporary (especially American) discussions of liturgical art, architecture and artifacts. The booklet *Environment and Art in Catholic Worship* n. 24 states the following: "By environment we mean the larger space in which the action of the assembly takes place. At its broadest, it is the setting of the building in its neighborhood, including outdoor spaces. More specifically it means the character of a particular space and how it affects the action of the assembly. There are elements in the environment, therefore, which contribute to the overall experience, e.g., the seating arrangement, the placement of liturgical centers of

action, temporary decoration, light, acoustics, spaciousness, etc. The environment is appropriate when it is beautiful, when it is hospitable, when it clearly invites and needs an assembly of people to complete it."

For example, see Mark G. Boyer, *The Liturgical Environment. What The Documents Say* (Collegeville: The Liturgical Press, 1990). Because we have already used the term "environment" in conjunction with our treatment of the use of creation in worship, specifically with regard to the contemporary confluence of environmental and liturgical theology, we will use the specific terms "art, architecture and artifacts" in this chapter.

2. To borrow from the title of Paul Waitman Hoon, *The Integrity of Worship. Ecumenical and Pastoral Studies in Liturgical Theology* (Nashville/New York: Abingdon Press, 1971) and more specifically from Don Saliers, "The Integrity of Sung Prayer," *Worship* 55 (July 1981) 290–303.

3. In addition to the reference above to the musical settings for the consecratory prayers at ordinations (see Chapter 5, 189 and fn. 55) the layout of the present *Sacramentary for Mass* is illustrative since in the main body of the text the Eucharistic prefaces, Good Friday solemn intercessions and the Easter Vigil *Exsultet* are set to music, the entire Order of Mass is set to music in the Sacramentary's Appendix III.

4. See, Pelagio Visentin, "Creazione—Storia della salvezza—Liturgia," *Rivista Liturgica* 77 (1990) 267.

5. A particularly forceful example of the comparatively inadequate treatment of the arts is reflected in the way liturgical arts are discussed in *L'Eglise en prière Vol. I*. They are treated in one section under the title "liturgical signs" and are almost ignored in discussions of individual rites in the succeeding three volumes. For important insight on this question see, Irénée-Henri Dalmais, "Symbolique liturgique et théologique de l'art roman," *La Maison Dieu* 123 (1975) 135–148. Also see, *The Study of Liturgy*, ed. Cheslyn Jones, et. al. (London: SPCK, 1978) where "The Setting of the Liturgy" (440–465) concerning "Music and Singing in the Liturgy," "Hymnody in Christian Worship" and "The Architectural Setting of the Liturgy and Vestments" (473–492) occupy approximately fifty pages in a handbook of 536 pages.

6. Recall the discussion above regarding the human manufacture of these or similarly produced "stable food and festive drink" in Chapter 4, 157–160 and 163–164.

7. In addition to the texts directly related to liturgy referred throughout this chapter, the following additional sources have helped form my thoughts on what is broadly called "aesthetics." Hans Urs Von Balthasar, *The Glory of the Lord: A Theological Aesthetics. Vol. I: Seeing the Form*. Trans. Erasmo Leiva-Merikakis, ed., Joseph Fessio (New York/San Francisco: Crossroad/Ignatius, 1982), *Symbol and Art in Worship*, eds. Luis Maldonado and David N. Power, Concilium vol. 132 (New York: Seabury Press, 1980), Don E. Saliers, *The Soul in Paraphrase: Prayer and the Religious Affections* (New York: Seabury, 1980) and Gerardus Van der Leeuw, *Sacred and Profane Beauty: The Holy in Art*, trans. David E. Green (New York: Holt, Rinehart and Winston, 1963).

8. Three works that include music, architecture, pictorial arts and artifacts as intrinsic parts of liturgical (and in particular Eucharistic) theology derived from the liturgy are Marion J. Hatchett's, *Sanctifying Life, Time and Space. An Introduction to Liturgical Study* (New York: Seabury, 1976), Edward Foley's *From Age to Age. How Christians Celebrated the Eucharist* (Chicago: Liturgy Training Publications, 1991) and Miri Rubin's *Corpus Christi. The Eucharist in Late Medieval Culture* (Oxford/NY: Oxford University Press, 1991). The first is a broad investigation of the liturgy that can be quite helpful as an outline for courses in liturgical studies. The second is more general and aimed at a wide audience. The third is more technical and aimed at the more restricted audience of the academy. However, all are helpful examples of factoring into systematic treatments of liturgy the liturgical arts, regarded here as essential and complementary sources for liturgical theology. Our particular interest is somewhat different from these authors (especially the last two) in terms of establishing method for liturgical theology in general, rather than elucidating a systematic liturgical theology of Eucharist.

9. Don E. Saliers, "Liturgical Aesthetics," *New Dictionary of Sacramental Worship* 31.

10. Ibid., 33. Recall here the operative principle throughout Part 2 about how symbolic engagement is intrinsic to liturgy.

11. For a summary of the (not totally smooth) passage from the Liturgy Constitution to *Musicam Sacram* see, A. Bugnini, *The Reform of the Liturgy* 898–914. Also see the helpful retrospective in J. Michael Joncas, "Re-Reading *Musicam Sacram:* Twenty-Five Years of Development in the Roman Rite Liturgical Music," *Worship* 66 (May 1992) 212–231. Translations from *Musicam Sacram* are from *DOL*.

12. See, Edward Foley, "Overview" of *Music in Catholic Worship* and *Liturgical Music Today* in *The Liturgy Documents. A Parish Resource* (Chicago, Ill.: Liturgy Training Publications, 1991) 270–273 and Andrew D. Ciferni, "Overview" of *Environment and Art in Catholic Worship* in *The Liturgy Documents* 314–316. In addition to the host of documents from the Sacred Congregation for Divine Worship about the importance of and appreciation of the postconciliar liturgical reform, the 1979 *Instruction on Liturgical Formation in Seminaries* by the Sacred Congregation for Catholic Education is most useful in this regard. In addition, see *Liturgical Formation in Seminaries. A Commentary* (Washington: USCC, 1984).

13. However, in the discussion that follows, especially section four of this chapter, some defects in these texts and possible defects in interpreting such documents will be noted.

14. The evolution of modern church legislation from Pius X to the Liturgy Constitution is amply documented elsewhere. For our purposes it is sufficient here to indicate that from *Tra le sollecitudini* of Pius X through the present documents of liturgical reform, music is regarded as an integral component of liturgical celebration (see, *Tra le sollecitudini* n. 1). Puis X extols Gregorian chant as the ideal musical style because of its aesthetic quality as true art, its

quality of holiness (meaning here that chant is not associated with the profane) and its universality (can be used throughout the world). Gregorian
chant also conforms to Pius's principles of "tradition and simplicity" (*Tra le
sollecitudini*, nn. 10-11, translation from Robert Hayburn in *Papal Legislation on
Sacred Music* [Collegeville, Minn.: The Liturgical Press, 1979] 227). It is also an
obvious example of the principle regarding the service role of music in the liturgy (n. 23). That many of these (and other of Pius's) principles are repeated
in subsequent Church documents is seen in *Musicae sacrae disciplina* (1955)
which uses Gregorian chant to exemplify its principle of universality. However, the latter transcended the restrictiveness of *Tra le sollecitudini* in allowing
the use of instruments other than the organ and in allowing the use of
vernacular hymns (nn. 36, 47, 62, 64). More will be said about hymns below.

15. *DOL* 4125.

16. *Musicam Sacram* n. 7 (*DOL* n. 4128): "The amount of singing determines
the gradations between the most solemn form of liturgical celebrations, in
which all the parts calling for singing are sung, and the most simple form, in
which nothing is sung. For the choice of parts to be sung, those should be
first that of their nature are more important and particularly those sung by
the priest or other ministers and answered by the congregation or sung by
the priest and congregation together. Later other parts, for the congregation
alone or the choir alone, may be added gradually."

17. While the task of articulating the elements of what might be termed a
liturgical aesthetic for the reformed liturgy is still in process, nonetheless to
our way of thinking, it would have been important to establish in these documents the value of aesthetics in shaping and celebrating the reformed liturgy.
The comments of Edward Foley in the "Overview" to these statements in *The
Liturgy Documents* 272–73 hint at this lack when they refer to the lack of at-
tending to "poetics" regarding liturgical language and to some possible questionable interpretations of what these documents call music that is "artistically
sound."

18. The introduction of this term in the General Instruction on the Liturgy of
the Hours (n. 273) and subsequent use in *Universi qui Officium* and *Musicam
sacram* has spawned a number of theoretical and practical commentaries on
the use of this principle in other liturgical celebrations.

19. The qualifying statement in the next paragraph (n. 15) is important: "at
the same time, it needs to be recognized that a certain musical integrity
within a liturgical prayer or rite can be achieved only by unity in the music
composition. Thus, it is recommended that for the acclamations in the Eucharistic prayer one music style be employed."

20. Edward Foley, "Overview," 273.

21. Secretariat for the Liturgy and Secretariat for Black Catholics, National
Conference of Catholic Bishops, *Plenty Good Room. The Spirit and Truth of
African American Catholic Worship.* (Washington: United States Catholic
Conference, 1990).

22. See, Chapter 2, 60–62.

23. As noted in Chapter 2, 60–61 and fn. 43.

24. See, John Jay Hughes, "Eucharistic Sacrifice. Transcending the Reformation Deadlock," *Worship* 43 (November 1969) 533.

25. See, Ralph Keifer, "Liturgical Text as Primary Source For Eucharistic Theology," *Worship* 51 (May 1977) 186–196 at 186.

26. Ibid., 190.

27. The number of artistic and theological commentaries on these mosaics abounds. Among them see the comparatively recent work of Gianfranco Bustacchini, *Ravenna. Capitale del Mosaico* (Ravenna: Cartolibreria Salbaroli, 1988).

28. See Chapter 4 above pp. 139–140 and fn. 32 for an overview of *Apostolic Constitutions* Book VIII.

29. For more background see, Giovanni Paolo Tesei, *Le Chiese di Roma* (Roma: Casa Anthropos, 1986) 54–55.

30. Another significant example of mosaics used lavishly and tastefully in a church building in the West is the cathedral in Monreale (outside of Palermo, Sicily). For a particularly thorough, artistically and theologically informed treatment see, Ernst Kitzinger, *I Mosaici di Monreale* (Palermo: S. F. Flaccovio, 1991).

31. See, *Le Chiese di Roma* 104. A related and highly formative issue concerns medieval altars and altarpieces, as documented in Jacob Burckhardt, *The Altarpiece in Renaissance Italy*, trans. and ed. Peter Humfrey, (Cambridge/New York: Cambridge University Press, 1988).

32. The present American edition of the ICEL Sacramentary published by the Catholic Book Publishing Co. leaves a great deal to be desired in this area. A glance at the present Italian altar Sacramentary and Missal (among other examples) only heightens one's awareness of the artistic deficiencies of the American Sacramentary.

33. Nothing can substitute for the twice daily lectures on site at Chartres by Malcolm Miller, the English language lecturer (who insists that he offers "lectures" not guided "tours"). Some helpful indications of the wonder that awaits (or of the wonder still remaining from) a Miller presentation are in his own books: *Chartres Cathedral* (Andover: Pitkin, 1985), *Chartres Cathedral: The Medieval Stained Glass and Sculpture* (Andover: Pitkin, 1980) and *Chartres: The Cathedral and the Old Town* (Andover: Pitkin, 1981). Also see Emile Male, *Notre-Dame de Chartres* (Paris: Flammarion, 1983).

34. See, among others, the two helpful works by Jean-Paul Deremble and Colette Manhes, *Les vitraux légendaires de Chartres* (Paris: Desclée de Brower, 1988) and *Le vitrail du Bon Samaritain, Chartres, Sens, Bourges* (Paris: Le Centurion, 1986).

35. See, Colette Deremble, "Les vitraux de Chartres et la liturgie," *La Maison Dieu* 177 (1989) 167–181.

36. See, for example, Roger S. Weick, et. al., *Time Sanctified. The Book of Hours in Medieval Art and Life* (New York: George Braziller, 1988).

37. For an historical perspective leading to contemporary insight, see, John G. Davies, "The Influence of Architecture on Liturgical Change," *Studia Liturgica* 9 (1973) 230–240.

38. First enunciated in *Tra le sollecitudini* n. 23.

39. Ibid., n. 3.

40. *Sacrosanctum Concilium*, n. 112; the phrase used here that music is intrinsic to every "solemn liturgy" is dropped in subsequent legislation.

41. It is at least notable that a distinction is made in the two articles about music in the liturgy in *The Study of Liturgy* as they are entitled "Music and Singing in the Liturgy" (by the Roman Catholic Joseph Gelineau) and "Hymnody in Christian Worship."

42. See, G. Wainwright, *Doxology*, specifically 198–217. Despite his reliance on liturgical texts throughout this work (especially hymns reflecting his own worship tradition) Wainwright appropriately argues against a liturgy that is overly didactic. In "Lex orandi and lex credendi—Strange Bedfellows? Some Refections on Worship and Doctrine," *Scottish Journal of Theology* 39 (1986) 233 Kenneth Stevenson notes that Wainwright's "love of quoting Wesley hymns is a refreshing tendency in a book of such density, and it is also extremely appropriate in a book which gives the overarching impression of having been conceived by a devout soul, of deep sincerity and passionate ecumenical zeal."

43. Our focus on these four moments of the Eucharist should be noted since some argue that the Gloria and the Sanctus are hymns regularly sung at Catholic Eucharist. More will be said about this below.

44. In this connection (in *Elements of Rite. A Handbook of Liturgical Style* (New York: Pueblo Publishing Co., 1982) 37) Aidan Kavanagh observes:

"The Roman Liturgy tends to resist metrical hymnody except in its liturgy of the hours. With the exception of several metrical sequences of relatively recent date, the Roman eucharist has never contained metrical hymns. Although these are now frequently included in eucharistic liturgies, especially in northern European cultures which have a rich tradition of such hymns stemming from non-Roman sources, the older pattern of antiphon with psalmody remains the preeminent norm in standard Roman eucharistic books. Unfortunately, the current English translations of these books make it difficult to observe this Roman tradition, except for the meditation chants between the lessons."

45. *DOL* n. 1416.

46. *Sacramentary for Mass* 51–52.

47. For example, one would need to sing all five verses of *Good King Wenceslaus* to appreciate its meaning!

48. Some of what is argued here coincides with the observations of Bernard Huijbers in *The Performing Audience: Six and a Half Essays on Music and Song in the Liturgy* (Cincinnati: North American Liturgy Resources, 1974 [2nd ed.]) Chapter 2 "Limits and Possibilities of the Song Form in the Liturgy" 29–44. Helpful in this connection are sections of Edward W. Pond's *A Select Study of the Liturgical Music of Bernard Huijbers: The Theological Principles Which Are Fundamental to His Music, and the Means by Which He Translated These Principles Into Music for the Assembly* unpublished doctoral dissertation from The Catholic University of America, 1991.

49. Not unrelated is the comment of Eric Routley: "if Catholics want hymn singing at Mass, they must candidly answer the question whether the change of congregational ethos required to give hymns a good soil to grow in is what the Catholic church really wants: if the answer is anything but 'Yes,' then hymns ought to be dropped and left to those Christian groups whose doctrine of congregational worship is founded in the Reformation." See, *Christian Hymns Observed* (London: A. R. Mowbray, 1983) 92. An allied set of observations about church *context* comes from S. Paul Schilling, *The Faith We Sing* (Philadelphia: Westminster, 1983) in which he discusses the function of hymns as credal formulary and indeed as *liturgy* itself in the non-liturgical churches.

50. See above, Chapter 5, 204.

51. See, Chapter 3, 92–94.

52. Of course, the best illustration of what we are arguing here would come from hearing the text sung, rather than describing it. In this absence, see *Graduale Romanum:*

Intr. 2.

Errí-bi-lis est * lo-cus i- ste : hic do-mus

De- i est, et porta cae- li : et vocá- bi- tur

au-la De- i. *T.P.* Al-le-lú- ia, alle- lú- ia.

Ps. Quam di- lécta tabérná-cu-la tu- a, Dómi- ne virtú-tum! *

concu-píscit, et dé- fi-cit á-nima me- a   in átri- a Dómi-

ni.   Gló-ri- a Patri.   E u o u a e.

53. See, Chapter 5, 178.

54. According to the *Lutheran Book of Worship* (Minneapolis: Augsburg, 1978) the Hymn of the Day may be sung before or after the sermon.

55. See the powerful collection by Carol Doran and Thomas H. Troeger, *New Hymns for the Lectionary. To Glorify the Maker's Name* (New York/Oxford: Oxford University Press, 1986).

56. Another example of what the inherent logic of the rite assumes and requires concerns the present liturgy for Passion (Palm) Sunday. Once the palm procession is over the texts of the liturgy (Scriptural and euchological) make no other reference to the Jesus's triumphant entry into Jerusalem. To conclude the liturgy with the singing of "All Glory Laud and Honor," for example, would be to miss the precise distinction between acclaiming Christ as King during the procession and emphasizing him as obedient servant of the Father's will, which led to his death on the cross, in the rest of the liturgy.

57. Anscar Chupungco, *Liturgies of the Future*, 172–84, specifically 180–81.

58. Among other recent studies, see *La Celebrazione del Triduo Pasquale. Anamnesis e Mimesis.* Studia Anselmiana 102. Analecta Liturgica 14. Ed., Ildebrando Scicolone (Rome: Editrice Anselmiana, 1990).

59. Liturgists will often term "historicization" that process whereby the unitive commemoration of Christ's paschal mystery is celebrated over time in such a way that the elongation to "three days" can be perceived to mean three historical reminiscences rather than one mystery commemorated over three days. That these positions are presently being nuanced, offering much material for liturgical theology, is exemplified in the collection *La Celebrazione del Triduo Pasquale.* Note especially Anscar Chupungco "Anamnesis and Mimesis in the Celebration of Easter Sunday," 259–271, Gabriel Ramis, "Cronología y dramatizacion de la Pasion en el triduo sacro de las liturgias occidentales," 99–177 and Jordi Pinell, "Dramatismo humano y misterio liturgico en la serie romana antigua de responsorios para el triduo sacro," 179–207.

60. See, for example, the discussion of one attempt at the indigenization of the Good Friday liturgy in Africa that remained very much on the level of historicization in Kevin W. Irwin, "Seminar on Sacramental and Liturgical Theology," *Proceedings of the Catholic Theological Society of America* 45 (1990) 113–114.

61. Recall Chapter 3, section four on "obedient listening" as constitutive of the theology of the Word, 116–118.

62. In the absence of a musical performance of this text see *Graduale Romanum:*

Grad. 5.

Chri-stus * factus est pro no- bis o-bé-di- ens us-que ad mor- tem, mor- tem au-tem cru- cis. ℣. Propter quod et De- us exal-tá-vit il-lum, et de- dit il-li no- men, quod est super o-mne * no- men.

63. Helpful in this regard in the short monograph by Edward Foley and Mary McGann *Music in the Eucharistic Prayer.* American Essays in Liturgy 8 (Collegeville: The Liturgical Press, 1988).

64. See, *The Parish Church* (London: Catholic Truth Society, 1984) 96pp. Significantly, this is the third implementation document from this conference, the other two being *The Parish Mass* and *Music in the Parish Mass.*

65. *Building and Reorganization of Churches* (Dublin: Veritas Publications, 1966 first edition considerably expanded to second version published in 1972) 55.

66. This recalls the theology of the proclaimed Word enunciated in Chapter 3, section four, 111–119.

67. See, Andrew Ciferni, "Overview," *The Liturgy Documents* 316.

68. A brief overview of what would be involved in such a study as buildings relate to the other aspects of liturgy is in Marion J. Hatchett, *Sanctifying Life, Time and Space,* 28–29, 49–50, 78–80, 95–96, 177–178.

Part 3

Text Shapes Context: Liturgical Theology

Chapter 7: Doxology and Ecumenism

The second part of the thesis *text shapes context* is used to show that the theology derived from the liturgy is inherently doxological and that liturgical theology can be most helpful in ecumenical sacramental conversations.

Chapter 8: Spirituality

The thesis is used to indicate that engaging in liturgy and in doing liturgical theology implies living a moral and spiritual life in conformity with the liturgy.

Chapter 7

Doxology and Ecumenism

From the outset we have argued a bipolar methodological thesis about liturgical theology—that *context is text* and that *text shapes context*. This argument underscores the essential *dialectical relationship* between contexts in which liturgical rites occur and the meaning of liturgical rites themselves. In chapters 3 to 6 our concern has been to articulate how varying contexts (including ecclesial, cultural, and personal factors) shape how the constitutive elements of liturgy are interpreted. Our focus now shifts to the second part of the methodological equation to determine (in this and the next chapter) some of the *implications intrinsic to liturgical engagement*.

In accord with our thesis these concern how *text shapes context* understanding "text" to mean enacted liturgy and "context" the lives of believers, both individual and communal. Our primary interest in this chapter will be to explore the contribution which liturgical theology, understood as *theologia secunda*,[1] can make to contemporary discussions about the nature of theology, namely that liturgical theology is "doxological,"[2] and how aspects of liturgical theology can contribute to discussions about the method to be used for engaging in ecumenical sacramental conversations, specifically mutual enrichment for participating Churches derived from liturgical theology. In the next chapter our focus will be on the life relation of engaging in liturgy, already understanding that *theologia tertia* is both constitutive and reflective of liturgical engagement and of the theology derived from that engagement. An underlying theme in both chapters reprises the argument noted in chapter 2[3] that "orthodoxy" means "right praise" revealed in the act of liturgy as much as (if not even more than) "right belief" reflected in correct Church teaching.[4] Throughout both chapters the second part of our thesis *context is text, text shapes context* will be applied specifically to the way one articulates doxological theology, the way one interprets liturgical rites for the theological insights these rites can contribute to ecumenical sacramental conversations (chapter 7) and the way liturgical rites derive from, shape our experience of and have ramifications for all of life (chapter 8).

This chapter has three parts. Part 1 situates the specific contribution of liturgical theology to shaping doxological theology in the context of contemporary discussions of theological language. Part 2 is divided into two sections concerning the nature of dogmatic statements and the evolving method for and progress in ecumenical sacramental conversations.[5] Part 3 offers our own methodological proposal for ecumenical conversations on specific sacraments as well as a proposal for conversations about a liturgical theology of sacraments that tries to get behind individual areas of remaining disagreement and place them in the new context provided by liturgical theology, understood as the theology derived from the liturgy presently celebrated in the Churches, which is remarkably similar in structure and content.

I. Liturgical Theology: Doxological Orthodoxy

As early as 1941 the Benedictine systematic theologian Anselm Stolz argued for an expansion of the conventional meaning of *theologia* and *theologein* beyond "speaking about God" to include the more traditional notions of "theology" as prayer and "speaking to God."[6] Clearly influenced by the patristic and monastic scholarship of his colleagues at Sant' Anselmo in Rome and by the wider developing *resourcesment* in Catholic theology, Stolz argued that in Hellenism *theologia* is a technical term for religious *poesia*, signifying the hymn, or hymnology[7] and that much patristic writing, especially that of St. Augustine, devolved from the understanding that theology is really speech *from* and *to* God as well as speech *about* God.[8] For Stolz the hymn is a direct prayer to God, the study of which, "hymnology," may simply be called "theology." In this theological enterprise the liturgy is particularly influential. As the Church's doxology it reflects and shapes both prayer and belief as intrinsically theological realities.

In a recent study of the import of the psalms and of Christian liturgy on the nature and shape of theology, Harvey Guthrie cites and agrees with Louis Bouyer's insight that "the first meaning of the Greek *theologia* . . . designates a hymn, a glorification of God by the *logos*, by [expressed human] thought. This thought is obviously rational in the highest degree, but rational in the way harmony is; it is an intellectual music whose spontaneous expression is therefore a liturgical chant and not some sort of hair-splitting or tedious labeling."[9]

This text is most congenial for Guthrie's argument in *Theology As Thanksgiving* (which title summarizes his argument) since in introducing the work he states that

"the *kanon*—the measuring rod, the standard, the norm—by which both ancient Israel and the early Church weighed the adequacy of theological statements was not one involving the content of those statements as such. On the contrary, that *kanon* was based on what emerged from liturgical forms, from cultic actions. It was based on what a community of faith knew and experienced and was involved in as it proclaimed its identity in worship."[10]

Towards the end he reprises this statement by saying that

". . . it was a norm rooted in the liturgy elicited by and appropriate as praise for God's revealing and saving involvement with a people in history. That form, that action, that norm was *eucharistia* which, like *todah* in ancient Israel, was thankful recital in the context of liturgical action in which the human community involved participated with God in the enjoyment of a sacrifice."[11]

Once again we can say that the liturgy as inherently doxological shapes both the Church's prayer and belief, which realities are intrinsically theological realities.

Congenial with this line of thought is Dietrich Ritschl's contention that for too long "nature and grace, reason and faith, scholarship and piety, theology and doxology, historical past and existential present have been separated from each other."[12] Hence in *Memory and Hope* he will argue for a doxological theology that reflects *Christus praesens* and our deification in Christ.[13] More recently Daniel W. Hardy and David F. Ford have taken up this call from a somewhat different perspective emphasizing the important place of prayer for understanding what theology is and for the way theologians should go about their craft.[14] It is therefore not surprising that they have criticized Geoffrey Wainwright's *Doxology* for being too systematic and for not giving attention to the inner dynamic of God's relating to humanity through "encounter."[15]

The recent (and regrettably all too brief) article relating liturgy and theology by the Trinitarian specialist Catherine Mowry LaCugna[16] provides much helpful insight, including the argument that liturgy restrains theology from becoming an "a-theological religious science" since it is the "ritual action by which we live and enact faith in the triune God"[17] which enactment of faith grounds all theology. LaCugna understands liturgy and theology to be *"intrinsically* related to each other because the 'inner moment' of both is doxology."[18] She asserts straightforwardly that "to do theology properly means to exhibit the unity of exegesis, liturgy, doctrine, confession, contemplation, and ethics."[19] For her, liturgy is a *mysterium salutis* that unites soteriology and doxology (among other things). Therefore theology can be nothing less than doxological. She then argues from her Trinitarian specialization that "the original context of both Christian faith and of what later became trinitarian doctrine was . . . doxological."[20]

She asserts that

"liturgy provides a constant check on the tendency of theological reason to over-emphasize one or the other dimension of our knowledge of God. Liturgy serves to prevent the type of theology which becomes fascinated with itself rather than with God. The activity of worship, in other words, accomplishes something which the theological *ratio* can never establish, viz., the unity of economy and theology."[21]

In language that reflects the important integration of liturgy and theology from a doxological perspective, she asserts that "it is proper to describe theology not as the *itinerarium in mentis Deum* but the *itinerarium in mysterium salutis,* and therefore, the *itinerarium doxologicum.*"[22]

In a particularly useful summary of her thesis LaCugna writes that

"as a 'science of the economy,' Christian theology is therefore concerned with (1) *diakonia,* actions and attitudes which serve the economy of God; (2) *koinonia,* structures of human community which display the communitarian nature of the God who is love;

(3) *doxology*, words and gestures and lives which give praise to God's glory."[23]

For our purposes both LaCugna's thesis and method are crucial to our understanding of what we call here *constitutive implications of liturgical theology*. To our way of thinking these implications concern both the method for doing theology itself and the way one ought to approach Christian spirituality as derived from the liturgy (to follow in chapter 8).[24]

In his recent collection of essays articulating what he calls his method of "postcritical theology," *The Craft of Theology*, Avery Dulles notes that the liturgy has regularly been recognized as a prime theological source and it is securely established in this role by (his articulation of) postcritical theology.[25] He asserts that "the contents of faith are known not by merely detached observation but by indwelling or participation . . ."[26] and that "if theology is not to regress, it must retain its close bonds with prayer and worship. In contemporary speculations about God theologians will do well to take account not only of abstract philosophical reasoning but also of the requirements of worship."[27] For Dulles

"a privileged locus for the apprehension of this subject matter is the worship of the Church, in which the biblical and traditional symbols are proclaimed and 're-presented' in ways that call for active participation (at least in mind and heart) on the part of the congregation. The interplay of symbols in community worship arouses and directs the worshipers' tacit powers of apprehension so as to instill a personal familiarity with the Christian mysteries."[28]

This is a particularly useful formulation for our purposes since our argument that *context is text* relies on the repeated representation and continual reappropriation of salvation in Christ through worship enacted in a variety of forms in a variety of ecclesial and cultural settings. To our way of thinking it is worship—particularly with its contemporary variety and varying contexts—that is the most native and true generative source for Christian theology which, as derived from the liturgy, is both essentially orthodox and doxological. To our way of thinking the theology derived from liturgy is best understood as "orthodox doxology."

269

In our understanding, doxological theology derives from the experience of God in liturgy whose intrinsic elements of Word, symbol, euchology and the arts disclose but do not dominate this unique experience of God. The doxology inherent in the act of liturgy and expressed through the liturgy orients participants primarily to the confession of praising God through ritual enactment. By their nature liturgical rites themselves are primarily oriented to doxological confession, which confession shapes doxological theology. This way of engaging in theology leads to an implicit critique of theological language that is overly intellectual or detached from personal confession of faith.

In one sense it is appropriate to assert that liturgy is the origin of doctrine because the liturgy expresses the living faith of the community of believers. At the same time, however, there is a mutual relationship between liturgy and theology because liturgy must be orthodox in the way it images and expresses the reality of God disclosed in the liturgy. A theological critique guaranteeing "right belief" is essential in order that the liturgy be (and ever become) as inadequate an expression of biblical and ecclesial faith in God as possible. Implicit here is the understanding that any humanly constructed rite must of necessity cede to the experience of the living God in prayer in general, and especially in liturgy whose forms foster, shape, and disclose the reality of God. That liturgy is essentially oriented toward communion with the living God is paramount in our appreciation of what liturgy is and what liturgical theology is about. One of the reasons why the liturgy is a *locus theologicus* par excellence is the *orthodox doxology* which it expresses and which derives from it.

One application of doxological theology to ecumenical dialogue on sacraments is the nature of the theological language which is likely to result from such conversations. As will be described more fully below, significant work has been done ecumenically on the hermeneutics of doctrinal statements, including the decrees of Trent on sacraments. An obvious example is the term "transubstantiation." Among other things, ecumenical progress has served to explore the meaning of this term and the extent to which it is required for Roman Catholic belief in the Eucharist. Pope Paul VI's encyclical *Mysterium Fidei* (1965) reflects something of an opening to contemporary explanations of Eucharistic presence as well as retaining the Tridentine teaching on the real presence and transubstantiation.[29] It would seem that a desired result of the search for a more explicitly doxological language derived from the Eucharistic liturgy would be terminology about the Eucharist that is less concerned with "substance" and "change" language (quite legitimate concerns at Trent and in subsequent Eucharistic catechesis) and more concerned with how the Eucharist is appreciated as (for example) necessarily symbolic, as requiring active participation and appropriation in the community of the Church.

Such a discussion would move dialogue participants and their respective Churches beyond terminology that was quite necessary and valuable in the past towards a language that is more reflective of the respective Church's tradition and contemporary belief as derived from its liturgical practice. This would obviously foster ecumenical honesty in the presumption that participants who theologize from the liturgy would reflect their Church's beliefs. At the same time it would advance toward an ecumenical consensus on the Eucharist that transcends the conventional language of individual Churches. In our understanding this means that the Liturgy of the Eucharist would provide the best resource for such dialogue. It would also provide a language that is more oriented toward doxology and liturgical participation than a former language that was more focused on the Eucharistic species of changed bread and wine. More generally, such an approach would require that those who evaluate ecumenical sacramental conversations would not merely examine agreed statements for the purpose of finding their own conventional terminology cited or affirmed, but also would appreciate the value of doxological terminology derived from the liturgy as this *lex orandi* is appreciated as the true source of the Church's *lex credendi*.[30]

Another reason for giving pride of place to the liturgy for developing theology is the *integral vision* of the theological enterprise and the *genetic vision* of reality that is disclosed in the liturgy. By "integral vision" we wish to assert that theology is a unitive discipline because its chief purpose is to disclose what Christian revelation and ecclesial faith professes about the living God. The word *integrity* is essential here as it refers both to liturgy and to theology. To our way of thinking there is an integrity in the act of worship in the sense that liturgy in its totality—namely, its *constitutive elements* of word, symbol, euchology, and the arts, and *the scope* of the ways that it reveals and discloses the work of the liv-

271

ing God "for our sakes and for our salvation"—comprises an integral and unifying experience of God. Individual acts of liturgy contribute to this totality but it is only liturgy in its entirety that can be considered *integral.*

For example, the many images of God or of the Church derived from the liturgy need to be taken together to articulate a liturgical theology of God or a liturgical theology of the Church. Similarly, the totality of images about our need for God or our incorporation into the Church grounds a theological anthropology developed from liturgy. In the same way, the pluriform images describing initiation or Eucharist from the present liturgical rites need to be articulated to develop an integral liturgical theology of initiation or Eucharist. Similarly, the images and likenesses of God as revealed in rites of initiation necessarily both complement yet differ from those expressed in rites of reconciliation. In addition, the divine images and likenesses disclosed in even the fascinatingly complex rites of Eucharist also necessarily both complement and differ from those expressed through rites of commitment, i.e., marriage and ordained ministries.

Similarly, the Liturgy of the Hours complements all of these rites in the sense that both nonsacramental and sacramental liturgy comprise the totality of Christian worship. To our way of thinking, such pluriform images and likenesses—in the sense of both describing the living God and revealing how the living God is experienced here and now in the Church—together form the most adequate basis on which to shape an integral theology understanding that theology includes the attempt to describe, among other things, the living God, the believing community of the Church and the nature of the human person as oriented toward relationship to and in the living God.

Thus the relationship between right praise and right belief can be probed fruitfully in liturgical theology in order that the *integrity of worship* as indicated here will influence and help to shape the *integrity of theology.* After decades of important work in articulating a truly contemporary method for engaging in theology in general (with such influential voices as Rahner, Schillebeeckx, and von Balthasar internationally and Lonergan in North America) and on various aspects of theology within theological specializations (e.g., Christology, anthropology etc.) many today would welcome a way to integrate theological knowledge which is both faithful to the

Church's belief and to the need to articulate this belief in ways that are appropriate in the present.

Thus our application of the classical argument about *lex orandi, lex credendi* concerns how to appropriate this maxim in a way that avoids a "fideism" in theology as well as a mere "philosophy of religion" approach to theology. To our way of thinking, just as the proper interpretation of the constitutive elements of liturgy depend in large measure on appreciating their *context* in terms of how they are related to each other and how they shape and are shaped by varying ecclesial and cultural contexts, so too our understanding of liturgical theology presumes that the way liturgical theology is developed and expressed is very much influenced by the variety in contemporary ecclesial and cultural contexts. To our way of thinking, theology derived from the liturgy—both the method for theology and content of theology—can spawn a number approaches to and emphases in theology depending on its ecclesial context which contexts can run the gamut from the enclosed monastery to foreign missionary or from cultural contexts that are as diverse as West is from the East. In such varied *contexts* it is the liturgy that supplies the measure in terms of a *regula fidei*, where such a "measure of the faith" is descriptive and schematic rather than one that is proscriptive and closed.[31]

That the liturgy also expresses and shapes a *genetic vision of reality* will be argued more fully in chapter eight on spirituality. It is sufficient here to indicate that methodologically we understand the liturgy to be the essential and constitutive framework within which theology is done for the craft of *theologia secunda* in terms of theology derived from the liturgy and also in terms of *theologia tertia* in terms of the ethical and spiritual import of liturgy for living the Christian life. *Theologia prima* and *secunda* necessarily yield a "third thing" that is constitutive of liturgical engagement and of engaging in liturgical theology.

Our emphasis thus far in this book on the proper genre of liturgy has required that its uniqueness as a privileged experience of God be respected. At this point we need to emphasize that it is precisely because liturgy is such a unique experience of the Trinity that it offers an incomparable framework within and from which to do theology. At the same time its uniqueness includes and implies that life be lived in harmony with what one experiences liturgically. Thus, liturgy offers both a unique experience and vision of the living God and necessarily leads to living life through, with and in the living God whom we worship through liturgy. As will be argued further in chapter 8, liturgy offers the most adequate experience and appreciation of God and of the human person. A liturgical theology reflective of the manifold aspects of Christian theology, held together and uniquely expressed in the liturgy, is complemented here in a spirituality that is reflective of the nature of the human person, described (in chapter 8) as Christian anthropology and Christian mission.[32]

Our understandings of liturgical theology and liturgical spirituality reflect our considerations of *symbol* already articulated throughout this book[33] and of *Orthodox doxology*. Our discussion of symbol reflected our thesis that *context is text* in the sense that we understand symbol to be inherently involving, so much so than without the active appropriation of the symbol by the believing assembly in the act of worship, the reality content of the symbol is diminished.[34] To our way of thinking, the community's continual reappropriation of liturgical symbols to enable these realities (especially Word, and elements from creation or human manufacture) to become true symbols is also required for developing liturgical theology. This means that our understanding of the task and method of liturgical theology requires a commitment to the God revealed and experienced through the liturgy, a responsiveness to how God is revealed and active in liturgy and a deepening conversion to gospel living as disclosed and experienced in the liturgy. Thus theology and spirituality derive from and are presumed results of engaging in liturgy.

That both liturgical theology and liturgical spirituality are inherently *doxological* is also operative here. We understand the languages of liturgy—Word, symbol, euchology, and the arts—to be intrinsically *doxological* because they are essentially oriented to the "right praise" of the living God. Thus, as these same languages serve the theological enterprise, they are no less doxological. To suggest that the language of liturgical theology is doxological means that by its nature it derives from prayer and reflects the faith reality that is Christian prayer. To our way of thinking the *doxological* nature of the language of liturgical theology prevents theological language from becoming too speculative or detached from the mystery of faith expressed in worship. The very notion

274

of *doxology* implies that both liturgical prayer and liturgical theology are mutually enriching and (where necessary) mutually corrective.

This doxological cast to theology and spirituality also implies that a prime value of each kind of language is *orthodox doxology* where the "orthodox" truth value of such language is not only its correctness in terms of belief but also (and again, more fundamentally) its correctness in terms of prayer. A principal reason why *doxology* is so important to the language of worship and of theology is that it is in the very act of liturgy that the realities with which theology is primarily concerned—God, Trinity, Christ, salvation, Church, etc.—are experienced in the Church's most privileged and unique manner. In the face of the experience of liturgy the participant-theologian can only offer the "thanks and praise" that is doxological language in prayer, doxological language in the grammar of theology and doxology in the shaping of one's perspective on life and how one lives the Christian life. "Doxology," in our understanding, signifies that which is experienced in worship and what is only able to be described inadequately—the mystery of the living God. Such a cast to theological language helps prevent it from becoming too presumptuous or definitive. In our understanding, theological language is at best descriptive and functions properly when it leads to deeper penetration into the mystery of the liturgy, the core of which is the experience of the living God, ever inviting the Church into a deeper penetration to the mysterious, saving ways of God.

It is especially at this point that our appreciation of the import of the theology of the liturgy (as described in chapters 3 to 6) comes into clearer focus. The theological description of what occurs in liturgy needs to be uppermost in the doing of liturgical theology precisely because the theology of liturgy as the accomplishment of "the work of our redemption" necessarily leads to a theology that is essentially dynamic, ecclesial and soteriological. Any of these categories, but especially these categories taken together, would require an approach to theology that involves the believing subject in deeper conversion to and penetration into the mystery of God. Thus what is required for the elements of liturgy to be themselves in terms of *involving symbols* is also required of the liturgical theologian in the sense of conversion and continual appropriation of the mysteries of salvation celebrated in the liturgy.

We understand that there is an intrinsic unity to liturgy and to the theology and spirituality derived from the liturgy in terms of how what is offered and experienced through liturgy is expressed in theological language describing the salvific meaning of the divine-human encounter that is liturgy and in terms of the rootedness in life and relationship to life of what is experienced in liturgy. Thus we understand the *context* for theology and spirituality to be provided by the *text* of liturgy, understanding *text* to mean liturgy's constitutive aspects and grammar. Here liturgy leads to a kind of theology and spirituality that permeates the believing community's whole life in such a way that liturgy necessarily (re)creates and (re)shapes both theology and spirituality derived from liturgy.

This deepens and makes more precise our thesis *context is text* in the sense that it goes beyond appreciating how differing ecclesial, cultural, and personal contexts shape the theological explanation and meaning of liturgy. Our thesis can now be expanded to include how the theological meaning of *liturgy as text* shapes our understanding of liturgical theology as an enterprise that is much wider than exploring or describing the theological meaning of liturgy. It now includes allowing liturgy to shape the very method and content of theology. Thus liturgy as *text* shapes the wider realities of theology and spirituality, so much so that our thesis now expands to include a concomitant emphasis on *text shapes context*. Here, emphasis on the varied realities of ecclesial life as experienced in the liturgy, understood as *context*, which (according to our thesis) must be brought to bear on our appreciation of the meaning of liturgy's constitutive elements, now shifts to allow the reality that is liturgy, *text*, to shape the lives of liturgical participants in terms of the kinds of theological enterprise they engage in as well as the fact that the Church's understanding of the spiritual life is essentially and intrinsically linked to its engagement in liturgy.

Simply put, to our way of thinking, both theology and spirituality are intrinsically related to the liturgy, so much so that they can be considered *constitutive implications* of engaging in the *theologia secunda* that is liturgical theology. The engagement in a liturgical rite is always an experience of something new both in terms of the meaning of the rite in terms of ecclesial and life contexts and in terms of the way that rite shapes right belief and right practice.

Furthermore, to be true to its source and nature, both the act of liturgy and the doing of liturgical theology must cede to the reality experienced in Word, sign and symbol and reflected upon—the power of God to make all things new.

The notion of theology as inherently *provisional* comprises an essential part of our understanding of liturgical theology. To our way of thinking, every act of liturgy is provisional in two senses. It is provisional in the sense that every act of liturgy is meant to cede to, and even more urgently to usher in, the reality it celebrates only imperfectly—the full experience of God's reign and kingdom. The classical use of the plea *maranatha* serves as a liturgical shorthand for the Christian prayer "thy kingdom come" and "let this world pass away." Hence any given act of liturgy is always provisional in that it is meant to lead to the full reality of the kingdom of God. Any given act of liturgy is also provisional in the sense that many aspects of the elements that constitute the liturgy have evolved and changed over the centuries, so much so that what may have been understood to be "traditional" at one time of the Church's life may in fact have only been "conventional" and have been changed either by evolving practice or by Church decree. The provisionality of liturgical forms enables our appreciation of them to be such that the present agenda of ongoing liturgical indigenization can only be welcomed as reflective of the Church's traditional response to its awareness of the changing ecclesial and cultural contexts in which the liturgy takes place. (The shift to the vernacular language being an obvious case in point when this meant shifting from Greek to Latin and in our own time from Latin to the variety of languages reflected in the present liturgical reform.)

Just as we have already argued that a main agenda for liturgical indigenization concerns establishing less and less (the least?) inadequate liturgical rite,[35] so we can assert that the agenda for liturgical theology is to articulate in less and less inadequate ways the theological description of what occurs in liturgy and the theology derived from liturgy. This particular link between liturgical rites and liturgical theology is their *inherent provisionality*. To use the term "provisional" here requires that one be appropriately tentative about all liturgical and theological formulations. The reason for such tentativeness includes the inherent inadequacy of all liturgical rites and liturgical theology in the sense that while each seeks to foster an experience of and appreciation for the core of Christian faith and tradition, any formulation is bound to fail to match the reality it is meant to reveal.

Even more important, however, is our argument that both liturgical rites and theology are meant to cede to assimilation into the mystery of God, which mystery is served, but never dominated, by liturgical rites and liturgical theology. Such an understanding helps to *contextualize* all liturgical rites and theological formulations as provisional. Thus self-criticism is built into every kind of theological formulation as it is built into the nature of liturgy itself, as the uniquely privileged but provisional means of experiencing God in the life of the Church here and now.

In terms of what has been argued in this section, we can say that the intrinsic doxological cast to liturgy, liturgical theology and liturgical spirituality serves as a continual reminder that each of these interrelated realities is by its nature provisional since even "right praise" will be unnecessary when the kingdom of God is fully and finally revealed. In the meantime liturgy, liturgical theology, and liturgical spirituality help to shape our experience of the living God. But even such a privileged experience necessarily points beyond itself to pure contemplation of and final assimilation into the living God. Thus, in our estimation, doxology and eschatology appropriately characterize liturgy, liturgical theology and liturgical spirituality.

II. Ecumenical Implications of Liturgical Theology

Among the more important shifts that have taken place regarding Roman Catholic participation in ecumenical matters in this century has been the shift in language in official documents from the requirement that non Catholics need to "return to Rome" for any possible reunion[36] to language about seeking a common ground for reunion,[37] from absolute avoidance of to participation in bilateral and multilateral ecumenical theological dialogues on national and international levels,[38] which participation has led to the Vatican's publishing official responses to the Anglican-Roman Catholic international dialogue[39] and to the Faith and Order document on "Baptism, Eucharist, and Ministry,"[40] and (more recently) from courses of instruction in Catholic institutions of higher learning about ecumenism to the inclusion of ecumenism as integral parts of the courses in Catholic theological curricula.[41] Our own concern in this section of this chapter is to indicate particular issues about ecumenical dialogue which can be enhanced by our argument about doxological theology and liturgical theology. Specifically, these concern the nature of dogmatic statements and the obvious growing interest in liturgical theology of specific sacraments. The last part of this section offers a critique of both the "Lima" liturgy and the Lima document on baptism, Eucharist, and ministry.

1. Nature of Dogmatic Statements. One of the lasting contributions to the contemporary study of theology within the Catholic Church and to engaging in theological conversation across denominational lines has been the way ecumenical dialogue has caused important work to be done on probing the meaning behind dogmatic terms that have been traditionally important in Catholicism. For example, discussions of Christ's presence in the Eucharist in the international Lutheran-Catholic dialogue led to careful wording in the "Agreed Statement"[42] to affirm common belief in the real presence and also to indicate the value of the term "transubstantiation" for Roman Catholics. The statement states:

"The eucharistic presence is continuous with all these modes of presence [baptism, the community, the Word] and is, at the same time, of a special character. Both traditions have used 'sacramental,' 'supernatural,' and 'spiritual.' These terms have different connotations in the two traditions, but they have in common a rejection of a spatial or natural manner of presence and a rejection of an understanding of the sacrament as only commemorative or figurative."[43]

When presenting the results of how their dialogue faced into the remaining differences in describing Christ's Eucharistic presence the statement asserts (n. 49) that the Catholic Church teaches that "Christ whole and entire" becomes present through the transformation of the whole substance of the bread and wine into the substance of the body and blood of Christ" and that this "wonderful and singular exchange is most aptly called transubstantiation by the Catholic Church." This latter phrase is particularly significant because it is taken from the decrees of the Council of Trent (DS 1652), whose use of *aptissime* ("most aptly") points to the value of the term "transubstantiation" yet does not say that its use is required for orthodox Catholic belief.[44] In the next paragraph the statement asserts how Lutherans have expressed the reality of Christ's Eucharistic presence "by speaking of a presence of Christ's body and blood in, with and under bread and wine—but not of transubstantiation" (n. 50). The statement concludes that these two positions must no longer be regarded as opposed in a way that leads to separation.

"The Lutheran tradition affirms the Catholic tradition that the consecrated elements do not simply remain bread and wine but rather, by the power of the creative word, are given as the body and blood of Christ.

"In this sense Lutherans also could occasionally speak, as does the Greek tradition, of a 'change.' The concept of transubstantiation for its part is intended as a confession and preservation of the mystery character of the eucharistic presence; it is not intended as an explanation of how this change occurs" (n. 51).

It is important to note that the statement is equally forthright when describing that differences remain both in liturgical practice over the *duration* of the Eucharistic presence (n. 52) and in the piety surrounding Eucharistic outside of the liturgy itself (nn. 54–55).[45]

Clearly, what is brought to bear on this kind of issue in ecumenical dialogue is both the important work on hermeneutics of conciliar statements within Roman Catholicism[46] and of the exigencies of ecumenical dialogue which foster reinterpretation of traditionally held positions. In line with our observations on doxological theology in section 1, we should like to suggest that the *doxological* value of dogmatic statements should be placed alongside their descriptive value and that this kind of equilibrium can help to sustain both the truth value of doctrines as well as their value as leading to deepening conversion to the God described through them. The intrinsic *doxological* content of such statements can thus help in their interpretation and then to a level of ecumenical dialogue that concerns a kind of rapprochement in belief that is a unity of doctrine, *oikonomia* and *diakonia* (to use LaCugna's terminology above). Doxology is thus a unitive system with prayer, thought and ethics as constitutive elements.

The Lutheran Edmund Schlink has called for a similar kind of theological language when he asserts the need for fully integrated dogma that does not so easily or neatly separate the confessional, the doxological, the kerygmatic, and the didactic elements of statements of faith.[47] For him that theology be done in a context of faith confession is essential since there is a difference between the believer's actual response in faith and the theological statements about his response. For him the root of all dogma is confession.[48] In a more explicitly worship-related context, Warren Quanbeck, another influential Lutheran theologian, states that theology should be closely related to the Church's life of worship and that, in turn, theology helps worship by its study of what Christian worship ought to be.[49]

Avery Dulles, himself a significant participant both in the USA Lutheran-Roman Catholic bilateral dialogues and the Roman Catholic who helped guide the final editing of the Lima text on baptism, Eucharist, and ministry, lends significant weight to the importance of careful hermeneutics for doctrinal statements when he notes that

"the role of theology in reception and interpretation is emphasized in the recent statement of the International Theological Commission on the hermeneutics of dogma. Dogmatic proclamation, according to this document, takes concrete form 'as a real, symbolic expression of the content of faith' and 'contains and makes present what it designates.' All doctrinal formulations, moreover, point beyond themselves to the mystery of God's own truth, which abides in the Church as a living subject. In a certain sense, therefore, even dogmatic declarations cannot be final. 'The definition of a dogma, therefore, is never just the end of a development, but always a new beginning. . . . After definition follows reception, i.e., the living assimilation of a dogma into the entire life of the Church and deeper penetration into the truth to which the dogma gives testimony.' "[50]

In our view, doxological theology derived from the liturgy can give the most adequate expression to this kind of theology. The kind of integral, doxological theology that we have argued for and the integration of liturgical theology with a spirituality derived from the liturgy (as argued here and in the next chapter) can help to flesh out these valuable insights.[51] In our view, the clearest demonstration of this kind of theological enterprise can be in ecumenical sacramental conversations.

2. Dialogue on Specific Sacraments. Roman Catholic participation in the dialogue that led to the Lima document was made possible not only by the Second Vatican Council's Decree on Ecumenism, it was also fostered by the kind of maturing in method and in theological sophistication that marked the Faith and Order Commission's work on sacraments, beginning with what can be considered tentative first steps at Lausanne in 1927.[52] The document resulting from this Faith and Order Conference reflected the method of "comparative ecclesiology" which was at work in this multilateral dialogue through the conference at Lund in 1952. This meant that participating members sought to determine exact areas of agreement and disagreement on a number of issues, including sacraments. This same method also marked the first stages of Roman Catholic participation in bilateral ecumenical dialogue after Vatican II, the results of which were impressive in terms of ecumenical honesty and in determining exact areas of disagreement.

The Lausanne document noted that the observance of sacraments was one of the characteristics of the Church (n. 20), that increased emphasis was being placed on sacraments at that time (n. 49), that the Lord's Supper (note use of biblical terminology here) was the Church's "most sacred act of worship" (n. 54) and that disagreements remained over the "mode and manner of the presence of our Lord; the conception of commemoration and the sacrifice; the relation of the elements to the grace conveyed; [and] the relation between the minister of this sacrament and the validity and efficacy of the rite" (n. 55).

These tentative first steps at Lausanne were strengthened and deepened at the 1937 Faith and Order Conference at Edinburgh[53] and were noted approvingly at the World Council of Churches Assembly at Amsterdam in 1948. However, a clear breakthrough for Faith and Order sacramental conversations occurred at Lund in 1952 both methodologically and regarding specific sacraments. Here the method shifted from "comparative ecclesiology" to a "Christological method" according to which divergences in faith, doctrine, and life were put in relation to the respective Church's belief in Christ, not on the basis of ecclesiological disagreements.

The introduction of the language of "mutual understanding" (n. 90) marked a new phase of ecumenical conversation and provided a method for it. The previous references to the ecclesiology of sacraments were significantly deepened here by the rather bold assertion (given the time and participants) that "worship, no less than Faith and Order, is essential to the being of the Church" (n. 90).

Participants agreed that "Word and Sacrament are both gifts of God and that in the preaching of the Word and the administration of the sacraments, God offers us His grace, imparts saving knowledge of Himself, and draws us into communion with Himself" (n. 96). At the same time the participants admitted particular disagreements about the relationship between the Eucharist[54] and Christ's eternal intercession and of the sacrificial nature of the Eucharist, specifically whether the proper understanding of sacrifice involves thanksgiving and obedient service, or whether in the Eucharist the Lord Jesus "unites the oblation once made by His body, the Church, with His own sacrifice" (n. 110).

What can now be considered something of a watershed in method for multilateral sacramental conversations is the phrase tucked into the summary statement from the World Council of Churches assembly at New Delhi (1961) which states that what is required is a new examination of the Eucharist away from the problem of a valid ministry to the whole Eucharistic action, which study demands the integration of and reflection on "eucharistic doctrines and liturgies" (n. 37). From now on the language of Faith and Order documents and contemporaneous bilateral dialogues on the Eucharist would speak in terms of the importance of the liturgical event of preaching, the role of the Spirit in Eucharistic enactment, the importance of the Eucharistic prayer in worship and in theology and the importance of memorial as a central way to describe the Eucharist.[55] Clearly the contemporaneous liturgical reforms of member Churches were significant in the growing seriousness and deepening communion among Churches on sacraments.[56] The principal appeal in Faith and Order conversations as well as in other contemporaneous bilateral conversations between the Roman Catholic and Protestant Churches has been to a recovery of the notion and reality of memorial and of the sacramental relation of the Eucharist to the cross. Dialogues with the Orthodox have made joint appeal to liturgy as an experience of the mystery of the Trinity and as the result of the action of the Trinity present among us.[57]

Deepening refinement in dialogue about baptism, Eucharist and ministry is seen from the Faith and Order Conference at Montreal in 1963, through the Conference at Bristol in 1967 and at Louvain in 1971. The discussion of "One Baptism, One Eucharist, And A Mutually Recognized Ministry" at the Faith and Order Conference at Aacra in 1974 and the detailed responses and commentaries by theologians and Church bodies alike paved the way for the significant Lima text in 1982. From our perspective the inclusion of a reference in the Lima text to reflection on the *theological meaning* of the Eucharistic liturgy was a most significant factor influencing the theological maturity seen in the Lima text.[58]
The text states:

"The best way towards unity in eucharistic celebration and communion is the renewal of the eucharist itself in the different churches in regard to teaching and liturgy. The churches should test their liturgies in light of the eucharistic agreement now in the process of attainment.

"The liturgical reform movement has brought the churches closer together in the manner of celebrating the Lord's Supper. However, a certain liturgical diversity compatible with our common eucharistic faith is recognized as a healthy and enriching fact. The affirmation of a common eucharistic faith does not imply uniformity in either liturgy or practice" (n. 28).

From our perspective we would add that theological reflection on liturgy is very significant because enacted liturgical rites create ecclesial contexts and Churches believe what Churches pray, especially at the Eucharist. While the Lima text and liturgy can be considered most significant because of what they represent in terms of progress and unity achieved, it is also important to point out how some of the built in limitations even here regarding method for doctrine and celebration can be transcended for deeper ecumenical rapprochement on sacraments. Because of our methodological concern throughout this book, the fact that a common Eucharistic liturgy was drafted for use at the Lima meeting (which has been used on a number of subsequent ecumenical occasions) requires that some observations be made on this liturgy and on the way the Lima document describes the Eucharist.

The Eucharist section of the Lima document is a surprisingly comprehensive treatment that is in line with current advances in theology, especially biblical studies, as exemplified in treating the "institution of the eucharist" n. 1, and in liturgy as seen in the frequent reference to liturgical terms such as *anamnesis*. On the one hand the use of terminology such as "the eucharist is the memorial of the crucified and risen Christ" (n. 5) reflects this liturgical influence; on the other, however, it leaves open (deliberately?) what it means by saying that this memorial is "still operative on behalf of mankind." The explicit conjunction of *anamnesis* and *parousia* (n. 6) is helpful today given the need for a Western reappropriation of the essentially eschatological nature of liturgical engagement. The accompanying statement that "representation and anticipation are expressed in thanksgiving and intercession" (n. 8) reiterates the conjunction of these two realities. The explicit reference to "intercession" here and in the accompanying "commentary" cannot but help to shape and to foster future reflection (both ecumenically and within Catholicism) about the propitiatory nature of the Eucharist. The section on Christ's presence in the Eucharist is particularly comprehensive, especially the assertion that "Christ's mode of presence in the eucharist is unique . . ." that Christ's statement "this is my body . . . blood" "is true, and this truth is fulfilled every time the eucharist is celebrated" (n. 13). The apparent agreement in this text is at least somewhat mitigated by the accompanying commentary stating "some . . . churches . . . do not link that presence so definitively with the signs of bread and wine."

A particular feature of the Lima text is the helpful section on the "invocation of the Spirit" (nn. 14–18) containing the reference "it is in virtue of the living word of Christ and by the power of the Holy Spirit that the bread and wine become the sacramental signs of Christ's body and blood" (n. 15). While one would not want to question the value of the assertions in n. 17 about the Church and the Spirit, the fact that they are not explicitly Eucharistic could cause some question about their importance in this particular (Eucharistic) section of the text. A similar question could be raised about nn. 24–25, concerning the Church's mission in the world, which paragraphs are part of the larger, and quite useful, section on the Eucharist as meal of the kingdom (nn. 22–26). It is at least questionable whether Roman Catholics could agree to the face value of the statement that the Eucharist is "entirely the gift of God" (n. 26) without any nuance about the requisite response to this gift in terms of offering and sacrifice.

The commentary on n. 28 on the Eucharistic liturgy (about which more is said below) about how "it is sometimes held that local food and drink serve better to anchor the eucharist in everyday life" is a notable inclusion and an indication of the present concern about liturgical indigenization. The references in the text's conclusion to Eucharistic practice are helpful in the sense that practice reflects belief and can sometimes mitigate theoretical agreement. Phrases such as "the eucharist should be celebrated frequently" (n. 30) and "every Christian should be encouraged to receive communion frequently" (n. 31) would seem to need more explanation. Issues such as daily versus weekly Eucharistic celebrations and the distribution of the Eucharist outside of Mass would certainly seem to require more attention. Here, Roman Catholic practice about frequency and the contemporary concern about what happens if local communities lack an ordained priest for regular celebrations of the Eucharist would seem to be important factors in such discussions. In addition there is the rather vague reference in the Eucharist section of BEM about the requirement of an ordained priest to preside at the Eucharist. The fact that "ministry" is a separate section of the text may well be the reason for this. At the same time, however, it would be important for this requirement in Roman Catholic and other Churches to be addressed here.

The Eucharistic liturgy of Lima certainly reflects the outline of the Eucharistic liturgy presented in n. 27 of the document and, from our point of view, is very telling about the limitations of this text. Succinctly put, the liturgy is heavily penitential, highly didactic and reflective of some Eucharistic practices that are at least debatable, if not highly questionable (e.g., from our perspective, hymn singing required at the conclusion and option at the beginning).

It is very significant that the liturgy is divided into three parts: liturgy of entrance, of the Word, and of the Eucharist. To delineate the "entrance" as one part of three, and not to note its complement in a conclusion is liturgically imbalanced. Greater emphasis on concluding rites would complement well the emphasis in the document on the living of the Eucharist in the world (nn. 22–24). However, this structural critique cedes to the deeper critique of how the liturgy of entrance emphasizes penitential elements: confession, absolution, Kyrie litany (with invocations asking for greater Church unity) and the Gloria with the central acclamation:

"Lord God, Lamb of God,
—You take away the sin of the world: have mercy on us;
You take away the sin of the world; receive our prayer.
—You are seated at the right hand of the Father:
    have mercy on us."

The Lima liturgy may be judged to be insufficiently courageous in overcoming the heavy penitential cast to this part of the conventional Eucharistic liturgy.[59] The theological difficulty with such a penitential emphasis here is the fact that it at least eclipses the purgative and sin forgiving aspect of the other, even more traditional aspects of the Eucharistic liturgy: proclamation of the Word, the explicit statement over the cup that the blood of the new covenant is "for the forgiveness of sins," the recitation of the Lord's Prayer ("forgive us our trespasses"), the exchange of the sign of peace, and the acclamation to the Lamb of God (at the breaking of the bread).

Unfortunately, the text of the "absolution" is liturgically curious (if not theologically askew) in that it concludes with:

"as a called and ordained minister of the Church
and by the authority of Jesus Christ,
I therefore declare to you
the entire forgiveness of all your sins . . . ."

In light of our argument above, that the traditional usage in liturgical prayer is the use of the plural form "we" and that this is expected because the ordained minister speaks in the name of and in communion with the whole community, this usage is at least liturgically and theologically curious. The highly didactic nature of the liturgy is also reflected in the entrance rite in the invocations to the *Kyrie* litany and to the (possible) use of the hymn to begin the liturgy.[60] Positively, the texts of three *Kyrie* invocations are all taken from the Scriptures (Eph 4:3-5, 1 Cor 10:16-17, and 2 Cor 5:18-20). Negatively these paraphrases are all far too long to be invocations and they are highly didactic in that the themes concern baptism, the breaking of the bread, and recognizing each other's ministries.[61] Here the Christological invocations to the *Kyrie* of the present Roman Catholic liturgy serve as a corrective to such a didactic text.

The "preparation" rite to the Liturgy of the Eucharist contains the present twin blessing prayers over bread and wine from the Catholic liturgy followed by the ecclesiological reference from the *Didache* with the acclamation *Maranatha! Come Lord Jesus!* Given the critique which the two "blessing" texts have received (that their sentiments belong more properly to the Eucharistic prayer itself) it is at least curious that these same texts are found here. In addition, given the important theological value of the *Didache* text and the eschatological value attached to its accompanying acclamation, it is at least debatable whether this text should be here or at another location, for example as part of the Eucharistic prayer, or as the conclusion to the liturgy. Even in the Lima liturgy the acclamation *Maranatha, the Lord comes!* follows the anamnesis and commemorations in the Eucharistic prayer.

The Eucharistic prayer repeats some at least debatable if not questionable usages, specifically a split epiclesis and the placing of the memorial acclamation after narrative of institution rather than after the anamnesis prayer itself. These conventional practices could well be adjusted in light of more traditional usages and contemporary liturgical scholarship. The helpful eschatological section of the Lima text is regrettably not reflected as fully in the liturgy, although the concluding "Thanksgiving Prayer" does end with the text:

"now that we have tasted of the banquet
you have prepared for us in the world to come,
may we all one day share together
the inheritance of the saints
in the life of your heavenly city. . . ."

Overall we would argue that the Lima liturgy is less impressive than the Lima document in terms of liturgical and theological sophistication. At the same time, this very critique is particularly pertinent given our thesis about liturgical theology, specifically here the theology derived from liturgy. Both texts may be said to reflect impressive, ongoing development in terms of ecumenical dialogue on the Eucharist. From the perspective of the "Christological method" of Faith and Order adopted since Lund in 1952 and the importance given to reflection on "eucharistic doctrines and liturgies" since New Delhi in 1961, certainly Lima is an outstanding outgrowth and product. We would also contend, however, that further progress in both bilateral and multilateral dialogue on sacraments can be enhanced by another approach to sacramental conversations, based on the kind of liturgical theology outlined in the next section.

III. Proposals for Method for Ecumenical Liturgical Theology

1. *Specific Sacraments, Method of Mutual Enrichment.* One of the more pressing agenda items faced by members of the Faith and Order Commission of the World Council of Churches and by participants in bilateral ecumenical sacramental conversations is how to move forward beyond even the very impressive results in the Lima text and from many other contemporary bilateral dialogues on the sacraments. We will argue that a fruitful methodological method would be firmly rooted in liturgical theology and based on determining areas wherein *mutual enrichment* would deepen present and ongoing *convergence* among the Churches. The basic approach here involves continual reappropriation of one's traditional doctrine in light of the self-criticism that derives from honest dialogue with another. In turn, this would lead to communal self-transcendence by the member Churches since the inadequacy of traditional and/or contemporary positions would come to light and would seek to be addressed and adjusted (where possible) precisely because of ecumenical contact. In the process member Churches would dialogue on the basis of their present (and presumably still evolving) liturgies in order that *lex orandi* can shape *lex credendi* within Church communions as well as across denominational lines.

In such a method, for example, for Roman Catholics to dialogue about the Eucharist would mean that they would approach the dialogue process concerned to sustain the truth of past dogmatic formulations, e.g., Trent, but not necessarily repeating these same formulations. They would be willing to admit the inadequacy of some of these traditional positions in order for a more complete sacramental theology to emerge. Here "inadequacy" is carefully chosen since the "correctness" of Trent is not at stake, it is presumed. In fact, we would argue that Catholics must be relied upon to reflect the Catholic tradition as fully as possible in the dialogue process. But in that very process we would assert that some *true* positions may also be *inadequate* and be in need of adjustment, refinement or enhancement. Hence, the truth of the Catholic doctrine on the real presence of Christ in the Eucharistic species would remain undisputed. However emphasis on the Eucharist as an experience now of the eschaton or of the life of the Church in the Trinity, insights intrinsic to the Church's present Eucharistic euchology and as emphasized, for example, in dialogue with the Orthodox, could be helpful additions to the traditional Catholic teaching on the real presence. Hence this method enables one to evaluate respective theological positions, not with the purpose of justifying an already preconceived position, but in order to evaluate one's particular tradition in the light of the others. This method would also be congenial with our treatment of doxology, namely, fruitful theologizing requires personal involvement and self-examination on the part of dialogue and liturgical participants.

Part of the issue here is moving dialogue participants from positions of seeming invulnerability to acknowledging common problems with self-criticism as well as with a view to scrutinizing another's position as these positions are evaluated in dialogue with a number of dialogue partners. Hence the value of a multilateral forum like that in the Faith and Order Commission. At the same time ongoing bilateral dialogues between and among specific Churches would help to sharpen areas of continuing dispute. Ongoing bilateral dialogues among those Churches whose theology and practice have been highly influenced by the Reformation would be essential to determine areas of actual disagreement as well as areas in which participating Churches might share similar but inadequate positions.

For example, for Anglicans, Lutherans, and Roman Catholics to scrutinize each other's positions may yield commonality and agreement. Yet, at the same time, when these very similar liturgical and theological traditions engage in dialogue with the Orthodox a whole host of avenues for enrichment emerge, particularly having to do with pneumatology, Trinity, and eschatology. Therefore, the very fact that the Reformation Churches have come to rather close agreement on some areas long held in dispute may belie the fact that these Churches, individually and with dialogue partners, need to move beyond these positions to incorporate theological and liturgical insight and theological depth from other Churches. Whereas the method of Faith and Order moved from comparative ecclesiology to a Christological method that ultimately emphasized convergence in sacraments, our method moves the emphasis on convergence to an approach that acknowledges inadequacy even in convergences and to mutual enrichment where particular traditions can gain the fullness it presently sees itself as lacking in that area of sacramental worship and teaching.

To base ecumenical dialogue on sacraments on theology derived from the liturgy is particularly congenial today since at present many denominations pray with the same texts (e.g., the Eucharistic prayer from Hippolytus' *Apostolic Tradition*) use the same or similar ritual gestures, environment, music, style of preaching, etc. and have adopted a model of liturgical reform in that is similarly open-ended and on-going.

Yet, in our method, these similarities themselves do not guarantee ecumenical convergence or unity.[62] A major argument of this book is that differing (ecclesiological, cultural, and personal) contexts within Roman Catholicism help to shape the meaning of liturgical rites and that these varying *contexts* give rise to varied meanings even when the same liturgical *texts* (meaning component elements of the rites) are used. From an ecumenical perspective the question is: does use of the same liturgical texts/rites lead to ecumenical convergence? On the one hand it does, since the same rites are operative. On the other hand it does not necessarily lead to convergence precisely because differing contexts foster a different hearing of the same text because theological traditions influence not only how liturgical texts are formulated but how they are heard and are understood. Or, in terms of this proposal, is there actually a different text heard because the *theological and ecclesial contexts* are different? Would not the sense of ecclesial interrelatedness within the Roman Catholic Church provide a way to deal with this?

Just as the use of the same words in liturgy does not lead to communality of comprehension of what these words mean in the sense argued here about *context*—thus making liturgical theology not a monolithic term—so the use of the same rituals or similar ritual structures across denominational lines does not automatically lead to unity among the Churches. Here, *context* implies variety of interpretation of liturgy. In fact, it ought not lead to uniformity precisely because such a model of liturgical or ecclesial unity is not desirable given the value of how varying *contexts* help to underscore a variety and complementarity in liturgical theology (as argued in Chapters 3 and 4). If local Churches within Roman Catholicism, with their varying ecclesial structures and spirits, are joined in communion through the liturgy as adapted for local need, then could not non-Catholic Churches be similarly joined through liturgy, especially when the same euchological texts are used? This is to suggest that the very variety of (especially inculturated) liturgy and liturgical theology derived from the liturgy offers a way for greater expansiveness in the self-understanding of the Church in general and in what ecclesial belonging signifies.

At the same time, in line with the argument presented above regarding liturgical theology in general, it should be recalled that the very ambiguity and symbolic nature of ritual action demands care in interpretation of any such liturgical texts or symbolic gestures. Many levels of interpretation help to determine ways of reaching ecumenical convergence, precisely because of the ambiguity of liturgical action. One cannot take liturgical texts out of their lived liturgical and ecclesial context. Hence, for example, to try to interpret Eastern sources requires appreciating their native context from the East historically and in their present usage.

What we have termed the "critical function of liturgical theology" plays a role here whereby the present euchology is placed alongside the tradition of preceding euchology in the Roman Catholic Church as well as preceding and present euchology among the Christian Churches. This suggests that probing the tradition and present liturgical euchology offers an ecclesially sanctioned framework for a truly integral liturgical theology. In such an articulation, variety and complementarity function to fill out what might well be lacking if one or another image from the Church's belief about a sacrament, for example, becloud the wider and more integral reality reflected in liturgical rites themselves.

The fact of a variety, if not a conflict, in interpretations helps to determine ways of reaching ecumenical *convergence* where convergence, not uniformity, is operative. The doing of liturgical theology in an ecumenical context allows for deeper comprehension of the varied mysteries of God, Christ and Church with different Churches expressing facets of these mysteries that others do not necessarily emphasize. Hence a complementarity of liturgical theologies helps to foster ecumenical reunion which is based on a complementarity of varied understandings of God, Christ, and Church derived from varied liturgical forms.

The model of ecumenical dialogue leading to convergence argued here implies that the way salvation is imaged in the liturgy and the way communities cooperate in experiencing salvation through the liturgy implies that the liturgy can be used as a particularly fruitful means for reexamining the faith/good works issue, with allowing for ecumenical convergence and mutual conversion based on the liturgy as the most traditional of theological sources.

For example, if our liturgical texts say something about our action and cooperation in achieving salvation, then a theological statement is being made about our involvement in salvation. The question arises about how does this aspect of the *lex orandi* affect the *lex credendi* in both Roman Catholic and Protestant Churches? This points to the particularly acute issue concerning the *mediation* of salvation through liturgy as understood by Lutherans and Roman Catholics (among others). This is reflected specifically in the cult of Mary and the saints as seen in the recent discussions in the American Roman Catholic-Lutheran dialogue on the role of Mary and the saints. Part of these deliberations has been to examine what liturgical texts say about such mediation and how theologians interpret (or do not interpret) them. A case in point is from the present Roman Catholic and Lutheran euchology. The present third Eucharistic prayer contains the text:

"May he make us an everlasting gift to you
and enable us to share in the inheritance of your saints,
with Mary, the virgin Mother of God;
with the apostles, the martyrs,
Saint N. and all your saints
on whose constant intercession we rely for help."[63]

The preface for All Saints day in the *Lutheran Book of Worship* contains the text:

"in the blessedness of your saints you have given us a glorious
pledge of the hope of our calling;
that moved by their witness and supported by their fellowship,
we may run with perseverance the race that is set before us
and with them receive the unfading crown of glory. . . ."[64]

Despite a clear reserve in the Lutheran text, there does seem to be
some area of acknowledgment of intercession in the *lex orandi* of
these Churches despite the serious division at the time of the
Reformation on this issue.

In light of our thesis the task of ecumenical dialogue now becomes that of determining the adequacy and correctness of the
contextual meanings when the same or similar liturgical rites are
used by different ecclesial bodies. For example, what degree of
communality in Eucharistic belief can be gained from the use of
Hippolytus' Eucharistic prayer? Another question arises when a
given Church determines the inadequacy of its Eucharistic liturgy
as the result of ecumenical dialogue on the Eucharist and proposes
textual or ritual adjustments, for example in the pneumatological
and eschatological nature of its texts. How does this adjusted rite
contribute to ecumenical agreement on the Eucharist? Simply put,
key issues here concern whether the same or similar *texts* create
the same *contexts* and what similarity in *context* is required for
there to be unity among the Churches understanding that "unity"
can mean, among other things, communion in one unified Church
or communion among various Churches using the same liturgical
structures which yield sufficient theological convergence as to
signify a communion of members in an entity wider than any
individual ecclesial body?[65]

Our overall thesis *text shapes context* raises significant issues for
the future of ecumenical dialogue at the very same time that it
offers significant prospects for real progress. Our particular approach here concerning *mutual enrichment* can also be brought to
bear on ecumenical sacramental dialogue in a number of ways.
Among the qualities that the ecumenical method of mutual enrichment requires is honesty in not ignoring areas of actual disagreement and humility to learn from dialogue partners. What is
offered in the next section is meant to build upon the important
effort and impressive results reflected in texts such as the Lima
document.

2. *Liturgical Theology of Sacraments in General.* The focus in this last section is away from dialogue on specific sacraments to an examination of five constitutive elements of every act of sacramental liturgy, a reexamination of which in ecumenical dialogue predicated on mutual enrichment may establish a fresh context toward appropriating the theological meaning of the liturgy of sacraments. The general categories of sacrament for this kind of ecumenical liturgical theology include: sacraments as Word events, sacraments as symbolic events, sacraments as experiences of the Trinity, sacraments as experiences of ecclesial solidarity, and sacraments as eschatological realities.

a. WORD EVENTS. The fact that every liturgical ritual revised after Vatican II contains a Liturgy of the Word[66] restores the proclamation of the Word to a place of prominence liturgically and reflects the fact that the Word is constitutive of the event of sacraments. In addition (as we argued above)[67] Word and sacrament are not two separate entities. Rather through the liturgy they are brought together into one whole—Word being specified by sacrament and sacrament extending the proclamation of the Word. Among recent magisterial statements solidifying this relationship[68] the following from the Introduction to the revised Lectionary for Mass states:

"The Church is nourished spiritually at the table
of God's word and at the table of the eucharist:
from one it grows in wisdom and from the other
it grows in holiness. In the word of God the divine
covenant is announced; in the eucharist the new and
everlasting covenant is renewed."[69]

One of the functions of the blessing prayers in sacraments is to bridge these two facets of the liturgy and to draw on images, metaphors, and symbols from the Scriptures to engage in blessing God and blessing symbolic elements for sacramental use.

One application of the theological value of the liturgical proclamation of the Word as constitutive of sacrament is its *anamnetic* character, that is its role in sacraments understood as "acts of memory" that enact what they proclaim.[70] This liturgical terminology can also be expressed by adjectives such as "performative" or "exhibitive," terms often used to indicate the power of the Word to effect what it announces. As Karl Rahner has stated:

"If we develop the basic character of the word spoken in and through the church as grace-event, as a basically manifestive word [exhibitives wort], that is, as present in the church as eschatological presence in the world of God's redemption, and if we allow for this word of and in the church the general existential and social variability of the human word, then we can arrive at a conception of 'sacrament' in which it can be understood within a theology of the word as a quite specific word-event, yet in which sacrament is not reduced, in its distinctive character, to the level of every other word legitimately spoken in the church."[71]

This has been effectively argued more recently by B. R. Brinkmann,[72] William Shea,[73] and Peter Fink[74] among others, some of whom derive insight from Paul Ricoeur on interpretation.[75] The Lima document states: "Since the *anamnesis* of Christ is the very content of the preached Word as it is of the Eucharistic meal, each reinforces the other. The celebration of the Eucharist properly includes the proclamation of the Word" (n. 12). Ritually, blessing prayers combine confession with anamnesis; theologically, blessing prayers combined with the proclamation of the Word enact the liturgical anamnesis.

This kind of traditional and now restored appreciation of the Word has a number of ecumenical implications. Especially in light of the discussions of Eucharistic intercelebration and intercommunion, it is important to reiterate that ecumenical Word services are significant theological realities and that through them a level of communality is achieved, despite the fact that this communality does not yet lead to full Eucharistic communion. Liturgical engagement in the progressive rediscovery and continuing self-disclosure of God ought to lead to directing energies away from only examining each other's sacramental doctrines and practices to examining their respective understandings of sacraments as incarnating and expressing the Word of God.

For example, such an investigation cannot but help in determining exact areas of disagreement about liturgies of penance. That the proclamation of the Word has classically been regarded as purgative and effective of sin forgiveness is capsulized in the phrase the deacon or priest says after proclaiming the gospel: *per evangelia dicta, deleantur nostra delicta*. It is theologically significant that all four of the revised Roman Catholic liturgies of penance contain liturgies of the Word. This fact sets a new and proper context for ecumenical discussions about how sins are forgiven. An appreciation of the revised *liturgy* of penance necessarily implies appreciation for variety in the Catholic rites for sin forgiveness, including baptism and the Eucharist itself. Thus a new situation is created within which to determine the theological meaning of rites for sin forgiveness since these rites are predicated on the proclaimed Word as an effective agent of forgiveness. Thus, in line with our method of mutual enrichment, we can argue that participants in ecumenical dialogues on sacraments might well direct their energies away from only comparing and examining each other's sacramental doctrines and practices to examining their respective understandings of sacraments as incarnating, expressing and effecting the Word of God.

b. SYMBOLIC REALITIES. Among the bases on which classical Roman Catholic sacramental theology is based is succinctly summarized in the phrase (already noted and briefly discussed)[76] *significando causant.* This doctrine presumes that creation is disclosive and reflective of the experience of God.[77] It also capitalizes on the value of human productivity and ingenuity in sacramental symbolization.[78]

Our particular treatment of symbol (above, chapter 4)[79] however, raises the important hermeneutical factor that sacramental symbols are best interpreted as the central means through which God works and is experienced in sacraments. Thus, in our view, to be faithful to the symbolic nature of sacraments implies being attentive to the Church community which engages in their use. This dialogical notion of sacraments based on their symbolic nature avoids an overstress on sacraments as objects and a "functionalism" which could lead to minimizing the *significando* factor in sacramental causality. As we already noted[80] the objectification of given symbolic elements used in liturgy can paradoxically diminish the *reality content* of the symbols upon which sacramental liturgy and liturgical theology is based, for at least two reasons. The first is that because symbolic *elements* complement the symbolic *Word* as essentially dialogical realities, to emphasize symbols as objects reduces their inherently dialogic character. The second is that the presumed ecclesial community, for whom and among whom symbols function in liturgy, can be eclipsed in a sacramental theology based on objectified symbols. It would be presumed, and hopefully emphasized, in a symbolically-oriented sacramental theology.

A number of ecumenical applications can be drawn from this symbolic foundation to sacramental theology. The first concerns examination of each others' approach to symbol as privileged means of mediating grace and the power of the divine. This focus necessarily includes questions about the use of creation in worship and of the human contribution to the means used to mediate salvation. (This is closely akin to, and should be discussed in relation to the knotty problem of "faith-good works.") A second (allied) factor concerns the inherently ecclesiological aspects of symbolic engagement as proper to sacramental liturgy. As a result of ecumenical dialogue, the extent to which different Churches converge on a theology of the power and use of symbol can set a new framework within which to discuss the symbolic mediation of salvation and the reality of the essentially symbolic presence of Christ in sacraments. More particularly with regard to the Eucharist, ecumenical conversations about "real presence" can now be set within the native liturgical context in which discussions about presence imply the Church community's experience of the unique Eucharistic presence of Christ and the way in which the Eucharistic liturgy itself describes the way the unique once-for-all sacrifice of Christ is mediated and experienced through the Eucharistic symbols. One concrete application for the Reformation Churches would be the intrinsic connection of Eucharistic liturgy to the Lord's day and the theological value placed on Eucharist as an essential complement to the proclaimed Word.

c. EXPERIENCES OF THE TRINITY. As we already discussed, a most significant voice in the early part of this century in terms of a Christological appreciation of the theology of liturgy was that of Odo Casel.[81] His emphasis on Christ's "mystery presence" in liturgy was a significant move toward revitalizing our understanding of how the paschal mystery itself is experienced through the liturgy.[82] Of particular advantage today is the clarity with which the paschal mystery is described and invoked as operative in the present revised liturgy. The disadvantage of this Christological emphasis, however, is that it can lead to a "Christomonism" (to use Congar's term) which may well reflect a Western preoccupation in liturgical theology but which can diminish the centrality of the role of the Trinity in liturgy. Clearly, at present, there is an obvious deepened emphasis on the role of the Spirit in most contemporary reformed liturgies when compared to their predecessors,[83] specifically in terms of the epicletic parts of the blessing prayers and the theological meaning derived from their use. What may be termed the *oikonomia* of sacraments really derives from the fact that the Father, Son, and Spirit are experienced in and through the liturgy in a unique way. Again, this is attested to in most contemporary revised liturgies. What derives from this theologically is increased emphasis on notions of divine indwelling through the experience of liturgy and the nuancing of grace language to be more self-consciously Trinitarian.

Among the ecumenical applications here using the mutual enrichment method of dialogue concerns both the liturgical rites themselves and the sacramental theology derived from them. The first level of discussion would concern the assessment of the adequacy of sacramental rites precisely in terms of the Trinitarian language used and not used. One concrete issue here concerns not only printed texts but the way introductory comments (e.g., penitential rite at the Eucharist) or other composed texts (e.g., intercessions) reflect this Trinitarian emphasis. With regard to the Western Churches specifically, one theological application would concern the way the liturgy of the Eucharist is fundamentally understood. Is it fundamentally regarded as a means of "ethical strength" or is it fundamentally a means of being drawn into the very mystery of the Trinity (which latter approach has obvious ecclesiological implications)? If the Reformation Churches were to gain mutual enrichment from the Eastern notions of *oikonomia* and *koinonia* one application of this would be to transcend the inadequacy of their similar positions emphasizing the ethical strength derived from liturgy. In the words of Avery Dulles,

"The Orthodox . . . possess an immensely rich heritage of Trinitarian and sacramental piety handed down from the Eastern fathers. They have a sense of spiritual communion (or *koinonia*) that supplements and partly corrects the more legalistic approach characteristic of the West."[84]

d. EXPERIENCES OF ECCLESIAL SOLIDARITY. It has become axiomatic in contemporary sacramental theology to speak of the intrinsic relationship between the Church and sacraments and even of the Church as sacrament. In contemporary English language literature the parallel is often drawn between Christ and the Church as "sacraments,"[85] with Christ often termed the "original" sacrament and the Church as the "ground" sacrament.[86] At the same time, some critics have appropriately pointed to the danger of making this parallel too neat and clear.[87] What is very helpful in reemphasizing the relationship between Church and the sacraments is that this emphasis underscores this traditional foundation for sacramental engagement and also provides a stimulus for drawing out the ecclesiological ramifications of the recently revised liturgical rites.

Part of this enhanced appreciation of what liturgical rites have to say about the Church as subject of liturgical action is that the Church at liturgy is essentially a self-transcending community and not one that should not presume on its self-sufficiency or be preoccupied with liturgical rites not intrinsically related to the rest of life. Instances in the Eucharistic liturgy that reinforce this self-transcending nature of the Church include the intercessions, collection of gifts for the poor, epicleses, prayers after Communion and dismissals.

Essentially the liturgical community is one that gathers in order to be sent forth. The kind of *communio* understood to occur liturgically is for the faith community to share as fully as possible in the mystery of God at liturgy in order that it might be drawn more deeply into unity with each other. This is meant to result, in turn, in the Church witnessing in the world to what is celebrated liturgically. For our purposes, therefore, it is preferable to speak in terms of "ecclesial solidarity" than merely of the Church at sacraments or even of *communio* in liturgy.

One specific application of the ecclesiology of sacramental liturgy for ecumenical sacramental conversations concerns the need to focus such conversations on both *ad intra* and *ad extra* notions of Church. Specifically this means making sure that the self-transcending and witnessing aspects of the liturgy are an obvious part of common understandings of sacraments. Here the question of ecclesiology and sacraments needs to include the reality of mutual self-transcendence. The theological point at issue here concerns sacraments as inherently conserving of the Church, and at the same time challenging of the Church towards communal self-transcendence. This should also influence discussions of liturgical presidency where the challenge to those who preside includes strong and effective leadership implying challenging the Church to be the Church both outside and inside sacraments. The burden of being a Church leader outside the liturgy, which leadership establishes that person's role as leader of liturgical prayer[88] implies leading that ecclesial community to become living witnesses of what is celebrated in the liturgy. Establishing this as an essential part of ministry and ordination discussions (while not limiting such discussions to this) might well help to contextualize discussions of participants from "high" and "low" Church perspectives on ordained ministry.

e. ESCHATOLOGICAL REALITIES. The renewed emphasis on liturgical *anamnesis* recontextualizes notions of eschatology in sacraments to their native setting as constitutive elements of liturgical prayer and liturgical theology. It also helps to draw out the traditional truth (concretized in Aquinas's theology) that sacraments are commemorative of what has gone before, Christ's paschal death and resurrection, demonstrative of what is brought about in us through Christ, grace in the believer, and prognostic of what is yet to be, future glory. This renewed emphasis on memorial as a central aspect of liturgical prayer makes a number of contributions to contemporary theology. These include the notion that eschatology is much wider than teleology, that justice and mission concerns of sacraments are intrinsically grounded in liturgy's eschatological nature, which grounding requires that justice and mission aspects of liturgy be emphasized as constitutive of what may be termed a "liturgical ethic" and that sacraments are to be regarded as intense moments of a kingdom inaugurated, but a kingdom which is not yet completed. Thus, *anamnesis* implies *maranatha*, the invitation for the Lord to come to draw all things to himself and bring the kingdom into completion and its full reality. This underscores what liturgical prayers themselves presume and state: that the liturgy is both eschatological and communal at the same time and that liturgical rites are for the community of the redeemed. Clearly, these emphases are particularly significant for the renewal of liturgical and sacramental theology within Church communions.

At the same time, this aspect of liturgical practice and theology also signals an implicit critique of liturgy on the eschatological basis that liturgy itself is a privileged but clearly a *provisional* experience of God which seeks its fulfillment in the eternal, heavenly liturgy in the kingdom. This further implies the provisionality of all liturgical forms, lest more status be granted them than is intrinsic to any liturgical forms.

Among the applications which this understanding can make to ecumenical sacramental conversations is appreciating how the present liturgies of sacraments emphasize their nature as realities which signify, foster, and build the kingdom as much as they are extensions here and now of the Incarnation. The presumed emphasis on an incarnational approach to liturgical theology is here nuanced by an emphasis on their intrinsic eschatological quality as well. Furthermore, the intrinsic challenge dimensions implied in sacramental engagement, and as presently at the forefront of some intrachurch and ecumenical discussions, are here seen to be intrinsic to the liturgical experience of sacraments and therefore as constitutive of a liturgical theology of sacraments.

Concretely, this means placing emphasis on ways the Churches together seek to realize the kingdom on earth both within and outside the experience of sacraments. The provisional character of sacramental rites leads to the insight about the provisional nature of the formulations of sacramental theology so that communities can see beyond both sacramental liturgy and theology toward the reality provisionally experienced through them—the living God of our salvation. A particular application of this would be to try to appreciate another's participation in discussions of intercommunion which may be very different from one's own precisely because their appreciation of what to expect from liturgical forms and theologies is very different. Hence ecumenical sacramental dialogue based on a mutual enrichment model can help communities whose ecclesiologies and sacramental doctrines are as different as Quakers are from the Orthodox to engage each other fruitfully and for mutual benefit precisely because the differences in their fundamental starting points are respected and probed for mutual benefit. The provisional nature of all sacramental doctrines has been influential on those Churches which have probed the issues underlying intercommunion, which discussions have led them to see the value of engaging in intercelebration and intercelebration as *means* of achieving unity. On the other hand, the classical

Roman Catholic position is to insure agreement on principal areas of Church doctrine and life before sharing in a common Eucharist which signifies the reality of already established substantial communion in theology and practice.

A particular pastoral aspect which the eschatological nature of sacraments touches on is how to appreciate sacraments as *signs of conversion*. This issue draws on a combination of both the eschatological and the symbolic in the sense that it places discussion of the way Churches celebrate (or "dispense") sacraments as crucial instances of appreciating how Churches understand themselves and how they will understand other Churches. If sacraments are approached as signs of ever deepening conversion, then the whole sacramental life of a given Church is seen in relation to becoming ever more faith-filled and responsive to the God of our salvation. This implies a contextualizing of sacramental forms and practice in order that the kingdom is ushered in, not glibly presumed to be experienced here and now.

This kind of approach also appropriately contextualizes tactics used to prepare people for sacraments. Clearly the present emphasis on preparation for (especially initiation) sacraments has led to a deepening in Catholic circles of contextualizing sacraments within the total life of the Church in ways that foster ever deepening conversion to God. At the same time, however, the very provisional nature of sacraments themselves requires that anything that might lead to a (semi-) Pelagian approach to sacramental preparation be avoided in order to allow sacraments themselves to be privileged means of deepening conversion to the living God. The assertion in the Wesley's Communion hymn "O Lord, at length, when sacraments shall cease" helps to specify the provisionality of sacraments; yet the use of that text at the Communion rite also solidifies the theology of sacraments as essential, privileged means to accomplish ever deepening conversion to God. Sacraments are, in essence, both a goal of preparation and a means of final preparation to meet the living God in eternity.

Our comment about sacraments as signs of deepening conversion is a fitting note on which to conclude this chapter because it concretizes much of its contents about the privileged yet provisional role of sacraments in the Christian life. We have argued here that the kind of theology that can be appropriately derived from reflection on the liturgy is *doxological*, which, by its nature, appropriately respects the liturgy as its generative and sustaining origin and source. At the same time it is intrinsically provisional in that it leads to experiencing the living God in ever deepening ways. In addition, the provisional nature of liturgical formulations, especially in the present reform, has led us to consider how to articulate a method for ecumenical sacramental conversations that respects the evolving nature of both liturgical forms and the sacramental theology that can be derived from them. This was concretized in our discussion of both the Lima document and its accompanying liturgy, both of which were appreciated and yet also critiqued. It is hoped that the brief comments on a possible future method for ecumenical sacramental conversations predicated on mutual enrichment, critique and convergence can help pave the way for even greater progress toward unity among the Churches in sacramental celebration and in a liturgical theology of sacraments.

Notes

1. Recalling the distinctions made above in chapter 2, 44–46.

2. For an example of the use of this term see, Erhard Griese, "Perspektiven einer liturgischen theologie," *Una Sancta* 24 (1969) 104.

3. See, chapter 2, 55.

4. In a sense this conventional distinction is somewhat artificial in that the classic dictum about *lex orandi, lex credendi* insists that the *orandi* contains and reflects both correct praise and belief at the same time.

5. The second section will include a brief critique of the adequacy of the "eucharistic liturgy of Lima" and the "Lima" document "Baptism, Eucharist and Ministry" because both of these are important contemporary expressions of ecumenical multilateral rapprochement on sacraments and will likely serve as something of a watershed in contemporary ecumenical progress on sacraments. The fact that the final drafting and approval of this significant document from the Faith and Order Commission of the World Council of Churches (Faith and Order Paper No. 111) took place in Lima, Peru in January, 1982 has caused these texts to be referred to as the "Lima liturgy" and the "Lima document," which text is also referred to as "BEM."

6. See, Anselm Stolz *Introductio in Sacram Theologiam* (Friburg/Rome: Herder, 1941) 5–21.

7. Ibid., 8.

8. Ibid., 5-8.

9. Harvey H. Guthrie. *Theology As Thanksgiving,* 213 citing Bouyer's *Eucharist,* 5.

10. Ibid., x.

11. Ibid., 181. Recall here the example offered above in chapter 4 about Eucharistic euchology whose interpretation today is very much influenced by the recent studies of Cesare Giraudo.

12. Dietrich Ritschl, *Memory and Hope* (New York: Macmillan, 1966) xiii.

13. See also the helpful insights of David B. Stevick, "Toward a Phenomenology of Praise," in Malcolm C. Burson, ed., *Worship Points the Way* (New York: Seabury, 1981) 151-166.

14. See, *Jubilate. Theology in Praise.* This work is less liturgically focused than the others already cited and is regrettably heavier on editorializing than on substantiated argumentation.

15. Ibid., 169-170. For a helpful review of this work and other recent writing on liturgical theology, including Kavanagh's *On Liturgical Theology* see, Teresa Berger, " 'Doxology'—'Jubilate'—'Liturgical Theology' Zum Verhältnis von Liturgie und Theologie: Publikationem aus dem englischsprachingen Raum," *Archif für Liturgiewissenschaft* 28 (1986) 247-255.

16. Catherine Mowry LaCugna, "Can Liturgy ever again be a Source for Theology?" *Studia Liturgica* 19 (1989) 1-16.

17. Ibid., 2.

18. Ibid., 3. She admits that we are "less accustomed to think of theology as doxological because we tend to identify it as a speculative discipline, speculative in the post-Enlightenment sense of 'conjecture' or 'theorizing,' not in the medieval-monastic sense of *speculum,* the contemplative mirror of knowledge."

19. Ibid., 4. She goes on to assert that "the subject of theology is the mystery of God who comes to us in Covenant and Christ, and who makes us partakers in the very life of God. In the language of antiquity, the subject matter of the science of theology is *theologia* made manifest in *oikonomia* ('management' or 'administration'), in the incarnation of the Son and the sending of the Spirit."

20. Ibid., 5. She also observes (4-5) that "liturgy . . . is the one place which kept alive some awareness of the trinitarian pattern of Christian faith, trinitarian not because of the number 'three' but because it was the ritual celebration of redemption by God through Christ in the power of the Spirit." "The original context of both Christian faith and of what later became trinitarian doctrine was as a matter of fact doxological. Doxology is the living language of faith in which praise is offered to God for the abundance of God's generous love."

21. Ibid., 8.

22. Ibid., 11.

23. Ibid.

24. In "Liturgy and Theology—An Ongoing Dialogue," *Studia Liturgica* 19 (1989) 14–16, an article that accompanies LaCugna's, Teresa Berger underscores LaCugna's methodological contribution and asserts its ecumenical and international ramifications. She then amplifies this assertion by citing the important recent work by M.-J. Krähe, L. Lies and A. Kallis on the liturgy-theology relationship.

25. Avery Dulles, *The Craft of Theology. From Symbol to System* (New York: Crossroad, 1992) 8.

26. Ibid.

27. Ibid., 9. He goes on to say that "the liturgy and the sense of the faithful are particular forms of tradition, which is likewise reckoned among the sources of theology. . . ." and that "tradition perpetuates itself not primarily by explicit statement but rather by gesture, deed and example, including ritual actions. " "The deeper insights of revelatory knowledge are imparted, not in the first instance through propositional discourse, but through participation in the life and worship of the Church" (18).

28. Ibid., 19.

29. David N. Power, "Eucharist," in *Systematic Theology* Vol. II, 263–64.

30. See, "Archbishop of Canterbury on Vatican Response [to ARCIC I Final Report]," *Origins* 21 (Dec. 19, 1991) 447 in which he states "if either communion requires that the other conform to its own theological formulations, further progress will be hazardous."

31. Our argument here is influenced by what Cipriano Vagaggini has termed his "gnoseological" theology. While his theological method is highly influenced by the unity of liturgy and theology in the patristic era, he is careful to argue that to imitate this method or to repeat the theological positions articulated then would be anachronistic and at variance with the nature of the theological enterprise. For Vagaggini, the term "gnoseological" underscores how "wisdom" (*gnosis*) and not just "knowledge" (*scientia*) are the desired results of engaging in theology.

32. See, chapter 8, 314–318.

33. Especially in chapters 3 and 4 above.

34. See above, chapter 4, 142–146.

35. See above, especially chapter 2, 69–74.

36. See, for example, the *monita* of the Holy Office in 1927 and 1948 denying Roman Catholics permission to participate in ecumenical dialogues, the first specifying Faith and Order: AAS 19 (1927) 278 and AAS 40 (1948) 257.

37. The beginning of the shift is evident in the Instruction of the Holy Office, *Ecclesia Catholica* (AAS 42 [1950] 142–147) enabling Roman Catholics and non Catholics to meet as equals (*par cum pari*) to discuss matters of the faith under the supervision of bishops or of the Holy See.

38. See, Decree on Ecumenism nn. 3-4. An excellent resource for multilateral and bilateral dialogues through the mid 1980s is James F. Puglisi and S. J. Voicu, *A Bibliography of Interchurch and Interconfessional Theological Dialogues* (Rome: Centro Pro Unione, 1984).

39. See, "Vatican Responds to ARCIC I Final Report [response developed jointly by the Congregation for the Doctrine of the Faith and the Pontifical Council for Promoting Christian Unity]," *Origins* 21 (Dec. 19, 1991) 441-447.

40. See, Vatican Response to WCC Document, "Baptism, Eucharist and Ministry: An Appraisal [from the Secretariat Promoting Christian Unity in consultation with the Congregation for the Doctrine of the Faith]," *Origins* 17 (Nov. 19, 1987) 401-416.

41. See, for example, Avery Dulles who states (in *The Craft of Theology* x) "ecumenism, I contend, is best understood not as a separate branch of theology but rather as a dimension of all good theology."

42. *The Eucharist*. Final Report of Joint Roman Catholic-Lutheran Commission (1978)," *Origins* 8 (January 11, 1979) 465-480.

43. *The Eucharist* n. 16.

44. See, among many others, the two helpful essays by Andre Duval, "Le culte eucharistique," and "Le sacrifice de la messe," in *Des sacrements au concile de Trente* 21-62, 63-150 and the more creative approach of David N. Power, *The Sacrifice We Offer*. The Tridentine Dogma and Its Reinterpretation (Edinburgh: T. and T. Clark, 1987).

45. The comment of Avery Dulles from *The Craft of Theology* 190 is germane here: "It is not altogether easy to separate the agreements from the disagreements." ". . . how fully do Catholics and Lutherans in the United States agree about the real presence of Christ in the Eucharist, as was claimed in 1967, if one group finds Christ present only in the actual administration of the sacrament while the other is committed to a real presence that persists after the eucharistic service is completed?"

46. In addition to Duval, the work of other commentators on Tridentine sacramental decrees such as Karl Rahner on penance and Cyrille Vogel on orders have been most helpful.

47. Edmund Schlink, *The Coming Christ and the Coming Church*. (Philadelphia: Fortress Press, 1968) 34.

48. Ibid., 43 and 79.

49. Warren Quanbeck, *Search for Understanding* (Minneapolis: Augsburg, 1972) 47.

50. Dulles, *The Craft of Theology*, 108, citing "On the Interpretation of Dogmas," *Origins* 20 (May 17, 1990) 12.

51. Dulles states (*The Craft of Theology* 192): "The task of ecumenism, as I see it, is not to choose between legalism, sacramentalism, and evangelical faith, but to discover ways of harmoniously integrating these values, without loss of

their respective strengths, into a plenitude that is, in the best sense of the word, Catholic."

52. A most useful summary of the Faith and Order progress is documented in Lukas Vischer, *A Documentary History of the Faith and Order Movement, 1927–1963.* (St. Louis: Bethany Press, 1963). Also see Lukas Vischer, *Foi et Constitution.* (Neuchatel: Delachaux et Niestlé, 1968).

53. Among the more important influences on the sacramental discussions at Edinburgh was the publication in 1930 of F.C.N. Hicks' *The Fullness of Sacrifice* (London: SPCK, 1930).

54. In the balance of this section on Faith and Order we will review progress on the Eucharist both as an example of progress on ecumenical sacramental dialogue and because particular difficulties surround ecumenical dialogue on the Eucharist itself.

55. See, among others, David N. Power, "Eucharist," 261–264.

56. See, among other helpful treatments, J.M.R. Tillard. "La réforme liturgique et le rapprochement des Eglises" in *Liturgia Opera Divina e Umana.* (Rome: Edizione Liturgiche, 1982) 251–240.

57. See, among others, David N. Power, "Eucharist," 261–66, as well as Harding Meyer and Lukas Vischer, eds., *Growth in Agreement: Reports and Agreed Statements of Ecumenical Conversations on a World Level* (New York: Paulist Press, and Geneva: World Council of Churches, 1984) and Joint International Commission for Roman Catholic/Orthodox Theological Dialogue, "The Church, the Eucharist and the Trinity," *Origins* 12 (1982) 157–160.

58. Our intention here is not to offer a complete commentary or critique of the Lima text or the Lima liturgy. Significant examples of these include, Max Thurian, ed., *Churches Respond to BEM.* Official Responses to the "Baptism, Eucharist and Ministry" text. Faith and Order Paper 129 (Geneva: World Council of Churches, 1986) and (from the Roman Catholic perspective) Michael A. Fahey, ed., *Catholic Perspectives on Baptism, Eucharist, and Ministry.* A Study Commissioned by the Catholic Theological Society of America (New York/Lanham: University of America Press, 1986). Rather our intention is to make some comments about the Eucharist as described in the document "Baptism, Eucharist and Ministry," and as celebrated according to the Lima liturgy. This will lead to section three to follow on proposals for future ecumenical sacramental conversations based on a liturgical theology of sacraments.

59. The brevity of the document's listing of the first three parts (out of twenty-one) of the eucharistic liturgy (n. 27) is belied here in such a heavy penitential introduction.

60. The first element of this liturgy is described as the "entrance psalm (with antiphon and *Gloria Patri*; or hymn)."

61. Curiously, this same text "recognize each other's ministries" is found next to last in the list of intercessions in this liturgy.

62. As I see it today the major limitation of my own doctoral thesis is that it listed textual similarities and even verbal similitude of the texts of the recently revised American Lutheran and Roman Catholic eucharistic liturgies. Positively, this work established data to work from regarding a theology of the Eucharist drawn from the liturgy. While this commonality is clearly significant the question left unanswered is how do these Churches "hear" and "interpret" even these very similar liturgies? In terms of our present work the question raised is whether common *texts* create common *contexts* in the sense of united churches.

63. The Latin text of the last phrase is: *et omnibus Sanctis, quorum intercessione perpetuo apud te confidimus adiuvari.*

64. Text from *Lutheran Book of Worship*. Ministers Desk Edition (Minneapolis: Augsburg, 1978) 292.

65. A related idea would be the kind of "federation" presumed in the notion of "sister churches."

66. This statement stands even for the present rites of penance and anointing of the sick. In the rite of penance the first of the three sacramental rites allows for a brief liturgy of the Word, the second and third forms require a full liturgy of the Word and the fourth of the rites contains a nonsacramental liturgy of penance predicated on a full liturgy of the Word. In the Rite for the Pastoral Care of the Sick and Anointing only in cases of emergency is the liturgy of the Word dispensed with.

67. See, chapter 3, 91–92.

68. On this intrinsic connection in conciliar and post conciliar documents see, among others, Liturgy Constitution n. 55 (DOL 55), Decree on the Ministry and Life of Priests n. 4 (DOL 259), Third Instruction on Implementing Sacrosanctum Concilium (*Liturgicae instaurationes*) n. 2 (DOL 513), Instruction on Worship of the Eucharist (*Eucharisticum Mysterium*) n. 10 (DOL 1239), and the General Instruction on the Roman Missal n. 8 (DOL 1398).

69. *Lectionary for Mass Introduction* n. 10 (revised edition). It is significant that the expansion in this revised edition of the Lectionary introduction deals largely with the theology of the Word as operative in the act of liturgy, and less with directives for celebration.

70. This draws on the liturgical theology of the Word articulated in chapter 3, 111–119.

71. See, Karl Rahner, "What is a Sacrament?" 276.

72. B. R. Brinkmann, "On Sacramental Man," *The Heythrop Journal* 13 (October, 1972) 371–401; 14 (January 1973) 5–34; 14 (April 1973) 162–189; 14 July, 1973) 280–306; 14 (October 1973) 396–416. Also see, A. Martinich, "Sacraments and Speech Acts," *The Heythrop Journal* 16 (1975) 289–303, 405–417.

73. William Shea "Sacraments and Meaning," *American Ecclesiastical Review* 169 (1975) 403–416.

74. Peter Fink, "Three Languages of Christian Sacraments," *Worship* 52 (November, 1978) 561-575.

75. See, among other works, Paul Ricoeur, "The Hermeneutics of Symbol and Philosophical Reflection," *International Philosophical Quarterly* 2 (1962) 191-218, and *Freud and Philosophy: An Essay on Interpretation* trans., Dennis Savage (New Haven: Yale University Press, 1970) 3-56, 344-551.

76. See, chapter 1, 12-14.

77. See, chapter 4, 130-132.

78. See, chapter 4, 157-160.

79. See, chapter 4, 142-151.

80. See, chapter 4, 143-146.

81. See, chapter 1, 21-23.

82. This is not to disparage "grace" language, the overuse of which Casel reacted to by his project. In fact, when properly understood, the use of grace-language can help to specify how each liturgy is a new event of salvation predicated on Christ's unique paschal death and resurrection.

83. See, among others, J.M.R. Tillard, "La reforme," 215 and 217.

84. Dulles, *The Craft of Theology*, 192-193.

85. Recall here the ground breaking work of Rahner, Schillebeeckx and Semmelroth.

86. See, among others, Kenan Osborne, "Methodology and Christian Sacraments," *Worship* 48 (September 1974) 536-549 and as expanded in *Sacramental Theology. A General Introduction* (New York/Mahwah, N.J.: Paulist Press, 1988) 33-48.

87. See, among others, Edward Kilmartin, "A Modern Approach to the Word of God and Sacraments in Christ: Perspectives and Principles," in *The Sacraments: God's Love and Mercy Actualized*, ed. Francis Eigo (Villanova: Villanova University Press, 1979) 59-109. Also, see one of the earliest critiques of Rahner by William van Roo, "Reflections on Karl Rahner's *Kirche und Sakramente*," *Gregorianum* 44 (1963) 465-500.

88. See, Herve Legrand, "The Presidency of the Eucharist according to Ancient Tradition," in *Living Bread, Saving Cup*, 196-221.

Chapter 8

Spirituality

This discussion builds upon our understanding of *liturgical theology*, as comprising the interrelationship among *lex orandi, lex credendi, lex vivendi*. We understand spirituality derived from the liturgy as the *lex vivendi* part of this equation. In this chapter we want to argue that the authenticity of liturgy resides in how the act of liturgy—summarized in accord with our thesis as *enacted texts in context*—derives from and impacts on all of human life. This argument presumes initial and deepening conversion on the part of liturgical participants—begun through the sacraments of initiation, sustained in regular engagement in liturgy (and other prayer) and expressed in the spirituality of daily living. In our understanding such liturgical engagement includes regular celebration of Eucharist, penance and the Hours[1] and occasional engagement in other kinds of liturgy, e.g., anointing of the sick, marriage, ordination and rites of profession, depending on individual contexts in life, i.e., aged, terminally ill, or one's vocation, i.e., married, ordained, and religious (including monastic, mendicant communities). As understood here, spirituality receives its focus and direction from liturgy and prayer as expressions of conversion and as signs and causes of deepening conversion.

Some working distinctions need to be made explicit as we begin this discussion, namely, that liturgy, prayer, and spirituality are intrinsically interrelated, that they are fundamentally theological realities, and that they are at the heart of the Christian way of life.[2] If one were to diagram how liturgy, prayer, and spirituality are interrelated, one could effectively use concentric circles.

The smallest of the circles would be *liturgy*. To our way of thinking its position in the center (as articulated in section 1 of this chapter) indicates that it is an essential and intrinsic part of both prayer and spirituality but that neither prayer nor spirituality is limited to the liturgy. This means that the enactment of liturgy is not coterminous with either prayer or spirituality and that liturgy has implications both for other forms of prayer and for spirituality.

The second concentric circle, larger than liturgy and smaller than spirituality, is *prayer,* understood as the direct and explicit communication with God in many and various ways.[3] In our understanding liturgy is a central form of prayer; but it is not the only act of prayer in which Christians should or do engage. Other kinds of Christian prayer—from mantras to meditation, from centering to contemplation—are here assumed and deemed essential for both engaging in the act of liturgy and for living the Christian life. The *way* one prays is less important in this configuration than the *fact* that one prays. (At the same time, however, we will indicate some forms of prayer which support liturgical prayer more directly and fully.) In section 1 of this chapter we will argue that there are anthropological and theological reasons why *liturgical* prayer is so central to leading the Christian life.

The third and largest of the concentric circles is *spirituality* understanding spirituality to mean *viewing* and *living* the Christian life as profoundly and explicitly graced in Christ and continually enlivened by the Trinity. Spirituality implies how one views all of life from the perspective of Christian revelation and faith and how one's life values and actual daily living are shaped by that revelation, enacted in the celebration of the liturgy. Spirituality thus relies on and is nurtured by both liturgy and prayer. Liturgy and prayer are its constant nourishment. They afford the means through which the Christian receives divine revelation and the lens through which the Christian views human life as graced and redeemed in Christ which grace and redemption is now made available through the Trinity and which is operative and experienced in all of life.

We will argue here that spirituality derived from liturgy is essentially integrative and that the *integral* vision of the Christian life experienced in liturgy derives from and leads to continuing to experience that integration in all of life. Thus liturgy derives from the *context* of human life and daily living. It also returns participants back to life with their vision of the Christian life sharpened and the challenge of living that vision the more clear. It relies on, and at times will articulate, aspects of what can be termed a "catholic," liturgical and sacramental vision of life (understanding, of course, that this vision is not particular to

Roman Catholicism). In our view, sacramentality derived from Christ's incarnation includes the discoverability of God in the human and that all of creation and human life reveals the divine. This integral vision of life is presumed and celebrated in liturgy. That the rest of life still needs to achieve the harmony expressed and experienced in liturgy is among the more precise tasks of spirituality.

In section 1 we will argue that participation in liturgy is the pivotal axis of Christian prayer, is essential for appreciating the inherent theological logic of the liturgy and for the way liturgy can and should be formative of other kinds of prayer. In section 2, we will argue that liturgy is essentially integrative in the sense that it shapes how we look at all of life as "this graced world"[4] and how liturgy is the essential means for disclosing what life really is and means for the Christian. In section 3 we will indicate what we regard as the mutual interrelationship of liturgy, ethics and eschatology, arguing that to speak of one is to speak of the other two at the same time and that together these three are central for Christian liturgical spirituality. In section 4 we will point to one specific application of liturgy for spirituality, specifically the way liturgy expresses the sacramentality of all creation, by pointing to the contemporary convergence in and challenge of environmental and liturgical ethics. In section 5 we will indicate some avenues for critiquing the present *lex orandi* in light of the argument of this chapter relating liturgy and spirituality and then offer a more specific critique about an integral vision of life and the essential ethical dimension of liturgical theology derived from liturgical celebration.

I. Theological Value of Liturgical Prayer

That modern and contemporary magisterial and canonical statements have continually referred to liturgy as the "official prayer of the church"[5] affords a key insight that summarizes important aspects of the theological and spiritual value of liturgy. More recently, however, liturgists and sacramental theologians have sought to go beyond such formulations (sometimes because of their legalistic tone) to articulate *why* liturgy has such a privileged place in the Church's life.[6] To our way of thinking, liturgy has such a privileged role in the prayer, the theology and the living of the Christian life because of all forms of prayer it is the most anthropologically and theologically "apt."[7] By its nature, liturgy has an anthropological and theological "fittingness." Liturgy is the most suitable means for human beings to pray because it respects and reflects their nature as *enfleshed* beings. Most particularly liturgy respects and reflects the way human beings interact and communicate.[8]

Anthropologically, the liturgy is apt in that it uses the common means of human communication—words, gestures, symbols, etc.—as the most appropriate way for human beings to engage in prayer. This anthropological foundation of liturgy grounds its dialogical character in the sense that (as we have argued above) word, symbol, and euchology are all intrinsically dialogical realities requiring responses for the act of liturgy to be itself—a reality participated in by the whole liturgical community by means of the (stylized) responses intrinsic to the act of liturgy, specifically words, gestures, and symbolic interaction. It also requires a response reflected in the rest of life in terms of how the liturgy shapes the Christian's worldview and how it shapes the conduct of one's life.

Liturgy is anthropologically fitting in the sense that the *combination* of using words, symbols, gestures, and silence in a whole ritual action articulates the way human beings communicate. It is their combination and intrinsic interrelatedness that makes the liturgy central as a unique ritual means of human communication which articulates how humans engage in the act of communicating with God and how God communicates with humans through means proper to humanity. Liturgy is most fitting anthropologically in the sense that it respects and uses the normal means of human communication to commune with God. (The use of "commune" here indicates a depth of interpersonal relationship not reflected in the term "communicate." The latter can mean passing on information; the former implies a commitment to the other. In liturgy it is a commitment to God ratified in ritual prayer.)

In addition, these essential elements of the liturgy are enacted in communal celebrations that respect and reflect the participants' personal and communal histories and the means humans use to "tell time." This is to assert that the rhythm of the seasons of a person's life—birth, childhood, adulthood, vocation in life, death—provide the anthropological grounding for the key ritual moments of baptism, chrismation, Eucharist (and penance) in sacramental initiation (whether at infancy or in adulthood, since "new life" is signified and expressed at both), the expression of vocational commitment most Christians make in marriage, profession, or ordination and rites of passage in anointing of the sick and funeral rites.

In addition, the genius of the liturgical year is that liturgical celebrations are predicated on the seasons (e.g., fall and winter for eschatology, spring for new life, as argued above, admitting at the same time the limitations of this example because of their reflecting the northern hemisphere).⁹ Similarly, the delineation of time based on the sun to situate day and night is used liturgically to articulate that each day is a new beginning in grace (especially in morning prayer) and each evening ushers in sentiments of thanks for the day and hope for eternal life in God (especially in evening prayer). The delineation of seven days for a week, resting not on cosmic phenomena but on Judaism's seven-day computation, places emphasis on Sunday as pivotal for ending one week and beginning another, hence the particular theological value of Sunday Eucharist as the explicit ratification of initiation through the Sunday Eucharistic celebration. The liturgy takes anthropology seriously in the way humans tell time and use this measuring of time to articulate how the grace, mercy and peace from God are both celebrated in time and are beyond time. They are experienced here and now and their fulfillment is yearned for in the kingdom of heaven, liturgy's fulfillment.

Liturgy is theologically "apt" in the sense that it incorporates and articulates a range of fundamental theological elements of Christianity. Taken together these theological elements can be regarded as "most fitting" in the sense that they reflect and respect the range of theological factors that should be incorporated in Christian prayer. This is to suggest, in the first place, that since every act of liturgy is a *Word event* wherein the Word of God is proclaimed and responded to, so every act of liturgy is necessarily regarded as an experience of divine revelation and of dialogue with God through the dynamic of revelation and response.

Every act of liturgical prayer is thus theologically fitting because it rests on the fundamental characteristic of biblical religion in terms of continuing the dialogue initiated by God with the chosen people in the Scriptures, sustained with those initiated into the liturgical assembly in the present and which dialogue always looks to its fulfillment in the kingdom. Thus liturgy can be regarded as theologically appropriate in the way it gives voice to divine revelation and enables the Word of God to achieve its purpose as always inviting and involving God's people into an ever deepening relationship with him. Parallel with this notion of the Word as theologically apt is the recollection of the fact that the blessing prayers that constitute a major portion of the liturgical complement to the Scriptures (especially in sacramental liturgy) also derive from words as a chief means of human communication.

Secondly, liturgy is theologically apt in that every act of liturgy is a *Church event* in that it enacts the community of believers into ever deepening communion with God and one another. Any privatized notions of personal prayer cede here to the theological reality that liturgy constitutes the Church at prayer. This statement implies first and foremost that God initiates, sustains, and accomplishes every act of liturgy by enabling the Church community to be drawn into these central saving mysteries again and again. Divine initiative in salvation is concretely expressed and experienced in what God does among us still through the liturgy. The fundamental reality of God having called and as still calling a people—not individuals only—into a deep and abiding experience of divine love and salvation is ratified and signified in liturgical prayer. The biblical God of relatedness and relationship is active in liturgy to continue to call and shape a people in the divine image and likeness. God's act of calling a people to himself is evidenced and accomplished in liturgical prayer in a unique way. Communal self-transcendence is thus a logical consequence of liturgical engagement. Liturgy is first and foremost about constituting the Church as the body of Christ on earth in the mystery of the Trinity. It is in relation to this foundation that it is a privileged means of personal sanctification.

Thirdly, liturgy is also theologically fitting in the *Trinitarian sense* that to experience the act of liturgy is to experience the three personed God, the Trinity, ever at work for our salvation.[10] Despite the legitimate critique often made today that Western liturgy ought to be more pneumatologically rich and specific in its euchology and in terms of the theology of liturgy derived from the *lex orandi*,[11] it is the Trinity that initiates, sustains, and completes every act of liturgy. Edward Kilmartin's assertions are helpful in this connection:

". . . Christ's personal presence in the community has a medium which affords a more intensive kind of presence. This medium is the Holy Spirit. The Spirit is the quasi-formal cause of our filial adoption: union with the Father, and so the basis of our intimate union with Christ and with one another in Christ. Through the presence of the Spirit of Christ in the believers the actual presence of Christ in the liturgy of the church is made possible. Christ and the believers are rendered mutually present to one another through the Spirit and so communicate with one another through the word of preaching and sacraments and offer acceptable worship to God."[12]

In our delineation of theological aptness of the liturgy, it is more appropriate to refer to the Trinity as a unity into which the Church is continually drawn, rather than separating (and thus seeming to have to choose between) liturgy's Christological and pneumatological dimensions. The Church is encountered by and repeatedly encounters the Trinity in liturgy. It is the Trinity who shapes the Church again and again through the liturgy. It is into the very life of the Trinity that the Church is drawn through liturgy. This Trinitarian focus for liturgical prayer resists any "functionalism" in terms of describing how God is operative in liturgy. It assures the liturgical community that Father, Son, and Spirit initiate and sustain every act of liturgy. It is the Trinity's very life that we share now through the liturgy, which we hope to share finally and fully in the kingdom of heaven.

Fourthly, liturgy is also theologically apt in the sense that the *soteriology* expressed in its euchology is theologically balanced and focused. This is to assert that the fullness and integrity of the paschal mystery as experienced in liturgy is almost always described in ways that balance suffering, passion, death, resurrection and exaltation. (It consciously avoids any kind of "passion piety" only or prayer that isolates one aspect of the logical and theological integrity of the whole paschal mystery.) The most concrete example of this is the anamnesis prayer and memorial acclamations. This kind of balanced theological formulation is derived from the Scriptures and is always ecclesiologically focused in that it describes how the Church experiences Christ's paschal mystery in liturgy.

Liturgical euchology serves this ecclesiological perspective by invariably referring to how what is experienced in the liturgy is from God and for our salvation. The classic couplet of Easter Preface I

"dying you destroyed our death
rising you restored our life"

indicates this balance in characteristically laconic Roman liturgical language. Euchological liturgical texts normatively use plural forms such as "we ask this through Christ our Lord." They also characteristically use the subjunctive, indicating how what we do liturgically is really to invite God to dwell among us again and to accomplish in us the salvation we pray for (e.g., *quaesumus*).[13]

It is particularly in soteriology (but not exclusively) that the anthropological and theological aptness of the liturgy meet in the sense that the ordinary and familiar human means of interaction which Jesus used to inaugurate the kingdom are still used in liturgy—Word, gesture, symbol. They are also anthropologically apt in the ways that specific combinations of texts, gestures, and symbols draw out particular aspects of the paschal mystery in ways that reflect particular needs. Hence the anthropological fittingness that water is used for baptismal bathing and washing, which water has been blessed with prayers reflecting water's life-giving and sanctifying properties.[14] Similarly, the Eucharist is most fittingly symbolized in bread and wine (themselves the product of the cycle of dying and rising in nature) and experienced in an act of ritual dining accompanied by the proclamation of the Church's central prayer of blessing, the Eucharistic prayer.[15] Similar fittingness extends to the imposition of hands and the sign of peace for forgiveness and reconciliation and salving the body with blessed oil for the anointing of the sick, etc.

To our way of thinking, it is in the liturgy uniquely that a balanced soteriology meets the human's need for God and for communion with others in God in the Church. These realities are most appropriately reflected in liturgy's symbolic engagement and euchology. Soteriology is also the locus for merging theological and anthropological aspects of liturgy in the sense that both in the incarnation and in liturgy, the flesh is the instrument of salvation.[16] This is to say that the Word was embodied in flesh for our salvation; the liturgy presumes the use of our bodies in ritual words and actions to deepen this salvation in and among us.

To speak of the theological fittingness of liturgy is to speak about the ways that the liturgical euchology articulates images, likenesses, metaphors, and names for God, the combination and juxtaposition of which discloses how the believing community experiences God in ever new ways but in ways that are paradigmatically described in the Scriptures and experienced through their liturgical proclamation.[17] The way the liturgy articulates prayer to God through Christ in the Holy Spirit and shapes how we experience this same triune God can be regarded as particularly reliable in the sense that one of the criteria involved in evaluating aspects of the *lex orandi* has traditionally been and is its theological (and thus, in our understanding, its spiritual) orthodoxy. Liturgical euchology is orthodox in the sense that it accurately reflects Christian belief,[18] and it is spiritually appropriate in the sense that it articulates (at least some of) the ways God acts in and among the Church (and enacts the Church) through the liturgy. At one and the same time theologically orthodox liturgical euchology both names God and our need for God. One example of the usefulness of this kind of orthodox prayer is that it continues to underscore how God acts in liturgy "for us" and "for our salvation" (in the words of the Creed). For example, in liturgy we pray less for *justice* in the world than we do for *the Just One* to come among us to renew the kingdom he inaugurated and established, which kingdom is renewed in and through the Church as it is renewed through the liturgy. This experience of God's justice through liturgy is what leads the Church to participate in the doing of just deeds in the contemporary world. This response is due, at least partly, to this liturgical participation.

From a slightly different perspective one needs to ask "what does the liturgy *do*" that makes it so important both in terms of the act of liturgical prayer and in terms of its implications for spirituality? A most appropriate response that comes from both the experience of liturgy itself and also from the tradition of systematic reflection on sacraments would assert that liturgy is an explicit enactment and experience of God that causes grace through the use of symbols themselves—*significando causant*.[19] Liturgical euchology continually reiterates this notion when it asks that God accomplish something for the liturgical community here and now on the basis of his having accomplished all salvation once and for all. The intrinsic relationship of engagement in ritual actions, of articulating the nature of the ritual action through liturgical euchology and of drawing out notions of what sacraments cause requires an integrated approach to appreciating liturgy and sacraments lest one factor be deemed more important than another. The liturgy *does* precisely this and by doing this it unleashes God's redemptive power here and now in new and different ways. It is precisely *through* the genres proper to the liturgy—blessing prayers, symbolic elements, and ritual gestures—that God *acts* among us and *causes* "the work of our redemption" to occur still and to be accomplished.

To our way of thinking the very notion of liturgical causality is anthropologically and theologically "apt" because on the one hand it avoids the danger of describing what the liturgy is and does in physicalist or realist categories,[20] and on the other it preserves the importance of the traditional category of causality in liturgical theology. Our contemporary experience of liturgy relies and draws on the once-for-all (*ephapax,*) unique act of salvation through Christ's paschal mystery. The liturgy uses and capitalizes on conventional notions of time here in the sense that what occurred once in time for our salvation occurs still through the liturgy. *Ephapax* salvation is continually experienced here and now. Classical liturgical terminology for this is *hodie* and *haec dies*. At Christmas we acclaim *hodie Christus natus est*. At Easter we acclaim *haec dies quam fecit Dominus*. These expressions offer the most useful theological foundation for the liturgy in that they link Christ's past deeds of salvation with our present experience of them.

Hence the present liturgy is not harkening back to "once upon a time." Rather it is our present experience of what has occurred in Christ, of what occurs still in Christ and of what will be fulfilled in the kingdom. The liturgy is thus both the same act of Christ's saving power and always a new act of salvation. What we do in liturgy is to "make anamnesis, memorial of this dynamic saving power in our lives, to make it penetrate ever more into the depths of our being."[21] It is also at the very same time "the future present" (to use Marianne Micks' term)[22] through which we experience even now what is yet to come—the final revelation at the end of time when Christ will bring time to an end—which revelation is Christ himself as the *eschatos*.[23] The focus is thus our *present* experience of salvation, which experience is articulated by euchological terminology often emphasizing this present experience of grace.

Thus, what liturgy "does" is enact the saving mysteries of Christ in the context of a believing and praying Church in an event whose elements are the most apt, anthropologically and theologically, which elements taken together comprise a ritual of prayer that has direct effects on and consequences for the Church for whom, with whom and among whom the liturgical action takes place. By the very "doing" of liturgy, the Church actualizes itself as the privileged locus where Christ's paschal mystery is operative for humanity here and now. Through liturgy, the Church enacts a paradigm against which other forms of devotion ought to be evaluated both anthropologically and theologically. Logically we now turn to the formative and evaluative nature of liturgy regarding both other acts of devotional prayer and other ways that prayer and spirituality are joined.

The Formative Role of Liturgy. To raise the question about the *formative* value of the liturgy implicitly raises the question about the relationship of liturgy to other kinds of prayer and devotional exercises and the theological and anthropological adequacy of such prayer and devotions. That one of the aims of the liturgical reform was to adapt and revise popular devotions where necessary is stated explicitly in the Liturgy Constitution n. 13:

"Popular devotions of the Christian people, provided they conform to the laws and norms of the Church, are to be highly recommended. . . . But these devotions should be so fashioned that they harmonize with the liturgical seasons, accord with the sacred liturgy, are in some way derived from it, and lead people to it, since in fact, the liturgy by its very nature far surpasses any of them."[24]

Hence the liturgy is to exercise the function of critiquing and shaping other forms of devotion. In our view this should be done in light of liturgy's anthropological and theological aptness. While this does not mean that all other acts of prayer and piety should imitate the liturgy, it does mean that these acts of devotion should, among other things, be theologically orthodox, offer a balanced soteriology, be Trinitarian in at least some of its formulations and be concerned with both the whole Church and the particular worshiping community. Concretely, this suggests that a balance of praise and petition, the acknowledgment of God as creator and redeemer of all life and as sustainer of life who continues to act in the Church as its unique redeemer needs to be factored into other prayer forms.

An equally important aspect regarding the formative nature of the liturgy concerns how other devotional practices can enable one to participate in the liturgy more fully for the sake of personal and communal spiritual renewal. In fact, to our way of thinking, the kind of spiritual renewal that is a chief aim of the present reform of the liturgy will only take place when it is supported by appropriate personal and domestic devotional practices which support what occurs in the liturgy itself.[25] Such devotional practices are, in our opinion, necessary so that liturgy can be experienced as fully as possible as the central act of Christian prayer.

In chapter 3 we argued that there is a theological and liturgical difference between *lectio divina* and the Liturgy of the Word, one aspect of which is that *lectio divina* is essentially reflection on the Scriptures ("holy reading") and the Liturgy of the Word is the enactment of the Word proclaimed ("holy happening").[26] However, the distinct advantage of *lectio divina* over other kinds of meditation and mental prayer as a devotional exercise is that it places one in direct relationship with the Scriptures themselves (as opposed to other inspirational writing). To our way of thinking it thus conforms with one of the aspects of the anthropological and theological aptness of the liturgy in the way it prepares one for the hearing and enactment of the Word in the liturgy and how it shapes one's perspective on life and life's values. Reflection on the Word in *lectio*[27] or reflection on the Scriptures in small groups can enhance the experience of the liturgical proclamation of the Word because these practices help one to shape one's worldview and values according to biblical revelation. They can also enhance the kind of "obedient listening" articulated above (in chapter 3).[28]

Another kind of liturgically appropriate devotion is what we will term "domestic ritual," that is, rituals engaged in by families or small groups that are patterned after the liturgy itself. Domestic forms of ritual prayer modelled on liturgical ritual are necessary, in our view, so that liturgical ritual itself can become "second nature" and sufficiently familiar that one can engage in it with less and less encumbrance or awkwardness. Chief among such domestic rituals is the family meal with blessings before and after it. In articulating the importance of the family meal we are intentionally arguing also for the liturgical and spiritual value of the *meal itself as ritual* in its own right because we understand it to be a chief means of underscoring familial belonging and identity.

The fact that fewer and fewer American families dine together regularly is detrimental first and fundamentally to family solidity. It is also detrimental to liturgical participation and therefore to valuing the liturgy itself. Without such domestic rites the family disintegrates into individuals living in "group homes" dining on "fast foods" brought in from elsewhere or prepared beforehand and heated up to be served at will. Thus the anthropological substratum on which liturgy is predicated—in this case the family meal—is lost. The meal as a domestic ritual helps to disclose the meaning of liturgical rituals in the way it values the very phenomenon of gathering together and of sharing food and drink in familiarity and love, and at times in festivity. The addition of blessing prayers derived from the themes of praise and thanksgiving of the Eucharistic prayer enhances and explicitates how this meal is a sacred event.

Another form of domestic ritual, or one that enhances the blessings at meals, could include reading Scripture, praying over it (at least part of which should be the psalms, thus appreciated as *the* Christian prayerbook), silence, intercessions, gestures, and song. Such an adaptation of the Liturgy of the Word could both insure familial relationships and enhance the value of dining together. It would also facilitate participation in liturgical ritual and thus enhance the value of such participation. Such experiences are particularly important for children in terms of societal and religious identity. The inclusion of this as a regular part of the family meal, for example, during the seasons of Advent-Christmas and Lent-Easter would be an important way of underscoring the importance of the way the liturgy "tells time" through the seasons and the way the liturgy in these seasons draws us into the paschal mystery.

Lectio divina and *domestic rituals* patterned after the liturgy itself are helpful ways of enhancing liturgical participation and of prizing liturgy as a central means of communal prayer. The enactment of the liturgy brings such prayer experiences to a fuller and more complete expression based largely on the anthropological and theological arguments we have put forth. In addition, these practices help to deepen individual's and the community's experience of the way the liturgy, in its uniqueness, is the privileged means of experiencing here and now how the work of our redemption accomplished by Christ is enacted for our salvation in the *hodie* of liturgical celebration.

II. Liturgy as Disclosive of Life

In the previous section we argued that a hallmark of liturgical spirituality, in line with what the liturgy implies for living the Christian life, concerns *causality* (through words, gestures, and symbols) in the sense of what the liturgy does to enable the Church to experience salvation. In this section we will argue that another hallmark of liturgical spirituality is how the liturgy illuminates what reality *is*. The purpose of this section is to illustrate the intrinsic relatedness of liturgy with all of life by arguing that the liturgy is a pedagogy for the way believers perceive and view all of life and that the power of liturgy is that it illuminates reality and unleashes its inherent meaning and power. This argument is built upon the notion that the community's engagement in the act of liturgy has consequences for life in the sense that the *way* it names things and the *fact* that it engages in naming things—both human and divine—is crucial for personal and communal identity. The Church's *lex orandi* therefore becomes all the more important because it shapes how believers perceive reality and how they engage in the act of naming it. The Church's *lex orandi* cannot but help to shape its *lex credendi* because in the doing of liturgy the Church is *aware* of itself—it hears and experiences itself—as it uses the various elements of liturgy to name and to articulate reality. In doing this it solidifies its identity and forges deeper communion with God and one another.

The act of doing liturgy is thus crucial for what the liturgy *causes* in liturgical enactment and for what it *causes* as implications for the Christian life. This is to say that just as *liturgical causality* enacts God's saving plan for humanity in the doing of liturgy, so too God's saving plan as disclosed in liturgy continues to shape—it is *causative*—how Christians look at life and experience life as disclosive of God's mysterious ways and plan of salvation. Liturgy is the pivotal means of uncovering the depth of reality, namely that in Christianity the ordinary is sacred. Liturgy is the pivotal means the Christian community has of reaffirming this belief, of saying that this is what it believes and of hearing others say that this is what they believe. The dynamic of liturgy thus includes affirming one's beliefs and engaging in communal acts affirming this belief. Liturgy rests on what one believes; it articulates what one believes in the community of the Church; it thus fosters deeper conversion and commitment to God.

For example in a particularly compelling section of chapter 31 of his *Rule,* St. Benedict asserts that the monastery cellarer shall show reverence for persons and things:

"(vs. 9) He must show every care and concern for the sick, children, guests and the poor, knowing for certain that he will be held accountable for all of them on the day of judgment. (vs. 10). He will regard all utensils and goods of the monastery as sacred vessels of the altar (vs. 11), aware that nothing is to be neglected."[29]

This short statement reflects the thorough incarnationalism of the *Rule,* articulates what is at the heart of the Benedictine life in terms of seeing and revering all aspects of creation and human life as a whole, and the harmony between work and prayer that is proper to Benedictine monasticism. The fact that showing reverence for the brethren and for the tools of the monastery should have such a striking role in the *Rule* is particularly noteworthy since cenobite monasticism places such a priority on liturgical prayer. A central idea and value in monasticism is thus the harmonious integration of all aspects of life seen from a particularly Christological and incarnational perspective. In Benedictine monasticism

"[h]uman life is a whole, and everything in creation is good. There is no aspect of life in this world that cannot, if rightly understood and used, contribute to leading us to our final end. Temporal reality and human endeavor are reflections of the perfections of God. Material things are *sacramenta,* symbols that reveal the goodness and beauty of the Creator. Consequently, Benedict can say that ordinary tools for work should be treated like the sacred vessels intended for liturgical use (31.10). It is only sin that has disfigured the beauty of creation and diverted things from their purpose. The monastic life is an effort to restore the lost paradise, to regain the image of God in man that has been distorted. Therefore, the temporal order cannot be despised or neglected. In the monk's life there is no area that can be exempted from subjection to the divine precepts and the regime of grace. This is no disincarnate spirituality; conversion embraces the whole of life."[30]

A contemporary perspective on how what is rightfully termed the Catholic approach to the sacramentality of life can influence spirituality as essentially linked to both sacramental and liturgical theology is offered by Philip J. Murnion. Particularly notable is his call for "Benedictine-like" communities that can reflect a new order for the world based on the principle of the sacramentality in all of life. He states that

"central to any notion of sacramentality is the fact of and a belief in the incarnation. We believe that in and through Christ there is a permanent union of God and this world, the divine and the human condition. We cannot look at the special actions we call the sacraments or the particular challenges faced by the church as sacrament without considering the present state of our world and our human condition, which are the flesh of God's presence among us."[31]

He then goes on to say

"the new order is one that recognizes explicitly, not begrudgingly, the community of all life, the interdependence of all persons, the symbiosis of human life and the environment. It also rewards relationships rather than acquisitions as the measure of success.
The distinctive traits of Catholicism are the convictions:
• That God has revealed and continues to reveal himself through the materials of human existence and that this revelation calls for a new way of life.
• That we come to understand who we are and what this means we must do in and through a community, a community of God's choosing rather than of our own convenience.
• That there is a communal or corporate process and authority for articulating the meaning of God's revelation and this way of life.
• That we respect human intelligence for structuring our shared understanding of revelation and relationships.
• That the fullest faithful expression of discipleship is in our actions, not just in our testimonies to belief.

• That we are the union of flesh and spirit such that we struggle to keep in tension the mystical flights of the spirit and the most basic concerns of the body and feel the tension between glory and sin within ourselves.

• That the sacramentality of Jesus discloses and makes possible the sacramentality of all life.''[32]

These examples illustrate what is at the heart of our understanding of liturgical spirituality, namely, that it is the liturgy that reveals the way things really are. Liturgy allows creation to be creation; it does not (and does not need to!) transform creation. Just as in Genesis 2 where human beings give the right names to things, so it is in the liturgy that the Church continues to give the right names to things and reveres creation as disclosive of the triune God. The activity of naming things is at its best in liturgical prayer in the sense that it is through liturgical language that we discover what reality really is. St. Benedict's admonition to the monastery cellarer is the admonition which the liturgy continually gives to the Church, namely, that all of life is sacred and that liturgy is the Church's continual reminder of life's sacredness. Thus we can say that liturgy *causes* believers to look at life through the prism of Christ, whose incarnation and paschal mystery become the filter through which they see the world as profoundly engraced and judge what is of real value and what really matters in life.

Thus, for example, it is in the liturgy of the anointing of the sick that we learn what is of real value in life in the sense that those anointed become sacramental signs to the rest of the Church and to the world that productivity, prowess, and performance are of little value compared with identification with God in suffering, in allowing suffering to teach us reliance on God and that the notion of "human fragility" is really both redundant and eminently hope-filled. Those anointed remind us about who *we* really are—those who experience divine life here and now and who are destined for the fullness of this divine life in eternity with God forever. In the meantime all created things, especially other human persons, are holy in themselves and disclose the holiness that is God.

The insight of the Orthodox theologian Alexander Schmemann is helpful in this regard:

"The whole creation depends on food. But the unique position of man [i.e., the human person] in the universe is that he alone is to *bless* God for the food and the life he receives from Him. He alone is to respond to God's blessing with his blessing. The significant fact about the life in the Garden is that man is to *name* things.

"To name a thing . . . is to bless God for it and in it. And in the Bible to bless God is not a 'religious' or a 'cultic' act, but the very *way of life*. God blessed the world, blessed the man, blessed the seventh day (that is, time), and this means that he filled all that exists with His love and goodness, made all this 'very good.' So the only *natural* (and not 'supernatural') reaction of man, to whom God gave this blessed and sanctified world, is to bless God in return, to thank him, to see the world as God sees it—and in this act of gratitude and adoration—to know, name and possess the world.

"The first, the basic definition of man is that he is *the priest*. He stands in the center of the world and unifies it in his act of blessing God, of both receiving the world from God and offering it to God—and by filling the world with this eucharist, he transforms his life, the one that he receives from the world, into life in God, into communion.

"The world was created as the 'matter,' the material of one all-embracing eucharist, and man was created as the priest of this cosmic sacrament."[33]

To appreciate the value of how liturgy is disclosive of life requires, among other things, that one "be attentive"[34] to the world and to the way liturgy shapes the Christian's worldview. To celebrate the liturgy implies that one bring to that celebration an appreciation of the world as graced and as the locus for divine self-revelation. To celebrate the liturgy implies seeing the world of the human and the divine as a unified whole with liturgy serving a mediating and integrating function. To celebrate the liturgy implies that one appreciate the value of what liturgy discloses, in terms of personal and communal conversion, in particular personal and communal self-transcendence. It also implies and requires an appreciation of what the liturgy demands in terms of conversion and self-transcendence. In our view it is in and through liturgy that reality is disclosed and affirmed.

In light of our anthropological and theological argument about the priority of liturgy, we can now assert that liturgy's use of "daily and domestic things" (to use David Power's term) concerns material elements and how they are experienced in ritual actions, which ritual actions disclose what these material elements really are. This is to argue that it is in the liturgy of baptism that we find out what water really is, for baptism involves an act of bathing in waters already deeply engraced. The act of baptizing by immersing in water articulates the value of the human action of bathing in such a way as to experience water's true life giving properties and water as part of God's "good" creation. Similarly, it is in the liturgy of the Eucharist that we find out what bread and wine really are as signs of abundance and divine favor. These products of human manufacture are used in the liturgical ritual of dining where blessing God and sharing food and drink enable us to experience their life sustaining properties understanding bread and wine as particularly poignant examples of the goodness of creation in that their manufacture relies on humanity's use of the goods of the earth.

It is only when this anthropological level of liturgical experience is appropriated and thematized theologically that we can discover and systematically describe what liturgy *does*. Liturgy discloses what life really is. To "use" liturgy this way is most appropriate because it is thus able to disclose what human life really is and what life with and in God means. What the liturgy does is place creation in its proper order and allows creation to be disclosed in its fullest depth. To experience God through the liturgy presumes the discoverability of the divine in human life and how the human is always the locus for us of discovering the divine. Liturgy is really the matrix of the anthropological and the theological. It is, in fact, theological anthropology enacted. In light of our thesis we can assert that liturgy is essential for Christian spirituality because it is the privileged locus for articulating how all of life is sacramental. Liturgical enactment only makes sense in light of what it orchestrates in terms of the *context* of human life.

III. Liturgy, Ethics, and Eschatology

The incarnational emphasis to liturgy and life described in the preceding section leads to questions about the ethical demands inherent in liturgy as liturgy relates to life. More explicitly this is to raise the more active aspects of living a spiritual life as disclosed in and derived from liturgy. With liturgy understood as *a* privileged locus but not *the* exclusive locus of experiencing God's presence, the argument in this section is designed as a complement to the incarnational emphasis in the preceding section and is aimed at drawing out some of its implications. It rests on the premise that all liturgy is as equally eschatological as it is incarnational and that the most appropriate place to locate a Christian ethic derived from liturgy is its eschatological nature which ethic then has important consequences for how one views and responds to human life.

To argue that liturgy is eschatological is to argue that the kingdom inaugurated in Christ's paschal mystery is most fully experienced here and now through the liturgy, and that liturgy's fulfillment is in the fully realized kingdom of heaven. Liturgy is the kingdom realized, looking to its complete realization in God's good time in the future. Liturgy is "the future present" as the Church, through the present liturgy, yearns for its fulfillment in its future in God. Liturgy is thus the present Church's privileged experience of what will one day be realized finally and fully. This is also to argue that while Christ is the fulfillment of God's promises, the Church's experience of this fulfillment still years for completion and perfection in heaven. This makes the liturgy "the future present" in the sense that it is the closest we come in this life to sharing directly and explicitly in God's eternal kingdom. Liturgy thus capitalizes on the transtemporal and metahistorical nature of the paschal mystery, in the sense that by its nature the paschal mystery is both in time and transcends time, it is an event within history and also an event outside of history. The genius of commemorating the liturgical year is that it enables us to experience salvation in time and according to time's seasons and to yearn for time's fulfillment in the endless day of eternal life.

Liturgy is both fulfillment and incompletion in the sense that every act of liturgy still yearns for its final completion in the heavenly liturgy (to adapt the image from the Letter to the Hebrews). This is also to argue that liturgy is fundamentally hope-filled in the sense that to experience liturgy is to experience hope as strength and comfort as the Church yearns for the perfection of liturgy in heaven. Thus the appropriateness of the early Church's frequent use of *maranatha* to conclude its liturgies. The intrinsic nature of the liturgical action as both a present and future reality is reflected in the use of *maranatha* in the *Didache* 10:5, which term is ambiguous in that it can signify at the same time the indicative, "the Lord comes" and the imperative "come, Lord Jesus." This acknowledgment of the incompleteness of liturgy is the first step in grounding the ethical demand of liturgical celebration in particular as well as for spirituality in general.

The notion of *lex agendi* and *lex vivendi* (argued methodologically in chapter two) implies that liturgical theology necessarily includes an ethic (*vivendi*) derived from the enactment of liturgy (*agendi*), specifically how one leads the Christian life outside the liturgy. Put a different way one could say that the *lex orandi/lex credendi* equation necessarily implies a *lex vivendi*—a liturgical ethic—derived from and articulated in conformity with the anthropological and theological vision of the liturgy argued in section one of this chapter. Our use of the term *lex vivendi* is relatively new, but not unprecedented, in the *orandi/credendi* equation.[35] It is meant to articulate both what has traditionally been implied as the ethical consequence of liturgical participation and as a way of giving this aspect of liturgy its proper place lest the liturgy become divorced from real life and the actual needs and concerns of persons here and now. The merging of these actual concerns with the liturgy as enacted together contribute to liturgy's authenticity. Without the explicitation of this life relatedness, the liturgy could become the preoccupation of the dilettante. As it is intended and experienced it is meant to be central to the very life of the whole Church.

Thus we want to argue that participating in the liturgy implies a fidelity to this ritual enactment that necessarily includes living a life in conformity with what the liturgy enacts—the kingdom of God among us here and now. This necessarily raises the question of divestment of the ego as a prerequisite in order to inhabit fully the languages of liturgy as these languages refer to life and to liturgy's potentiality to transform our view of life and life itself. The way that the liturgy deals with ethics sets up a model in the sense that liturgy continually acclaims and draws the community more fully into the mystery of God's love. This becomes the basis on which ethical demands are made. It is not that in living the ethical life that we *earn* salvation. The primacy of the overarching love of God grounds any response to that love in terms of right conduct. To return "again and again" to the liturgy is to experience continually God's reconciling love in order that this love might so overtake us as to enable us to extend this love to others more and more spontaneously and fully.

To our way of thinking this means attention to the eschatological aspect of liturgy as both "waiting in joyful hope" for the Lord's return as well as living and working in the world continually assessing how and where the kingdom of God is not yet fully realized and becoming more fully agents and ministers of that kingdom on earth. The eschatological nature of the liturgy is thus the most appropriate grounding for liturgical ethics in that it is the most compelling locus and avenue for articulating *precisely why* liturgical engagement necessarily has ethical consequences. The more fully this ethical aspect can be argued in terms of liturgical theology—understanding *eschatology* as the key to such an argument—the more substantial will be our appreciation of and commitment to living a liturgical ethic. Hence, to our way of thinking, it is eschatology that grounds the *ethical dimension* of liturgy by linking liturgy with life here and now, particularly in linking liturgy with social justice, mission, service, and love. Because even this graced world is imperfect and because the kingdom manifest in liturgy is not yet fully realized in all of life, the liturgy implies and requires that those who participate in liturgy seek to extend the kingdom's manifestation here and now through actions that conform with the liturgy, itself understood as the enactment of the kingdom.

This is to argue that liturgy is intrinsically *pastoral* (and reflection on it is essentially a pastoral discipline) in the sense that it concerns people engaged in liturgy in specific ecclesial and life contexts. Liturgical actions are meant to draw people more fully into the mystery of Christ experienced through the liturgy, one effect of which is to enable believers to live more fully the Christian life experienced in the liturgy. Hence the appropriateness of raising ethical dimensions of liturgical engagement.

The category of liturgical eschatology also implies an awareness of the provisional nature of all liturgy and the truth that all cultic forms are meant to lead to experiencing the full reality of Christ made manifest in all of life here on earth and as he will be fully manifest at his second coming. In the meantime liturgy is required for less than perfect Christians and for Christians whose response to liturgy is less than perfect. This is to say that one must remain cautious about not "judging" too quickly or determining too fully or applying too readily criteria for evaluating how effective liturgical celebration has been in fostering an ethical life. The regular engagement in the ritual repertoire of the liturgy should, *over time,* lead to forming how one looks at life and how one ought to lead the Christian life. Results should not be either judged or required immediately. Recall here the parable of the sower (Mark 4:1-9 and par.) where it is only over time that real rootedness in Christ's Word can be determined and whether the yield is thirty, sixty or a hundredfold (4:8).

Similarly instructive is the Lukan parable of the withered fig tree (Luke 13:1-9). (Its use as part of the gospel on the fifth Sunday of Lent "C" cycle is illustrative of our thesis in the sense that the *context* of Lent certainly colors the hearing and interpretation of this *text*.) After yielding no produce for three years the owner ordered "cut it down" (vs. 7). The vinedresser offered a different solution: that he would fertilize it and care for it for one more year, after which time "if it bears fruit, well and good; but if not, you can cut it down" (vs. 9). The application here is that *over time* the liturgy should be formative of spirituality in terms of how one views life, how one's appreciation of liturgical prayer deepens and grows and how one's ethics in life reflect what one celebrates and experiences in liturgy. To the question "are our allegiances what they ought to be?" the most helpful response this side of the kingdom is "not fully," which response implicitly argues for the need for repeated liturgical engagement until the kingdom is fully realized.

In line with our argument in chapter 3 about the word as an act of transfiguration,[36] we would argue here that all acts of liturgy can be regarded as privileged moments of transfiguration in the sense that they are moments of experiencing the fullness of Christ as fully as is possible in this life. The point of ascending "God's holy mountain" for repeated experiences of the liturgy is in order for the Church to be more and more fully transformed into the transfigured, risen and ascended Christ.[37]

This paradigm is helpful in that it insists on the unique value of the transfiguration for the three apostles. In our view the initial experience of transfiguration is sacramental initiation, clearly a most unique and formative experience of God. However, as the early Church came to experience, initiation fervor is not uniformly sustained; hence the need for regular engagement in the Eucharist as the renewal of the covenant of baptism and for a liturgy of penance for serious post baptismal sins. Paradigmatic here is the fact that the apostles' fervor in experiencing the transfiguration (Mark 9:2-8 and par.) was not sustained. In fact, it is severely damaged (if not lost) almost immediately (Mark 9:33-37) when the disciples' preoccupation was their discussion of "who is the greatest?" (vs. 10). Hence the need for the Church to engage in the liturgy on a continual basis. The ascent to the mountain of transfiguration is because of our need; its consequence is returning to the rest of life to live what we have experienced in liturgy. The link between the two is the transformative experience of liturgy.

The use of this "transfiguration" paradigm helps in our appreciation of the intrinsic interrelationship among liturgy, ethics and eschatology in the sense that what is experienced provisionally in liturgy, God's rule and kingdom, leads to ethical consequences. The reality of injustice, oppression, imperfection, pain, and suffering, even in this graced world, needs addressing. An ethical consequence of the liturgy implies facing into these human needs and responding to them. At the same time eschatology is the operative category for liturgy and ethics in that liturgy offers sure hope in the midst of apparent defeat and all liturgical and ethical engagement necessarily cedes to the full reality of Christ who is final reconciler and healer. The ethical efforts of even the most perfect Christians are flawed and imperfect in the sense that they always need to point to the perfection of and in Christ. A spirituality derived from the liturgy is thus expressly eschatological in the sense that it offers hope derived from the liturgy, not "quick fix" solutions to life's deepest problems, especially lack of harmony and oppression among nations whose stock in trade is enmity, or in the face of terminal human suffering that knows no remedy except death itself.

Thus one of the real contributions of repeated liturgical engagement is to offer hope in the midst of life's sorrows and human imperfections. Liturgical spirituality is superficial if it seems to promise solutions to all of life's problems. It is equally superficial if its preoccupation is well-executed rituals. Liturgical spirituality is authentic if it draws believing communities more and more fully into the mystery of Christ as personally and communally experienced in liturgy, the very experience of which sustains hope in the midst of the fragility of human life.

IV. Convergence: Creation and Liturgical Theology and Ethics

As we have argued above, the very use of creation in liturgy shows reverence for creation through which and in which the incarnate God is disclosed and discovered. The very fact of using material creation has traditionally been understood to reflect back to the creator and to imply an understanding that rests on the sound foundation of theological anthropology.[38] Intrinsically connected to the use of creation in worship is how its very use transcends the problem of a spiritual/material dualism against nature and for the divine.[39] Our concern in this section is to capitalize on this usage as a truly "catholic" principle of liturgical theology and to indicate points of convergence for creation and liturgical theology and ethics.

One way of addressing the intrinsic relationship between creation and liturgical/sacramental theology is through liturgical participation as understood in two ways. First, liturgical *participation* is grounded in what God does for the believing Church drawing it into the very being of God through the liturgical experience of the paschal mystery. Here participation means the act of "taking part in"—of being drawn into and of sharing the very life of God through liturgy. Second, the believing Church assembled at liturgy ratifies this divine act by partaking in the ritual act of liturgy through (among other things) words, gestures, symbols, and the arts. Thus the divine and human elements in liturgy complement each other with the divine always taking precedence in terms of God's initiative in liturgy but which also requires human action that is proper to the human person. Hence the value of the community's engagement in liturgy through things which are anthropologically apt. The way this *participation* takes place is through the use of creation in worship. The theological predication of this participation is the incarnation and an incarnational approach to and appreciation of reality.

We have already noted that one useful example of an integral approach to liturgy and spirituality derived from the liturgy is the *Rule* of St. Benedict and as lived in the Benedictine tradition. The mendicant tradition of St. Francis of Assisi stands alongside the monastic as a helpful example of an integral view of the Christian life predicated on a wide notion of sacramentality and of incarnationalism. Pope John Paul II asserted as much when he said:

"In 1979, I proclaimed Saint Francis of Assisi as the heavenly
Patron of those who promote ecology (cf. Apostolic Letter *Inter
Sanctos:* AAS 71 (1979) 1509f). He offers an example of genuine
and deep respect for the integrity of creation. As a friend of the
poor who was loved by God's creatures, Saint Francis invited all
of creation—animal, plants, natural forces, even Brother Sun and
Sister Moon—to give honor and praise to the Lord. The poor man
of Assisi gives us striking witness that when we are at peace with
God we are better able to devote ourselves to building up that
peace with all creation which is inseparable from peace among all
peoples. It is my hope that the inspiration of St. Francis will help
us to keep ever alive a sense of 'fraternity' with all those good
and beautiful things which almighty God has created. And may
he remind us of our serious obligation to respect and watch over
them with care, in light of that greater and higher fraternity that
exists within the human family" (n. 16).[40]

The Franciscan tradition's prizing of conventual liturgy (both the
Eucharist and Hours) of preaching and of their particular kind of
communal life stands as another significant example how the principle of the sacramentality of human life functions in the Christian
life as well as how the sacramentality of creation functions in this
specific context.[41]

In our view the linking of theology and ethics (in the preceding
section) as experienced together in and as a result of the act of liturgy and the example of the Benedictine and Franciscan traditions
both reflects an appropriate theology of creation and grounds a
proper environmental, ecological ethic. The contribution of liturgical theology to the contemporary discussion of environmental theology and ethics is that these are well grounded in the liturgy and
that the consequences of liturgical engagement necessarily include
care for the environment.

This particular moment in history affords a unique opportunity
to articulate important strands of convergence between liturgical
studies and creation theology, the combination of which articulates
theological depth and argues for the preservation of creation for
the integrity and quality of liturgical and sacramental engagement.
The present reform of the liturgy builds on the Roman rite's use
of and reverence for symbol and symbolic engagement and maximizes such engagement because it is precisely through these

means that God is revealed and encountered. The rubrical directives in the reformed liturgy for greater use of elements from creation in worship,[42] either as they exist in nature or as they are manufactured from nature, are faithful to the tradition of the Roman rite. They also transcend the minimalist approach to symbolic interaction in liturgy and sacraments that resulted from the rubrical precision and fixity of the Roman rite after Trent. That the contemporary liturgy maximizes symbolic engagement makes the kind of theological statement that substantiates the contemporary concern for the environment because the very act of liturgy is imperiled when creation is threatened. The foundations upon which the very appropriate revival in Roman Catholic circles of a theology of symbol for liturgical and sacramental theology are similarly imperiled because of the diminished quality of the earth's resources. At the same time, however, the rootedness of Christian liturgy in creation needs to be articulated all the more today in order that liturgical and sacramental theology may be faithful to its anthropological roots and articulate a theology in harmony with the revised rites.

A creation focus for the theology of liturgy would ground the liturgical act as anthropologically apt (as we have already argued). A creation focus for the theology of liturgy and sacraments would ground the global relatedness and cosmic import of every act of worship, the paradigm for which (at least in the northern hemisphere) would be the annual spring feast of Easter when the location of the moon and the rebirth of the earth provides the requisite cosmic context for the sacred rites of being reincorporated annually in the deepest sense possible in Christ's paschal mystery.

A creation focus for liturgical theology could lead to appropriate emphasis on liturgy as an experience of God's "power and might" in continuing the salvific deeds of creation and redemption. Such an appreciation would lead to the response of liturgical participants to praise and thank God for all these good gifts. The awesomeness of creation and the ecstatic as a factor of the human person's response would be operative here. A creation focus for liturgical theology would ground and express the Trinitarian theology of worship by emphasizing how the Trinity was operative in creation and is operative in sustaining creation as an expression of God's nature and goodness.

A creation focus for liturgical theology would ground the appropriateness of symbolic integrity and the fullness of symbolic interaction in the celebration of liturgy because it is through creation and symbolic elements that God is discovered, revealed and encountered.[43] A creation focus for liturgical theology would offer the most appropriate category within which the value of aesthetics would be argued. Such an argument would emphasize how that which is aesthetically pleasing reflects the glory of God and how aesthetically-pleasing arts and artifacts are intrinsic to the experience of liturgy (and to engaging in liturgical theology). Just as the categories of the good, true and beautiful are being revived as crucial for contemporary ethics, the theology developed from the reformed liturgy necessarily includes them and gives them shape.

A creation focus for liturgical theology would necessarily imply and argue for the value of quality construction and the use of quality materials in Church construction. Just as some liturgical symbols are the result of human ingenuity and productivity, so the construction of church buildings and liturgical spaces articulates the creative spirit and human manufacture intrinsic to the liturgy. John Paul II addressed this point when he said:

"Finally, the aesthetic value of creation cannot be overlooked. Our very contact with nature has a deep restorative power; contemplation of its magnificence imparts peace and serenity. The Bible speaks again and again of the goodness and beauty of creation, which is called to glorify God (cf. Gen 1:4ff.; Ps 8:2; 104:1ff.; Wis 13:3-5; Sir 39:16, 33; 43:1, 9). More difficult perhaps, but no less profound, is the contemplation of the works of human ingenuity. Even cities can have a beauty all their own, one that ought to motivate people to care for their surroundings. Good urban planning is an important part of environmental protection, and respect for the natural contours of the land is an indispensable prerequisite for ecologically sound development. The relationship between a good aesthetic education and the maintenance of a healthy environment cannot be overlooked."[44]

A creation focus to liturgical theology could broaden categories of salvation which focus too intensely on an (individual or collective) experience of sin forgiveness to wider notions that include cosmic regeneration and renewal. In such a worldview the human person's need for salvation would be located in the fact that cos-

mic regeneration is still incomplete. The "groaning of creation" itself is the groaning of humanity for a deeper experience of
harmony, integration and of cosmic regeneration.

A creation focus for the theology of worship gives specificity to
the *lex vivendi* in that responding in life to what one celebrates
would necessarily include environmental concerns. The most apt
way of combining creation theology with creation ethics in Roman
Catholicism is precisely through the liturgy itself. Here sacramentality is presumed and creation is revered. An ethical response to
liturgy necessarily leads to an environmental ethic. Put somewhat
differently this is to assert that since the ecological crisis is often
linked to the concern for justice, the liturgy as the locus for meeting the Just One[45] becomes the logical and most traditional locus
for grounding the justice of environmental ethics. Another way
the liturgy offers the most useful avenue for environmental ethics
concerns the way it articulates a theology and practice allied with
the just distribution of the world's resources. The evolution and
theological meaning of the rites surrounding the presentation of
the gifts in the Roman rite are both complex and theologically
rich.[46] Whatever can be said of them historically and in the present reform, it is clear that intrinsic to these rites is a collection of
goods for the poor. The texts from Hippolytus' *Apostolic Tradition*
for the "offerings of the faithful" (specifically oil, cheese and
olives and other offerings) reflect both a "theology of earthly
realities"[47] and a theology linking liturgy with social justice.[48]
Edward Kilmartin observes that our understanding of the Eucharist should include "the relationship between the service of
God in the liturgy and the service of humankind in the world."

"The collections at the Eucharist should be interpreted as a symbolic expression of this consecration to God. The use made of
these collections should not be self-serving but should correspond
to the wider horizon of the Christian community's social obliga-
tions. It should be taken for granted that the normal recipients are
God's poor. In this way the community is enabled consciously to
actualize the relation between worship and social justice."[49]

In fact the present General Instruction on the Roman Missal specifies that the rite of the "preparation of the gifts" is "also the time
to receive money or other gifts for the church or the poor brought

by the faithful or collected at the Mass" (GIRM n. 49) and that at the Evening Mass of the Lord's Supper on Holy Thursday "at the beginning of the Eucharist, there may be a procession of the faithful with gifts for the poor."[50]

In our view the association of this collection with presenting bread and wine is theologically rich and ethically poignant. At the very moment when the goods of this earth are brought forth for consecration and Communion, the Church also brings forth the earth's produce for the poor. That the connection between these two facets of this rite is food is most significant in that food thus grounds a liturgically inspired creation theology and ethic. The theological statement being made here is that we draw near to God in the Eucharist through our sharing in the goods of this earth, which sharing implies demonstrable sharing in the more equitable distribution of the world's goods and resources. This is to assert that at the very moment when we take bread and wine and through them represent creation back to God we simultaneously commit ourselves to sharing creation with all God's creatures. Liturgy once again becomes the obvious key to link a truly catholic (as well as Roman Catholic) theology of creation and ethic of the environment. In our understanding, therefore, there is at present a timely and significant convergence between creation theology and ethics through articulating a theology of liturgy. That this convergence is particularly noted in the Benedectine and Franciscan traditions within Roman Catholicism is pertinent in our understanding because of the role of creation and liturgy in each of these lived religious traditions. Once again, in the doing of the liturgy the Church articulates what it believes and the consequences those beliefs have for ethical living. Thus to articulate a liturgical spirituality means to articulate the role of creation in liturgy and the ethical consequences of the liturgy for both creation theology and creation ethics. For this reason the liturgy, to our way of thinking, offers the most traditional foundation for an environmental ethic. Regrettably this foundation has often been ignored, although presumed both liturgically and theologically.[51]

V. Critique of and by the Liturgy

In this section the customary application of the critical liturgiology is divided into two, namely some critical observations about what is not included or emphasized in the present *lex orandi* in light of the argument of this chapter and then some of the direct ways that participation in liturgy can critique other forms of prayer and spirituality.

Especially in light of the previous section's assertions about convergence between creation and liturgical theology it is appropriate to recall here the critique offered about liturgical euchology in general (above in chapter 4[52]) concerning the lack of attention given to praise for creation in the present prefaces and Eucharistic prayers in the Roman rite. Regrettably this classic location for praising God for creation is all but eclipsed (except for the briefest references in Eucharistic prayer four) in favor of moving directly to praise for Christ and the paschal mystery. A contribution which contemporary theologies of creation can make to Eucharistic euchology is to emphasize the Christological and Trinitarian axis of creation (and thus of creation theology)—lest it be doomed to a theology which acclaims a "generic" God or to the heresy of pantheism. The specific Christological and pneumatological mediating functions in creation and in sustaining creation in being can easily and legitimately be included into Eucharistic anaphoras. The Christological link to creation is clear in the evidence from classical anaphoras which move from creation to redemption. The inclusion of an explicitly pneumatological cast to praise for creation at the epiclesis might well be one avenue to explore, especially in light of the revived interest in this part of the Eucharistic prayer and the fact that part of its function in the present Roman anaphoras is for the transformation of bread and wine.

Another location for more explicit acknowledgment of the glory of creation and offering praise and thanks for creation would be in the prayers over the gifts immediately preceding the preface dialogue. Precisely because these prayers have often been criticized as too "proleptic" in praying for what only the transformed gifts can bring us, this might be a most appropriate location for more in depth acknowledgment of creation as grace filled and grace bearing.

A second critique concerns the present theology of some presidential prayers in the Eucharist, specifically the prayers after Communion. The General Instruction on the Roman Missal states that "in the prayer after communion, the priest petitions for the effects of the mystery just celebrated. . . ." (56, k). Sometimes these prayers speak directly to what we have termed spirituality derived from the liturgy by speaking of connecting the celebration of the Eucharist with daily living. One particularly apt example is from Thursday of the Second Week of Easter. The present translation reads:

"Almighty and ever-living Lord,
you restored us to life
by raising Christ from death.
Strengthen us by this Easter sacrament;
may we feel its saving power in our daily lives."

The Latin is taken from the old Gelasian Sacramentary and some newly composed phrases. In light of the stated acknowledgment of the Lord's restoring us to eternal life (the Latin is *aeternam vitam*) by Christ's resurrection (*in Christi resurrectione nos reparas*) we confidently and humbly ask that the fruits of this Easter sacrament (*fructum in nobis paschalis multiplica sacramenti*) may strengthen us against our weakness and the forces of evil in the world. This succinct text draws on an image used in the opening prayer for the same day, that the Eucharist may be fruitful in our lives (*fructiferum nobis omni tempore sentiamus*). It clearly ends by asking that by this sacrament, God would enable us to experience its saving power in all of life.

Other prayers after Communion speak helpfully about the eschatological dimension of the Eucharist. Not surprisingly, because it coheres with the theology of the season, one example is from the first Sunday of Advent. The translation presently adopted by the ICEL subcommittee revising of these translations reads:

"Lord our God,
grant that we who journey through this passing world
may learn from the sacrament we have celebrated
to cherish the things of heaven
and to cling to the treasures that never pass away."[53]

The accompanying explanatory note from ICEL states that the translated phrase "the sacrament we have just celebrated" (*frequentata mysteria*) refers to the entire celebration, not just Communion. The rendering "to cherish the things of heaven/and to cling to the treasures that never pass away" is certainly an improvement over the 1973 ICEL version: "teach us to love heaven . . . [and] guide our way on earth." Overall the prayer may be judged a helpful expression of the connection between the Eucharist and the eschatological banquet in the kingdom of heaven.

Less successful, however, are some prayers after Communion which betray what might be called a "tinged" eschatology in the sense that they reflect near disdain for the things of this world, including creation. One example is from the prayer after Communion for Tuesday of the First Week of Lent whose present translation reads:

"Lord,
may we who receive this sacrament
restrain our earthly desires
and grow in love for the things of heaven."

The Latin phrase *terrena desideria mitigantes* might also be rendered "to control our longing for the things of this world"; its complement, *discamus amare caelestia,* might be rendered "and teach us to love the things of heaven." The difficulty here is how those things that are "earthly" or "of this world" are to be regarded in the sense that in an incarnational perspective this good earth has been redeemed and is the locus where we work out our salvation. That even this good earth is not to be preferred to "a new heavens and a new earth" is clear; however, that it might be disdained in the meantime is an unfortunate sentiment for prayer, one that is theologically questionable, if not theologically unjustified.

The point here is that the petitions constitutive of the prayers after Communion in the present revised liturgy offer a helpful locus for underscoring how liturgy relates to spirituality, in particular to life lived outside the liturgy. These are poorly used when they do not claim the intrinsic value of creation and the world. This is all the more regrettable when the critical eye cast on such texts views them through the lens of the paschal mystery just celebrated in the Eucharist (*context*). The eschatological hope of the final integration and regeneration of creation is experienced through the liturgy, however provisionally. This same hope should critique prayers that are unnecessarily pejorative of the world.

The other side of the coin regarding liturgical spirituality expresses what the traditional and present reformed liturgy offers to critique forms of prayer and devotion that are not in harmony with the liturgy. The theological premise for this section is our argument favoring liturgy as the most apt expression of prayer and as the most apt source for developing one's spirituality. The close association of the anthropological and the theological is seen in the first example concerning the community of the Church— both a human need and a divine reality.

That the liturgy is an ecclesial event is paramount for appreciating liturgy itself; it is equally paramount in establishing the principle that all prayer should move believers beyond self-absorption and self-concern. One application of this principle regarding participating in the liturgy itself changes the question about whether to engage in liturgy from "what do I get out of the liturgy?" to "how does my participation help to constitute the Church and usher in the kingdom." If in fact the liturgical community is the *ecclesia*, the community called into being by God ("the people you have gathered here before you") then the members of this community can be expected to have demands made upon them to participate in liturgy as constitutive of Church belonging. Ultimately a chief lesson of liturgical praying is communal and personal self-transcendence.

By its nature all Christian identification is communal in the sense that we are initiated into a community and our relatedness to God is through identification with that community. This is nowhere seen more clearly than in the liturgy. The critique which this offers to other forms of prayer and devotion is that these ought not to be concerned with oneself or individuals only. This is not to argue that all forms of prayer are to be done in common by groups. Rather it is to argue that all prayer and devotion ought lead us to being other-concerned in terms of the experience of liturgical prayer itself, in terms of interceding for others in both liturgical prayer and personal prayer, and that personal prayer and devotions make us the more committed to both the Church community and to the wider world.

That the liturgy always orients participants to leading a deeper spiritual life, a life lived in conformity with the liturgy, requires that liturgical enactment and ritual performance (again, to use an unfortunate term because of extrinsic connotations, but in this case this usage is thus more understandable) be looked to not just for its own sake as a pleasing aesthetic experience but because of what it both discloses and demands about leading one's life. The necessary complement to well executed liturgical rituals is life lived in greater conformity with Christ and in harmony with his gospel and paschal mystery.

The fundamental connection between eschatology and justice (argued in section three) can be appropriately expanded to include other forms of discipleship as intrinsically related to what the liturgy celebrates. The critique which this offers to movements stressing the urgency of certain needs (that are indeed quite legitimate) is that they find their grounding in the anthropology and theology of the liturgy. Specifically, this is to ground "justice and peace" concerns so that they are viewed as expressions of experiencing the Just One and the Prince of Peace through the liturgy. Such a grounding also helps prevent these (or similar) concerns from becoming trivialized or marginalized as passing, contemporary concerns rather than that which is experienced in and springs from the heart of the Church.

Allied with this critique is the assertion that the liturgy is always hopeful in the sense that it offers support and strength to believers here and now for the journey of leading the Christian life on earth until we are called from this life to see God face to face. This means that spirituality derived from the liturgy must always be similarly hope-filled and optimistic. To suggest this is to assert that the Christian life is ultimately hopeful itself and that Christians need to be optimistic in the sense that whatever evil has been produced and unleashed on the earth by sinning is not more powerful than the Lord of the universe, and that the world's final restoration is the divine will and an act to which we conform ourselves. Existentially this is to assert that whatever one says about the world, it is ultimately the place where our salvation will be worked out. Theologically this is to assert that whatever may be said about grace and participating in the divine life, our experience of these realities will occur here and now on this good earth. That the liturgy is the matrix of the anthropological and the theological has been part of our argument throughout this chapter. It is appropriate to conclude this treatment by asserting that in a similar fashion by asserting that a liturgical spirituality properly so called derives from this same matrix, especially given its incarnational nature and eschatological exigencies.

We asserted at the beginning of this chapter that *lex orandi* and *lex credendi* are meant to yield a new thing—*lex vivendi*. The ultimate aim of this *lex vivendi* is living the Christian life in conformity with Christian revelation, both as revealed by God and as that revelation makes demands upon us. Throughout our argument, the essential interrelationship between liturgy and life has been our focus because liturgy derives from the ordinary and returns us to the ordinary, graced in an extraordinary way in Christ. A chief characteristic of the spiritual life to our way of thinking is its *integration* of all facets of life in Christ. The liturgy is the axis and chief means to accomplish this. This includes both the enactment of the liturgy and leading a life in conformity with the liturgy. The ultimate goal will be reached when this integration is so harmonious as to be termed *congruent*.

To our way of thinking, any real evaluation of how effective the liturgy has been or is can only be done *over time*. In the *meantime* the liturgy is the chief source for experiencing God in ways that are most apt both because of the anthropological substratum of the act of liturgy itself and for the conduct of one's spiritual life. At the same time (as we have argued) by its nature the liturgy is also provisional. It necessarily looks to the day when there will only be the praise of the heavenly liturgy. In the words of St. Augustine:

"then we shall be free to contemplate
then we will contemplate and we will love,
we will love and chant canticles of praise.
We will be attentive to these at the end
at the feast which has no end" (*De civitate Dei*, 32, 30).[54]

Until that time the liturgy as well as *lex orandi, lex credendi* and *lex vivendi* are all of a piece and (should) make all the difference in terms of our relationship to God and to one another.

In accord with the dialectical thesis of this book, two things matter. That the *text* of the liturgy be interpreted in relation to the *context* of our communal and personal lives and that the *context* of all of life be lived in harmony with the *text* of enacted liturgy so that liturgy and life can be intrinsically and keenly related. It is the Christian's prayer that they might eventually become congruent.

Notes

1. The Hours is an obvious inclusion for religious and hopefully for the whole Christian people as the celebration of the Hours becomes more common in parishes and other ecclesial settings.

2. These distinctions build upon those established in my own book, *Liturgy, Prayer and Spirituality* (New York/Mahwah: Paulist Press, 1984) 7–22; also see my essay on "Liturgy," in the *New Dictionary of Catholic Spirituality*, ed. Michael J. Downey (Collegeville, Minn.: The Liturgical Press, 1993). For other ways of evaluating this relationship see, among others, Don E. Saliers, *Worship and Spirituality* (Philadelphia: Westminster, 1984) and Shawn Madigan, *Spirituality Rooted in Liturgy* (Washington: Pastoral Press, 1988).

3. A useful treatment of classical prayer and spiritual traditions and contemporary expressions of both is by Robin Maas and Gabriel O'Donnell, eds., *Spiritual Traditions for the Contemporary Church* (Nashville: Abingdon, 1990).

4. To use Michael Himes' description from "This Graced World. Trinity, Grace and the Sacraments," *Church* 1 (Spring 1985) 3–12. I am indebted to him for a most helpful conversation expanding on this article, which insights are reflected in this chapter.

5. Canon 834 of the 1983 *Code of Canon Law* states:
"1. The Church fulfills its office of sanctifying in a special way through the liturgy, which is indeed the exercise of the priestly office of Jesus Christ; in it through sensible signs the sanctification of humankind is signified and effected in a manner proper to each of the signs and the whole of the public worship of God is carried out by the Mystical Body of Jesus Christ, that is, by the Head and the members.
"2. This worship takes place when it is carried out in the name of the Church by persons lawfully deputed and through acts approved by the authority of the Church."
This is of particular interest because para. 1 is slightly modified from n. 7 of The Liturgy Constitution and para. 2 is from canon 1256 of the 1917 Code. Also see, Matias Augé, "Preghiera Liturgica e non Liturgica. Alcune riflessioni su un dibattito ancora in atto," *Traditio et Progressio*, Studi Liturgici in onore del Adrien Nocent, ed. Giustino Farnedi. Studia Anselmiana 95. Analecta Liturgica 12. (Roma: Editrice Anselmiana, 1988) 35–44.

6. See, for example, Raymond Didier, *Les sacrements de la foi. La Paque dans ses signes.* (Paris: Editions du Centurion, 1975) 7–17, on the need to articulate "why" sacraments are important. His approach is both anthropological and ecclesiological.

7. One example of how the anthropological fittingness of sacraments can ground a treatise on sacraments in general is in Carlo Rochetta, *Sacramentaria Fondamentale*. Dal "mysterium" al "sacramentum." (Bologna: Edizioni Dehoniane, 1989) esp. 11–91.

8. From a different, but nonetheless complementary perspective, see Armando Cuva, "Linee di Antropologica Liturgica," *Salesianium* 36 (1974) 3–31.

9. For example, see above, chapter 4, 133–135.

10. Two of the more helpful systematic treatments of the Spirit and the Trinity that have influenced my thought are Heribert Mühlen, *Una Mystica Persona. Die Kirche als das Mysterium der Identitat des Heiligen Geistes in Christus und den Christen: Eine Person in vielen Personen* (Munich: F. Schöningh, 1967) and William Hill, *The Three Personed God. The Trinity As A Mystery of Salvation* (Washington: Catholic University, 1982). In addition, the following helpful reflections on the Trinity in liturgy that have influenced our thought are Edward Kilmartin, *Christian Liturgy*, Jean Corbon, *The Wellspring of Worship*, trans., M. J. O'Connell (N.Y./Mahwah: Paulist Press, 1988, from the 1980 French original) and Constantin Andronikoff, *Le sens de la liturgie. La relation entre Dieu et l'homme* (Paris: Les Editions du Cerf, 1988).

11. See the trenchant critique and argument along these lines by Edward Kilmartin in *Christian Liturgy* as well as in "A Modern Approach to the Word of God and Sacraments of Christ: Perspectives and Principles," 59–109.

12. "A Modern Approach to the Word of God," 87.

13. See above, Chapter 5, fn. 41.

14. Recall the discussion of initiation euchology above, chapter 4, 147–151.

15. Recall the discussion of the fittingness of the use of bread and wine above, chapter 4, 157–160.

16. This draws on the traditional argument about liturgy and sacraments from Tertullian, *caro salutis est cardo* in *De Carnis Resurrectione* 9, see, Cipriano Vagaggini, *Caro Salutis Est Cardo—Corporetá. Eucaristia e Liturgia* (Rome: Desclée, 1966).

17. Recall the discussion above, chapter 3, 111–116 about the proclamation of the Word as being an act of creation, of transfiguration and of the kingdom.

18. This is not to ignore the fact that at times in history the liturgy was in need of correction because of defective theology, not to say heterodoxy. Nor is it to ignore the fact that (as already noted) the Roman Missal after Trent was regarded as having been in need of "correction." The assertion of having confidence in liturgical euchology is intended to respect the process and results which euchology has undergone to be sanctioned for liturgical use.

19. See above, chapter 1, 6–15, where in our historical overview we argued that the essentially symbolic nature of liturgical engagement has been evident in the theological descriptions of what the liturgy accomplishes from the patristic era through at least high scholasticism. Even as it was recast in Peter Lombard's description—that sacraments *cause* grace by signifying—the modifying *significando* remained closely attached to the action of causing. From then on it remained, and remains, a hallmark of (Roman Catholic) sacramental teaching. Part of the creativity, not to say excitement, in contemporary sacramental theology is the restoration of this maxim to a position of promi-

nence which has led contemporary theologians to emphasize systematic reflection on the symbols (including persons, word, elements, texts etc.) and symbolic interaction intrinsic to the liturgy.

20. A review of magisterial teaching about the Eucharist discloses how careful the Church has been to safeguard the symbolic nature and causality of this sacrament, even at times when crassly realistic or overly physicalist explanations of the Eucharist abounded in popular catechesis and literature. See, among others, Andre Duval, *Des sacrements au concile de Trente*, "Le sacrifice de la messe," 61–150, Alexander Gerken, *Teologia dell'eucaristia*, Burkhard Neunheuser, *L'Eucharistie. II. Au Moyen age et à l'époque moderne*, trans., A. Liefooghe (Paris: Les Editions du Cerf, 1966, German original 1963) and David N. Power, "Eucharist," 277–280.

21. Robert Taft, "Toward A Theology of the Christian Feast," in *Beyond East and West. Problems in Liturgical Understanding* (Washington: Pastoral Press, 1984) 7.

22. See, Marianne Micks, *The Future Present. The Phenomenon of Worship* (New York: Seabury, 1970). The book's two sections are appropriately divided into "summoning the future" and "shaping the present."

23. To borrow Patrick Regan's term, quoted in Taft, "Toward a Theology of the Christian Feast," 3.

24. DOL 13.

25. This is to utilize the rather common distinction often made between liturgical "reform" and "renewal." The former concerns changing forms and can be achieved by *fiat*. The latter concerns the renewal of spirit which is a chief aim of liturgical engagement. Renewal is the far more difficult process to engage in and to assess, but it is the process which liturgical reform is meant to serve.

26. See above, chapter 3, 86–90.

27. A contemporary application of *lectio divina* as an appropriate lenten practice is in Kevin W. Irwin, "The Good News of Repentance and Conversion," in *Repentance and Reconciliation in the Church* (Collegeville: The Liturgical Press, 1987) 44–52. Also see Andre Boland, "Lectio Divina et lecture spirituelle," *DTC* IX: 470–510.

28. See, chapter 3, 116–119.

29. Translation from Timothy Fry, et. al., *RB 80. The Rule of Saint Benedict* (Collegeville: The Liturgical Press, 1981) 229. Rembert Weakland's use of this same term is notable in his "Introduction" to Michael Skelley's, *The Liturgy of the World. Karl Rahner's Theology of Worship* (Collegeville: The Liturgical Press, A Pueblo book, 1991) 9.

30. Taken from the commentary on the *Rule* entitled "The Abbot," in *RB 80*, 370.

31. "A Sacramental Church in the Modern World," *Origins* 14 (June 21, 1984) 85.

32. Ibid., 85–86.

33. Alexander Schmemann, *Sacraments and Orthodoxy* (New York: Herder and Herder, 1963) 15–16. The title of the British edition of this work on sacraments from the Orthodox perspective is the more apt *For The Life of the World*.

34. See, Bernard J. Lonergan, *Method in Theology* (London: Darton, Longman and Todd, 1972) 127–132, where he lists "experience" as the first functional specialty of theology and uses the exhortation "be attentive" to illustrate it.

35. Recall, for example, M. Augé, "Pro sancta Ecclesia."

36. See, chapter 3, 114–115.

37. For some helpful resonances of our relating liturgy and spirituality see, Robert P. Imbelli and Thomas H. Groome, "Signposts Towards a Pastoral Theology," *Theological Studies* 53 (March 1992) 127–137.

38. One generally helpful summary of Karl Rahner's thought in this regard in the (second half of) Michael Skelley, *The Liturgy of the World* 85–158.

39. See, "Ecumenical Forum," "Creation and Culture: an Ecumenical Challenge" *The Ecumenical Review* 37 (Oct., 1985) 509–510 quoting the Orthodox theologian Emilie Dierking Lisenko who "pointed to the spiritual/material dualism, and to a certain arrogance against nature. In the Eastern Christian vision God did not create the world for the sake of human welfare *per se* and thus for exploitation, but as an element for human communication with God, the human person being a priest for eucharistic celebration of the world. Liturgy comprehends the whole of creation and shows definitely a communal orientation. The fall expresses human love for the world as an end in itself, separating it from God and thus from its very source of life. Nature is not evil, salvation is for all of creation." "Everything exists because God existed first. Therefore, grace is prior to creation. The world has only a relative independence, and is—in its goodness—God's self-expression. Nothing in creation is essentially unclean. Sin is a secondary concept, and redemption means restoration. Some idea of a continuous creation is necessary. Nature must be seen as a single coherent event."

40. John Paul II, "Peace With All Creation: World Day of Peace [Jan. 1, 1990]," *Origins* 19 (Dec. 14, 1989) n. 16.

41. Some indications of the similarities and differences between the Benedictine and Franciscan traditions as they bear on showing reverence for creation are found in René Dubois, "Franciscan Conservation verses Benedictine Stewardship," In David and Eileen Spring, eds., *Ecology and Religion in History* (New York: Harper and Row, 1975) 114–136.

42. For example, *General Instruction of the Roman Missal* nn. 281–285 about bread and wine for the Eucharist.

43. One of the premises of *Environment and Art in Catholic Worship* is this kind of authenticity in sign and symbolic interaction in liturgy; see nn. 12–26 for some theoretical grounding for the document.

44. "Peace With All of Creation," n. 14.

45. This recalls the classical Advent refrain "let the clouds rain down the Just One" from Isa 45:8, presently used at the entrance antiphon on the Fourth Sunday of Advent.

46. See above, chapter 4, 163–166.

47. See, commentary in Lucien Deiss, *Springtime of the Liturgy*, trans., Matthew O'Connell (Collegeville: The Liturgical Press, 1979) 132–133.

48. See the very helpful essay by Edward J. Kilmartin, "The Sacrifice of Thanksgiving and Social Justice," in Mark Searle, ed., *Liturgy and Social Justice* (Collegeville: The Liturgical Press, 1980) esp. 70–71.

49. Ibid.

50. *Sacramentary for Mass*, 137.

51. One can only muse about whether "pantheism" for theology in general and/or "companation" in Eucharistic theology in particular are at the root of ignoring the role of creation in articulating a theology of liturgy.

52. See above, chapter 5, 203–204.

53. *Second Progress Report on the Roman Missal* (Washington: ICEL, 1990) 19.

54. Quoted in A. Verheul, "La Liturgie comme louange à Dieu," *Questions Liturgiques* 64 (1963) 44.

Bibliography

Agourides, B. "The Bible in the Orthodox Church: The biblical substance and vision of Orthodox worship and spirituality," *Scripture Bulletin* 10 (Summer 1979) 11–16.

Alberigo, Giuseppe. "Dalla uniformità liturgica del concilio di Trento al pluralismo del Vaticano II," *Rivista Liturgica* 69 (1982) 604–619.

Albertine, Richard. "The Problem of the (double) Epiclesis in the Roman Eucharistic Prayers," *Ephemerides Liturgicae* 91 (1977) 193–202.

Aldazábal, Jose. "El libro liturgico como pédagogía de la celebracíon," *Phase* n. 116 (1980) 111–124.

Alessio, Luis. "La liturgia y la fe," *Notitiae* 15 (1979) 578–583.

Alsteens, André. "Liturgie, théologie et sens de l'aujourd'hui," *Paroisse et Liturgie* 50 (1968) 387–400.

Amaldoss, M. *Do Sacraments Change? Variable and Invariable Elements in Sacramental Rites.* Bangalore, India: Thelogical Publications In India, 1979.

Amalorpavadass, D.S. "Theological Reflections on Inculturation," *Studia Liturgica* 20 (1990) 36–54, 116–136.

Anamnesis 1, La Liturgia, Momento nella storia della salvezza, eds. B. Neunheuser, S. Marsili, M. Augé and R. Civil. Casale Monferrato: Marietti, 1974.

Anamnesis 2. La Liturgia. Panorama storico generale, eds. S. Marsili et. al. Casale Monferrato: Marietti, 1978.

Anamnesis 3/2. Eucarista. Teologia e storia della celebrazione, eds. S. Marsili, A. Nocent, M. Augé, A. J. Chupungco. Casale Monferrato Marietta, 1983.

Andronikoff, Constantin. *Le sens de la liturgie.* La relation entre Dieu et l'homme. Paris: Les Editions du Cerf, 1988.

"Archbishop of Canterbury on Vatican Response [to ARCIC I Final Report]," *Origins* 21 (Dec. 19, 1991) 447.

Aubert, Roger "Liturgie et Magistère ordinaire," *Questions Liturgiques* 33 (1952) 5–16.

Augé, Matias. *Liturgia. Storia, Celebrazione, Teologia, Spiritualità.* Milano/Torino: Edizioni Paoline, 1992.

Augé, Matias. " 'Pro sancta Ecclesia': una espressioni della 'lex orandi' in sintonia con la 'lex credendi' a la 'lex vivendi,' " *Notitiae* 26 (1990) 566–584.

Austin, Gerard, ed. *Fountain of Life.* Washington: Pastoral Press, 1991.

Baptism, Eucharist and Ministry. Faith and Order Paper No. 111. Geneva: World Council of Churches, 1982.

Bargellini, E. and G. Remoni. "Letture e Formule Euchogiche nel Nuovo Messale Romano," *Vita Monastica* 43 (1989) 9–23.

Barsotti, Divo. *Liturgia e Teologia.* Milan, 1956.

Barsotti, Divo. *Il Mistero cristiano e la Parola di Dio.* Firenze: Editrice Fiorentina, 1954.

Baumer, Iso. "Interaktion—Zeichen—Symbol. Ansätze zu einer Deutung liturgischen und volkfrommen Tuns," *Liturgisches Jahrbuch* 31 (1981) 9–35.

Baumstark, Anton. *Comparative Liturgy,* ed. F. L. Cross. Westminster, Md.: Newman Press, 1958.

Beauduin, Lambert. "Eassai del manuel fondamental de liturgie (I and II)," *Questions Liturgiques* 3 (1913) 143–148, 271–280.

Beauduin, Lambert. *La piété de l'Eglise.* Louvain: Mont-César, 1914.

Bebis, George S. "Worship in the Orthodox Church," *Greek Orthodox Theological Review* 22 (1977) 429–443.

Beguerie, Philippe. "La Bible née de la liturgie," *La Maison Dieu* n. 126 (1976) 108–116.

Békés, Gerard J. "Parola e Sacramento. Il rapporto tra due fattori nella partecipazione alla salvezza," *Ecclesia Orans* 8/3 (1991) 261–276.

Berger, Teresa. " 'Doxology'—'Jubilate'—'Liturgical Theology' Zum Verhältnis von Liturgie und Theologie: Publikationem aus dem englischsprachingen Raum," *Archif für Liturgiewissenschaft* 28 (1986) 247–255.

Berger, Teresa. "Lex orandi—lex credendi—lex agendi. Auf dem Weg zu einer okumenisch konesensfähigen, Verhältnisbestimmung von Liturgie, Theologie und Ethik," *Archif für Liturgiewissenschaft* 27 (1985) 425–432.

Berger, Teresa. "Liturgy and Theology—An Ongoing Dialogue," *Studia Liturgica* 19 (1989) 14–16.

Berger, Teresa. "Liturgy—a Forgotten Subject Matter of Theology?" *Studia Liturgica* 17 (1987) 10–18.

Berger, Teresa. "Unity in and Through Doxology? Reflections on Worship Studies in the World Council of Churches," *Studia Liturgica* 16 (1986/87) 1–12.

Bernal, José Manuel. "Liturgia y ortodoxia. Apuntes historicos," *Phase* n. 17 (1977) 53–63.

Bernard, Charles André. *Théologie symbolique*. Paris: Téqui, 1980.

La Bibbia nella Liturgia. Rome: Marietti, 1987.

Boehringer, Hans. "A Response to the Keynote [by Mary Collins]," *Worship* 49 (February 1975) 103–106.

Boland, Andre. "Lectio Divina et lecture spirituelle," *Dictionnaire de Théologie catholique* IX: 470–510.

Bonaccorso, Giorgio. *Introduzione allo studio della Liturgia* "Caro Salutis Cardo" Sussidi, I. Padova: Edizioni Messagero, 1990.

Bornet, Roger. "Pour une interprétation comparative de la réforme liturgique," *Questions Liturgiques* 67 (1986) 1–32.

Bossy, John. *Christianity in the West 1400–1700*. New York: Oxford University Press, 1985.

Bossy, John. "The Mass as Social Institution, 1200–1700," *Past and Present* 100 (1983) 29–61.

Bouley, Allan. *From Freedom to Formula*. The Evolution of the Eucharistic Prayer from Oral Improvisation to Written Texts. Studies in Christian Antiquity, n. 21. Washington: Catholic University of America Press, 1981.

Bouyer, Louis. *Eucharist*. Theology and Spirituality of the Eucharistic Prayer, trans. Charles Underhill Quinn. Notre Dame, Ind.: University of Notre Dame Press, 1968.

Bouyer, Louis. *Liturgical Piety*. Notre Dame, Ind.: University of Notre Dame Press, 1955.

Boyer, Mark G. *The Liturgical Environment*. What The Documents Say. Collegeville: The Liturgical Press, 1990.

Bradshaw, Paul. *Daily Prayer in the Early Church*. New York: Oxford University Press, 1982.

Braga, Carlo. "Il valore ecclesiale della norma liturgica," *Ambrosius* 65 (1989) 356–373.

Bright, John. *A History of Israel.* Philadelphia: Westminster, 1959.

Brilioth, Yngve. *Eucharistic Faith and Practice, Evangelical and Catholic,* trans. A. G. Hebert. London: SPCK, 1930, reprinted 1965.

Brinkmann, B. R. "On Sacramental Man," *The Heythrop Journal* 13 (October, 1972) 371-401; 14 (January, 1973) 5-34; 14 (April, 1973) 162-189; 14 (July, 1973) 280-306; 14 (October, 1973) 396-416.

Brinkman, Matrien E. "A Creation Theology for Canberra?" *The Ecumenical Review* 42 (April 1990) 150-156.

"British Bishops: The Convergence and Agreement Achieved," *Origins* 21 (Dec. 19, 1991) 448.

Britt, Matthew. *The Hymns of the Breviary and Missal.* New York: Benziger Brothers, 1922.

Brock, Sebastian P., "The Consecration of the Water in the Oldest Manuscripts of the Syrian Orthodox Baptismal Liturgy," *Orientalia Christiana Periodica* 37 (1971) 317-332.

Brovelli, Franco, "Movimento liturgico e spiritualità cristiana," *Rivista Liturgica* 73 (1986) 469-490.

Brovelli, Franco, "Per uno studio della liturgia," *Scuola Cattolica* 104 (1976) 567-635.

Brovelli, Franco, "Rassegna bibliografica: spunti di metodo e di interpretazione," *Ritorno alla Liturgia. Saggi di Studio sul Movimento Liturgico,* ed. F. Brovelli. Rome: Edizioni Liturgiche, 1989, 19-45.

Brovelli, Franco, "Storia della movimento liturgico nel nostro seculo: dati, attese e linee di approfondimento," *Ephemerides Liturgicae* 53 (1985) 217-238.

Brunner, Peter, "Theologie Göttesdienstes," *Bemühngen um die einigende Wahrheit.* Gottingen: Vandenhoeck und Ruprecht, 1977, 163-188.

Brunner, Peter. *Worship in the Name of Jesus,* trans. M. H. Bertram. St. Louis: Concordia, 1968.

Bruylants, Pierre. *Les oraisons du Missel Romain, Texte et Histoire.* Vol. I and II. Louvain: Mont Cesar, 1952.

Bugnini, Annibale. *The Reform of the Liturgy, 1948-1975,* trans. Matthew J. O'Connell. Collegeville: The Liturgical Press, 1990.

Burckhardt, Jacob. *The Altarpiece in Renaissance Italy,* trans. and ed. Peter Humfrey. Cambridge/N.Y.: Cambridge University Press, 1988.

Burghardt, Walter J., "A Theologian's Challenge to Liturgy," *Theological Studies* 35 (1974) 233–48.

Bustacchini, Gianfranco. *Ravenna. Capitale del Mosaico.* Ravenna: Cartolibreria Salbaroli, 1988.

Butler, J. F. "Presuppositions in Modern Theologies of the Place of Worship," *Studia Liturgia* 3 (1965) 210–226.

Bynum, Caroline Walker. *Docere Verbo et Exemplo.* An Aspect of Twelfth Century Spirituality. Harvard Theological Studies n. 31. Missoula/Ann Arbor: Scholars Press, 1979.

Calati, Benedetto. "Teologia ascetico-mistica e liturgia," *Rivista Liturgica* n. 57 (1971) 219–237.

Callewaert, R. S. "Pour situer le renuoveau liturgie dans sa contexte: l'apport de la théologie, de la philosophie et des sciences humaines," *Paroisse et Liturgie* 50 (1968) 135–146.

Cambridge History of the Bible. Volumes I and II. Cambridge: Cambridge University Press, 1970.

Camps, J. "La palabra de Dios es celebrada," *Phase* n. 10 (1970) 141–157.

Capelle, Bernard. "Autorité de la liturgie chez les Pères," *Recherches de théologie ancienne et médiévale* 21 (1954) 5–22.

Capelle, Bernard. "La liturgie, soutien de la foi," *Questions Liturgiques* 32 (1951) 100–111.

Capelle, Bernard. "Mission doctrinal et spirituelle de la Liturgie," *Questions Liturgiques* 29 (1948) 165–177.

Capelle, Bernard. *Travaux liturgiques de doctrine et d'histoire.* Louvain, 1955–67.

Cappuyns, M. "Liturgie et Théologie," *Questions Liturgiques* 19 (1934) 249–272.

Cappuyns, M. "L'origine des Capitula pseudo—célestiniens contre le semi-pélagianisme," *Revue Bénédictine* 41 (1929) 156–170.

Caprioli, A. "Linee di recerca per uno statuto teologico della liturgia," *Communio* 41 (1978) 35–44.

Cardinali, B. "La nuova edizione di *L'Eglise en prière*," *Rivista Liturgica* n. 73 (1986) 704–712.

Carideo, A. "Parola e celebrazione: catechesi all interno della celebrazione," *Rivista Liturgica* 59 (1972) 490–496.

Carideo, A. "Urgenza di una rinnovata ricerca sui fondamenti biblici della teologia liturgica," *Rivista Liturgica* 65 (1978) 589–594.

Carminati, Giancarlo. "Una teoria semiologica del linguaggio liturgico: una verifica sull 'Ordo Missae,' " *Ephemerides Liturgicae* 102 (1988) 184–233.

Casel, Odo. *The Mystery of Christian Worship,* ed. Burkhard Neunheuser. Westminster, Md.: Newman Press, 1962.

Castillo, José Maria. *Simbolos de Libertad.* Teologia de los sacramentos. Salamanca: Ediciones Sigueme, 1981.

"Catholic-Lutheran Agreed Statement on the Eucharist." *Origins* 8 (Jan. 11, 1979) 465–480.

Catholic Perspectives on Baptism, Eucharist, and Ministry. A Study Commissioned by the Catholic Theological Society of America. Ed. Michael Fahey. New York/Lanham: University of America Press, 1986.

La Celebrazione del Triduo Pasquale. Anamnesis e Mimesis, ed. Ildebrando Scicolone. Studia Anselmiana 102. Analecta Liturgica 14. Rome: Editrice Anselmiana, 1990.

Chauvet, Louis-Marie. *Du symbolique au symbole. Essai sur les sacrements.* Paris: Les Editions du Cerf, 1979.

Chauvet, Louis-Marie. "Place et fonction de l'histoire dans une théologie des sacrements," *Revue de l'Institute Catholique* 24 (1987) 49–65.

Chauvet, Louis-Marie. "La ritualité chrétienne dans le cercle infernal du symbole," *La Maison Dieu* n. 133 (1978) 31–77.

Chauvet, Louis-Marie. *Symbole et sacrement.* Une relecture de l'existence chrétienne. Paris: Les Editions du Cerf, 1987.

Chavasse, A. "L'oratio 'super sindonem' dans la liturgie romaine," *Revue Bénedictine* 70 (1960) 313–23.

Chenis, Carol. *Fondamenti teorici dell'arte sacra.* Magistero post-conciliare. Rome: Libreria Ateneo Salesiano, 1991.

Chiesa Oggi. Architettura e communicazione. Milan: Di Baio Editore, 1992.

Chryssides, G. D. "Subject and Object in Worship," *Religious Studies* 23 (1987) 367–375.

Chupungco, Anscar J. *Cultural Adaptation of the Liturgy.* New York/Mahwah: Paulist Press, 1982.

Chupungco, Anscar J. *The Cosmic Elements of Christian Passover.* Studia Anselmiana 72. Analecta Liturgica 3. Rome: Editrice Anselmiana, 1977.

Chupungco, Anscar J. *Liturgies of the Future*. New York/Mahwah: Paulist Press, 1989.

Ciobotea, D. I. "The Role of the Liturgy in Orthodox Theological Education," *St. Vladimir's Theological Quarterly* 31 (1987) 101–122.

Collins, John. "Isaiah," in *The Collegeville Biblical Commentary*, eds. Dianne Bergant and Robert J. Karris. Collegeville: Liturgical Press, 1989, 411–452.

Collins, Mary, "Critical Questions for Liturgical Theology," *Worship* 53 (July 1979) 302–317.

Collins, Mary, "Liturgical Methodology and the Cultural Evolution of Worship in the United States," *Worship* 49 (February 1975) 85–102.

Collins, Mary, "The Public Language of Ministry," *Official Ministry in a New Age*, Permanent Seminar Studies No. 3, ed. James H. Provost. Washington: Canon Law Society of America, 1981, 7–40.

Congar, Yves. *Diversity and Communion*, trans. John Bowden. Mystic, Conn.: Twenty-Third Publications, 1984.

Congar, Yves. *La foi et la théologie*. Le Mystère chrétien, I. Paris: Desclée, 1962.

Congar, Yves. *L'Homme devant Dieu*. Vol. I. Lyons: Editions Montaigne Aubiere, 1963.

Congar, Yves. *Tradition and Traditions*, trans. Michael Naseby and Thomas Rainborough. New York: Macmillan, 1966.

Congregation for the Doctrine of the Faith, "On the Interpretation of Dogmas," *Origins* 20 (May 17, 1990) 1–16.

Corbon, Jean. *The Wellspring of Worship*, trans. Matthew O'Connell. New York/Mahwah: Paulist Press, 1988.

Cornehl, P. "Theorie des Gottesdienstes—Ein Prospekt," *Theologische Quartalschrift* 159 (1979) 178–195.

Costa, Eugenio. "La celebrazione come catchesi integrale." *Rivista Liturgica* 60 (1973) 633–642.

Cross, F. L., ed. *St. Cyril of Jerusalem. Lectures on the Christian Sacraments*. London: SPCK, 1951.

Cuva, Armando. "Linee di Antropologica Liturgica," *Salesianium* 36 (1974) 3–31.

Dalmais, I. H. "La Bible vivant dans l'Eglise," *La Maison Dieu* n. 126 (1976) 7–23.

Dalmais, I. H. *Introduction to the Liturgy*, trans. Roger Capel. Baltimore, Md.: Helicon, 1961.

Dalmais, I. H. "La liturgie comme lieu théologique," *La Maison Dieu* n. 78 (1964) 97–106.

Dalmais, I. H. "Le Mysterion, Contribution a une théologie de la liturgie," *La Maison Dieu* n. 158 (1984) 14–50.

Dalmais, I. H. "Symbolique liturgique et théologique de l'art romain," *La Maison Dieu* n. 123 (1975) 135–148.

Davies, J. G. "The Influence of Architecture upon Liturgical Change," *Studia Liturgica* 9 (1973) 230–240.

Debuyst, Frédéric. "Espace et foi, l'oeuvre exemplaire d'Emil Steffan," *La Maison Dieu* n. 174 (1988) 119–130.

De Clerck, Paul. "La tradition en acte. La prière eucharistique," *La Maison Dieu* n. 178 (1989) 81–92.

De Clerck, Paul. " 'Lex orandi lex credendi,' sens original et avatars historiques d'un adage équivoque," *Questions Liturgiques* 59 (1978) 193–212.

De Clerck, Paul. La *"prière universelle"* dans les liturgies latines anciennes. Temoinages partistiques et textes liturgiques. Liturgiewissenschaftliche Quellen und Forschungen, n. 62. Münster: Aschendorff, 1977.

De Clerck, Paul. "Théologie, histoire et tradition. Accents majeurs d'un débat," *La Maison Dieu* n. 181 (1990) 119–130.

Defois, G. "Typologie du rassemblement chrétien aujourd'hui," *Sacrements de Jesus Christ*, ed. L. M. Chauvet. Paris: Desclée, 1983, 161–182.

Deiss, Lucien. *Springtime of the Liturgy*, trans. Matthew O'Connell. Collegeville: The Liturgical Press, 1979.

Dekkers, Eloi. "Creativité et orthodoxie dans la 'lex orandi,' " *La Maison Dieu* n. 111 (1972) 20–30.

Dens, Pierre. *Tractatus de sacramentis in genere*. Mecheln, 1850.

Deremble, Colette. "Les vitraux de Chartres et la liturgie," *La Maison Dieu* n. 177 (1989) 167–181.

Deremble, Jean-Paul and Colette Manhes. *Les vitraux légendaires de Chartres*. Paris: Desclée de Brower, 1988.

Deremble, Jean-Paul and Colette Manhes. *Le vitrail du Bon Samaritain, Chartres, Sens, Bourges*. Paris: Le Centurion, 1986.

De Vogüé, Adalbert, ed. and comment. *La Règle de saint Benoit*. Sources Chrétiennes 185. Paris: Les Editions du Cerf, 1972.

De Vogüé, Adalbert. "Le sens de l'office divin," *Revue d'Ascétique et de Mystique* 42 (1966) 391–404, 43 (1967) 21–33.

De Vries, Wilhelm. "Lex supplicandi, lex credendi," *Ephemerides Liturgicae* 47 (1933) 48–58.

De Waal, Victor, "Worship and Theology," *Liturgy Restored*, ed. Kenneth Stevenson. London: SPCK, 1982, 109–121.

De Zan, Renato. "Punti Salienti dei 'Praenotanda' dell 'Ordo Lectionum Missae' 1981," *Rivista Liturgica* 70 (1983) 691–703.

Didier, Raymond. *Les sacrements de la foi. La Paque dans ses signes*. Paris: Editions du Centurion, 1975.

Dimitrios I, *Orthodoxy and the Ecological Crisis*. Gland, Switzerland: World Wide Fund for Nature International, 1990.

Documents on the Liturgy 1963–1979. Conciliar, Papal and Curial Texts. International Commission on English in the Liturgy. Trans. Thomas O'Brien. Collegeville: The Liturgical Press, 1982.

Doncoeur, Paul. "Bible et liturgie: conditions d'une tension féconde," *Etudes* 194 (1957) 95–105.

Donghi, A. "Nella lode la Chiesa celebra la propria fede." *Mysterion. Miescellanea, Salvatore Marsili*. Torino: Elle di Ci, 1981, 161–192.

Doran, Carol and Thomas H. Troeger. *New Hymns for the Lectionary*. To Glorify the Maker's Name. New York/Oxford: Oxford University Press, 1986.

Dubois, Rene. "Franciscan Conservation verses Benedictine Steward-ship," *Ecology and Religion in History*, eds. David and Eileen Spring. New York: Harper and Row, 1975, 114–136.

Dufort, Jean-Marie. "Le langage de l'espérance dans la prière liturgique," *Science et esprit* 26 (1974) 233–250.

Dufrasne, Dieudonné. "Qu'est-ce que l'homélie actualise?" *Communautés et Liturgiques* 59 (1977) 39–44.

Duke, Robert W. "Word Spoken and Broken in Ritual," *Worship* 61 (January 1987) 61–72.

Dulles, Avery. *The Craft of Theology*. From Symbol to System. New York: Crossroad, 1992.

Dumas, Antoine. "Les prefaces du nouveau missel," *Ephemerides Liturgicae* 85 (1971) 16-28.

Dumas, Antoine. "Pour mieux comprendre les textes liturgiques du Missel Romain," *Notitiae* 6 (1970) 194-213.

Dumas, Antoine. "Les préfaces du nouveau Missel," *Ephemerides Liturgicae* 85 (1971) 16-28.

Dumas, Antoine. "Les sources du nouveau missel romain," *Notitiae* no. 7 (1971) 37-42, 74-77, 94-95, 134-136, 276-280, 409-410.

Dürig, W. "Zur Interpretation des Axioms 'Legem credendi lex statuat supplicandi,'" *Veritate Catholicae*, eds. A. Zeigenaus, F. Courth, P. Schafer. Aschaffenburg: Pattloch, 1985, 226-236.

Duval, Andre. *Des sacrements au concile de Trente.* Paris: Les Editions du Cerf, 1985.

L'Englise en prière. I Principes de la Liturgie, ed. A. G. Martimort. Paris: Desclee, 1983.

Einig, Maternus. "Liturgische und mystagogische Predigt," *Freiburger Zeitschrift für Philosophie und Theologie* 18 (1971) 322-333.

Eliade, Mircea. *Cosmos and Myth*, trans., Willard Trask. New York: Harper Torchbooks, 1959.

Ellebracht, Mary Pierre. *Remarks on the Vocabulary of the Ancient Orations in the Missale Romanum.* Nijmegen/Utrecht: Dekker and Van De Vegt, 1966.

Empereur, James L. *Models of Liturgical Theology.* Bramcote/Nottingham: Grove Books, 1987.

Empereur, James L. *Worship: Exploring the Sacred.* Washington, D.C.: The Pastoral Press, 1987.

Empereur, James L. "The Theological Experience," *Chicago Studies* 16 (Spring 1977) 45-62.

Espeja, J. "La Iglesia, comunidad liturgica segun Sto. Tomas," *Teologia Espiritual* 27 (1965) 487-499.

Eucaristia sfida alle Chiese divise, ed. Luigi Sartore. Padua: Edizioni Messaggero, 1984, 197-221.

The Eucharist. Final Report of Joint Roman Catholic-Lutheran Commission (1978)," *Origins* 8 (January 11, 1979) 465-480.

Fede a Rito, eds. D. Sartore, G. Gavaert, I. DeSandre, E. Costa. Collana Studi di liturgia 3. Bologna: Dehoniane, 1975.

Federer, Karl. *Liturgie und Glaube. Eine theologiegeschichtliche Untersuchung.* Paradosis IV. Legem credendi lex statuat supplicandi. Fribourg: Paulus-verlag, 1950.

Fernandez, Pedro. "Estructura semiologica de la Liturgia," *Salmanticensis* 22/3 (1975) 457–497.

Fernandez, Pedro. "La liturgia, disciplina principal o nuava dimension de la Teologia," *Ciencia tomista* 98 (1971) 581–610.

Fernandez, Pedro. "La liturgia, imagen de este siglo que pasa," *Studium* 14 (1974) 97–117.

Fernandez, Pedro. "La liturgia, quehacer teologico. Estudio sobre una definicion." *Salmanticensis* 20 (1973) 203–271.

Fernandez, Pedro. "Liturgia y teologia en la *Summa* de Santo Tomás," *Angelicum* 51 (1974) 383–418.

Fernandez, Pedro. "Liturgia y teologia. Historia de un problema metodologico," *Ciencia tomista* 99 (1972) 135–179.

Fernandez, Pedro. "Liturgia y teologia. Una cuestion metodolgica," *Ecclesia Orans* 6 (1989) 261–283.

Fernandez, Pedro. "Teologia de la liturgia en la *Summa* de Santo Tomas," *Ciencia tomista* 101 (1974) 253–305.

Fernandez, Pedro. "Teologia de la Oracion Liturgica," *Cienca tomista* 107 (1980) 355–402.

Ferrari, Giuseppe. "La dimesione teologica nella Liturgia di S. Basilio," *Nicolaus* 8 (1980) 138–144.

Ferriere, Cinette, "A propos de 'Dieu-potier.' Images de la création et foi chrétienne en Dieu créateur," *Pariosse et Liturgie* 48 (1966) 533–548.

Fink, Peter E. "The Challenge of God's Koinonia," *Worship* 59 (September 1985) 386–403.

Fink, Peter E. "Living the Sacrifice of Christ," *Worship* 59 (March 1985) 133–148.

Fink, Peter E. "Public and Private Moments in Christian Prayer," *Worship* 58 (November 1984) 482–499.

Fink, Peter E. "The Sacrament of Orders: Some Liturgical Reflections," *Worship* (November 1982) 482–502.

Fink, Peter E. "Three Languages of Christian Sacraments," *Worship* 52 (November 1978) 561–575.

Fink, Peter E. "Towards a Liturgical Theology," *Worship* 47 (December 1973) 601–609.

Fisch, Thomas, ed. *Liturgy and Tradition*. Theological Reflections of Alexander Schmemann. Crestwood: St. Vladimir's Press, 1990.

Fischer, Balthasar. "Les titres chretiens des psaumes dans le nouvel office divin," *La Maison Dieu* n. 135 (1978) 148–157.

Fischer, J.D.C. *Christian Initiation: Baptism in the Medieval West*. London: SPCK, 1965.

Foley, Edward. *From Age to Age. How Christians Celebrated the Eucharist*. Chicago: Liturgy Training Publications, 1991.

Foley, Edward and Mary McGann. *Music in the Eucharistic Prayer*. American Essays in Liturgy 8. Collegeville: The Liturgical Press, 1988.

Foley, Edward, Kathleen Hughes and Gilbert Ostdiek, "The Preparatory Rites: A case study in Liturgical Ecology," *Worship* 67 (January 1993) 17–38.

Fontaine, Gaston. "Commentarium ad Ordinem Lectionum Missae," *Notitiae* 5 (1969) 256–282.

Frattalone, R. "La celebrazione liturgica: premesse antropologico-teologiche," *Ephemerides Liturgicae* 92 (1978) 245–260.

Fry, Timothy, et. al., eds. *RB 80. The Rule of Saint Benedict*. Collegeville: The Liturgical Press, 1981.

Galadza, Peter. "The Role of Icons in Byzantine Worship," *Studia Liturgica* 21 (1991) 113–135.

Gantoy, Robert. "La Bible dans la liturgie: pourquoi, comment," *Communautés et Liturgies* 59 (1977) 25–35.

Gargano, Innocenzo. "L'uso della Bibbia nella Liturgia: l'esegesi 'Spirituale' Oggi," *La Bibbia nella Liturgia*, 83–95.

Garijo Guembe, M. M. "Uberlegunger für einen Dialog zwishen Orthodoxie und Katholizisimus im Hinblick den Satz 'lex orandi—lex credendi,' *Theologische Jahrbuch* (1988) 145–163.

Gartner, H., and Merz, M. "Prolegomena für eine integrative Metholde in der Liturgiewissenschaft. Zugleich ein Versuch zur Gewinnung der empirischen Dimension," *Archif für Liturgiewissenschaft* 24 (1982) 165–189.

Geffré, Claude. "Du symbolisme au symbole: les sacrements," *La Maison Dieu* n. 142 (1980) 49–56.

Gerhards, Albert. "La doxologie, un chapitre définitif de l'histoire du dogme?" *Trinité et liturgie.* Conf. St. Serge 30, eds. A. Triacca and A. Pistoia. Rome: Edizioni Liturgiche, 1984, 103–118.

Gerken, Alexander. *Teologia dell'eucaristia,* trans., Battista Mabritto and Angelo Bressan. Alba: Edizioni Paoline, 1977, German original 1972.

Giraudo, Cesare. "La Celebrazione della Parola di Dio nella Scrittura," *Rivista Liturgica* 73 (1986) 593–615.

Giraudo, Cesare. *Eucaristia per la Chiesa.* Prospettive teologiche sull'eucaristia a partire dalla "lex orandi." Aloisiana 22. Brescia: Editrice Morcelliana, 1989.

Giraudo, Cesare. *La Struttura Letteraria della Preghiera Eucaristica. Saggio sulla genesi letteraria di una forma. Toda veterotestamentaria, Beraka giudaica, Anafora critsiana* Analecta Biblica 92. Rome: Biblical Institute Press, 1981.

Goenagga, J. A. "La homilia: acto sacramentale y de magistero," *Phase* n. 16 (1976) 339–358.

Griese, Erhard. "Perspektiven einer liturgischen theologie," *Una Sancta* 24 (1969) 102–113.

Grossi, Vittorino. "I Padri della Chiesa e la teologia liturgica." *Rassegna di Teologia* 24 (1983) 126–137.

Gryson, Roger. *The Ministry of Women in the Early Church,* trans. Jean Leporte and Mary Louise Hall. Collegeville: The Liturgical Press, 1976.

Gueranger, Prosper. *Institutions liturgiques, I, II, III.* Le Mans-Paris, 1940-51.

Gueranger, Prosper. *Institutions liturgiques. Extraits.* Montreal: Editions de Chire, 1977.

Gueranger, Prosper. *The Liturgical Year,* trans. Laurence Shepherd. Westminster: Newman Press, 1952ff.

Gueranger, Prosper. "Valeur dogmatique de la liturgie," *Auxiliaire Catholique* 5 (1846) 96–119.

Guiver, George. *Company of Voices.* Daily Prayer and the People of God. New York: Pueblo, 1988.

Guroian, V. "Bible and Ethics. An Ecclesial and Liturgical Interpretation," *Journal of Religious Ethics* 18/1 (1990) 129–157.

Guthrie, Harvey H. *Theology As Thanksgiving.* From Israel's Psalms to the Church's Eucharist. New York: Seabury, 1981.

Gy, Pierre-Marie. "Culte et culture. Point de vue théologique," *La Maison Dieu* n. 159 (1984) 83–89.

Gy, Pierre-Marie. *La Liturgie dans l'histoire*. Paris: Editions Saint-Paul/Cerf, 1990.

Gy, Pierre-Marie. "La liturgie entre la fonction didactique et la mystagogie," *La Maison Dieu* n. 177 (1989) 7–18.

Gy, Pierre-Marie. "La trésor des hymnes," *La Maison Dieu* n. 173 (1988) 19–40.

Hameline, J. Y. "Passage d'Ecriture," *La Maison Dieu* n. 126 (1976) 71–82.

Hanggi, Anton and Irmgard Pahl, eds. *Prex Eucharistica* Textus e variis liturgiis antiquioribus selecti. Fribourg: Editions Universitaires, 1968.

Hardy, Daniel W. and David F. Ford. *Jubilate. Theology in Praise*. London: Darton, Longman, Todd, 1984.

Hatchett, Marion J. *Sanctifying Life, Time and Space*. An Introduction to Liturgical Study. New York:Seabury, 1976.

Häussling, Angelus. "Die kritische Funktion der Liturgiewissenschaft," *Liturgie und Gesellschaft*, ed. Hans Meyer. Innsbruck: Tyrolia Verlag, 1970, 103–130.

Häussling, Angelus. "Liturgiewissenschaft Zwei Jahrzehnte nach Konzilsbeginnen," *Archif für Liturgiewissenschaft* 24 (1982) 1–18.

Häussling, Angelus. *Mönchskonvent und Eucharistiefeier: Eine Studie über die Messe in der abendlandischen Klosterliturgie des frühen Mittelalters und zur Geschichte der Messhaufigkeit*. Liturgiewissenschaftliche Quellen und Forschungen 58. Münster-Westfalen: Aschendorff, 1972.

Hayburn, Robert. *Papal Legislation on Sacred Music*. Collegeville: The Liturgical Press, 1979.

Henkey, Charles H. "Liturgical Theology," *Yearbook of Liturgical Studies* 4 (1963) 77–107.

Hering, H. "De loco theologico liturgiae apud Sanctum Thomam," *Pastor Bonus* 5 (1941) 456–464.

Hermans, Jo. "L'etude de la liturgie comme discipline théologique. Problèms et méthodes," *Revue Théologique de Louvain* 18 (1987) 337–360.

Herwegen, Ildephonse. "L'Ecriture sainte dans la Liturgie," *La Maison Dieu* n. 5 (1946) 7–20.

Hill, William. *The Three Personed God. The Trinity As A Mystery of Salvation.* Washington: The Catholic University of America Press, 1982.

Himes, Michael J. "This Graced World: Trinity, Grace and Sacraments," *Church* 1 (Spring 1985) 3-12.

Himes, Michael J. and Kenneth R. Himes, "The Sacrament of Creation," *Commonweal* 117 (Jan 26, 1990) 42-49.

Hinson, E. Glen. "The Theology and Experience of Worship: A Baptist View," *Greek Orthodox Theological Review* 22 (1977) 417-443.

Hoffman, Lawrence. *Beyond the Text: A Holistic Approach to Liturgy.* Bloomington/Indianapolis: Indiana University Press, 1987.

Hoon, Paul Waitman. *The Integrity of Worship.* Ecumenical and Pastoral Studies in Liturgical Theology. Nashville/New York: Abingdon Press, 1971.

Houssiau, Albert. "La liturgie," *Initiation à la pratique de la théologie,* eds. Bernard Lauret and Francois Refoulè. Paris: Les Editions du Cerf, 1983, 5:155-201.

Houssiau, Albert. "La liturgie, bien priveliegié de la théologie sacramentaire," *Questions Liturgiques* 54 (1973) 7-12.

Houssiau, Albert. "Pratique, vérité et situation. A propos sur la théologie sacramentaire," *Revue Théologique de Louvain* 10 (1979) 40-50.

Houssiau, Albert. "La redecouverte de la liturgie par la théologie sacramentaire (1950-1980)," *La Maison Dieu* n. 149 (1982) 27-55.

Houssiau, Albert. "Le service de la Parole," *Questions Liturgiques* 65 (1984) 203-212.

Houssiau, Albert. "The Theological Significance of the New Ordination Rite," *Louvain Studies* 3 (Spring 1970) 31-40.

Hughes, John Jay "Eucharistic Sacrifice. Transcending the Reformation Deadlock," *Worship* 43 (November 1969) 532-544.

Huijbers, Bernard. *The Performing Audience: Six and a Half Essays on Music and Song in the Liturgy.* Second ed. Cincinnati: North American Liturgy Resources, 1974.

Hyde, Clark. "The Bible in the Church: The Lectionary as Paradigm," *Worship* 61 (July 1987) 323-336.

The Hymnal for the Hours. Chicago: GIA, 1989.

366

Ignatios IV, "Behold, I Make All Things New," *The Ecumenical Review* 42 (April 1990) 122–131.

Imbelli, Robert P. and Thomas H. Groome, "Signposts Towards a Pastoral Theology," *Theological Studies* 53 (March 1992) 127–137.

Irwin, Kevin W. *American Lutherans and Roman Catholics in Dialogue on the Eucharist: A Methodological Critique and Proposal*, Studia Anselmiana 76, Sacramentum 5. Rome: Editrice Anselmiana, 1979.

Irwin, Kevin W. "The Good News of Repentance and Conversion," in *Repentance and Reconciliation in the Church*, ed. Michael Henchal. Collegeville: The Liturgical Press, 1987, 32–54.

Irwin, Kevin W. *Liturgy, Prayer and Spirituality*. New York/Mahwah: Paulist Press, 1984.

Irwin, Kevin W. "On Monastic Priesthood," *The American Benedictine Review* 41 (September 1990) 225–262.

Irwin, Kevin W. "The Official Vatican Response to BEM: Baptism," *Ecumenical Trends* 17 (March 1988) 33–37.

Irwin, Kevin W. "Toward a Theological Anthropology of Sacraments," in *A Promise of Presence*. Studies in Honor of David N. Power, eds. Michael Downey and Richard Fragomini. Washington: Pastoral Press, 29–43.

Isambert, Francios. *Rite et efficacité symbolique*. Paris: Les Editions du Cerf, 1979.

Jasper, R. C. D. and G. J. Cuming, eds. *Prayers of the Eucharist: Early and Reformed*. Third ed. New York: Pueblo, 1987.

Jennings, Theodore W. "Ritual Studies and Liturgical Theology: An Invitation to Dialogue," *Journal of Ritual Studies* 1 (1987) 35–56.

John Paul II, "Peace With All Creation: World Day of Peace [Jan. 1, 1990]," *Origins* 19 (Dec. 14, 1989) 465–468.

Johnson, Cuthbert. *Prosper Gueranger (1805–1875): A Liturgical Theologian*. An Introduction to his liturgical writings and work. Analecta Liturgica 9. Rome: Studia Anselmiana, 1984.

Joint International Commission for Roman Catholic/Orthodox Theological Dialogue, "The Church, the Eucharist and the Trinity," *Origins* 12 (Aug. 12, 1982) 157–160.

Joncas, Jan Michael. *Hymnum Tuae Gloriae Canimus*. Toward an Analysis of the Vocal and Musical Expression of the Eucharistic Prayer in the Roman

Rite: Tradition, Principles, Method. Rome: Pont. Athenaeum S. Anselmo, Thesis ad Lauream n. 168, 1991.

Joncas, Jan Michael. "Re-Reading *Musicam Sacram:* Twenty-Five Years of Development in the Roman Rite Liturgical Music," *Worship* 66 (May 1992) 212–231.

Jossua, J. P. "Parole de Dieu et liturgie," in *La liturgie après Vatican II.* Paris: Les Editions du Cerf, 1967, 141–146.

Kallis, A. "Theologie als Doxologie. Der Stellenwert der Liturgie in den orthodoxen Kirchen und Theologie," *Theologische Jahrbuch* (1988) 137–144.

Kavanagh, Aidan. *Elements of Rite.* A Handbook of Liturgical Style. New York: Pueblo, 1982.

Kavanagh, Aidan. *On Liturgical Theology.* New York: Pueblo, 1984.

Kavanagh, Aidan. "Primary Theology and Liturgical Act," *Worship* 57 (July 1983) 321–324.

Keenan, Joseph. "The Importance of the Creation Motif in a Eucharistic Prayer," *Worship* 53 (July 1979) 341–356.

Keifer, Ralph A. "Liturgical Text as Primary Source For Eucharistic Theology," *Worship* 51 (May 1977) 186–196.

Kelleher, Margaret Mary. "Liturgical Theology: A Task and a Method," *Worship* 62 (January 1988) 2–25.

Kelleher, Margaret Mary. "Liturgy: An Ecclesial Act of Meaning," *Worship* 59 (November 1985) 482–497.

Kelleher, Margaret Mary. "Liturgy as a Source for Sacramental Theology," *Questions Liturgiques* 72 (1991) 25–42.

Kiesling, Christopher. "The Sacramental Character and the Liturgy," *The Thomist* 27 (1963) 385–412.

Kilmartin, Edward J. *Christian Liturgy.* Theology and Practice I. Systematic Theology of Liturgy. Kansas City: Sheed and Ward, 1988.

Kilmartin, Edward J. "Liturgical Theology," *Worship* 50 (July 1976) 312–315.

Kilmartin, Edward J. "A Modern Approach to the Word of God and Sacraments of Christ: Perspectives and Principles," *The Sacraments: God's Love and Mercy Actualized,* ed. Francis Eigo. Villanova: Villanova University Press, 1979, 59–109.

Kilmartin, Edward J. "The Official Vatican Response to BEM: Eucharist," *Ecumenical Trends* 17 (March 1988) 37–40.

Kilmartin, Edward J. *The Particular Liturgy of the Individual Church.* The Theological Basis and Practical Consequences. Placid Lectures Series 7. Bangalore, India: Dharmaram Publications, 1987.

Kilmartin, Edward J. "A Roman Catholic Response," in James F. White. *Sacraments as God's Self Giving.* Nashville: Abingdon, 1983, 135–140.

Kilmartin, Edward J. "The Sacrifice of Thanksgiving and Social Justice," *Liturgy and Social Justice,* ed. Mark Searle. Collegeville: The Liturgical Press, 1980, 53–71.

Kilmartin, Edward J. "Theology of the Sacraments: Toward A New Understanding of the Chief Rites of the Church of Jesus Christ." *Alternative Futures for Worship,* Volume I, ed. Regis A. Duffy. Collegeville: The Liturgical Press, 1984, 123–175.

Kimbrough, S. T. "Hymns Are Theology," *Theology Today* 42 (1985) 59–68.

Kitzinger, Ernst. *I Mosaici di Monreale.* Palermo: S. F. Flaccovio, 1991.

Kleinheyer, Bruno. *Sakramentliche Feiern I.* Die Feiern der Eingliederung in die Kirche. Gottesdienst der Kirche. Handbuch der Liturgiewissenschaft, 7, 1. Regensburg: Verlag Friedrich Pustet, 1989.

Krahe, M.-J. " 'Psalmen, Hymnen und Lieder, wie der Geist sie eingibt.' Doxologie als Ursprung und Zeil aller Theologie," in H. Becker and R. Kaczynski, eds., *Liturgie und Dichtung. Ein interdisziplinares Kompendium,* Vol. 2. Interdisziplinare reflexion. Pietas Liturgica 2. St. Ottilien, 1983, 923–957.

Krosnicki, Thomas. "Preparing the Gifts: Clarifying the Rite," *Worship* 65 (1991) 149–159,

LaCugna, Catherine Mowry. "Can Liturgy ever again be a Source for Theology?" *Studia Liturgica* 19 (1989) 1–16.

Lathrop, Gordon. "Holy Things. Foundations for Liturgical Theology." *Institute of Liturgical Studies.* Number 7. Valparaiso: Valparaiso Institute, 1991.

Lathrop, Gordon, *Holy Things. Foundations for Liturgical Theology.* Minneapolis: Fortress, 1993.

Lathrop, Gordon, "A Rebirth of Images: On the Use of the Bible in Liturgy," *Worship* 58 (July 1984) 291–304.

369

Lebrun, Dominique. "L'homélie redevenue acte liturgique?" *La Maison Dieu* n. 177 (1989) 121–147.

Leclercq, Jean. "L sermon, acte liturgique," *La Maison Dieu* n. 8 (1946) 27–37.

Lecuyer, Joseph. "Réflexions sur la théologie du culte selon S. Thomas." *Revue Thomiste* 55 (1955) 339–362.

LeGall, Robert. "Pour une conception integrale de la liturgie," *Questions Liturgiques* 65 (1984) 181–202.

Lehman, Karl. "Gottesdienst als Ausdruck des Glaubens. Plädoyer für ein neues Gespräch zwischen Liturgiewissenschaft und Dogmatischen Theologie," *Liturgisches Jahrbuch* 30 (1980) 197–214.

Lescrauwaet, Jos. "Confessional Aspects in Contemporary Theology. Confessing the Faith inthe Liturgy." *Post Ecumenical Christianity*. Concilium 54, ed. Hans Kung. New York: Herder and Herder, 1970, 119–125.

Lex Orandi. Lex Credendi. Miscellannea in onore di P. Cipriano Vagaggini, eds. G. Békés and G. Farnedi. Studia Anselmiania 79. Sacramentum 6. Roma: Editrice Anselmiana, 1980.

Lies, Lothar. "Teologie als eulogisches Haldeln," *Zeitschrift für katholische Theologie* 107 (1985) 76–91.

Liturgia e Adattamento. Dimensioni Culuale e Teologico-Pastorali, eds. A. Pistoia, A. M. Triacca. Rome: Editrice Liturgicae, 1990.

Liturgia Opera Divina e Umana. Rome: Edizione Liturgiche, 1982.

Liturgia e Parola di Dio. "Assemblee in ascolto della Parola." Atti della XLI Settimana Liturgica Nazionale. Rome: Edizioni Liturgiche, 1991.

Liturgia e Spiritialità. Atti della XX Settimana di Studio dell'Associazione Professori di Liturgia. Rome: Edizioni Liturgiche, 1992.

Liturgical Formation in Seminaries. A Commentary. Washington: USCC, 1984.

Liturgical Practice in the Fathers, eds. Thomas K. Carroll and Thomas Halton. Wilmington: Glazier, 1988.

Liturgie et Anthropologie, eds. A. M. Triacca and A. Pistoia. Rome: Edizioni Liturgiche, 1990.

Liturgie, éthique et peuple de Dieu. Conf. St. Serge 37, eds. A. M. Triacca and A. Pistoia. Rome: Editrice Liturgicae, 1991.

La liturgie expression de la foi. Conf. St. Serge 25. Rome: Edizioni Liturgiche, 1979.

La liturgie, son sens, son esprit, sa méthode. Liturgie et Théologie, eds.
A. Pistoia, A. M. Triacca. Rome: Edizioni Liturgiche, 1982.

Liturgy: A Creative Tradition. Concilium Vol. 162. Eds. Mary Collins and
David Power. New York: Seabury, 1983.

The Liturgy Documents. A Parish Resource. Chicago: Liturgy Training Publications, 1991.

Llopis, Joan. "Algunas Claves del Arte de la Celebracion," *Phase* n. 29
(1989) 303–312.

Lonergan, Bernard J. *Method in Theology.* London: Darton, Longman and
Todd, 1972.

Lopez Martin, Julian. *En el Espiritu y la verdad.* Salamanca: Segretariado
Trinitario, 1987.

Lopez Martin, Julian. "Funcion didascalica de la liturgia en el mistero
trinitario," *Estudios Trinitarios* 12 (1978) 3–52.

Lopez Martin, Julian. "La fe y su celebracion," *Burgense* 23 (1982)
141–196.

Louvel, F. "La proclamation de la Parole de Dieu," *La Maison Dieu* n. 20
(1950) 72–82.

Lukken, Gerard. "La liturgie comme lieu théologique irremplacable."
Questions Liturgiques 56 (1975) 97–112.

Lukken, Gerard. "Semiotics and the Study of Liturgy," *Studia Liturgica* 17
(1987) 108–117.

Lukken, Gerard. *Original Sin in the Roman Sacramentaria and the Early Baptismal Liturgy.* Leiden: Brill, 1973.

Lukken, Gerard. "Plaidoyer pour una approche intégrale de la liturgie
comme lieu théologique: un défi à toute la théologie," *Questions Liturgiques* 68 (1987) 242–255.

Lukken, Gerard. "The Unique Expression of Faith in the Liturgy," *Liturgical Expression of Faith.* Concilim 82, eds. Herman Schmidt and David
Power. New York: Herder and Herder, 1973, 11–21.

Lutheran Book of Worship. Prepared by the churches participating in the
Inter-Lutheran Commission on Worship. Minneapolis: Augsburg, 1978.

Lutheran Book of Worship. Ministers Desk Edition. Minneapolis: Augsburg,
1978.

McGuire, Joan M. "The Official Vatican Response to BEM: Ministry," *Ecumenical Trends* 17 (March 1988) 41-43.

McKenna, John. "The Epiclesis Revisited: A Look at Modern Eucharistic Prayers," *Ephemerides Liturgicae* 99 (1985) 314-336.

McMahon, L. M. "Towards a Theology of the Liturgy: Dom Odo Casel and the Mysterientheorie," *Studia Liturgica* 3 (1965) 129-154.

Maas, Robin and Gabriel O'Donnell, et. al. *Spiritual Traditions for the Contemporary Church*. Nashville: Abingdon, 1990.

Macquarrie, John, "Creation and Environment," *Ecology and Religion in History*. New York: Harper and Row, 1975, 32-47.

Madigan, Shawn. *Spirituality Rooted in Liturgy*. Washington: Pastoral Press, 1988.

Maggiani, Silvano. "La 'Liturgia della Parola': Sequenze Rituali Costitutive," *Rivista Liturgica* 73 (1986) 633-645.

Magrassi, Mariano. "Linee teologiche del nuovo *'Ordo Missae,'* Il Nuovo Rito della Messa, Liturgia N.S. 8. Rome: Edizioni Liturgiche, 1969, 39-57.

Magrassi, Mariano. "Teologia e Liturgia dei Sacramenti," *Rivista Liturgica* 49 (1962) 152-165.

Magrassi, Mariano. *Vivere La Liturgia*. Noci: La Scala, 1978.

Maldonado, Luis. "Celebracion y expression de la fe," *Estudios Trinitarios* 19 (1985) 91-105.

Maldonado, Luis. "El Estilo 'Catequetico' de Celebracion," *Phase* n. 29 (1989) 313-320.

Maldonado, Luis. "Liturgia y Experiencia Cristiana en algunes epocas historicas," *Phase* n. 25 (1985) 365-378.

Maldonado, Luis and Pedro Fernandez, "La Celebracion Liturgica: Fenomenologia y Teologia de la Celebracion," *La Celebracion en la Iglesia*. Vol. I. Liturgia y Sacramentologia Fundamental, Third ed., ed. Dionisio Borobio. Salamanca: Ediciones Sigueme, 1991.

Male, Emile. *Notre-Dame de Chartres*. Paris: Flammarion, 1983.

Marsili, Salvatore. "Cristo si fa presente nella sua parola," *Rivista Liturgica* n. 70 (1983) 671-690.

Marsili, Salvatore. "Dedicazione senza Consecrazione. Ossia: teologia liturgica in una storia rituale," *Rivista Liturgica* n. 66 (1979) 578-601.

Marsili, Salvatore. *I segni del Mistero di Cristo*. Teologia liturgica dei sacramenti. Roma: Edizioni Liturgiche, 1987.

Marsili, Salvatore. "La liturgia attraverso i secoli: Costituzione, Liturgia, Messa," *Rivista Liturgica* n. 52 (1964) 309–330.

Marsili, Salvatore. "La Liturgia del Popolo sacerdotale," *Rivista Liturgica* n. 56 (1969) 194–209.

Marsili, Salvatore. "Liturgia e Devozioni: Tra Storia e Teologia," *Rivista Liturgica* n. 63 (1976) 174–198.

Marsili, Salvatore. "Liturgia e Teologia," *Rivista Liturgica* n. 59 (1972) 455–473.

Marsili, Salvatore. "La Liturgia, mistagogia e culmine della preghiera cristiana," *Rivista Liturgica* n. 65 (1978) 184–191.

Marsili, Salvatore. "La Liturgia nel Concilio Vaticano II," *Rivista Liturgica* n. 50 (1963) 259–272.

Marsili, Salvatore. "La Liturgia nella Strutturazione della Teologia," *Rivista Liturgica* n. 57 (1971) 153–172.

Marsili, Salvatore. "Il mistero di Cristo," *Rivista Liturgica* n. 26 (1939) 73–78.

Marsili, Salvatore. *Mistero di Cristo e Liturgia nello Spirito*. Vatican City: Libreria Editrice Vaticana, 1986.

Marsili, Salvatore. "Le orazioni della Messa nel nuovo Messale. Teologia e pratica della preghiera liturgica," *Rivista Liturgica* n. 58 (1971) 70–91.

Marsili, Salvatore. "Orientamento teologico della liturgia delle ore," *Ora et Labora* 26 (1971) 108–117.

Marsili, Salvatore. "La parola nel culto," *Rivista Liturgica* n.53 (1966) 149–164.

Marsili, Salvatore. "Il problema liturgico," *Rivista Liturgica* n. 26 (1939) 15–19.

Marsili, Salvatore. "Riforma liturgica dell'alto," *Rivista Liturgica* n. 51 (1964) 76–91.

Marsili, Salvatore. "Teologia della celebrazione eucaristica. Note sul nuovo 'Ordo Missae,'" *Rivista Liturgica* n. 57 (1970) 93–114.

Marsili, Salvatore. "Theologhia," *Rivista Liturgica* n. 22 (1935) 273–277.

Martinich, A. "Sacraments and Speech Acts," *The Heythrop Journal* 16 (1975) 289–303, 405–417.

Martini, Carlo. "The School of the Word," *Worship* 61 (May 1987) 194–198.

Mason, David R. "An examination of 'worship' as a key for reexamining the God problem," *Journal of Religion* 55 (1975) 76–94.

Mazza, Enrico. *Mystagogy*. A Liturgical Theology in the Patristic Age, trans. Matthew O'Connell. New York: Pueblo, 1989.

Mercker, H. ed. *Bibliographie Romano Guardini (1885–1968). Guardinis Werke. Veroffentlichungen uber Guardini*. Paderborn: F. Schöningh, 1978.

Messale di Ogni Giorno. Roma/Milano: Editoriale Consortium, 1984.

Il Messale Romano del Vaticano II. Orazionale e Lezionario. Vol. I and II. Torino: Elle Di Ci, 1984.

Meyer, Hans Bernhard. *Eucharistie*. Geschichte, Theologie, Pastoral. Handbuch der Liturgiewissenschaft 4. Regensburg: Friedrich Pustet, 1989.

Meyer, Hans B. "Liturgische Theologie oder Theologie des Gottesdienstes," *Zeitschrift für katholische Theologie* 86 (1964) 327–331.

Meyer, Hans B. "Temps et liturgie. Remarques anthropologiques sur le temps liturgique," *La Maison Dieu* n. 148 (1982) 7–37.

Meyer, Hans B. "The Social Significance of the Liturgy," *Politics and Liturgy*. Concilium 92. New York: Herder, 1974, 34–50.

Meyer, Harding and Lukas Vischer, eds., *Growth in Agreement: Reports and Agreed Statements of Ecumenical Conversations on a World Level*. New York: Paulist Press, and Geneva: World Council of Churches, 1984.

Micks, Marianne. *The Future Present*. The Phenomenon of Worship. New York: Seabury, 1970.

Miller, Malcolm. *Chartres Cathedral*. Andover: Pitkin, 1985.

Miller, Malcolm. *Chartres Cathedral: The Medieval Stained Glass and Sculpture*. Andover: Pitkin, 1980.

Miller, Malcolm. *Chartres: The Cathedral and the Old Town*. Andover: Pitkin, 1981.

Mitchell, Leonel L. "The Liturgical Roots of Theology," *Time and Community*, ed. J. Neil Alexander. Washington: Pastoral Press, 1990, 243–254.

Mitchell, Nathan. "Dissolution of the Rite of Christian Initiation," in *Made, Not Born*, ed. John Gallen. Notre Dame, Ind.: University of Notre Dame Press, 1976, 50–82.

Moltmann, Jurgen. *The Future of Creation.* Collected Essays, trans. Margaret Kohl. Philadelphia: Fortress Press, 1987.

Moltmann, Jurgen. *God in Creation.* A New Theology of Creation and the Spirit of God. San Francisco: Harper and Row, 1985.

Mpongo, L. "Le Rite Zairois de la Messe," *Spiritus* 19 (1978) 436–441.

Mühlen, Heribert. *Una Mystica Persona.* Die Kirche als das Mysterium der Identität des Heiligen Geistes in Christus und den Christen: Eine Person in vielen Personen. Munich: F. Schöningh, 1967.

Murnion, Phillip J. "A Sacramental Church in the Modern World," *Origins* 14 (June 21, 1984) 81–90.

Mveng, E. "Christ, Liturgie et Culture," *Bulletin of African Theology* 2 (1980) 247–255.

Nakagaki, Frank. "Metodo integrale. Discorso sulla metodologia nell'interpretazione dei testi eucologici," *Fons Vivus.* Miscellanea Liturgica in Memoria di Don Eusebio Maria Vismara, ed. A. Cuva. Zurich: Pas. Verlag, 1971, 269–286.

Nelle Vostre Assemblee. Vols. *I and II.* Teologia pastorale delle celebrazioni liturgiche. Second ed. Brescia: Queriniana, 1975.

Neunheuser, Burkhard. "Der Beitrag der Liturgie zur theologischen Erneurung," *Gregorianum* 50 (1969) 589–614.

Neunheuser, Burkhard. *L'Eucharistie.* II. Au Moyen age et à l'époque moderne, trans., A. Liefooghe. Paris: Les Editions du Cerf, 1966, German original 1963.

Neunheuser, Burkhard. "Liturgiewissenschaft: Exakte Geschichtsforschung oder (und) Theologie der Liturgie," *Ecclesia Orans* 4 (1987) 7–102.

Neunheuser, Burkhard. "Pluralismo è uniformità nella Liturgia della Chiesa locale," *Rivista Liturgica* n. 59 (1972) 71–92.

The New Dictionary of Sacramental Worship, ed. Peter Fink. Collegeville: The Liturgical Press, 1990.

The New Dictionary of Theology, ed. J. Komonchak et. al. Wilmington: Michael Glazier: The Liturgical Press, 1987.

Newman, David R. "Observations on Method in Liturgical Theology," *Worship* 57 (July 1983) 377–384.

Nicholls, William. *Jacob's Ladder: The Meaning of Worship,* Ecumenical Studies in Worship, No. 4. Richmond: John Knox Press, 1958.

Nocent, Adrien. "Les apologies dans la célébration eucharistiques," in *Liturgie et rémission des péchés*. Rome: Edizione Liturgiche, 1975, 179–196.

Novella, Guido. "Priorità della Parola nella vita della Chiesa," *Rivista Liturgica* n. 71 (1984) 9–19.

Nuevo Misal del Vaticano II, eds. Jaime Sancho y Gabril. Ramis/Bilbao: Ediciones Mensajero/Editorial Desclée de Brouwer, 1989.

Nuovo Dizionario di Liturgia, eds. Domenico Sartore and Achille M. Triacca. Roma: Edizioni Paoline, 1984.

Oliana, Guido. "Liturgia: «*fonte e culmine*» della teologia e della spiritualità presbyterale," *Ephemerides Liturgiche* 102 (1988) 456–476.

Olivar, A. "Quelques remarques historiques sur la prédication comme action liturgique dans l'ancienne," *Melanges Liturgiques offerts R. P. Dom Bernard Botte*. Louvain: Mont Cesar, 1972, 429–443.

Oppenheim, Philippus. *Principia theologiae liturgicae*. Turin: Marietti, 1947.

Orianne, Jean. "Baptism. An Enquiry on the Evocative Force of the Symbolism of the Baptismal Rites," *Lumen Vitae* 26 (1971) 623–648.

Orthodoxy and the Ecological Crisis. The Ecumenical Patriarchate, World Wide Fund for Nature International, 1990.

Osborne, Kenan. "Methodology and Christian Sacraments," *Worship* 48 (September 1974) 536–549.

Osborne, Kenan. *Sacramental Theology. A General Introduction*. New York/Mahwah, N.J.: Paulist Press, 1988.

Pagliarani, Vittorio, "A proposto di Teologia della Celebrazione Eucaristica," *Divinitas* 14 (1970) 59–71.

Pannenberg, Wolfart. "Analogie und Doxologie," *Dogma und Denkstrukturen*, ed. W. Joest. Göttingen: Vandenhoeck and Ruprecht, 1963, 96–115.

Parente, Pietro. "La sacramentalita nella sua vera prospettiva teologica," *Divinitas* 20 (1976) 272–281.

Parola e Sacramento nella Comunità di Salvezza. Padova: Centro Azione Liturgica, 1974, 81–104.

La Parole dans la liturgie. Lex Orandi 48. Paris: Les Editions du Cerf, 1975.

La Parole dans la liturgie. Semaine liturgique de l'Institut Saint-Serge. Paris: Cerf, 1970.

Paschale Mysterium, Studi in memoria dell'Abate Prof. Salvatore Marsili, ed. Giustino Farnedi. Studia Anselmiana 91, Analecta Liturgica 10. Rome: Editrica Anselmiana, 1986.

Pascher, Joseph. "Theologische Erkentnis aus der Liturgie," *Einsicht und Glaube*, eds. J. Ratzinger and H. Fries, Freiburg: Herder, 1962, 243-258.

Pascual De Aguilar, J. A. *Liturgia y Vida Cristiana*. Madrid, 1962.

Pilla, Anthony "Christian Faith and the Environment," *Origins* 20 (Nov. 1, 1990) 333-338.

Pinell, Jordi. "Per uno studio scientifico della liturgia. Orientamenti ed ooporionzo do un programma," *Rivista Liturgica* n. 57 (1971) 248-260

Pinto, M. *O valor teològico da liturgia*. Coleccao "Criterio" 27. Braga: Livraria Cruz, 1952.

Pontificale Romanum De Ordinatione Diaconi, Presbyteri, et Episcopi. Vatican City: Typis Polyglottis Vaticanis, 1968.

Portalié, E. "Célestin I. Lettre contre les Sémipélagiens et les Capitula annexés," *Dictionnaire de Théologie Catholique* II, 2052-2061.

Power, David N. "Cult to Culture: The Liturgical Foundation of Theology," *Worship* 54 (November 1980) 482-495.

Power, David N. "Doxology: the Praise of God in Worship, Doctrine and Life," *Worship* 55 (January 1981) 61-69.

Power, David N. *Ministers of Christ and His Church*. The Theology of the Priesthood. London: G. Chapman, 1969.

Power, David N. "People at Liturgy," *Twenty Years of Concilium— Retrospect and Prospect*. Concilium 170, eds. Paul Brand, Edward Schillebeeckx and Anton Weiler. Edinburgh: T. and T. Clark, 1983, 8-14.

Power, David N. "Response: Liturgy, Memory and the Absence of God," *Worship* 57 (July 1983) 326-329.

Power, David N. *The Sacrifice We Offer*. The Tridentine Dogma and Its Reinterpretation. Edinburgh: T. and T. Clark, 1987.

Power, David N. "Two Expressions of Faith: Worship and Theology," *Liturgical Experience of Faith*. Concilium 82. New York: Herder and Herder, 1973, 95-103.

Power, David N. "Unripe Grapes: the Critical Function of Liturgical Theology," *Worship* 52 (September 1978) 386-399.

Power, David N. *Unsearchable Riches: The Symbolic Nature of the Liturgy*. New York: Pueblo, 1984.

Powers, Joseph M. "Liturgical Theology I," *Worship* 50 (July 1976) 307–312.

Progress Report on the Revision of the Roman Missal. Washington: International Committee on English in the Liturgy, 1988.

Progress Report on the Revision of the Roman Missal, Second. Washington: International Committee on English in the Liturgy, 1990.

Progress Report on the Revision of the Roman Missal, Third. Washington: International Committee on English in the Liturgy, 1992.

Prenter, R. "Worship and Creation," *Studia Liturgica* 2 (1963) 82–95.

Puglisi, James F. and S. J. Voicu. *A Bibliography of Interchurch and Interconfessional Theological Dialogues.* Rome: Centro Pro Unione, 1984.

Quilotti, R. "L'Ecclesiologia del Messale Romano," *Sacra Doctrina* 32 (1987) 564–589, 621–664.

Rahner, Karl. *The Church and the Sacraments,* trans., W. J. O'Hara. New York: Herder and Herder, 1963.

Rahner, Karl. "The Presence of Christ in the Sacrament of the Lord's Supper," *Theological Investigations, Vol. IV,* trans. Kevin Smyth. Baltimore: Helicon Press, 1966.

Rahner, Karl. "What is a Sacrament?" *Worship* 47 (May 1973) 275–76.

Ramis, G. "La liturgia expression de fe," *Phase* n. 19 (1979) 519–523.

Ramshaw-Schmidt, Gail. *Christ in Sacred Speech. The Meaning of Liturgical Language.* Philadelphia: Fortress Press, 1986.

Reifenberg, Hermann. "Brauchen wir eine zweite Liturgiereform?" *Bibel und Liturgie* 47 (1974) 209–230.

Renaudin, Paulus. "De auctoritate sacrae Liturgicae in rebus fidei," *Divus Thomas* 13 (1935) 41–54.

Richter, Klemens. "Die Liturgiewissenschaft im Studium der Theologie heute," *Liturgisches Jahrbuch* 32 (1982) 46–63, 89–107.

Richter, Klemens, ed. *Liturgie—ein vergessenes Thema der Theologie?* Freiburg/Basel/Wein: Herder, 1987.

Ricoeur, Paul. *Freud and Philosophy: An Essay on Interpretation* trans., Dennis Savage. New Haven: Yale University Press, 1970.

Ricoeur, Paul. "The Hermeneutics of Symbol and Philosophical Reflection," *International Philosophical Quarterly* 2 (1962) 191–218.

Ricoeur, Paul. "The Model of the Text: Meaningful Action Considered as Text." *Hermeneutics and the Human Sciences*, ed. and trans. J. B. Thompson. Cambridge: Cambridge University Press, 1981, 197–221.

Righetti, Mario. *Manuale di storia liturgia* I. Milano: Áncora, 1964.

Riley, Hugh M. *Christian Initiation*. Studies in Christian Antiquity, Vol. 17. Washington: Catholic University of America Press, 1974.

Rinaudo, S. " 'Rinnovamento nello Spirito' e partecipazione attiva alla liturgia," *Rivista Liturgica* n. 67 (1980) 495–505.

Ritschl, Dietrich. *Memory and Hope*. New York: Macmillan, 1966.

Roberts, Eileen. "The *Exsultet* in Twelfth Century Sicily as an Indicator of Manuscript Provenance," *Ecclesia Orans* 5 (1988) 157–164.

Rochetta, Carlo. *Sacramentaria Fondamentale*. Dal "mysterion" al "sacramentum" Bologna: Dehoniane, 1989.

Rogers, Elizabeth, trans. and ed. *Peter Lombard and the Sacramental System*. Merrick: Richwood, 1976, reprinted from 1917 original.

The Roman Pontifical. Volume I. Washington: International Commission on English in the Liturgy, 1978.

Rooney, Marcel. "Eucharistic Concelebration, Twenty-Five Years of Development," *Ecclesia Orans* 6 (1989) 117–129.

Rordorf, Willy, et. al. *The Eucharist of the Early Christians*, trans. Matthew O'Connell. New York: Pueblo, 1978.

Rordorf, Willy. "Liturgie et eschatologie," *Ephemerides Liturgiche* 94 (1980) 385–395.

Rose, André. "La parole vivante de Dieu dans la liturgie," *La Maison Dieu* n. 82 (1965) 43–58.

Rose, André. "La repartition des psaumes dans le cycle liturgique," *La Maison Dieu* n. 105 (1971) 66–102.

Routley, Eric. *Christian Hymns Observed*. London: A. R. Mowbray, 1983.

Rubin, Miri. *Corpus Christi. The Eucharist is Late Medieval Culture*. Oxford/NY: Oxford University Press, 1991.

Runyon, Theodore. "The World as Original Sacrament," *Worship* 54 (November 1980) 495–511.

Sacramentarium Veronense, ed. L. C. Mohlberg. Rerum Ecclesiasticarum Documenta 1. Rome: Herder, 1956.

Saint Michael's Daily Missal. English translation of the Missale Romanum. Authorised for public use by the Hierarchy of England and Wales. Alcester and Dublin: Goodliffe Neale, 1973.

Salaun, Pierre, "Pas de sacrement sans parole de Dieu," *Paroisse et Liturgie* 48 (1966) 623–629.

Saliers, Don E. "The Integrity of Sung Prayer," *Worship* 55 (July 1981) 290–303.

Saliers, Don E. *The Soul in Paraphrase: Prayer and the Religious Affections.* New York: Seabury, 1980.

Saliers, Don E. "Theology and Prayer: Some Conceptual Reminders," *Worship* 48 (April 1974) 230–235.

Saliers, Don E. *Worship and Spirituality.* Philadelphia, Pa.: Westminster, 1984.

Salmon, Pierre. "De l'interpretation des psaumes dans la liturgie aux origens de l'Office divin," *La Maison Dieu* n. 33 (1953) 21–55.

Sanon, Anselme. "Cultural Rooting of the Liturgy in Africa since Vatican II," in *Liturgy: A Creative Tradition.* Concilium 162, eds. Mary Collins and David Power. New York: Seabury Press, 1983, 61–70.

Sartori, Luigi, ed. *Teologia e liturgia.* Bologna: Dehoniane, 1974.

Schillebeeckx, Edward. *Christ the Sacrament of the Encounter With God.* New York: Sheed and Ward, 1963.

Schillebeeckx, Edward. "The Liturgy and Theology," *Revelation and Theology* Vol. 1. New York: Sheed and Ward, 1967.

Schilling, S. Paul. *The Faith We Sing.* Philadelphia: Westminster, 1983.

Schleck, C. A. "Integration of Dogmatic Theology with the Liturgy," *Yearbook of Liturgical Studies* 1 (1960) 41–64.

Schlink, Edmund. *The Coming Christ and the Coming Church.* Philadelphia: Fortress Press, 1968.

Schmemann, Alexander. *Introduction to Liturgical Theology,* trans. Asheleigh Moorhouse. London: The Faith Press, 1966.

Schmemann, Alexander. "Liturgy and Theology," *The Greek Orthodox Theological Review* 17 (1972) 86–100.

Schmemann, Alexander. *Sacraments and Orthodoxy.* New York: Herder and Herder, 1965.

Schmemann, Alexander. "Theology and Liturgical Tradition," in *Worship in Scripture and Tradition*, ed. Massey H. Shepherd. New York: Oxford University Press, 1963, 165–178.

Schmidt, Herman. "Lex orandi, lex credendi in recentioribus documentis pontificiis," *Periodica* 40 (1951) 5–28.

Schneider, Theodor. *Zeicher der Nähe Gottes. Grundriss der Sakramententheologie*. Mainz: Matthias-Grünewald, 1979.

Schnitker, Thaddaus A. and Wolfgang A. Slaby, *Concordantia verbalia Missalis Romani*. Westfalen: Aschendorff, 1983.

Scicolone, Ildebrando. "Libri Liturgici," in *Nuovo Dizionario di Liturgia* 701–713.

Searle, Mark. "Liturgy as Metaphor," *Worship* 55 (March 1981) 98–120.

Searle, Mark. "The Narrative Quality of Christian Liturgy," *Chicago Studies* 21 (Spring 1982) 73–84.

Searle, Mark. "New Tasks, New Methods: The Emergence of Pastoral Liturgical Studies," *Worship* 57 (July 1983) 291–308.

Searle, Mark. "The Pedagogical Function of the Liturgy," *Worship* 55 (July 1981) 332–359.

Searle, Mark. "Reflections on Liturgical Reform," *Worship* 56 (September 1982) 411–430.

Searle, Mark. "Renewing the Liturgy—Again," *Commonweal* 115 (November 18, 1988) 617–622.

Seasoltz, Kevin. "Anthropology and Liturgical Theology: Search for a Compatible Methodology," *Liturgy and Human Passage*. Concilium 112, eds. David Power and Luis Maldonado. New York: Seabury, 1979, 3–13.

Seasoltz, Kevin. Book Review of *Anamnesis* in *Worship* 60 (January 1986) 84–86.

Seasoltz, R. Kevin, ed. *Living Bread, Saving Cup*. Readings on the Eucharist. Collegeville: The Liturgical Press, 1982.

Semmelroth, Otto. *Church and Sacrament*, trans. Emily Schossberger. Notre Dame: Fides Publishers, 1963.

Senn, Frank. *New Eucharistic Prayers*. An Ecumenical Study of their Development and Structure. NewYork/Mahwah: Paulist Press, 1987.

Serra, Dominic E., "The Blessing of Basptismal Water at the Paschal Vigil in the Post Vatican II Rite," *Ecclesia Orans* 7 (1990) 343–368.

Shaping English Liturgy, eds., Peter Finn and James Schellman. Washington: The Pastoral Press, 1990.

Shea, William. "Sacraments and Meaning," *American Ecclesiastical Review* 169 (1975) 403–416.

Skelley, Michael. *The Liturgy of the World. Karl Rahner's Theology of Worship*. Collegeville: Liturgical Press, A Pueblo book, 1991.

Sloyan, Gerard. "The Bible as the Book of the Church," *Worship* 60 (January 1986) 9–21.

Sloyan, Gerard. "Is Church Teaching Neglected When the Lectionary Is Preached?" *Worship* 61 (March 1987) 126–140.

Sloyan, Gerard. "The Lectionary as a Context for Interpretation," *Interpretation* 31 (1977) 131–138.

Sloyan, Gerard. "Some Suggestions for a Three-Year Lectionary," *Worship* 63 (November 1989) 521–535.

Sloyan, Gerard. "Word and Sacrament in the Life of the Spirit," *Liturgy* 5/3 (1986) 59–69.

Stenzel, A. "Les Modes de transmission de lá Revelation," in *Mysterium Salutis*, Vol. 3. Paris: Les Editions du Cerf, 1969.

Stevenson, Kenneth. "The Ceremonies of Light—Their Shape and Function in the Paschal Vigil Liturgy," *Ephemerides Liturgicae* 99 (1985) 170–185.

Stevenson, Kenneth. "Lex orandi and lex credendi—Strange Bedfellows? Some Reflections on Worship and Doctrine," *Scottish Journal of Theology* 39 (1986) 225–241.

Stevenson, Kenneth. "The Origins and Development of Candlemas: A Struggle for Identity and Coherence?" *Ephemerides Liturgicae* 102 (1988) 316–346.

Stevick, Daniel B. "The Language of Prayer," *Worship* 52 (November 1978) 542–560.

Stevick, Daniel B. "Toward a Phenomenology of Praise," in *Worship Points the Way*, ed. Malcolm C. Bruson. New York: Seabury Press, 1981, 151–166.

Stuhlmueller, Carroll. "Deutero-Isaiah and Trito-Isaiah," in *The New Jerome Biblical Commentary*, eds. Raymond E. Brown, Joseph A. Fitzmyer and Roland E. Murphy. Englewood Cliffs: Prentice Hall, 1989, 329–348.

Stolz, Anselm. *Introductio in Sacram Theologiam*. Friburg/Rome: Herder, 1941.

The Study of Liturgy, ed. Cheslyn Jones, Geoffrey Wainwright and Edward Yarnold London: SPCK, 1978.

Summa Theologiae. Blackfriars edition, Vol. 56. Latin text and English translation. New York: McGraw-Hill, 1975.

The Summit Choirbook. Summit: Monastery of Our Lady of the Rosary, 1983.

Symbol and Art in Worship. Concilium Vol. 132, eds. Luis Maldonado and David N. Power. New York: Seabury Press, 1980.

Systematic Theology, eds. Francis Schüssler Fiorenza and John P. Galvin. Roman Catholic Perspectives. Vol. I and II. Minneapolis: Fortress Press, 1991.

Taft, Robert. *Beyond East and West*. Problems in Liturgical Understanding. Washington: Pastoral Press, 1984.

Taft, Robert. "Ex Oriente Lux? Some Reflections on Eucharistic Concelebration," *Worship* 54 (July 1980) 308-325.

Taft, Robert. "Liturgy as Theology," *Worship* 56 (March 1982) 113-117.

Taft, Robert. *The Liturgy of the Hours in East and West*. Collegeville: The Liturgical Press, 1986.

Taft, Robert. "Response to the Berakah Award: Anamnesis," *Worship* 59 (July 1985) 305-325.

Taft, Robert. "The Structural Analysis of Liturgical Units: An Essay in Methodology," *Worship* 52 (July 1978) 314-329.

Tamburrino, Pio. "Lex orandi—Lex credendi. Per un discorso liturgico nell'ecumenismo," *Rivista Liturgica* n. 68 (1981) 313-321.

Tarruel, Gibert J. "Los formularios de la benedicion del auga," *Ephemerides Liturgicae* 88 (1974) 275-309.

Tena, Pedro. "La Celebracion del Mistero: Identidad Interna y Forma Externa," *Phase* n. 29 (1989) 271-286.

Teologia e Liturgia, eds. L. Sartori, G. Barbaglio, E. Ruffini, E. Lodi. Bologna: Dehoniane, 1974.

Tesei, Giovanni Paolo. *Le Chiese di Roma*. Roma: Casa Anthropos, 1986.

Theodorou, E. "Theologie und Liturgie," *Theologia* 55/1 (1984) 169-192.

Theodorou, E. "Unité de la foi et pluralismo liturgico," *L'Eglise dans la liturgie*. Rome: Edizioni Liturgiche, 1980, 377-394.

Thurian, Max and Geoffrey Wainwright, eds., *Baptism and Eucharist: Ecumenical Convergence in Celebration*. Geneva: World Council of Churches and Grand Rapids, Mich.: Eerdmans, 1983, 136–209.

Thurian, Max, ed. *Churches Respond to BEM*. Official Responses to the "Baptism, Eucharist and Ministry." Geneva: World Council of Churches, 1986.

Thurian, Max. "Créativité et spontanéité dans la Liturgie," *Notitiae* 14 (1978) 169–175.

Thurian, Max, ed. *Ecumenical Perspectives on Baptism, Eucharist and Ministry*. Geneva: World Council of Churches, 1983.

Traditio et Progressio. Studi Liturgici in onore del Adrien Nocent, ed. Giustino Farnedi. Studia Anselmiana 95. Analecta Liturgica 12. Roma: Editrice Anselmiana, 1988.

Traets, Cor. "La Liturgie rencontre de Dieu dans le Christ," *Questions Liturgiques* 67 (1986) 214–234.

Traets, Cor. "Orientations pour une théologie des sacrements," *Questions Liturgiques* 53 (1972) 97–118.

Traets, Cor. "Rite et liturgie sacramentelle," *Questions Liturgiques* 55 (January 1974) 11–31.

Triacca, Achille M. " 'Confessio—professio—celebratio fidei.' Pedagogia alla fede," *Crescita dell 'uomo nella Catechesi dei Padri*, ed. S. Felici. Rome: Libreria Ateneo Salesiano, 1987, 229–258.

Triacca, Achille M. "In margine alla seconda edizione dell 'Ordo Lectionum Missae.' La celebrazione della Parola di Dio, fointe della vita spirituale dei fedeli." *Notitiae* 18 (1982) 243–280.

Triacca, Achille M. and Burkhard Neunheuser, "Il libro liturgico e la celebrazione: ieri e oggi," *Rivista Liturgica* n. 63 (1976) 57–76.

Triacca, Achille M. "La liturgia educa alla liturgia," *Rivista Liturgica* n. 58 (1971) 261–275.

Triacca, Achille M. "Partecipazione alla celebrazione liturgica: Per un 'bilancio pastorale' a vent'anni della Costituzione sulla Liturgia," *Notitiae* 20 (1984) 12–36.

Triacca, Achille M. "Teología y liturgia de la epiclesis en la tradición oriental y occidental," *Phase* n. 25 (1985) 379–424.

Triacca, Achille M. "L'uso delle citazioni liturgiche nel magistero extraliturgico di Giovanni Paolo II," *Notitiae* 24 (1988) 790–816.

Triacca, Achille M. "Valore Teologico della 'Liturgia della Parola.'"
Rivista Liturgica n. 73 (1986) 616–632.

Triacca, Achille M. "Vers une théologie liturgique de l'eschatologie,"
Eschatologie et liturgie, Conf. St. Serge 31, eds. A. M. Triacca and A.
Pistoia. Rome: Edizioni Liturgiche, 1985, 293–312.

Turck, André, "Le Rite et la Parole dans la reforme liturgique," *Paroisse et
Liturgie* 47 (1965) 383–392.

Una Liturgia per l'uomo. La liturgie pastorale e i suoi compiti. "Caro Salutis
Cardo" 5, ed. Pelagio Visotin, et. al. Padova: Edizioni Messaggero, 1986

Vagaggini, Cipriano. *The Canon of the Mass and Liturgical Reform,* trans.
Peter Coughlan. Staten Island: Alba House, 1967.

Vagaggini, Cipriano. *Caro Salutis Est Cardo—Corporetá, Eucaristia e Liturgia.*
Rome: Desclée, 1966.

Vagaggini, Cipriano. "La liturgia rinnovata e le esigenze dell'annunzio
della parola di Dio," *Seminarium* 31 (1979) 85–117.

Vagaggini, Cipriano. "De principiis generalibus ad Sacram Liturgiam instaurandam atque fovendam," *Ephemerides Liturgicae* 78 (1964) 187–200.

Vagaggini, Cipriano. "Prospetto di un saggio su simbolismo e linguaggio
teologico," *Symbolisme et Théologie.* Studia Anselmiana 64. Sacramentum 2.
Rome: Editrice Anselmiana, 1974, 297–307.

Vagaggini, Cipriano. "Riflesioni in prospettiva teologica sui dieci anni di
riforma liturgica e sulla aporia del problema liturgico in questo
momento," *Rivista Liturgica* n. 41 (1974) 35–72.

Vagaggini, Cipriano. "Teologia," *Nuovo Dizionario di Teologia,* eds.
Giuseppe Barbaglio and Severino Dianich. Rome: Edizioni Pauline, 1977,
1597–1711.

Vagaggini, Cipriano, *Theological Dimensions of the Liturgy.* A General Treatise on the Theology of the Liturgy, trans. Leonard J. Doyle and W.A.
Jurgens. Collegeville: The Liturgical Press, 1976.

Vahaniani, Gabriel. "Pour une Ethique des sacrements," *Revue des
Sciences Religieuses* 75/2 (1989) 277–292.

Vajta, Vilmos. "Creation and Worship," *Studia Liturgica* 2 (1963) 29–46.

Van der Leeuw, Gerardus. *Sacred and Profane Beauty: The Holy in Art,*
trans. David E. Green. New York: Holt, Rinehart and Winston, 1963.

Vandenbroucke, Francois. "Sur la théologie de la liturgie," *Nouvelle Revue
théologique* 92 (1970) 135–164.

van Roo, William. "Reflections on Karl Rahner's *Kirche und Sakramente,*" *Gregorianum* 44 (1963) 465–500.

"Vatican Responds to ARCIC I Final Report [response developed jointly by the Congregation for the Doctrine of the Faith and the Pontifical Council for Promoting Christian Unity]," *Origins* 21 (Dec. 19, 1991) 441–447.

"Vatican Response to WCC Document: *Baptism, Eucharist and Ministry: An Appraisal,*" *Origins* 17 (Nov. 19, 1987) 401–416.

Venturi, Gianfranco, "Il Lezionario, Catechesi Narativa della Chiesa," *Rivista Liturgica* n. 71 (1984) 52–79.

Verheul, Ambrose. *Introduction to the Liturgy,* trans. Margaret Clarke. Collegeville: The Liturgical Press, 1968.

Verheul, Ambrose. "La Liturgie comme louange à Dieu," *Questions Liturgiques* 64 (1963) 19–44.

Verheul, Ambrose. "Le service de la Parole. Essai d'une approche de théologie pastorale," *Questions Liturgiques* 56 (1975) 225–256.

Vinel, J. A., "L'argument liturgique opposé par Saint Augustin aux Pélagiens," *Questions Liturgiques* 68 (1987) 209–241.

Vischer, Lukas. *A Documentary History of the Faith and Order Movement, 1927–1963.* St. Louis: Bethany Press, 1963.

Vischer, Lukas. *Foi et Constitution.* Neuchatel: Delachaux et Niestlé, 1968.

Vischer, Lukas. "Giver of Life—Sustain Your Creation," *The Ecumenical Review* 42 (April 1990) 143–149.

Visentin, Pelagio, "Creazione—Storia della salvezza—Liturgia," *Rivista Liturgica* n. 77 (1990) 252–268.

Visentin, Pelagio. *Culmen et Fons.* Raccolta di Studi di Liturgia e Spiritualità. "Caro Salutis Cardo" Studi 3 & 4, eds. R. Cecolin and F. Trolese. Padova: Edizioni Messaggero, 1987.

Visentin, Pelagio, "L'insegnamento della Dogmatica in rapporto alla Liturgia," *Rivista Liturgica* n. 58 (1971) 186–211.

Visentin, Pelagio, "L'Istituto di Liturgia pastorale di S. Giustina—Padova: dati e prospettive," *Notitiae* 20 (1984) 559–567.

Visentin, Pelagio. "Lo studio della teologia nella Liturgia," *Introduzione agli studi liturgici.* Rome, 1962, 189–223.

Vogel, Cyrille and William G. Storey. *Medieval Liturgy: An Introduction to the Sources.* Washington: Pastoral Press, 1986.

Vogel, Cyrille, "Une mutation cultuelle inexpliquée: le passage de l'Eucharistie communitaire à la messe privée," *Revue des sceinces religieuses* 54 (1980) 231–250.

von Allmen, Jean-Jacques. "La sens théologique de la prière commune," *La Maison Dieu* n. 116 (1973) 74–88.

von Allmen, Jean-Jacques. "A Short Theology of the Place of Worship," *Studia Liturgica* 3 (1964) 155–171.

von Allmen, Jean-Jacques. "The Theological Meaning of Common Prayer." *Studia Liturgica* 10 (1971) 125–136.

Von Balthasar, Hans Urs. *The Glory of the Lord: A Theological Aesthetics. Vol. I: Seeing the Form*, trans., Erasmo Leiva-Merikakis, ed., Joseph Fessio. NY/San Francisco: Crossroad/Ignatius, 1982.

von Rad, Gerhard. *Old Testament Theology*. Vol One, trans., D. M. G. Stalker. New York: Harper and Row, 1962.

Vorgrimler, Herbert. "Liturgie als Thema der Dogmatik," *Theologische Jahrbuch* (1988) 126–136.

Wainwright, Geoffrey. *Doxology*. The Praise of God in Worship, Doctrine, and Life. A Systematic Theology. New York: Oxford University Press, 1980.

Wainwright, Geoffrey. *Eucharist and Eschatology*. London: Epworth Press, 1971.

Wainwright, Geoffrey. "Der Gottesdienst als 'Locus Theologicus,' oder: Der Gottesdienst als Quelle und Thema der Theologie." *Kerygma und Dogma* 28 (1982) 248–258.

Wainwright, Geoffrey. " 'E pluribus unum' Questions of Unity and Diversity on the Ecumenical and Liturgical Scene in the U.S.A.," *Communio Sanctorum*. Melanges Offerts à Jean-Jacques von Allmen. Geneva: Labor et Fides, 1982, 291–305.

Wainwright, Geoffrey. "In Praise of God," *Worship* 53 (November 1979) 496–511.

Wainwright, Geoffrey. "A Language in Which We Speak to God," *Worship* 57 (July 1983) 309–21.

Wainwright, Geoffrey. "The Praise of God in the Theological Reflection of the Church," *Interpretation* 39 (1985) 35–45.

Walsh, Liam G., "Liturgy in the Theology of St. Thomas," *The Thomist* 38 (1974) 557–583.

Walsh, Liam G. *Sacraments of Initiation*. Theology Library Series 7. London: Geoffrey Chapman, 1988.

Walton, Janet, "Ecclesiastical and Feminist Blessing: Women as Objects and Subjects of the Power of Blessing," in *Blessing and Power*, Concilium vol. 178, eds. David Power and Mary Collins. Edinburgh: T. & T. Clark, 1985, 73–80.

Ward, Anthony and Cuthbert Johnson. *The Prefaces of the Roman Missal. A Source Compendium with Concordance and Indicies*. Rome: Tipografia Poliglotta Vaticana, 1989.

Weber, M. J. "L'enseignement dogmatique de la Liturgie," *La Vie Bénédictine* 47 (1939) 79–85.

Weick, Roger S. et. al. *Time Sanctified. The Book of Hours in Medieval Art and Life*. New York: George Braziller, 1988.

Wiener, Claude. "L'exégèse et l'annonce de la parole de Dieu," *Paroisse et Liturgie* 52 (1970) 29–36.

Willis, G. G. *Essays in Early Roman Liturgy*. Alcuin Club Collections 46. London: SPCK, 1964.

Willis, G. G. *Further Essays in Early Roman Liturgy*. Alcuin Club Collections 50. London: SPCK, 1968.

Winter, Gibson. *Liberating Creation. Foundations of Religious Social Ethics*. New York: Crossroad, 1981.

Yarnold, Edward. *The Awe-Inspiring Rites of Initiation. Baptismal Homilies of the Fourth Century*. Slough: St. Paul, 1971.

Zimmermann, J. A. "Toward a Theology of Liturgical Meditation," *Eglise et Théologie* 14 (1983) 155–180.

Zizoulas, John. *Being As Communion*. Studies in Personhood and the Church. Crestwood: St. Vladimir's Press, 1985.